REMNANTS
of the HEART

RoseMarie Dalbow

REMNANTS OF THE HEART

iUniverse books may be ordered through booksellers or by contacting:

iUniverse
1663 Liberty Drive
Bloomington, IN 47403
www.iuniverse.com
1-800-Authors (1-800-288-4677)

ISBN: 978-1-5320-1325-6 (sc)
ISBN: 978-1-5320-1326-3 (e)

Library of Congress Control Number: 2016920991

Print information available on the last page.

iUniverse rev. date: 02/23/2017

I dedicate this book to my husband Herb and my children David, Kevin, Rachele, Mark, Ryan and Jillian, without whom there would be no reason for this book. I thank God for the tenacity to complete this labor of love and for blessing our family so abundantly.

REMNANTS *of the* HEART

"God gave us memories so that we might have roses in December."

James M. Barrie

For as long as I can remember, I wanted to be the best mother ever. I thought about it in my early teens. I prayed about it all my life and still came up short. Wanting to be the best doesn't make it so. I was impatient, I raised my voice often but I love my children fiercely. I told them every day. They were good kids, well behaved, intelligent, sensitive to others, generous, loving and at times comedic. They were my dream come true.

My daughter Rachele used to say that after having her three sons, she truly believes that I had to raise my voice just to be heard amid the chaos with six children. She was giving me a pass. We laughed but it's still there, the regret for not doing more… for not being more.

Memories elicit sentiment, laughter, tears of joy and pain, pangs of regret, feelings of passion, dreams realized and dreams unfulfilled. My life has been, and still is, a collage of events, colored most often by the faces of my six wonderful, uniquely talented children.

Although I do not hear voices, I may as well be hearing them because that inner voice is so insistent and persistent at times. I do not have visions either. However, I have this picture in my mind of Jesus throwing up his hands in exasperation when I screw things up and saying, "Roe, I keep trying to guide you in the right direction but you keep veering off. You ask for My help, then proceed to act on your own". Of course, Jesus would

1

not be exasperated with me. That is my own perception. He loves me too much. He loves us all that much.

I was very good at telling God how to fix things. I prayed for all the things and situations that I knew would change my life for the better. We've all heard the saying "Be careful what you pray for. You might get it." Trust me on this one. Leave the fixing to God. God has given us everything we need to make good decisions. We need to do our best, then leave the rest…to Him.

I am blessed abundantly in so many ways. I feel close to my children. They've forgiven my impatience, my yelling, my rigid ways. God has forgiven me too, it's so difficult to forgive myself. I didn't listen very well to the Holy Spirit back then. I've always clung to my religion, almost like a safety net. Long ago, though, it was more out of fear. Don't miss Mass, it's a mortal sin. Don't do this, don't do that. I heard it from my parents, from the nuns who taught me, from the pulpit. I grew up. I would never think of missing Mass. I never turned away from my faith even when tragedy struck. I not only go to Mass on Sunday but try to go a couple times during the week. I go, not out of fear, but out of love. I don't recall when that changed. Probably about thirty years ago. I couldn't go a day, not an hour without talking to Jesus.

My patience has increased. My son, Ryan has been an inspiration to me. His faith is so strong. He wanted so to join the police force. He became a corrections officer first, as a step that would help him attain his dream. He prayed about it, asked me to pray and to ask family and friends to pray. We stormed the heavens with prayer. Ryan took test after test. Written tests, physical tests, psychological tests, over and over and over. I lost track of how many townships he applied to. He excelled at everything. Yet, when there's only one or two openings and twenty or more applicants, nepotism prevailed.

Ryan would go down to the Police Station in our town just to make sure his application was kept in the current file. He got to know everyone. He had friends in the police department. Time and again, others were chosen to fill positions. I'd get my hopes up and finally, after six years of this I said to Ryan, "Don't you ever get discouraged or angry?" He said, "Mom, didn't you tell me that prayers aren't always answered when we want them to be. God may have a reason to wait and when the time is right, it will happen." When I heard Ryan calmly saying those words to me, I thanked God for my wonderful son. I also remember thinking I must have done something right to raise such a trusting, faith-filled son.

Ryan was right. He persevered, he prayed and he never doubted that his dream would come to fruition. A year after that conversation, a total of seven years, he became a police officer in the township that he wanted as his first choice. I cried a river of tears, tears of joy, the day my Ryan graduated from the police academy. My heart ached with gratitude to God. He, indeed, had chosen the right time to answer our prayers. He also gave me more material for my CCD (Confraternity of Christian Doctrine) students. I passed Ryan's photo, in uniform, around and several students said, "I know him! I've seen him". It was now a tangible source for them, when someone they looked up to, had prayed that long.

MY CHILDREN: MY TREASURES FROM GOD

PSALM 127 : 3 BEHOLD, CHILDREN ARE A HERITAGE FROM THE LORD, THE FRUIT OF THE WOMB IS A REWARD.

I want to preface these chapters with a memory from my early teen years. I remember praying to our Blessed Mother to intervene for me when the time came for me to get married. I told her that I wanted to have 'a lot' of children. She obviously listened and took my request to her Son.

You can do anything, Father. Let my children remember the good times, the hugs, the kisses, the praise, which wasn't enough. Please erase from their memories the yelling, the impatience and all the times that I was too busy to really listen to them—Please…..

You may get emotional and mental whiplash reading this book. It is not written entirely in sequence - - - I tried. My mind meanders from one thought to another. My writing is indicative of that. There is, however, a filament connecting everything, God, family and all the highs and lows that ensue. I would experience miracles and adversity, as does everyone. I heartily agree with Charles Koch's father who told his children to "Remember that often adversity is a blessing in disguise and certainly a character builder".

DAVID BRIAN, my firstborn was born in the spring, just shy of our first year wedding anniversary in 1963. He was 8 lbs. 6 oz. God, was he beautiful! He still is. He was born in Brunswick, Maine where my first husband, George, was stationed at the Naval Base. I was five months short of turning 19. I had no family there and just a few friends—more like acquaintances. I was painfully shy and had difficulty making close friends.

I went into labor on Wednesday and didn't have David until Saturday morning. It was a good experience, though long and painful. I remember walking the halls with my IV pole and watching the nurses bathe the babies, in the nursery, at 1:00 am. I just couldn't sleep. Any pain medication just slowed the labor, so I opted to go without. The hospital was beautiful. It was all on one floor. Rooms were decorated like your own bedroom would be.

There was snow on the ground, even though it was April. I saw my first deer outside my window. He was a magnificent creature, regal looking. I was mesmerized. What a gift from God. I think that's why my son, David, is such a lover of the woods and everything in it.

The first time I lay eyes on David, seconds after he was born, I was overwhelmed with joy, unlike anything I had ever experienced. I felt as if I would burst from all the love that was welling up inside me. I thought of myself as mature even though I wouldn't be nineteen for another five months. I felt confident in being able to care for my baby even though I had no one to help me. I was ten years old when my twin brother and sister, Joe and Mary were born. I helped my mother with everything, feeding, bathing, diapering. It came naturally.

4

It wasn't until years later that I realized how unprepared I was, for this overwhelming responsibility. It was my first night in the hospital. I was sleeping when a very considerate nurse woke me with a flashlight instead of turning the glaring ceiling lights on. She had David wrapped in a blanket in one arm and a cup of hot chocolate with whipped cream in her other hand. She knew that I wasn't a coffee drinker. She said that they forgot to ask me if I was going to bottle feed or breast feed. I hadn't even given it a thought until that moment. I looked down at my chest, shrugged and said "I guess that's why God made them. I'll nurse." One of the best decisions I ever made.

One of the most unusual things that happened to me at the hospital, bears telling. It's a cute, human interest story. While in Maine, during my pregnancy, my husband and I would take walks into town. Temperatures were in the 20's but I had a craving for black and white milkshakes, despite the frigid weather. We would go almost every night to a "Five and Dime" store that had a fountain where they would make milkshakes. We'd sit at the counter. I smiled at the ladies behind the counter, but was too timid to strike up a conversation. Anyway, my third day in the hospital I had a visitor. One of the women from the soda fountain walked into my room with a milkshake. I was shocked. The town was so small, that when I didn't show up at the store, they assumed I had my baby and went to the only hospital there. What would the world be like if we all took the time to show others we cared.

I've gotten off track. I do that a lot. Back to my precious son. David was a good baby but somehow never looked like a baby. He looked too wise for a little child. He had a serious grown up side to his nature. He walked at eight months! My brother Eddie was always coaxing him to walk across the room. It didn't take long. I didn't think this was unusual because I had no other children to compare him to. Everyone else told me it was highly unusual. At thirteen months, when his brother, Kevin was born, David was helping me by getting diapers and doing small tasks. No wonder he has such a strong work ethic. He's been working since he was one year old. He was so creative. One of my favorite memories is of David playing quietly by my side, while I rested. He made dozens of airplanes out of my bobby pins. He displayed patience and determination, so rare in such a young child.

CHILDHOOD MEMORIES AND MISHAPS

St. Bartholomew's Grade School in Philadelphia was a two mile walk from our home. There were no school buses at that time. I got a call from the nurse that David had hurt his arm. The nurse didn't think it was bad because David wasn't making a fuss. He was nine years old. I didn't have a car so I walked to the school to get him and we walked home together. He seemed fine and thanked me for coming to get him.

When we got home, I helped him take his jacket off, very cautiously, and a wave of nausea hit me as I saw David's obviously broken arm, turned at an angle to such a degree, that I couldn't believe he wasn't screaming. I called George and asked him to come home to take us to the hospital. A few years later at Evans School in N. J. I got another call about David. He somehow had bit his tongue and almost severed the tip. Another time he got hit in the throat with a hockey puck.

Our first home was on Scattergood St. in the Frankford section of Philadelphia. We had a small row home with no yard, just a front porch. Later my dad built us a back porch. The park was too far for the kids, nobody had a yard, so our kids, the Moores and the Stumpo kids played hide and seek in the nearby cemetery, or as they dubbed it, "The Cem".

Years later, as an adult, David was working on a house across the street from our house. I was out front, David was on the second floor of the neighbor's house. He waved to me, then threw a sheet of aluminum out of the window. Next thing I see was David walking rapidly out the front door towards our house. Instinctively, I ran in the house got my keys, purse and a white towel. As David reached me I asked "what do you have?" He was holding his forearm and when he removed his hand, blood spurted and I could see clear to the muscle. I wrapped his arm in the towel and drove to the hospital where they stitched him up. He came back and insisted on finishing the job. Talk about a dynamic work ethic. When he threw the metal sheet out the window, it sliced his arm.

DAVID'S OTHER INTERESTS

David is an avid hunter. He wastes nothing. He and his family eat venison all year long. What most people do not realize is that a truly good hunter respects nature even more so than the average person. I've heard David describe sitting high in a tree and watching the sun rise, watching a doe with her fawn. There are times when that's all he did—just watched. I've come to realize that the woods are his church.

David's expertise extends to fishing also. He's won so many tournaments and though I don't fish, I've heard the stories about how skilled David is at this sport also. He's like a magnet, he just knows where to drop his lines. Of course, I believe that there's Someone more in control than we are, guiding him. God does that for those who learn to keep Him first. This does not mean that we won't have problems. Problems are a part of life.

David is also blessed with architectural talent. He's been doing construction, wood working, designing, building and restoring homes for most of his life. I remember one time when David was so young, about nineteen, and he took me to see some work that he had done on an old house in Clementon, N.J. He had done the sheet rock and was proud of his work, rightfully so. The old house looked new inside. Keep in mind that David is blessed, and sometimes cursed, with being a perfectionist. He has no patience or tolerance of mediocrity. He's so demanding of himself, and, of course, others who work for him. Let's put it this way. If you're designing or having a house built and want something unique and constructed to exceed every standard set by those in charge, you'd want my son to build it. There is no better.

However, as proud and impressed as I was with David's work, I probably didn't have a clue just how good David really was at what he did. Then the inspector came by to check out the job, directing a flashlight at the walls, trying to find seams. I'll never forget this guy looking with disbelief and saying "Who the hell did this rock?" I assumed that was short for sheetrock. David knew, even then, that he had a gift. He proudly answered, "I did.". The inspector said, "I don't believe it. I don't see any seams." He was looking in awe at this young teenager who had done a better job than most professionals. My son, the craftsman. Talk about using the talents God gives you. He must be so pleased with my firstborn. I am.

David was so confident about his abilities to be the best in his field. Years later he was inundated with requests to do remodeling. He was earning an amazing reputation for excellence. He had to start turning people down. Too many jobs, not enough time…I asked him how he chose the jobs that he would take on. He told potential clients to get three estimates, pick the most expensive one, double it and then he would do it. Ironically, they consistently hired him. You've heard the saying "Time is money." People were willing to pay more because he excelled at what he did and he did it in half the time as anyone else.

The first cut on a piece of wood had to be accurate otherwise, you're wasting time and people's money. I recall him saying that when he was still very young. There were many instances I witnessed firsthand. I wanted a picnic table, a big one to accommodate our big family. It was last minute request. I remember looking out in the back yard to see David working in what appeared to be a speeded up video. He was nailing boards together, would stoop down to "eyeball" his project from time to time. An hour and a half later the massive table was done. I never saw him measure anything. The table was on the ground which I'm sure wasn't exactly level. When completed, it took several people to lift it to the basketball court. He placed a level on it…dead center.

Another time David was going to put a new roof on for us. He usually starts early but went fishing that morning and arrived at our home about 10:00 am. He hauled all the shingles up to the roof with no help. Our neighbor who had just had a roof put on his house, came over to talk to me. He said that he had three guys and it took them three days to complete the job. He wanted to know how many helpers David had coming. I said "None." He laughed and said it'd take him all week. I told him that

David said he'd have it done that day. The neighbor said, that's impossible because we had the same exact house. I told him that was why my son was in such great demand. Our neighbor was gone all day. When he returned, David was already gone. The roof was done! I had a tough time convincing him that David didn't have help. Let's put it this way, I told him, David wouldn't even use a nail gun. It slowed him down.

I write the way I talk, nothing in sequence. I ramble sometimes, or as my children would say, most times. So, at my age, when the memories strike, I switch gears and write while they're fresh. I just remembered a special time with David, not too long ago. We had a home in the Poconos, lakefront... Lake Wynooska, a very extraordinary place, at least to our family. It was a hot sultry day. Our entire family was up for the weekend. The lake was like glass, the sun was starting to set, casting a golden glow on the water. David and I were floating in large black inner tubes, talking. He motioned me to be quiet and then pointed to a beaver on a tiny island, not too far from us. The beaver was gnawing at a small tree or bush. He then swam, carrying it in his mouth. He dove underwater, barely rippling the water. He swam under us. Not a big event, but when you love nature as much as we do and have the opportunity to witness closely, God's beautiful creatures, it is a gift.

Another memory comes into focus. It was after Mark went home to heaven. David came over with a small ice chest filled with beer. He sat down at the kitchen table and asked me to join him. I actually think it was the first beer I ever had. For some reason (probably the company), I really enjoyed that. It tasted so good. Again, I can't say it often enough that I treasure any time spent with my kids.

David is 43 now and he's building his dream home in upstate New York, to escape the rat race, to get back to nature, permanently. The thought of him being five hours away, bothers me. Yet, I am so happy for him.

2007 NEW YORK – DAVID'S CABIN

Sat under the stars with David, outside his cabin. The fire in the burning barrel warmed us outside while the wine coolers warmed us inside. God, it's so beautiful here. Next day David took me to the stream on his quad. I lay down on the grassy bank, warm, with the sun on me, eyes closed, listening to the babbling water and the birds chirping. This must be what heaven is like...I don't want to go home.

David started this. We would never have dreamed of going to New York. Now, we're in love with the area and the people who are so warm and friendly. We had lunch at a sports bar in the quaint town of Oxford. There was a town square that made us feel as if we had stepped back in time. We had four drinks, a large pizza and bought drinks for three people at the bar. The bill for seven drinks and a pizza was an unbelievable $26.00. In the end, we paid even less because the bartender and another guy treated us to drinks also. I was feeling real good when we left. I don't know how they make any money. Although we would go up to New York almost every weekend for several months, we didn't find our dream home. David insists all we did was spend time in restaurants and church and didn't look at enough places. However, we did make a concerted effort and also ate out and went to church. Those things were important to us as part and parcel of the whole experience. David is not a "people person", we are.

HUMOROUS MEMORY

One of the funniest memories I have of Herb (my hubby) and David together was also a big surprise to me. I learned something new about Herb. David came over with a patch that he wanted sewn on a jacket. I told him I didn't know how to use a sewing machine even though I had one. I can hand sew a beautiful hem but that was the extent of my expertise in this area. David thought I was kidding. I guess children think that their moms can do everything.

When he realized I was serious, he looked disappointed. Sorry. Herb to the rescue. He said to David, "Come with me. I'll do it." The bench for the sewing machine was a small one for one person. To this day, I regret not having my camera ready. I followed them down to see my husband (200+ lbs.) and my 6'2" son sitting side by side on this tiny bench. They could fit only one cheek each on the seat. Herb had his glasses on the tip of his nose and was expertly guiding the patch.

I had forgotten about this incident until I recently saw a "Duck Dynasty" episode with Uncle Si showing Miss Kay's daughter-in-laws how to make an apron without a pattern. They were amazed that he could use a sewing machine. He responded that he was in the service in Vietnam and when you're in the military, you learn to do everything for yourself. That is so true. Herb also served in Vietnam.

One of the greatest gifts that my son has given me is the way he treats my husband, Herb. Though they are so different in so many things, their differences complement each other. The mutual love and respect between them is obvious.

Thank you, God, for loving me enough to bless me with David…..

DAVID'S FAMILY PARTY JULY 13, 14 and 15, 2012

This weekend was reminiscent of the Poconos when Herb and I had all those July 4th parties. It was a crazy, miraculous weekend filled with surprises and unexpected emotions. We almost didn't make it. I got stung by a wasp and my arm swelled up and became painful and inflamed. Luckily, I got to see the doctor and get Prednisone for my allergic reaction.

In my haste to pack my medicines, Xanax, so I could sleep, I failed to pack my Prevalite, which I literally need to be able to eat. With David having only one bathroom and so many people staying over, I couldn't chance eating and tying up the bathroom all day. Sorry to gross anyone out with details, but this was disastrous for me. Especially, since David is a gourmet cook and always has something special planned. I was annoyed with myself but then thought about how I wanted to lose weight—so water and tea were all I'd have that weekend.

We had our first miracle of the weekend, though some might not see it that way. Herb suggested we go to the Walmart Pharmacy in this little 'hick' town. I laughed because I had just spoken with my pharmacist at Shop Rite in N.J. a few weeks ago and he told me that out of the several thousands of prescriptions he fills, I'm the only one on Prevalite. It was something that had to be special ordered. I explained my situation to the pharmacist in this little New York town, hoping I could get two packets, which would get me through two days. I gave him my license, my Rx bottle of something else that had my name and the pharmacy on it. He called the number then said that my Rx had to be called in by my doctor. Of course, since it was Saturday, he wasn't in. He said that he couldn't do it. He wasn't even sure he had it, anyway. As I thanked him for trying, and started to walk away, he found a half box of Prevalite and called me back. He handed me two packets and said, "Don't tell anyone what I just did." We left with a heartfelt thank you.

Considering David's culinary expertise, I was ecstatic. I thoroughly enjoyed the steak and chicken kabobs, marinated steaks, pulled chicken that he had rubbed with spices and smoked for days, then tossed with an apricot sesame sauce that was to die for. Jillian, this is just the kind of treat you and Mark would appreciate. Can you smell it? I made German potato salad, Ryan made a pasta salad and Kelly made mac and cheese. Jane made Texas salsa and brownies. I have passed her recipe for Texas salsa on to at least six people and have made this dish at least ten times since then. It's sooo good. Maybe I should include the recipe in the book.

Accommodations were superb. We had David's room with a wraparound view of the mountains and pond (It's more like a small lake). Rebel, his cat slept with us and Dakota, his yellow Lab would wake me with her huge head on my pillow giving me a morning kiss. We loved it.

David built his home from the ground up. It belongs in "Better Homes and Gardens". The chandelier and railing up the stairs are made from deer antlers. It's rustic, natural and so obvious that David values the gifts-of-nature, he uses to adorn his home with. Your picture, Jillian, is on his dresser, along with Mark's and daddy and grandpop standing in front of a train.

Jake is five now and he swam across the entire lake with Ryan and me on either side of him. It's a long swim and just a few feet from the opposite bank, he said, "I need help". He barely placed a hand on Ryan's shoulder, to assure himself. Ry encouraged him "You can do it Jake. You're almost there!" He swam the rest of the distance, unassisted. He's so brave.

Later, Jake and Ry walked through the icy creek to get minnows and crayfish. I followed from a distance, savoring the beautiful picture of father and son. In a deeper part of the creek, Jake had to swim. It's difficult to believe that he's only five. I pitched a bucket of thirty-five balls to him and he only missed hitting three. Jen and Ry are always practicing with both Jake and Kenzie.

At night, a massive bonfire illuminates everything and marshmallows are toasted and stories told. Kids on the wooden swing are slowing down, getting sleepy from a day filled with constant activity. For Herb and me, the walks are special, a time just to relax, be romantic and appreciate how much we love God's abundant gifts of nature.

Beautiful sight of Ryan and David fishing in early morning from the dock. The mist is hovering over the lake. I'm so glad that we're early risers. Life's too short to sleep it away. I feel Mark and Jillian's presence. For me, it's palpable. They are here at David's. Otherwise, I probably wouldn't feel the peacefulness that permeates me.

David took Herb up the mountain on the quad. He's taken me several times but this is a first for Herb. He was amazed at how rough and steep the ride was and was impressed with the way David had hauled logs down the mountain to make a clearing on high. I don't know how much longer he'll be able to do this brutally hard labor. He's forty-nine and looks ten years younger with a physique of someone even younger, muscle bound and sinewy. He has a strong work ethic and admires Herb for the same, although he would love to see Herb retire.

UPDATE: 2013

David, my first born is fifty years old. I find that hard to believe. Of course, he looks a decade younger. He is thoroughly enjoying his life in New York. He continues to work in construction. We look forward each summer when he has the family stay for the weekend. His home is beautiful and reflects his unique talents. He's made furniture from the trees on his forty-three acres, a recent increase in acreage from the original seventeen acres. His staircase is made of antlers, as is his chandelier. There is a real tree in his kitchen, with a squirrel climbing up it. The stone hearth of his fireplace is made with stones he brought up from his streambed. Some have fossils on them. He never tires of the serenity and laid back life style. I still miss him but a five hour drive remedies that.

UPDATE 2014

David and Jayne were married in May, in Delaware. It was a beautiful church wedding. The reception was at a Yacht Club that provided a serene, classy setting. We met Jayne's parents and sister and her many friends, for the first time. I am so happy for David. He is blessed to have met and fallen in love with such a wonderful caring woman.

This is a first marriage for both of them. I know that Jayne has been a foster parent to several children and that she works with young adults with Down Syndrome. Her creative side was apparent at a second reception in a state park. Centerpieces for the picnic tables were rustic yet elegant. David sawed circles from a tree and Jayne had jars of wildflowers and vases wrapped in twine. Favors were tiny fir trees in a burlap bag. All the elements used were from the woods. Both Jayne and David love gardening and landscaping together.

A WARM MEMORY

It was autumn of 1962 and I was pregnant with David. George was given two hours notice to be at the Navy Base, packed and ready to ship out. I was alone for several weeks. The Catholic Church was walking distance from our apartment so I would attend Mass every Sunday. I also would get overwhelming waves of nausea (morning sickness was kicking in) about half way through the Mass. I'd sit down until it passed.

About the fourth time this happened, the priest was preparing to say the Gospel. Since I sat in the third pew, the priest was able to see me clearly. He apologized to the congregation and said he'd be right back. He came off the altar, gently took me by the arm and walked me over to the convent which was opposite the church. He said he noticed, more than once, all the color drain from my face. I told him why. He told me that I did not have to come to Mass until that passed. Of course, I still felt I should. When one of the nuns opened the door, he asked her to fix me something to eat and take good care of me. He went back to church. Although, this next memory may seem inconsequential, it was important to me. Sister fixed me bacon and eggs and gave me a cup of coffee laced with sugar and real cream. It was my first cup of coffee. It tasted so good and the memory of a very caring priest and sister still lingers like the aroma of that coffee.

I had another embarrassing moment in the church setting. Since Brunswick, Maine was so close to the Canadian border, many of the people spoke French. The Mass was even in French, so when it came time for me to go to Confession, I labored through my high school French. After struggling to grasp for words, the priest (a different one from above), asked if it would be any easier for me to speak in English. I could feel myself blushing when I realized how I must have sounded, and all the time he allowed me to go through that. He didn't laugh at me but I'm sure that story must have provided some well-intentioned laughter for years to come.

RARE ENTRY IN MY JOURNAL - JANUARY 31, 1988

8:30 Mass with Ryan; food shopping afterwards; Jillian washed the car after coming home from a Halloween sleepover party at Cheryl's. David and Ryan are watching the Super Bowl and baby David is asleep on the sofa. While I was in my bedroom on the phone, David brought me in a cup of tea. I feel so filled with love for him. Little things mean a lot!"

KEVIN BRICE, my second born....I so wanted another boy. He was born the following spring in 1964, thirteen months after David. Another prayer answered. Kevin was always a contented baby. His smile was almost constant. Tears were rare. He slept ten hours the first night home from the hospital. He was my biggest baby, 9 lbs. 4 ¾ oz. He, also, to this day, has the biggest heart.

My memories of Kevin are warm and fuzzy, like he was. He had a head full of blond peach fuzz that was almost like a brush haircut, or 'spiked' as they call it today, but it was soft as down.

I was at Mass today, Friday 10-6-06, and I couldn't concentrate. It was as if a magnet was drawing me back to memories of Kevin. I could see him in the bottom bunk on Dock Road. in Atco, propped up on pillows. Sheba, our black German Shepard was lying on the bed with him. Kev was strumming his guitar. The other children were watching TV or playing outside. Television held very little interest for Kevin.

Kevin did enjoy the fort that he and David made out back and the ramps for their bikes. We had two acres of land. Only now as I recall those childhood structures, do I realize the danger that could have befallen them. If memory serves me well, there was an underground fort. I realize it must have been their guardian angels protecting them from a cave-in or serious injury when they played "Evil Knievel".

Sometimes Kevin would go out to the fort alone and say the rosary. One of the other children told me about this. There was a time that I thought Kevin would be a priest. God had other plans. However, Kevin did become an altar boy.

Kevin has ministered to so many people in his life by sharing time, money, even his home with an ongoing parade of relatives and friends. He and his wife, Trudi, are so generous. They married as teenagers and have grown together in the most beautiful way, sharing everything they have, with others.

In Church I realized for the first time that my Kevin is so much like my father was. You couldn't have a better role model than my Dad. I've never heard Kevin talk unkindly about anyone, even when the whole group is chiming in. He says only positive things. He is a strong and gentle man. Maybe that's why he was so open and sensitive to what I call spiritual insight.

I can recall this incident as if it occurred yesterday. It was summer on Dock Rd. We had just finished eating dinner and David, Rachele and Mark raced out back to play. Kevin stayed behind to help me with the dishes. I was pregnant and almost due to have Gene Ryan. Kevin didn't want me bending over to load the dishwasher. He said I'd "scrunch" the baby. Anyway, as we cleaned up, we talked. Very matter of factly, Kevin said that he knew that "one of us kids is going to die young;" I was appalled at his words and said "Kevin, why would you say such a thing?" He was only eleven years old, but so adamant and sure of what he said. He said it without fear or trepidation. I asked if he had had a bad dream. He answered "No.". He explained that he didn't dream it but he *knew*, without a doubt, that it would happen. He just wasn't sure whether it would be him or one of the other children. Again, this was explained by Kevin very calmly. He was completely at peace with this revelation.

I eventually erased that conversation from my memory—so I thought. Twelve years later, my son, Mark, Kevin's younger brother by two years, died in a diving accident at the age of twenty. Then, the memories of that conversation came flooding back. I realized that this tragedy was revealed to Kevin because he was so open to God in his life. If only we could all be that open and trusting. We can, but in this materialistic, hedonistic and anti-God world, it takes a lot of ongoing hard work on a daily basis.

I'm remembering a couple of things that happened when Kevin was a toddler and a six year old. As I said before, Kevin was the most contented little boy, never complaining. The first time I saw Kevin cry for being reprimanded, he was about three years old. He and David were sitting on the sofa and I saw two tears trickle down Kevin's cheeks. I said, "Kevin, you're crying". He said "No I'm not. My eyes are just sweating". My heart broke. He was trying to be so stoic. I hugged him tight. Years later, I sent this story to Reader's Digest and was so disappointed that they didn't publish it.

When Kevin was six years old, he and his sister, Rachele had their tonsils taken out. As they were both being wheeled out of the operating room I leaned over Kevin and asked how he felt. He said, "I feel fine Mommy" then proceeded to throw up. Again, he was not a complainer.

An incident that bears mentioning, is the fact that there were no hospital rooms for Kevin and Rachele. Beds were rolled into the sunroom that had an emergency door. My brother Joe was in high school at the time and offered to stay overnight in the room with them. You see, it was twenty-two degrees outside and there was concern that Kevin or Rachele might get up to go to the bathroom, become disoriented and lock themselves out if they pushed on the emergency door. If my memory serves me well on this one, it was my dad who was so worried. Joe slept sitting up all night and went to school the next day right from the hospital. What a generous thing to do. Thanks, Joe!

Another memory of Kevin's thoughtfulness was in August 1975 during a heat wave. I was in the hospital having Ryan. Children weren't allowed in for visiting then but Kev made homemade water ice for me and sent it in with George. It was sooo good, but just the thought that he would do that for me was so touching. He's a wonderful adult but he was an exceptional child. Kevin has a penchant for giving the most thoughtful, meaningful gifts. I have come home to beautiful bouquets of flowers after surgery. There have been subtle surprises such as a magnolia tree planted in our front yard. Kevin knows how I've always admired their beautiful tree. He leaves gifts of nature when nobody is home. He wants no fuss made. A river birch tree also appeared in our front yard. He waits until we're at church, digs the holes and plants these treasures. Trudi said that Kevin does this on his own.

Kevin's musical talent became evident at my sister Mary's wedding. Kevin, Rachele and Mark were in the wedding. I don't even recall how it came about but the three of them were on the stage and the DJ played "Jeremiah was a Bullfrog". Kevin and Mark in their tuxes looked so handsome and Rachele in her gown was adorable. Nobody was prepared for this little trio when Kevin took the microphone and began belting out the song, hair flying, moving on the stage like he was a hired professional. I was so proud of them all, but Kevin stole the show. It gave me a glimpse into the future of what was to come.

Kevin's talent is phenomenal. He's a self-taught musician. He's also a talented artist. His paintings are beautiful and detail oriented. He writes his own music, lyrics, plays guitar, banjo, violin and keyboard and cello. His songs reflect his life, memories and other people's lives, patriotism and his love for his wife and family. Each time I hear one of his songs it becomes my favorite. Now I accept that they're all my favorites. They evoke so many memories, like in "Nine and Ten" which is about he and his brother, David when they were nine and ten years old. "We Still Give", about the bombing in Oklahoma and the Twin Towers, is a heart wrenching tribute, and "The Overcrowded Bed" which speaks of the closeness of his family. He sings of a storm, with the rain and thunder and lightning, and what a perfect night it is and no one has a clue. All of my children and I share those sentiments. We love stormy weather. Yet, to hear Kevin put all those thoughts to music is amazing. He is also a published author of short stories and poetry. Did I say that I am so proud of him?

Kevin also dedicated a song about Mark to me on my wedding day. A few people were whispering, "not today. Kevin must have read their minds because he said "Mom has been talking about Mark all day anyway". It was so beautiful and touching. It had to be difficult for Kevin, but it *was* the perfect gift for me. The song was "I See Your Face In The Water", one more incidence of how close Mark and Kevin were to each other, even scuba diving together. This was another prayer answered because I was praying that Kevin would play his guitar and sing at our wedding. Yet, I didn't want to put him under any pressure. I think that my pride in Kevin was obvious as he picked up his guitar. I hugged my precious son as did my new husband. I am so blessed.

I am so proud of my Kevin, quiet, yet profound, unbelievably talented in his music and his art work, yet humble, caring and compassionate with all. I love you Kev Brice.

MAY 2013 UPDATE

Over the years, before we even realize what's happening, new rituals evolve. Sunday morning Herb and I leave for Mass. Several hours later we return to a bag hanging on the front door, every Sunday. Kevin leaves all the leftovers from their meals for that week, as a treat for "Buster" and his friends. Buster is one of our many turkey buzzards that do us the service of cleaning up for us. One time Kevin had so much food that within minutes of putting it out in our feeding area, there were twenty-four buzzards. They were on the ground, in the trees, flying around and even fighting each other over the tasty morsels.

Trudi and Kevin leave so much meat on the chicken carcasses or ham bones, that Herb threatens to go out back and graze if I continue to limit his intake, for health reasons, of course. Soon it became an exchange. Since we don't see that much of each other, despite the close geographical proximity, I started writing notes to Kevin and taping them on the front door. I also leave a treat for him, usually cut up fruit or homemade baked goods. For awhile there we had a book exchange. I learned more about our founding fathers from books that Kevin shared with me. Benjamin Franklin's biography was more like a tome. I felt like I knew him personally by the time I finished it. I also shared books about Reagan and Kennedy and my favorite of all, Abraham Lincoln.

There's a lesson in all of this. Though these things may seem trivial to others, to me they bring me smiles, laughs and absolute joy. One of the most treasured gifts we can give to our family and friends is time. Yet, in this day of modern conveniences and progress that I believe are meant to facilitate our tasks, it seems they impede them. Time, due to numerous obligations, is a rare commodity. That's why my little exchange with Kevin is one of the highlights of my week.

Kevin and Trudi's jobs are stressful yet necessary. I don't know how they can do all that they do, carrying two large mortgages in N.J. and their Pocono home. On top of that, Kevin recently undertook a renovation project outside their beautiful home. Humble, as he is, he never mentioned it in his e-mails. We happened to stop by unexpectedly and were shocked, jaw dropping shocked at the gorgeous tropical oasis he created. There seems to be no end to his talents. Trudi and Kevin love the beach but hated the traffic jams in order to get to the beach. Kevin got creative and brought the beach to them. He had part of his yard excavated, then brought in several tons of sand, six inches deep to be exact. There's also a Tiki Bar with hand carved stools.

Kevin and Herb share their love of animals, all animals. On his way over our home on Sundays, he passes a farm market with horses in the back of their property. He'd bring food for the horses and gave them a treat before stopping at our place. Both have shared photos by e-mail if they come across an animal at work. Herb has sent photos of groundhogs, which nobody else seems to like. He had all the guys in work standing around watching the mother and babies. Kevin sent a photo of a fox that was in one of his towers at work. Since Herb made birdfeeders for us and for Kevin and Trudi, that are right outside our kitchen windows, we've also become avid bird watchers. Kevin's feeder was empty one time, but not for long. The squirrels were actually tapping at their window, creatures of habit that they are. Simple things are treasures too.

We've been told in Scripture not to waste our talents but to make them grow. How proud God must be of all you've accomplished, Kevin. I know that I am. You have made my heart well up time and time again. I love you so much Kev Brice.

MEMORY OF KEVIN AND MARK

Trudi related this story to me many years ago and it recently surfaced in our conversation. Kevin and Mark were very close to each other and would do just about everything together, even scuba diving. Mark even lived with Trudi and Kevin for a short time. One night when the three of them were watching TV together, there was a show about one of the islands. The beaches were white, the water crystal clear and teeming with colorful fish. Kevin said, "We'll have to plan a trip there." Trudi, excited about the thought of a vacation on a tropic island responded "Really, Kev?" He looked at Trudi with surprise and said, "Not you Trudi. I meant Mark and me." We had a good laugh about that.

HUMOROUS MEMORY

Kevin was always doing odd jobs in the neighborhood. He mowed lawns, shoveled snow and one day he was on a ladder cleaning leaves out of gutters for a neighbor. He must have disturbed a nest because he was attacked by a squirrel. That house still stands and is on a corner opposite Jenny's mom's house.

TEEN MEMORY

As I said before, Kevin is a talented artist as well as phenomenal musician. He employed his artistic skills and graphic design and embroidered the logos for the rock groups "Kiss", "Rolling Stones" and "Pink Floyd" on the back of his jacket. Rachele seems to remember that somehow battery acid got on it and ruined it. All those hours, all those weeks of work, lost. I wish I had a picture of it. I can only see it in my mind.

RACHELE'S MEMORY OF KEVIN

Rachele wanted to learn to play the guitar and Kevin was going to teach her. He took her to the music store in the Berlin Farmer's Market. The owner asked Rachele if she played the guitar. She said no, then he asked Kevin if he did. When Kevin replied "yes", he took a guitar down from a display and handed it to him. Kevin, of course, began to play. The owner was impressed and Kevin was so into his music that he was unaware that people passing by stopped to listen and came in the store. Rachele said it is one of her fondest memories of Kevin. Twenty-five years later I visited the store to buy some sheet music for my piano. I got talking with the owner who happened to be a Vietnam vet. He shared photos of the plane he flew. I shared stories of my children and, of course, pulled out my photo album I carry with me. He kept going back to the photos of Rachele and Kevin, saying that he remembered them. They had been in his shop. Confirmation received!

UPDATE 2015

Kevin, Trudi, Steven and Nikki all work in the cellular wireless industry. Kevin, Steven and Nikki work for the same company. Kevin is a Construction Manager. Steven and Nikki are Project Managers. Trudi works from home for two different companies as Group Operations Coordinator. She is in the process of training Steven's wife, Amber, to work with her. What a unique dynamic of the whole family working together. It works out well for Steven and Amber's little girl, Courtney. With different hours and days off, they juggle their schedules so that my little great granddaughter always has a family member to care for her. Trudi redecorated her home office before Courtney was born. Since Trudi works from home, Courtney shares her space which is designed for a little princess. Trudi's waited a long time for her precious granddaughter and she is literally, not letting her out of her sight. Courtney's crib is opposite Trudi's desk. Beautiful!

RACHELE, my first little girl, was born on my 21st birthday in late summer of 1965, sixteen months after Kevin. She weighed seven pounds 14 ounces. I still remember the day that you were born and my first look at you. You were chubby with dark hair. You looked like a little Italian baby. Within six months you were blond. Aunt Lorraine said that you looked like my mother. You were so beautiful….still are. My first little girl. What a gift for my 21st birthday.

To avoid any confusion, I want to clarify the use of Rachele's name and her nickname Chele, which is actually the last part of her name. She uses that name on her drawings and poetry and also she loves it because my father called her Shelly. Even though it's spelled differently, it's pronounced the same way. I continue to use both names when talking to her and writing about her.

It's close to midnight. I've had a wonderful, spirit-filled day. I've shared it with Herb but there is a part of me that aches to share it with you, Chele. I'm really feeling your absence more than ever and hoping it's not too long before you get your phone. I miss our talks, our laughter, our political discussions, your spiritual insights, the sound of your voice. I don't doubt that God's plan for you is the best but I'm having difficulty adjusting to it, even though I know that you love your new home and life in Missouri.

I admire you, honey, for the way you've nurtured your boys. You probably doubt your effectiveness, at times, like all mothers do, but all you need do is to read the journals you've kept for them. I wish that I had done that, consistently, like you did. Now I rely on memories and I'm so afraid of losing them. My journal entries help but they were few and far between.

WARM MEMORIES

I close my eyes and I can see you in the corner, behind the table, pulling out tissues, one by one until you appeared to be standing in a snowdrift. I see you walk to the edge of the diving board in high school and make the sign of the cross...in a public school. You do the same before your gymnastic routine. I am so proud of you. You've taught your boys to say "Thank you" to anyone in uniform. They've been taught, also, to go up to handicapped people and acknowledge them.

I'm standing in the back of a classroom at Our Lady of Mount Carmel while you talk to a roomful of teenagers who do not want to be there. There are also a half dozen teachers present. You talk about Mark and about your best friend, Jesus. You are dressed in camouflage. The unruly teens become so quiet you can hear a pin drop. The only sound....teachers crying softly, me crying and the kids too. You have a gift with words, with your faith. I am blessed to be your mother.

24

Your talents are many, your diving, your black belt status in Karate. Your poetry is profound. You've written volumes, some of it published. Your art is beautiful and evocative.

I can see you with Grandpop on the swing on Peach Road in Marlton Lakes. He loved you so much, his "Shelly Bird". I see you in the lake with him, in the waves at Margate. I see you with your "Good & Plenty" bag.... the hamburgers and the slurpees were such an extravagant treat for us. I haven't cried for my father in years, but I'm crying now, picturing the both of you together. Where has all the time gone. Like a misty morning, it's evaporated in the blink of an eye. I miss you Chele. I miss us. I love you like crazy.

I see you with 'Kenzie. The love and pride you have in her is so apparent, as if she was your own little girl. We walked to the play park together. It was obvious that she loved being with you and your boys and that they loved and doted on her.

You put her mittens on and brought snow in for her to make snowmen, when it was too cold to take her outside. You had tea parties and taught her sign language. You and I even did that together. You did so many art projects with her and baked with her. The one project that you did for Christmas was so time consuming and so thoughtful. You helped her to make bookmarks for everyone, using her fingerprints as a base for an object that was meaningful to each person. Pop-Pop calls 'Kenzie, "Angel Face". His bookmark had an angel on it. The body is Kenzie's fingerprint. As I write this, Herb is reading a book and using his bookmark. My bookmark is in my "Good News". I loved reading to Makenzie about spiders, teaching her about ladybugs and seeing her delight when she found the real thing outside. My bookmark has ladybugs and a spider. Of course, the bodies are her fingerprints. Herb laminated them so we'll have them forever. I miss you so much Chele...I miss all the things we did together for Makenzie.

Remember the lunch we had at Chauncy's before you left for Missouri? We sat in the car until the song "Jesus, Take the Wheel" by Carrie Underwood was over. We laughed and we talked at length, with anticipation about your move to Missouri. The waitress gave you the candles on the table to take home. All three of us shared experiences about attending Catholic school…and laughed some more. Then we went home to Blue Anchor and napped! How weird is that. God gave you a respite from your ongoing trials at El's parents' house. You were refreshed when you left. Rachele was the caretaker for her husband's elderly parents who had numerous health issues including diabetes and dementia. You have done so much with the gifts that God gave you. You've made a safe haven for you and your boys in Missouri. I'm so proud of you.

You as well as your brothers have had some difficult times with your dad. With David and Kevin, as they got older, it was physical. With you, Rachele, it was emotional. You were always doing things to get your dad's attention, unsuccessfully. My heart still aches as I recall you sitting at the kitchen table with your 16th birthday cake. Daddy had called and said he'd be home by dinner time and we'd sing to you then. You were thrilled. I wanted to light the candles at 9:00pm and you said "No, mom, not yet. Wait just a little longer." Such a special landmark birthday. At 11:00 pm you finally went to bed in tears. He came home at 2:00 am.

Years pass and despite our divorce, things improve. You're an adult now. You get to spend some quality time with your father—an Eagles game, River Dance, and visiting some military landmarks that were so meaningful to you.

UPDATE: 2010 SKY DIVING MIRACLE

Jillian came home in July of 2008. She and Rachele had made plans for Rachele's birthday, coming up in September. Jillian said that she would be coming back in October to visit and would make arrangements for her sister to sky dive for the first time. It was to be her birthday gift for Rachele. Jillian loved sky diving and would jump often. She wanted her sister to experience it also. Tragedy struck at the end of July when Jillian was taken from us. It was not to be.

Rachele talked of doing it on her own, to honor Jillian's last wish for her. However, the cost was prohibitive. She talks every day to her sister so I suggested she ask Jillian to intercede for her to fulfill Jillian's wish for her. I said that she couldn't do it on her own, but she had to have more pull up in heaven than we do down here. In July 2010 there was the annual Fourth of July Fair in Mountain View, Missouri. They have had it for decades. This year they would have an added attraction. Freefall Express Sky Diving from Mt. Vernon, Missouri would be at the fair. They also had a lottery so Rachele bought a ticket. She won! Thanks Jillian.

Rachele's sons were so upset with her. They tried to talk her out of it. She told them she'd be fine because her sister would be with her. She told the boys that if anything did happen to her, they would also be fine because she had her affairs in order. Also, she wanted them to know that if anything did happen, they should remember she died happy. This, of course, increased their apprehension.

Rachele could not contain her excitement. I talked to her before she jumped. She was wearing her sister's Atlanta Sky Dive t-shirt. She had Jillian's photo with her. Jillian was in her sky diving gear in the picture. She was going to jump with Jillian's photo in her hand and release it when she released the chute. She was in tandem with an instructor who was sensitive to her situation. Since he had lost his father recently and they would skydive together, he had released his father's ashes on his next jump. He assured her that Jillian would be with her the whole way.

Rachele called minutes after she landed. She was elated, screeching with joy, crying. She kept thanking Jesus and Jillian for this wonderful opportunity. We have watched the video of her in the plane before she jumped, the jump and the landing. It was amazing. Her excitement in the video was almost tangible to us, as we watched. Ask and you shall receive.

UPDATE: 2013

Rachele has been in Missouri for seven years. We continue to talk on the phone several times a week and sometimes several times a day. She has been

27

through a divorce as well as fourteen surgeries on her jaw and collarbone. She has improvised because of her disability and manages to do just about anything from repairs in the house to minor car repairs. She has always been mechanically inclined. Her three sons help, but for the most part, she is self-sufficient. She raises chickens and even put a turkey on the table that she got during hunting season with a crossbow, for which she needs a license because of her disability with her shoulder. I just found out recently that she keeps her 9mm semi-automatic pistol on top of her Bible, to remind her of the grave responsibility that goes along with ownership and the gravity of any consequences that come with using it for protection.

Rachele has been separated from her first husband, Elwood, for seven years and divorced for five years. He is the father of her three sons. Over the course of the last few years, they have had an amicable relationship. I have some good memories of Elwood. He had a great respect and appreciation for our military. His grandfather and father were war veterans. I can't say that we were close because he would keep his distance. However, there were times that he expressed affection and respect for me. Chele confirmed that he felt an affinity towards me which greatly surprised me. They had been married a year and El had yet to address me by name. It irked me so one day I asked him to please do me the courtesy of calling me by name. He was ten years younger than me and ten years older than Rachele. I said call me mom, call me Rose, just call me something, out of respect. From that day on he called me Rose.

On several Christmases, Elwood wrapped up and gifted me with a few of his antique books that he treasured. He did this on his own and Rachele was just as shocked as I was to be the recipient of these rare books. We both did share a love of books. Those books are so valuable to me, because of the thought behind them.

Herb and I were at Walmart in Missouri shortly before Rachele's wedding to Tom. We literally bumped into Elwood. He hugged me warmly, we talked for awhile and he asked me to give Rachele his best wishes. Another time, I got a phone call from El. He had heard that I was diagnosed with cancer and just wanted to let me know that he was thinking of me and wished me well. That call meant so much. El lives in Missouri also, a short distance from Rachele. They have a cordial relationship. She even invites him to holiday dinners because he's alone.

Rachele has a love and respect for Native American History, as well as for all things of nature. We share that in common. She has met her soulmate in Thomas, whom she will marry in September of this year. Herb and I have not formally met him in person, but have had conversations over the phone. She says that he's so much like Herb, that it's uncanny. That is a blessing. Despite the fact that Rachele is in her forties, Thomas called Herb to ask permission to request her hand in marriage. Of course, Herb said as long as you treat Rachele well and take care of her, permission granted. We are anticipating Rachele and Thomas' wedding with great joy, as well as seeing our grandsons again. We'll be staying at Joann and Jerry's farm so it will be a reunion of sorts. We've been friends for over forty years.

RACHELE'S INJURY

Rachele is adventurous and loved rock climbing before her shoulder injury. It all started with an injury to her jaw. She and her husband El were wrestling and his elbow connected with her jaw. She said it hurt for a few weeks but she brushed it off, saying it'll get better. It wasn't until she went to the dentist that x rays revealed that her jaw had been broken. She was having all kinds of problems with pain, clicking and inability to open her mouth wide. Sometimes she would open her mouth and would have difficulty closing it. By this time she needed a metal implant which her body rejected.

The doctor decided the best option for Rachele was to take a part of her collarbone to use to repair her jaw. Her body wouldn't reject that. However, she ended up with another serious problem. The bones can regenerate and fill in the area from where the bone was taken. In Rachele's case this didn't happen because the surgeon cut completely through the bone. She did not realize this at first. Her shoulder appeared to be coming out of the socket. In reality, the shoulder and socket together were dislocating, giving the appearance of her shoulder dropping to her chest area.

There were a total of fourteen surgeries over a period of ten years. Pieces of the left collarbone were used to reconstruct the right jaw. Likewise, part of the right collar bone was used to reconstruct the left jaw. The curvature of the bone fit like a puzzle. Both surgeries were necessary in order to align everything.

The last surgery for Rachele was the most frightening. X rays revealed a long fragile shard of collar bone pointed towards her left lung and heart. At this time Rachele was in the process of becoming a black belt in karate. That goal of hers came to fruition but not without a lot of pain. Little did she realize the risk until she saw the x ray. I'll never forget the sickening feeling that came over me when I first viewed the x ray. She would have one more surgery to endure. Of course, this was a different surgeon. Dr. Williams was one of the best in the country.

The surgery would be done at Presbyterian Hospital in Philadelphia. The surgeon planned to take a section of her tibia and reconstruct the collarbone. The surgery would be eight hours long. Rachele was out of surgery in just a few hours. The doctor and his entourage came in to talk to Rachele and told her that they were unable to do what he had planned. There just wasn't enough stable bone to support the reconstruction. Herb and I will never forget the sickening feeling when the doctor told her that she had two choices and neither was good. She could undergo fusion or learn to live with it. She has chosen to live with it. Not only that, but she has learned to laugh about it. Don't ever complain about pain to her. She's in constant pain but says "Pain lets me know I'm alive." She's also fond of quoting a military motto, "Pain is weakness leaving the body."

Although Rachele's injury is no laughing matter, her attitude and acceptance of it provide a good example to the rest of us. We've all been present at some time when her shoulder dislocates. For someone who witnesses this for the first time, it can be upsetting. Visually, her deformity is obvious because the shoulder and socket are in her chest area. It's extremely painful but there are ways to get it back. Usually, a hard thrust against a wall will do it. Not always, though, as it has deteriorated even more over the years.

She couldn't get it back one time, nor could her son Jamie so he took her to the emergency room. They were all stumped.

Dr. Berger has kept in touch with Rachele and me and has gone out of his way at times, attempting to find a doctor or hospital with a solution. They can replace hips and knees but can't fix my daughter. Anyway, we went to a wedding shower for someone in our extended family. My sisters had never seen Rachele when her shoulder was dislocated. We were sitting together when Rachele motioned to me to quietly leave with her to go to the ladies' room. My sister saw us get up and noticed Rachele and gasped. It's not a pretty sight.

By then, Mary, Diane and my mother were with us. They're praying the rosary. Mom is saying "Oh, My God" and crying. Rachele said she'd be fine and for them to go back. They stayed. Mary was insistent on helping. She said that there must be something she could do. Rachele said there was. "Aunt Mary, please go to the bar and get me a double shot of Jack Daniels." When Mary realized she was serious, she got the shots. Rachele downed them, gave it a few minutes to take the edge off the pain.

Thrusting against the wall had become ineffective. Her doctors had come up with another solution. Jamie, her son, had used it effectively many times. Finding an area to do this was tricky. She didn't want to make a scene. We found a large cubby where the pay phones were. Rachele would lie down on her back on the floor (which thankfully, was carpeted), yuk! The thought of all those germs in that carpet grosses me out. She walked me through what I would have to do. I took my shoe off, placed the heel of my foot in her axillary area (armpit) and had to pull on her arm with all my strength. She said to pull hard and fast otherwise it wouldn't work.

Keep in mind, the cubby wasn't long enough to give us enough room for total privacy. Rachele's legs from her knees to her feet were visible to people walking by. As they turned to look, it appeared as if I was standing on her. One person actually wanted to use the phone, then left abruptly. Chele let out one large moan, stood up, dusted herself off and went back to her seat. The rest of us stood there shaking and traumatized. When things settled down, Rachele and I couldn't stop laughing just wondering what went through everyone's mind on witnessing this bizarre event. I'm sure there were those who thought I was insensitive but I follow my daughter's lead in this instance. She refuses to be a victim and finds the humor in everything.

MILITARY

Rachele is very knowledgeable about the Military, Constitution, History and the Bible. She has an amazing wealth of knowledge and an eidetic memory. After high school, her father had taken her to the Naval Shipyard in Philadelphia where she got her physical and was sworn into the Navy. However, she was given an honorable discharge several weeks later when they realized she did not have her high school diploma. She had completed twelve years of school, receiving good grades in all but one subject, Algebra. She also walked with her graduating class, in cap and gown, but she was handed a blank scroll. She was supposed to go to summer school for algebra. On completion of that course, she would receive her diploma but she never followed through. This is something Rachele regrets not doing. I know my daughter and I know she would have "kicked ass" in the Navy.

TRIP TO ATLANTA

Chele' and I flew to Atlanta to visit Jillian and had a great time. We had half the people on the plane laughing and joining us in conversation. I sat opposite the lavatory door and would hold it open when someone came down to use it. Chele' would say "We know what you're doing". People were laughing and asking if they should tip me, in jest. We met guys from Sicklerville who were going to Missouri to hunt. We had such a good time then. However, fast forward a few years and we would have been escorted off the plane. You would have thought we were drinking but we weren't.

Jillian showed us such a good time, including taking us to our first I Max movie. We were able to take our "Dirty Martinis" into the theatre. Jillian's friends Tom and Dan were with us. Once again we stirred things up and got everyone laughing before the movie started. You could tell that Chele' and I didn't get out too often.

Another night we were with a group of Jillian's friends and went to an upscale restaurant. While waiting for our table, we ordered drinks at the bar. Rachele ordered a highball and the bartender looked at her and said "What?" He had no idea what that was. This place had every fancy drink you could imagine. She was trying to explain how to make her favorite drink and ended up behind the bar, making it by herself.

At the hotel we asked to have a wake-up call at 6:00 am and a cab for 7:30 to take us to the nearest Catholic Church. Mass was at 8:00 am. The cab was prompt. We went in to the church and Mass had just started. Of course, the Mass is the same all over the world, so we knew all the prayers by heart and were caught off guard by one phrase that sounded unfamiliar. We looked at each other with a question on our lips….what just happened?

On the way up to receive Communion, Chele' saw a bulletin in the pew and frantically pointed to St. John's Episcopal Church. She asked what I was going to do. I said I was going to receive Communion. She figured I'd feel guilty and go looking for the Catholic church. I said that we fulfilled our Sunday obligation with good intentions. The cab driver was the one who made the mistake. Also, Episcopal, Lutheran, Catholic….we all have the same God. We did have a laugh over that. Oh, Rachele, after we left the church, said "That priest was hot!" He was actor Kevin Bacon's double.

TRIP TO MISSOURI

Rachele and I flew to St. Louis, Missouri then rented a car for the next two hundred miles, which would get us to Mountain View, Missouri to visit our friends, the Conley's. Rachele had not seen her "long ago, childhood friends", as Maureen had so succinctly phrased it. It had been twenty-eight years but when Rachele, Maureen and Michele were reunited, the years melted away and it was like they had never been separated.

However, before we got there we had more traveling to do. It was a crazy road trip with Rachele driving and me navigating. We stopped for gas and met the owner, "Skeeter", who gave us directions after I got us lost for four hours. He sent us down a back road where there were no signs of life. No houses, stores, street lights etc. We had gone about twenty miles then out of nowhere there was a yard sale and the car screeched to a halt.

Chele was talking to me as she got out of the car. She turned her head for a second and when she looked back, I was gone!! "Mom" she screamed, "Where are you?" Unaware of what was about to happen, I opened my door and disappeared into a deep ditch. Chele ran around and was frantic when she saw me sprawled in the ditch. I had had a hip replacement months ago. I could not stop laughing. When she realized that I was okay, we both laughed.

Of course, we couldn't pass up the yard sale. The man was very nice but looked strange, with only one tooth in his entire mouth. Another fifteen miles, no more houses, but we did pass a group of hillbillies camped by the road. They had a fire going and what appeared to be, jugs of moonshine. This was not looking good.

We went another twenty miles, it was desolate and starting to get dark. By this time I was convinced that Skeeter sent us down this deserted road so he could follow us. I was praying out loud, asking Jesus to be with us. I was nearing panic attack mode. Chele was still laughing at me, reliving the moment when I disappeared into the ditch. She got a lot of mileage out of that escapade.

Skeeter never showed up and we finally arrived at the Conley's farm. The next big hurdle came at bedtime when Chele with her bad shoulder and me with my new hip had trouble getting in and out of the king sized water bed we were sharing. All in all, it was a memorable trip and Chele got to see the twenty acres she had bought, a few months before, three miles from the Conley farm.

I'm changing gears here because the water bed reminded me of something Herb did when we stayed with Joann and Jerry. We, also, slept in the waterbed. When we stripped the bed before we left, Herb employed his sense of humor and crisscrossed two huge pieces of duct tape on the bed, as if covering up a hole. That got a good laugh, after the initial shock.

RACHELE AND TOM'S WEDDING

The wedding was beautiful and Rachele is truly amazing and talented in so many areas. She orchestrated the whole wedding and reception. She made her veil and all the bouquets for her and her bridal party. Her bouquet had a cameo with a picture of Jillian in it. She included Mark and Jillian in every possible way. Mark's favorite color, pink and his favorite flower, pink roses were on the tables along with purple irises (Jillian's favorite.) Her bridesmaids gowns were sage green, Jillian's favorite color. She even made her wedding cake with pink roses and purple irises. Little bits of Scripture were everywhere, dangling from the wine bottles and at the place settings. The wedding was in St. John Vianney Catholic Church, since Rachele had been granted an annulment.

There were so many touching moments. One was the father, daughter dance where Herb and Chele' danced to Brad Paisley's "The Man He Didn't Have To Be". They both cried as did I. Another treasured moment was when Brandon asked me to dance.

Rachele also had what can only be described as a heavenly gift, on her wedding day. I'm sure it was one more indication of Jillian and Mark's presence. There were beautiful Easter Lilies blooming in the small garden by the front entrance to the church...on September 14. Rachele, like me, has come to expect miracles but never takes them for granted. She starts her day with the St. Michael Chaplet at 6:00 am on EWTN TV, then the Rosary at 6:30 am. She finds it gives her the best start to her day.

Her gift table had my mother's crocheted table cover on it. My mother had made it when she was pregnant with me, making it seventy years old. On the table was a memorial vase with a pink rose for Mark, a purple iris for Jillian and a white rose for her father. There was also a note attached, with these words "These flowers bloom as a symbol of a life and love remembered." As she walked down the aisle in the church, Kevin's rendition of "Amazing Grace" was playing. It was wonderful seeing Rachele so happy. Our grandsons Jamie, Tyler and Brandon, unbelievably, are now men—very handsome men. Where has all the time gone?

Our trip to Missouri was uneventful. However, on the way home we made up for it. We only had two days there because Herb only gets two weeks vacation. He's been working at the Philadelphia airport for thirty-six years. Every five years a new contract is drawn up and they may change companies, so vacation time starts over again, no accumulation. Four of those days were spent traveling. We flew on previous trips and the luggage was lost and with the nearest airport in Springfield, we'd still have to rent a car and drive several hours. Driving eliminated some problems.

I'm being redundant, yet it's worth repeating. Rachele and Tom's wedding was beautiful and so worth the trip. The trip home, however, was one I would not want to repeat. I've always wanted to travel but this trip cured me of that. There are some people who think that your life will run smoothly if you are Christ centered. While that may be the case sometimes, remember that Jesus promised us that He would be our refuge in a storm. He did NOT say that there wouldn't be any storms.

Herb and I got up at 4:00am and left the Conleys at 5:00 am. It was still dark, it was Sunday but the priest at Rachele's wedding said that their 4:00 pm Saturday wedding Mass fulfilled our Sunday obligation, so we were on our way. The highway was devoid of traffic. Herb anticipated a very easy ride home. An hour and a half into the drive, a small deer came out of nowhere. Another two seconds and we would have missed him. The front right bumper hit him in the rear. He continued running into the woods. We were travelling at sixty-five miles an hour.

Herb got out of the car to survey the damage and said everything looked good. We both said a prayer of thanks that we were okay and it appeared the car was too. Of course, Herb was very upset about the deer. Days later he was still stressing about it. We continued on our way then stopped for coffee. When we came out of McDonalds, there was a puddle of what appeared to be antifreeze under the car. He assumed it was the radiator so we called AAA for a tow to the nearest repair shop. The guy who came to tow us said that he knew of a radiator shop in the next town, which was Rolla. He drove us there but the shop was now out of business.

He wanted to drop us and the car at the nearest motel, which was decrepit looking. He had another call and was anxious to drop us off anywhere. I said "You can't just leave us here. Aren't you supposed to keep us from being stranded?" He asked, "Where do you want to go?" I told him that we didn't know where to go since we're from out of state. He unloaded the car and left us there. As the characters on "Duck Dynasty" would say, "He gone!" (That is not a typo. There is no "s" in that phrase).

We checked into the "Bates Motel" while trying to figure out our next move. Did I mention that it was my birthday, also Rachele's birthday. Herb called AAA to explain the situation, after talking with Joann back at the farm. Her daughter Melissa and her son-in-law David have a garage and work on cars together. We arranged for a tow back to our starting point, Mountain View. In the meantime, David called a shop in Springfield Missouri and had them agree to deliver a new radiator for our car. It was a Sunday and most places were closed. Since David and Melissa normally do business with this company, they were good enough to travel several hours to bring it to them.

David didn't want us to get another tow to his shop. He felt badly for us and said he'd drive the two hours to Rolla with the new part. We were amazed at the generosity of time and talent that David offered to us. We insisted on coming back to their place. The two hour ride back to Mountain View in the cab of the truck was horrendous in terms of pressure on my back and hip and Herb's back. It was such a rough ride. Keep in mind, though, that from the instant we got in the car, the tow truck and the second tow truck, we continued thanking God for protecting us. As Herb repeated several times, it could have been much worse. We were safe and the car would be fixed instead of totaled.

We got to David and Melissa's. They were both looking for the leak. Are you ready? There is no leak, yet we had both seen it dripping. Herb told them that I did pray about the car. David said "Why is it so hard for people to believe in miracles." We're always trying to figure out what God has in store for us. While Herb and David and Melissa were checking the car out further, I was looking at some of the cars that David and Melissa had for sale. They also do restorations. Anyway, I saw a car that I fell in love with, that was inexpensive and thought that maybe this is why we had to come back. Had we been able to facilitate the paperwork, I would have left our car and drove the other car home. Again, it was Sunday and it would mean staying over another day or two and Herb couldn't afford the time off.

Back to the garage, one last shot. David noticed that a small hose was cut. Melissa got some water to put in the windshield wiper reservoir. Sure enough, it leaked out. Apparently, the slight dent in the fender was enough to nick the hose. Herb felt foolish that he hadn't checked further, something he always insists on doing. After all, he is a mechanic. He was thrown off by the color of the green fluid, because of the smell, thinking it was antifreeze.

Herb said that the Duck Dynasty crew has nothing on him, with all the stupid things that they do. He said he'd fit right in. If Uncle Si had been with us he'd probably want to blow up this piece of junk. Herb, however, is not letting go of this Trooper yet. It's a diehard and he's going to run it into the ground.

Herb is determined that I not write this story. He threatened to delete it. Then he threatened to bypass the rest stop after I drank a quart of water. No deal. I'm writing this as we're heading home in our perfectly good 1995 Trooper. He'll never get rid of this car. He asked if I was still writing about this incident, which is very humbling to him. I said it was a great story and the kids would get a laugh out of it. He asked how I'd feel about walking the rest of the way home. Actually, with Herb's overactive sense of humor, even he was laughing as hard as I was. You're a good sport hon.

RACHELE'S POEM TO ME

Rachele has written hundreds of poems. Some have been published in "Great Poems of the Western World". Poetry has always been a love of Chele's since she was in grade school. It just seems to flow effortlessly. It is a gift from God. This poem was written in 2010, four years after she moved to Missouri. Of course, I love this poem. Rachele tends to see the best in me, remember the good times and filter out the negative…so generous and loving.

MY MOTHER, MY FRIEND

Scared and alone, six kids in tow,
What to do now, she just didn't know.
With courage and faith and nights full of tears
My mom said a prayer, then faced all her fears.

Gave strength to her daughters and strength to her sons
Leaving nothing for herself when the day was done.
Many years passed and along came a man
With love in his heart and a ring in his hand.

Once again, her sweet smile reached her green eyes
And she ended each day with embraces and soft sighs.
Her children, now older, with babes of their own,
She recalls the memory of children now grown.

Laments the loss of a daughter and son
And often wonders what might have been.
But still her faith carries her through
To make wonderful memories bright and new.

Plane rides and theatres, ditches and drinks,
Living for God no matter what anyone thinks.
Overlapped laughter of mother and child
Shining through on our faces, the love held inside

Friendship forged from tears and worry
It's nice now a days to not have to hurry.
Now it's long distance calls and boxes from home
Though miles apart, I'm not alone.

At night on my pillow, my head does lay
And I listen to crickets and frogs as they play.
The yip of the coyote and hoot of the owl
Reminds me of how blessed I am now.

As I say my prayers and the moon does rise
I can see in my head, my mother's bright eyes
And I thank the Lord for it all at day's end,
But especially for my mother, my friend

MARK TODD was born at Holy Redeemer Hospital in 1966, weighing in at 8 lbs. 8 oz. He was beautiful! There was fifteen months between Rachele and Mark. David, Kevin and Rachele were all toddlers and fussed over him as if they were miniature parents. Markie thrived on the attention.

Mark was about six years old and had a sling shot. Yes, we knew about it. They were cautioned about safety issues so as not to poke out anyone's eye., just like in the "Christmas Story". He did kill a small bird with it. I found out afterwards when I found him very upset and experiencing a wave of guilt. He was placing a cross that he had made out of sticks, over the grave of the little bird he had buried. He had never expected to hit it….tough lesson.

One of the sweetest memories I have of Mark, and there are many, was when Mark was working at "Moby Dick's" restaurant. He was dating someone much older than he was. Kathy was a teacher. She is also the mother of Mark's daughter, Natalie Rose. More on that later, Anyway, Kathy had just gotten a brand new convertible sports car. She told Mark to take it, on his lunch break. I was home washing windows. Mark came in so excited and grabbed my hand and said, "Let's go, Mom." He insisted that I drive, so I went 25 mph in our West Berlin neighborhood. Mark moaned and said, "Mom, it's a sports car. You need to go on Rte. 73 and feel the power." Ten minutes later, he was saying, "Slow down, Mom. You're going to get a ticket." I felt the power. Just a half-hour out of my day, a day that I will never forget. Mark could have gotten one of his many friends and taken them for a ride, but he chose to share that moment with me.

Another vivid memory I have of Mark took place after Natalie, his daughter, was born. He was a single parent and on that note, he decided to go to "Parents Without Partners" one night. I tried to talk him out of it, to no avail. We were waiting in line outside the Silver Lake Inn. Admission was $5.00. Mark was having second thoughts. He said, "Most of the women that were in line, looked old enough to be grandmothers." I said, "What do you think I am!" He then said that I didn't look like a grandmother. What a great compliment from my nineteen year old son.

Mark decided to stay, but we agreed not to let anyone know that he was my son. Except for one person, nobody knew. We had a lot of fun with that. I was in the ladies' room combing my hair, when two girls in their late twenties, early thirties were talking about this "gorgeous hunk". The one girl was describing Mark, tall, blonde, built, etc. She was on a mission to get his attention. I wanted to say, "Stay away from him. He's my son", but I promised to keep it a secret.

Another girl that I knew, was in her thirties and regularly came to PWP. She was beautiful, to the point that every head turned toward her when she came in. She had a very suggestive way of dancing. I used to feel sorry for the guys she danced with. Actually, she wasn't dancing with them. She was using them so she could go out on the floor and do her incredibly athletic moves and show off. They were no match for her and she actually made fools of them. I told Mark that she was "bad news". Of course, that made her more of a challenge for him

She asked him to dance, on a ladies' choice. When the fast tunes were played, she pulled him out on the dance floor. He was more than willing as he found her very attractive. Her time in the limelight was over. Mark knew what she was doing and played along. Only difference this time, was that there was a circle of women around Mark, cheering him on as he matched this girl step for step, then outdid her with a few splits and moves of his own. Ironically, Mark became a challenge for this girl and although they did date a few times, Mark decided that she wasn't his type. Needless to say, I was relieved.

That same night there was another incident, which made us both laugh. Mark was talking to some people he knew and I was with a friend, across the room from the bar. I noticed someone staring at me. My friend confirmed that he was aware of this before I was. It made me uncomfortable so I just turned my back. Then Mark comes over to me and says "Mom, come with me. I want you to meet someone". Mark took me over to the bar. The guy he wanted me to meet happened to be the one who was leering at me. He was just taking a sip of his drink when Mark said "I'd like you to meet my mother." The guy started to choke on his drink, coughing and sputtering, then stood up straight and became the perfect gentleman. It turned out that the guy was a diving instructor of Mark's. We did have a lot of laughs that night. Mark isn't here physically, but he's here.

SISTER CARMEL AND MARK

Long after Mark was in heaven, the stories about Mark and Sister Carmel still surfaced from time to time. Mark was voted the class clown and lived up to his title. Sister Carmel was so tiny and Mark towered over her. She recalled him in the doorways, swinging from the upper molding. He did make her laugh, however, there was one day he pushed her to the limit. She called me and said, "RoseMarie, I don't know what to do with Mark." I asked what he had done now. She seemed flustered.

Keep in mind that Mark excelled in school despite his antics. Sister explained that she had given an assignment to draw a picture of a man, nothing else. It was religion class and she was going to make a point about something. The pictures the kids drew were of a man fishing, swimming, doing everything under the sun. She repeated her instructions. Draw a man, nothing else. Mark then drew an anatomically correct male figure.

The class roared, Sister was mortified. However, when she told me the story, she also said "I guess all he did was what I told him to do."

We both laughed. I feel sure that Mark is still teasing Sister Carmel in heaven.

MORE MEMORIES OF TEEN YEARS

Mark would always have girls calling him. One time when he had just started dating, he told me he had a date and that the girls were picking him up because they had a car. He did not. He was in the bathroom combing his gorgeous blonde curls when the girls came. One was blonde, one was brunette, both were so pretty. I went in to tell Mark that they were here. I asked him which one was his date. He said "Both." I assumed it would be a double date but he was treating them both to dinner. They were okay with that.

Mark's entrepreneurial side surfaced in eighth grade. He would earn money raking leaves or clearing snow for neighbors. One night I walked into the kitchen to an assembly line. He had spent his money on lunchmeat and snacks and was making dozens of sandwiches and selling lunches at a profit in school. He never ceased to amaze me.

He never lacked in self-confidence. He thought nothing of taking his nephew Steven, diaper bag and all on a date, to give Kevin and Trudi some free time. He loved Steven so much. There was a time that Steven was in the hospital for tests. He was very sick. Mark was working at the Phoenix Room at the racetrack. He was done work at 2:00 am, at which time he would go to the hospital to see his little buddy. Trudi and Kev had gone to get coffee in the cafeteria and when they came back, Mark was there with tears streaming down his face.

FLASHBACK

When David, Kevin, Mark and Rachele were teenagers and Jillian and Mark were toddlers and I was a single parent, we pinched a lot of pennies. The house was kept cool to keep heating costs down. We'd have the fireplace going and would place loose bricks in the front of the screen so they would absorb the heat. On cold nights the kids would take a hot brick wrapped in a towel and place it in their bed under the covers. David was too proud to do that. After several days of hearing the oohs and aahs of crawling into a warm bed, he discreetly came down and grabbed a brick when he thought I wasn't looking.

Mark would try to make a point about how cold it was by wearing his royal blue knit hat to bed. One morning he called me in to show me the scorch mark made by the brick, on his bottom sheet. Old fashioned remedies… everyone had a good laugh. Oh, I still have my Mark's blue hat.

MARK'S DIVING ACCIDENT 1987

Our lives are changed forever. It's been more than two decades since that day, yet, the pain remains intact. Time does not heal. We just learn to hone our coping skills. Mark was with his best friend Greg, at the pool near his apartment in proximity to Camden County College where he was attending classes. He dove from a lifeguard stand but the stand was not secured to the ground. It fell backwards, cutting Mark short from the pool. He struck his neck before entering the water. Greg pulled him out and administered CPR.

We saw him first in the emergency room at John F. Kennedy in Stratford. He looked just as beautiful as ever. I thought he would be alright. He HAD to be. Our priests came, our friends, Mark's friends lined the hall, some sitting on the floor crying. He never regained consciousness. It was just a matter of days when the doctor came to discuss organ donation. I remember thinking, "Oh My God! This is real. He's not going to sit up and hug me or take me for another sports car ride or for another lunch. No more jokes and laughter. I'll never be able to smile or laugh again without my Markie Spark.

The floodgates are open and even though it's twenty-five years since that day, I feel as if I'll never be able to stop crying. I miss you sooo much Mark.

Happiness is situational. Joy, however can be experienced in spite of tragedy. I miss my Mark every single day but I am also blessed with having a closeness with my children. Yet, it's at family gatherings that I miss Mark the most. There's always that empty seat at the table or one less body doing flips off the diving board. I do find joy in my memories of Mark. Some are painfully touching, others are hilariously funny.

MARK'S WEDDING GIFT TO ME, A MIRACLE

Mark is alive and well. Just not here. I have so much comfort knowing that I will be with him again. He wasn't physically here for Herb's and my wedding day, but he was with me. The night before our wedding day I bought flowers at ShopRite, to take to the cemetery for Mark. It was after ten at night so there was nobody in the florist section to wrap or price the flowers. I just started pulling out flowers that I knew Rachele and Jillian would be carrying in their bouquets. There were a half dozen different types of flowers, most of which I couldn't identify, except for stargazer lilies. I had a beautiful, nicely rounded bouquet for Mark.

As I gathered the flowers, I talked to Mark, telling him these flowers were just like his sisters would be carrying the next day. I was ready to leave and realized that I hadn't put a rose in the bouquet. I would be carrying roses. The only roses they had were long stemmed. When I placed two roses in the center of the bouquet, it looked ridiculous. They were so much taller than all the other flowers. I went to the cemetery and had my talk with Mark, and my cry, then apologized for the odd arrangement of flowers. I couldn't cut the stem to the rose, so it just jutted out.

Next day I prayed so hard that I would have a sign from Mark that he was with me. At the house, before the wedding, the florist delivered the flowers for me and my girls. She wanted to talk to me but seemed nervous. She normally did not deliver the flowers. She just arranged them. This morning was different, though. While she was getting the flowers ready, the card with my name and address fell on the floor. She couldn't believe it at first, then realized I was Mark's mother. She was a friend of Mark's and although it was six years since Mark had gone to heaven, this girl thought of him all the time because she would pass our house. She talked about his kindness and his sense of humor and she wanted me to know that she had loved him as a friend and had not forgotten him. We both cried and she apologized for making me cry on my wedding day. I hugged her and said that they were tears of joy and thanked her for this gift. I thanked God for this answer to my prayer. Little did I know there was more to come.

We went to Luciens for the reception and the maitre d came to me to tell me that there was a problem with the flowers I had ordered for the tables. I had ordered gold and burgundy chrysanthemums, perfect for October. She showed me my order slip that she had given the florist. She couldn't understand how such a huge mistake had been made. She said that I wouldn't have to pay for them and apologized profusely. When I saw the flowers on the table, I got the chills. On each and every table was the exact bouquet I had taken to Mark at the cemetery. A few people remarked about the odd arrangement, the two long stemmed roses poking out from the center of each bouquet. I kept hearing "I don't know how this could have happened." I smiled, looked up and said "I do."

Mark had a sense of humor that wouldn't quit. He could make me laugh in the middle of me reprimanding him. He'd hike up the waist of his pants, to his armpits and act like a nerd just to get a laugh. We had a half wall divider between the dining room and kitchen. It had spindles on it. Mark would hang on them, make sounds like a monkey and swing from one to the other. No matter how much I yelled for him to stop, he wouldn't until I laughed. He always said that he wanted to see me smile, laugh and be happy. You've given me so many good memories to draw from, Mark. Along with yours and those of your brothers and sisters, and the ongoing "works in progress" that we all live each day, you'll be glad to know, Mark, I am happy honey. I am very happy.

UPDATE: 2010

Once again, God has granted me a gift. We have a picture of Jillian & Mark on the memorial book which sits on a pedestal near the Blessed Mother in our church. People walking up to receive Communion pass by and see their names and photos. One day after Mass a man came up to me, introduced himself as the father of one of my CCD students and told me he used to work with Mark at Lucien's and knew him well. Twenty-four years later God is letting me know that Mark is remembered by people who cared about him. This is so uplifting to me. His son Devon was in my CCD class for three years and we have become friends with his entire family.

Devon and his family were here for a swim party in 2015. He is now a junior in high school, a wrestler and a lector at church. This young boy was in my CCD class for several years. Now, he towers over me, is a lifeguard and serving his community and church. He exudes confidence, humility and respect. I am so proud of him.

UPDATE 2014

It is the twenty sixth anniversary of Mark's homecoming (heaven). Rachele had called me the night before. She knew it was always a difficult day for me and that I would go to Mass and try to keep busy. Although this next paragraph seems disconnected, bear with me.

Herb and I have a casual friendship with a young girl, Linda, that we met at church when they were both attending classes to convert to Catholicism. Eventually, Linda asked Herb to be godfather to her daughter, Lila. Linda was a single parent and did not have anyone else who was Catholic, who could stand for her. Herb said yes.

There is no easy way to say this. Though Linda does not label herself a medium (someone who connects with those who have passed on), that is her gift. I was initially upset when she would tell me that Jillian and sometimes Mark would "speak" with her. I was actually angry the first time she told me these things. Why would they talk to her and not me! Keep in mind she had never met Jillian. She had never been to our home where I have many pictures of Jillian displayed. Anyway, as time went on I realized there were things she was telling me that she or anyone else couldn't possibly know. Yet, she did and was so accurate to the point of being eerie.

On this anniversary of Mark's I took a mug of tea outside and talked to him. It was a beautiful day, yet my heart ached. I heard the sound of a kitten crying. It was coming from under the deck. I got a flashlight and looked under the deck to see a tiny, pitiful black and white kitten with mud caked on his face and whiskers. He looked about four weeks old. I coaxed him out and cleaned him up with a warm washcloth and tried to get him to eat something. He didn't seem to know how to eat. He obviously was still nursing but his mother was nowhere to be found. He curled up in a soft blanket and went to sleep.

I went to Mass and was surprised that so many people greeted me afterwards, sharing memories of Mark even though twenty-six years had passed. That was a gift. My friend Maureen took me to breakfast. I even did some shopping and had a very uplifting day. This was very unusual for my children's anniversaries. Normally, depression would take hold.

I went home and found a message from Rachele, asking me to call her. She, also, knew Linda and had gotten a call from her. She told Rachele that she saw me smiling and laughing and Jillian and Mark were on either side of me. She said, "Your mom's having a great day!" Rachele told Linda that she was wrong and asked if Linda knew what day it was. She did not. Rachele told her it was Mark's anniversary and I never had a good day then. Linda insisted, saying she was sorry but she was just telling her what she saw.

Then Rachele said, "I think Linda is losing it." Because Linda said that she saw Mark and Jillian touch their fingers to their lips as if to say "Be quiet. We have a surprise for mom." Then she said that they bent down and when they stood up, they had kittens in each of their hands. When I had told Rachele about the kitten, she was stunned. When I told her I had a really good day she couldn't believe it. After hearing about Linda's account of the kittens I thought, please, don't let there be others. Fast forward, yes there were others that showed up days later. But the little black and white one was our favorite. We named him Silas. Our grandson Jake called him Silas Robertson after Uncle Si on Duck Dynasty.

LUCIENS OLD TAVERN

Lucien's holds many good memories for me. My son, Mark worked there as a waiter. Many years later Herb and I had our wedding reception there. We had Ryan and Jenny's rehearsal dinner there. Nikki and Bobby were also married there. I never realized all the history behind Lucien's until I came across a book "The Inn Book", a field guide to Old Inns and Good Food by Kathleen Neuer, written and published in 1974. The following is from that book.

"Things have changed in the last two centuries to be sure. This little ole tavern isn't so little anymore, and you need a knowledgeable guide—maybe an on-site dig—to separate the old sticks and stones from the shiny new additions. Speaking of ghosts, Lucien still greets guests as they enter, smiling from a portrait on the wall, and from beyond the grave still dictates the menus and the recipes. A good restaurateur has to be egotist or despot. Lucien, it appears, was a bit of both. He left the old place to his employees who own and operate it as if he were theirs."

My Mark felt so at home in this place. They almost immediately promoted him from busboy, the job he had applied for, to waiter. Lucien's was then, and still is a very classy place. Although now, they do strictly catering for weddings and other occasions. Mark had wanted me to come and see him work. He also wanted me to meet a few people he worked with. This was not the easiest thing for me to do. I was single again and had never been to a bar until my late thirties. I was still not entirely comfortable going places alone. However, at Lucien's, with my son there I was at ease.

Mark had me sit at the bar (another big step for me) and he introduced me to the bartender. He had given him specific instructions to take care of his mom. Joe would not only make the latest drinks that were popular, but also kept a variety of appetizers coming out from the kitchen. Mark had told him that I loved to eat and sample new things. The kitchen staff seemed only too happy to have feedback on their original creations.

While sitting there I was able to observe Mark and the other waiters. Mark had a gift for getting along with other people. He had more tables than anyone, yet he seemed relaxed, interacting with his customers. He complimented Mrs. Curtis' new hairstyle (very observant) and discussed football scores with her husband. As they would take the last sip of their drink, a new one would appear as if by magic. Mark juggled all his tables with the greatest of ease.

Mark and I had talked about his job before. He had been a busboy before this. I always encouraged him to be observant of people and he would be able to discern something of interest to them, giving him openings to converse with them. It was obvious that people loved him. That's why he had so many more tables than the other waiters. I was so impressed and proud of him, not just his accomplishments but the way he treated others.

Mark was a hard and tireless worker. He actually got into trouble at another restaurant, Pier III in Atco, N.J., for doing too much! The waitresses loved him because he often would help them serve when things got too busy. One of the waitresses told me that all the other busboys would stand around until it was time to clear tables. Mark could not stand to be idle or to see the girls work so hard. He seemed to be determined to know everyone's job description, so he could pitch in whenever needed.

Mark even cooked for me when he was home. I was in nursing school and had to study at night, so Mark would offer to make something. He really was a fantastic cook for one so young.

One of the things I could never seem to get right in the kitchen was the dressing for Caesar Salad. Mark made an exceptionally good Caesar salad, rubbing the bowl with fresh garlic, cracking the egg, squeezing the right amount of fresh lemon juice and he did it all at the tableside of the customers—what confidence. He promised to show me how to make this specialty but never got the chance. It's strange, the things we do under duress, not thinking clearly. I remember as if it were yesterday, running into the emergency room to be with Mark, after his diving accident. It didn't seem real. This wasn't happening. I remember telling him I loved him. Then I started rambling nonsensically about how he had to teach me to make the Caesar salad. Maybe it was denial or sheer terror. I expected him to open his eyes and say "Okay mom.", but he didn't....and my life changed forever.

PAINFUL REALIZATION

People have asked me how I was able to deal with the loss of my son, Mark. I don't know that I ever did completely "deal" with the devastation of losing my precious son. I miss him everyday, yet, I know that he is still with us. We all have our stories of how we believe Mark still intervenes in our lives. Ryan has several stories that he can relate, whether it was in extremely rough surf in Ocean City when he was surfing alone and was struck in the head by his surfboard as the waves tossed it around. He had promised me that he would not go surfing alone. He insisted that he had not been alone, that Mark was with him. There was also the time that Ryan swerved his truck on Route 73 to avoid hitting someone who changed directions at the last minute without signaling. His truck rolled over, and when he opened his eyes, he was looking at the asphalt. He came out without a scratch. He knew that Mark was there protecting him. Even stranger is the fact that Route 73 always has a high traffic volume, but not that day at that time.

There were several catalysts that made me realize that I could not continue in a constant state of depression. It wasn't fair to my other children, yet, I wasn't able to see that at the time. The first time that hit home was when I was standing at the stove cooking dinner, crying quietly. David had just walked in and, without me even turning around, knew I was upset. All he said was "Mark?" and I responded yes. He came up behind me, put his arms around me and said, "You still have me, mom." Such a simple statement and, at the same time, so profound. David was right. David's words began to help me heal. The pain was still there but I knew that, with God's help, I could still live a good life. I have so many wonderful children and grandchildren. If I didn't get on with my life, I'd be cheating all of them.

As often happens, with a change of attitude, the heart doesn't always follow. I knew what I had to do but found it difficult to do it. I would have good days and then a totally unrelated incident would jolt me afresh with wracking pain. One time I was with a friend at the Berlin Farmer's Market, outside at the flea market. I was enjoying the sunny day and found myself smiling at times. My eyes glanced down at someone walking by. I didn't even see their face, just their feet. This person had on Italian leather loafers and was not wearing socks. My Mark wore the same type of shoes with no socks. I had made such a point of having the undertaker, our friend Jim Giosa, make sure that we could see that Mark was not wearing socks. It was so important to me to see that little patch of bare skin on Mark's ankle.

There were so many recurring memories it was becoming increasingly difficult to pick myself up each time, so to speak. I knew that I could not do it alone. I begged for God's help. At this time, if my memory serves me well, it had been about two years since Mark had gone home to heaven. Ask and you shall receive. I needed to get a second job to help in paying the bills. I applied for a job with Bayada and was assigned a case in a nearby town. I was to care for a young man, twenty years old, in his home. When I arrived at the house, Bob was in a wheelchair with a tray in front of him. He had on thick glasses, his head was bobbing up and down and he was drooling. He required total care. He had to be tube fed, bathed, diapered, etc. He was nonverbal but his parents seemed to think he was responding positively to me. I spent time with him, talking to him as I did whatever needed to be done. Having worked with handicapped children and young adults for years, I was comfortable. I believed that this was what God wanted me to do. It didn't matter if I was told that the person wasn't aware I was there. I always talked to them, or read or attempted to interact with them as if they were aware.

After Bob's shower, I was tucking him into his bed, still talking to him and even kidding around with him. On the wide windowsill beside his bed were several 5"x 7" and 8"x10" frames with photos of this tall, dark and handsome guy. One photo was of the prom with this young man in a tux and his beautiful girlfriend, in another he was in a football uniform, holding his helmet, his arm encircling his girl. There was no resemblance at all between the boy in the photos and the boy in the bed, yet I knew that they were one and the same. I stood staring at the photos when his mother walked in and confirmed that they were all of Bob. I was trembling and a wave of nausea hit. I continued to talk to Bob and finally said goodnight to him and his family.

In my car, the tears I had been holding back, spilled over and wouldn't stop. I had asked God to help me deal with losing Mark. I never expected it to happen this way. All the way home I thanked Jesus for taking Mark home to be with Him. My Mark, the athlete, the daredevil and risk taker who squeezed every ounce of life out of every situation, who did wheelies on his dirt bike and rode it into the lake, who surfed in summer and winter, who scuba dived with his brothers, who loved to dance....I thought of him in that chair like Bob and I knew that Mark is much happier where he is now. He's probably catapulting from cloud to cloud and filling the heavens with his ever present joy and laughter.

How do I handle it? With God's help. Thank you God for the twenty wonderful years with Mark. Thank you for trusting him to my care. You must love me so much. More than I ever realized.

Another memory of Mark just flitted through my thoughts. Mark had asked me to meet him at the Diamond Diner in Cherry Hill to see him compete in a break dancing contest. He would be coming over after he was done work at the Phoenix Room at the Garden State Racetrack. A friend and I went to the restaurant early. Keeping with my still reticent nature, I chose a booth in the back, where I could still see the dance floor. I thought that Mark may have been embarrassed if everyone knew that his mother was there. Boy! was I insecure. I should have known better. He came bounding in, headed right for me, gave me a hug and called several people over to meet me. Needless to say, he won the contest and I have another memory for my storage bank.

My faith sustains me, my memories of "Markie Spark" are tangible and I have the very last words Mark spoke to me. He had visited me that day, left and called later from his apartment. He wanted to let me know that he would help me get rid of some wood that was under our little porch. He had forgotten to tell me that when he was over. Then he told me that he loved me. I said the same thing to him too. Because he was always joking around, he got serious and repeated it. "Mom, I mean I *really* love you." I love you too Mark.

GENE RYAN

"SOME MEN ARE DRAWN TO OCEANS. THEY CANNOT BREATHE UNLESS THE AIR IS SCENTED WITH A SALTY MIST."

This quote by Earl Hamner (The Waltons), epitomizes my youngest son. He and his family seem to have an ongoing love affair with the ocean. They swim and surf no matter what the weather or the season is. Sometimes I swear that they have salt water running through their veins.

Gene Ryan was born in the summer of 1975 in the middle of a heat wave. You would think by now that I would have the labor routine down to a science, this being my fifth baby. However, since this birth was to be my second 'frank' breech presentation, (Rachele was the first), it wasn't quite that simple.

A couple of weeks before Ryan was born, he was in the perfect position for a normal delivery. Then George and I saw the movie "Jaws". The scene where one of the men was underwater checking the damage to the boat, a dead body floated into view. I screamed and was terrified, my heart pounding. I felt Ryan shift in my body. Next day we went to the doctor and he was totally taken aback when he said that the baby had shifted and was in a breech position.

I was walking in our front yard on Dock Road., Atco, N.J., when I went into labor. We had a tree, heavy with sour cherries that I gorged myself on. After about six hours of pains, ever increasing in number and intensity, George and I made our first trip to the E.R. My doctor met us there. Apparently, I was not ready to deliver, but why waste a trip and an opportunity.

John F. Kennedy hospital in Stratford, N.J. was a teaching hospital. Since a 'frank breech' (buttocks first) presentation was not an everyday occurrence, I was asked if I would be receptive to being examined by the doctors in training. This was a great opportunity for them. How else would they learn. I agreed. George and I didn't know what we were having but when one of the young doctors examined me, he became so excited at being able to tell the sex, that he let it slip. I don't believe that George heard him, but I did. We were having another boy. I was ecstatic! After all the exams, I was sent home to wait and continue my labor. It never stopped. Breech births, many times, cause erratic labors and take longer. At least, that's what I was told. It held true, both times for me.

I feel blessed to have had six normal deliveries. Years later when I was in nursing school and on a rotation in Labor and Delivery, I realized how lucky I was. The doctors when confronted with a breech presentation, automatically did a C section. They said it was too risky for mother and baby. Considering that my babies were so big, it increased the risk. Needless to say, Someone was watching over me.

Gene Ryan weighed in at 8lbs. 10oz. He was perfect and perfectly beautiful. I was in my room just long enough for the nurse to tell me to stay put for a few hours because of the difficult delivery. My excitement overcame me. I was on a 'high', as I always was after having my babies. As soon as the nurse left, I got up and went to the nursery to check on Ryan.

Keep in mind, that I thought I was done having babies after Mark was born. Here it is, nine years later. It's like being given a second chance to bring a new life into the world. It definitely doesn't get any better than that.

I remember holding Ryan and nursing him and my tears would be dripping all over his little face. I was even more in awe this time around because I was older and more appreciative. Ryan was such a good baby and had so much attention from his older brothers and sister. Kevin wrote a song for him and gave him some crazy, cute sobriquet. "Bunky boo boy Ryan".

Ryan would be on a blanket on the floor, surrounded by his brothers and sister. They would shower him with attention. Even Sheba, our German Shepherd was so possessive with him. She wouldn't let anyone but us get close to him. She would stand, like a sentry at his cradle and growl if a stranger or one of the kid's friends got too close.

George had made a cradle before Ryan was born. It was absolutely beautiful. When our friend Father Bober came to visit, he brought a visiting Bishop from India. Anyway, the Bishop blessed the cradle. That cradle meant so much to me.

Lorraine and Paul, our friends from Philadelphia, were Ryan's godparents. They bought his christening gown and placed two hats in with the gown. One was a little boys cap and the other was a little girl's frilly bonnet. Since this definitely was our last baby, I asked Lorraine why she would give me a girl's hat too. She nonchalantly said it was for the baby we would have the following year. I laughed and said, "No way!" A few months later, I was pregnant with Jillian and thrilled about it. Now the two babies would grow up together. Lorraine just grinned from ear to ear when she saw our precious daughter in her bonnet.

We had a beautiful rancher, built by George and Jerry Conley on a country road in Atco, at this time. We also had two acres. I'd walk Ryan, in his stroller, to the end of the road across from our neighbors, the Newmans. They had a seventeen acre farm. Anyway, we'd pick and eat blueberries until we were sated. Gene Ryan and his stroller were stained with the juice from these luscious gems.

We were in a financial bind at this time. The Newmans would bring strawberries, peas, squash and other vegetables to us. This helped so much. When Ryan was born, instead of a baby gift, we got a chicken and all the fixings. They were so generous. They used to have a dog named "Charlie Brown", who would run over to greet Gene Ryan. He would giggle every time he saw him.

Norm Newman is in his late eighties, as is Evelyn. I still visit once a month. On a recent visit, my memory was jarred by an old lawnmower on their property. The engine was not in it. There was this huge gaping hole. I started to say, "Norm, do you remember the day George left for a business trip and....." Norm laughed and finished reminiscing for me. He said, "I sure do remember the day Gene Ryan got his head stuck in a similar lawn mower without the engine. Norm came to the rescue. Then he shook his head in disbelief as he said, "And now, Gene Ryan's a police officer. Where did the time go?"

MORE CHILDHOOD MEMORIES

Ryan loved eating vegetables picked right from our garden, tomatoes, peppers etc. He wasn't much for cookies and sweets. He'd think nothing of biting into a tomato, warm from the sun, juice dripping down his little chin.

One event that I don't like to recall occurred when Ryan was about eighteen months old. It was in our kitchen. I had the oven on. The light was on in the oven also. He was just a few feet away from me when I heard a scream and saw him with his tiny hands up against the oven door. He must have been trying to see inside. Oven doors weren't insulated well back then. We took him to the emergency room where they applied Silvadene cream and bandaged his tiny hand. It was heartbreaking. Of course, I felt terrible and guilt ridden. He was so good and didn't even complain. He did heal uneventfully. It was one palm that was burned. It looked like a bad sunburn. This was one time I should have put him in the playpen. He would have been able to watch me cook from there. Maybe this is why I'm such a proponent of playpens, although they seem to be a thing of the past.

SEPTEMBER 26, 1979 10:30 pm JOURNAL ENTRY

This is an entry from a journal that I rarely wrote in. My entries were few and far between. This one brought back a memory with such clarity, I felt as if I had traveled back in time.

"I just came home from St. Ed's Parish and the "Visitors for Christ Program" to see all of you sleeping so soundly.

Ryan, you're all cuddled up to Mark in his bed, while the trundle bed (your bed) is empty. I look back on this day and see so many beautiful moments to be thankful for. I hollered at Jillian today for being naughty. You heard your sister crying Ryan, and came running, asking what happened. When I told you, you put your arm around your little sister and said, "C'mon babe, I'll take care of you." You took her into the bathroom, got a tissue and holding Jillian's head still with one hand, wiped her tears away with your other hand. Then you held the tissue to her nose and told her to "blow". You kissed her and said she'd be alright. How precious you babies are to me.

Later that day, you and Jillian had a fight over raisins. Jillian, you wanted them all and grabbed Ryan's bowl too. He pulled them away and so on it went. Are these the two angels from this morning? Naptime was the same old routine. I lay you down in your crib Jillian and you'll ask for your list of "comfys"... your hanky, then a cover, your Winnie the Pooh baby pillow, Baby Anne and last of all you need to "Kip Ry" (kiss Ryan). He climbs in your crib, leans down and kisses you and says "I love you babe." Jillian, you tell Ryan that you love him too. Are these the same precious angels who were fighting over raisins an hour ago?

You talked to Jesus this morning Ryan. I love to hear you do this. We could all learn from you. You looked up at His picture held up your foot and said, "Thank you for my sneakers Jesus and my cereal and Babe and the sun and my toys. Jillian, you just say "Hi God." David treated you to lollipops later. You babies are loved more than you'll ever know.

When daddy left for work, you kissed him, Ryan, and told him to be careful. Your love for everyone just pours forth in so many little ways. This afternoon you spent a half hour raking a pile of leaves and were so proud of it. You also thanked me after dinner and said it was good. How beautiful the world would be if we were as complimentary to others as you are.

You had a nice treat today. Rachele brought you each your own bag of cheese twists from school. More often than not, the little bit of spending money your

2

brothers and sister have, is spent on the "babies." How generous all of you are. Goodnight my children....know that daddy and I love you very much."

Ryan was, and still is, close to all his brothers. One of my fondest memories is of Mark taking him on his bike when he delivered papers. I also remember Mark teaching him to shoot baskets. Ryan loves to surf even when the waves are dangerously high. He knows that Mark is there protecting him. He's also an avid hunter and fisherman. His daughter, Makenzie already takes after him in that respect. She's had her picture in the local paper several times for her catches.

Ryan has a timely sense of humor. He would leave me silly notes in an effort to make me laugh and usually succeeded. He was also very sensitive. One incident stands out in my mind. I was in a Hallmark store buying a card, when I heard one salesgirl call to another to "show this young man some cards that would be appropriate for his mother, however, it was for no special reason". Since the card displays were so high, I couldn't see over them to see who was talking. I remember thinking "I hope that mother appreciates her wonderful son". Later that evening, Ryan gave me a card for no reason, expressing his love. He was the boy who had been in the Hallmark store that day. Needless to say, I cried tears of joy, thanking God for my wonderful son.

Another treasured memory took place in the woods in Medford. It was a very cold day and Ryan had brought me to the woods to show me where he hunted. I also saw his tree stand and got butterflies in my stomach, seeing how high up it was. I kept my fears to myself. I was so happy, even honored, that he had wanted to share this with me. I can still smell the woodsy scent and hear the crunch of leaves, the memory is that vivid. Afterwards we went to McDonald's for breakfast.

MORE MEMORIES

Ryan's first car was a red Ford Mustang. Herb drove Ryan to the car dealer to pick up the car. He didn't have the car insured yet, so we couldn't go for a ride, but we did the next best thing. Ryan was so proud of his car and wanted me to check it out. I remember that it was a bitterly cold day, but we sat in the car with the engine running and the heater warming us. He had the radio turned up loud and Jimmy Buffett was singing "Margaritaville". Ry and I sang along at the top of our lungs.

Ryan's love of surfing brings forth another memory. He was taking a course in criminal law and had to write an essay. He wrote at length about a time that he went surfing in the aftermath of a storm. Of course, I did not know about this at the time. This was a dangerous situation, but Ryan is a risk taker, like Mark was and Jillian is. I had elicited a promise from him that he would never surf alone. Yet, after reading this eloquent, sensitive, loving tribute to his brother, Mark, I realized that he had gone alone. What happened that day was frightening and given the circumstances, could have been tragic. He sustained a head injury from his surfboard, which was tossed around in the rough surf. He was also pinned to the bottom of the ocean, disoriented in trying to discern which direction to swim. However, Ryan made it clear that he wasn't alone. His brother Mark was with him. This speaks of love, trust and an unshakeable faith.

Ryan has also added running to his activities, as do Jen and Kenzie and Jake. To date, he had participated in "Tough Mudder" obstacle courses that benefit "Wounded Warriors Foundation and other charities. Jenny has recently completed one course with him. Kenzie is awaiting her turn which will come in a few years.

As mentioned previously, Ryan's dream came to fruition. He is a police officer of the highest caliber. God had richly blessed him with his extraordinary family, many wonderful friends and the respect of all who know him. The closeness he has with his brothers, is one of my greatest joys. I am so proud of Ryan for so many reasons. He is a wonderful faith-filled man, phenomenal father, husband and police officer. These are not just my words and observations but those of whom he works with and those who have the privilege of knowing him. Once again, God has blessed me with the gift of yet, one more extraordinary son.

JILLIAN MARIE, my baby girl.....my last born.

I relive Jillian's birthday, her actual birth, as I do with all of my children, on their special day. They feign abhorrence of this practice, yet, I know they will miss it, if I ever stop trying to reminisce. Now, I do it quietly. It brings me profound joy to be able to remember details and emotions as if it were yesterday, recalling their birth. It is indeed a gift, because, in other things, my memory fails me. Jillian was born fifteen months after Gene Ryan and weighed 8 lbs, 10 ½ ounces. I can see Dr. Berger holding Jillian up in front of him, saying, "She has piano fingers." God, was she beautiful! I wish that I could go back in time to hold her close to me, one more time, in that delivery room. I wish that I could describe the feeling of holding my baby girl, but the only word that comes to mind is "ineffable", Jillian's favorite word.

Jillian, the baby and "Babe" to her brother, Ryan was, and still is, so loved by all her brothers and sister. On her last visit home, her oldest brother, David showed her just how much he loved her. While that may not sound very profound, it was, considering David's not one to get involved when someone is experiencing problems as Jillian was. Unconditional love is a gift not to be taken for granted. Without going into detail I can recall the day after David had talked to Jillian. She was leaning against the stove drinking her tea and grinning from ear to ear. I asked her what she was smiling about. She replied "David loves me mom. I mean he REALLY loves me." I'm sure she had already known that but now she felt it.

Just a bit of trivia that not everyone in our family knows. Jillian was baptized "Gillian Marie". I loved the British spelling of her name. Years later I had it changed to "Jillian" because of the teasing she got, using the nickname Gilligan from Gilligan's Island.

Jillian's talents abound. Her musical ability began to surface when she was in first grade. I remember her standing on our tiny deck on Franklin Avenue with an Alabama tape playing. She sang "Mountain Music" at the top of her lungs. I was shocked at how good she was. This tiny little wisp of a girl was belting the song out like she was on stage. She wasn't standing still either. Holding her "mike" she was dancing around with movements like a pro. This ability was obviously innate.

Jillian has a beautiful voice, she's a self-taught guitarist and singer. She's a writer of lyrics that evoke strong emotions and touch the soul. There are so many things that Jillian does to perfection. She's a graphic designer and a massage therapist. God must be pleased with you Jillian for using and perfecting the talents that He blessed you with. Always remember, every breath, every good thing on this earth is a gift from God. Anything not good usually comes from us turning away from Him. We all do it, over and over. Yet, He's always there loving us and forgiving us, if we ask.

Jillian was on the evening news for a segment in kick boxing. She's done a Chili's Restaurant commercial. Thankfully, Rachele taped it and we still have it along with her skydiving DVD. She piloted a small plane and has run numerous races to raise money for "Make a Wish Foundation" and other noble causes. I have photos of her riding a bicycle and white water rafting with large groups for charitable causes. She is the only girl in these groups.

A HUMOROUS MEMORY

Jillian is now a certified massage therapist. She relates to me how at the end of the day, she was responsible for laundering and folding all the towels she used. This is one time that she said she was not happy, inheriting my OCD (Obsessive Compulsive Disorder.) Both my girls loved doing laundry, just like me. The problem came when she opened the closet to put her neatly folded towels away—folded just as I had taught her. Fold in half, then half again, then in thirds so no open edges show. All the other towels in the closet were folded 'wrong'. She said "Mom, I couldn't leave until I refolded every towel in the closet. It would have bothered me all night." Sorry honey.

TIME MARCHES ON

Where have the years gone…If I close my eyes and go back in time, I'm rocking you while you nurse. I can hear and feel your little rosebud mouth, sucking. It was so easy to give you what you wanted and needed then. Oh, that I could give you anything that you want or need now. I can almost smell your baby soft scent. I can't seem to stop crying. I wish you were here so that I could hold you close. I am so grateful that God blessed me with you, Jillian.

It seems appropriate to me that I end these pages with words that I read a long time ago. They touched me so deeply because they were my feelings, but author, Barbara Kingsolver penned these words in her novel, "The Poisonwood Bible". I read them every year to Jillian on her birthday. She told me that she loved hearing these words, year after year.

"A mother's body remembers her babies—the folds of soft flesh, the softly furred scalp against her nose. Each child has its own entreaties to body and soul. It's the last one, though, that overtakes you. But the last one: the baby who trails her scent like a flag of surrender through your life when there will be no more coming after—oh, that's love by a different name. She is the babe you hold in your arms for an hour after she's gone to sleep. If you put her down in the crib, she might wake up changed and fly away. So instead you rock by the window, drinking the light from her skin, breathing her exhaled dreams. Your heart bays to the double crescent moons of closed lashes on her cheeks. She's the one you can't put down." I started the day as I do each day, with prayer and thanksgiving. I cannot conceive of not doing this. Despite my concerns about our children, retirement, finances etc., we are so blessed!!

JILLIAN'S BIRTHDAY! JOURNAL ENTRY

My baby girl just got a wonderful job and sounds so happy, despite her serious problems. Other gifts flow in abundance. I woke up this morning, Herb woke up, the sun is streaming in the windows, warming me as I write. Outside temperature is in the low 30's. The trees are stark and bare but I have my sight to see them, not everyone does. The annoying sound of traffic, even through closed windows, reminds me that I have my hearing. Oh, thank you, Jesus, for my sense of taste. I love to eat…and savor the warmth of your wine, too. Thank You for grapes, fresh fruit, hot water for my bath and a thermostat to make us comfortable with so little effort. Jillian never took these things for granted and was very vocal about it. Thermostats and hot baths were at the top of her list.

Thank you for our health and for good doctors when our health fails. Thank you for my new hip. On my walk, thanks for Your gifts You leave in my path, the crimson leaf, the pine branch with tiny, perfectly formed pine cones and even a clear, sea green cat's eye marble and smiles from people. Please don't ever let me hurry so much that I take these things for granted.

Thank You, especially, for my faith. I would not have survived without You. I know that, like I know my name. Thank you for my children and my husband and our many good friends. Thank you for laughter. Herb and I seem to do so much of that, especially during our scrabble games. With all the aches, pains and limited mobility, thank you again for humor.

I am thankful especially today, on Jillian's birthday, for her. I ache to see her in so much emotional pain. She is not aware of what a gift she is to me, to her father and brothers and sister and to all who know her. She's dealing with tremendous problems now.….Depression and the debilitating end result it entails. She's struggling with ridding herself of prescription drugs, an addiction in part, made easy by a doctor who isn't conscientious about his patients. My baby girl is so strong, though she doesn't see it or feel it, but I do. Besides, if we did everything based on feelings alone, they'll screw us up.

GEORGIA

Our relationship when Jillian was in high school was strained. She rebelled, as do most teenagers. She became very moody. Back then I didn't give it much thought. Hindsight, however, indicates the onset of bipolar disorder. Years later, I spoke with my family physician who had a nephew with this disorder. He said that it usually takes about eight years to get an accurate diagnosis. Then there is the trial and error of combinations of different drugs. He also said that sometimes the drugs can exacerbate the situation. That may take years to fine tune.

She wasn't happy in school anymore. One of her teachers told me that she excelled at everything and in hindsight, said that she needed something more challenging but by that time Jillian was headed south. As she matured, our relationship became close. But that wasn't until she moved to Georgia. Jillian wanted so much for her family to visit her and see her in her new home, her new life in Georgia. She took such pride in taking Herb and me to her place of work and all the unique attractions in Georgia. Years later Kevin and Rachele would visit her there. Although, Herb and I didn't go often due to financial circumstances, I am so glad that we did get to go a half dozen times, meet her friends and eat at some of her favorite restaurants.

Jillian was nineteen when she went to Georgia. She has been on her own for over ten years. She survived on her own, made friends, was successful in her work and did things so frightening to me—jumping out of airplanes, climbing mountains, rock climbing blind folded, which was an exercise in learning how to trust your partner in extreme circumstances (I still have difficulty watching the video of that), riding a motorcycle, making presentations in front of large groups of people. I actually am thankful that she's done these things and I'm so proud of her. Of course, ambivalence allows my fears in. Then, a balance—I couldn't and I wouldn't stop her if I could. I don't want her to be afraid of everything, like I was.

Prayer was the element that erased my fears for her. I can't do anything. God can do everything, so I left her in God's hands. He's kept her safe from most dangers. However, He will not force her to do anything. Free will is His gift to us. I guess, how we use it, is our gift to Him. The same applies to our talents.

RoseMarie Dalbow

TEEN MEMORIES

Jillian, my precious baby has so many talents. Her personality and smile alone, can brighten a room. It's a joy to see and hear someone so gorgeous, inside and out, express herself is such an articulate manner. She has a love of language. I like to think that I fostered and encouraged that. She, also, has a love for animals, especially, abused ones. She's volunteered at the animal shelters. So many of us may express similar feelings, then sit back and do nothing.

Jillian, even at the age of fifteen, was altruistic. She worked at Archway School that summer with handicapped children. There were several teens her age and older. Most of them viewed this as a social opportunity, gathering around the pool and all but ignoring the children. Although Jillian had chosen the most medically involved child to work with, she also ended up changing diapers for some of the other children because their caretakers were too busy. Rather than throw stones at the others she did what was best for the children.

The child who was her sole responsibility was blind, deaf, in a wheelchair, had no communication skills, didn't smile and required total care. With no training, Jillian immersed herself into improving this little girl's life in little more than a month. Since I was working at Archway as a nurse, I was able to witness firsthand how Jillian was bonding with this child. I walked by the classroom one time to see Jillian on the floor with this child, her arms wrapped around the little girl, her hands on the child's hands. She had a ball in her hands, would let her feel the ball, then form her hands to make the sign for ball. She did this repeatedly for days, teaching her sign language for many other words too.

Another time I went to the room because I had heard extremely loud music. There was Jillian lying on the floor, as was the little girl, with her ear right next to the tape player. She, though deaf, must have felt the vibrations because she was tapping her hand on the floor. Of course, Jillian then taught her the sign for music.

It was not all work for this little girl. Jillian also would take her to the pool. The end result of her weeks of working with this child were almost miraculous. This little girl left Archway summer camp, smiling and able to communicate her basic wants and needs with sign language, all because of *my* little girl. I could almost hear the angels saying, "Well done Jillian!"

JILLIAN & SIGN LANGUAGE

Another memory surfaces and I recall Jillian at age thirteen, asking to go with me to Camden County Public Library in Voorhees for a sign language class. I was thrilled that she wanted to do this. However, when I went to sign us up, I was told it was for adults only. It wasn't too often that I challenged people, but on this issue I felt it was wrong to keep my Jillian out of the class. She certainly wouldn't be disruptive like a younger child. She was willing to learn what most young teenagers wouldn't have time for.

I asked if we could strike up a compromise, allowing Jillian to sit in on two classes and see how she did. There were about a dozen other adults. They all agreed that it was a reasonable request. Jillian stayed for all the classes. Our final day would determine how much we learned. We were to sign, without verbalizing, a brief biography of our interests, hobbies and other personal information. Everyone was able to do this but it was a struggle—a slow, struggle, grasping for the correct signs. Jillian's turn left everyone including the instructor stunned. She signed expertly, rapidly and was so fluent that nobody except the instructor knew what she said. The rest of us, in trying to interpret each other's signing, were halting, to say the least. It was like playing charades. I was so proud of my baby girl.

There was another incident involving language (not sign language) when Jillian was in fifth grade. She wrote a composition and used the word "eudaemonia". I had not used this or taught this to Jillian. This speaks to her love of language. She'd walk around with a thesaurus. The teacher accused her of making up words. Jillian insisted it was a word and was used appropriately. The teacher told her it wasn't in the dictionary. Jillian respectfully told her that she needed a bigger dictionary. The teacher apologized the next day. How proud I was!

<u>JILLIAN & HERB</u>

Jillian's relationship with Herb was close. She would tell him and me how much she loved him. She was ten when they met. She wanted so badly to go on his motorcycle. I knew he was a safe driver and so one time I allowed her to do so. He had gotten her a helmet. I was driving the car behind them. She looked so tiny. She was ecstatic about the ride and it instilled in her a desire to get a motorcycle when she was old enough. She did follow through on that and loved to ride. She had the bike for several years before it was stolen. Secretly, I was relieved. She never got another bike.

One of the other things she enjoyed were the foot massages that Herb was famous for (in our small family circle). She couldn't get enough of them. There was such an ease to their relationship. I loved watching them. Another bit of trivia, Trudi said Herb gave the best backrubs. All our girls spoiled him, but he, in turn, spoiled them too. Just recently, I had a flashback of Jillian, like I stepped back in time, when Kenzie flopped on the couch and automatically kicked her shoes off and was getting a foot massage from Pop-Pop. Her feet were always cold and Pop-Pop's hands are always warm. I do the same thing every night.

One of the best surprises I had was orchestrated by Herb and Jillian for one of my birthdays. Keep in mind that we didn't see Jillian every year so it was a big occasion when we did. Jillian had called me one afternoon just to talk but there was a lot of static so she said she'd call back. Herb came home shortly after, kissed me then went to his office and sat at the computer. I stayed in the office reading a book, keeping him company and waiting for Jillian's call. All of a sudden Herb said he smelled something burning. It wouldn't be the first time I left the stove unattended. I ran into the dining room and there in the kitchen doorway was Jillian.

I screamed, "Jillian's home!" and to hear Jillian tell it, I was screaming, clapping my hands, jumping up and down and running in place in midair before I grabbed her in a bear hug. She couldn't stop laughing. She said, "Mom, you looked so funny. She said I looked like a little kid on Christmas morning. I'm yelling for Herb and he's right behind me. Jillian asked us

68

not to tell anyone that she was home. She just wanted a quiet visit for my birthday. She had been in the car with Herb when she called me and complained of the static. It was the best birthday surprise ever.

Jillian's gifts were so thoughtful. She gave me a St. Joseph carved rosary. She knew he was my favorite saint. She also gave me a pearl rosary that she had gotten in the Cathedral in Paris, France. She framed a photo she had taken of my laundry blowing in the breeze and if you think that's strange, then you haven't read my chapter on "Laundry". Of course, she had to include a culinary treat, artichokes in white wine and a small statue of "Our Lady of Mt. Carmel", which is our parish.

When Herb had emergency open heart surgery, she came home. She was so worried about him. I didn't realize until later, when George told me, that she had asked to use her father's frequent flier miles for the trip from Georgia. Jillian was with us when Herb's blood pressure dropped drastically his first night home and he became faint. Together we got him into bed. She again expressed to me, how much she loved him. She even asked me if I thought he would walk her down the aisle when she got married. I assured her that Herb and her father would probably share that honor. She usually thought positive about most situations, but this time, it was obvious that she was scared of losing him. Herb's love for her was just as strong. It is still heart wrenching for him to pass the gate at the airport where he would pick her up. He has to pass that gate daily.

JILLIAN'S CRY FOR HELP

Jillian was still struggling with prescription drugs and was extremely frustrated with the doctors who were more interested in writing prescriptions, than counseling and finding the right combination of drugs for someone who was bipolar. She seemed to be more knowledgeable than the doctors about her diagnosis. She'd run information by me, I'd do some research and we'd concur at times.

One time she checked herself into the hospital wanting to get some help in ridding herself of her dependence on these drugs. One of the drugs was Xanax. I was familiar with that because I had been on it for years. I literally cannot fall asleep naturally. As Jillian did, I also stayed up for days at a time without sleep. Herb made jokes about it, saying it was great. He'd go to bed at night and wake up the next morning to a freshly painted room. I'd just paint around him because I couldn't sleep. Might as well be productive if I was going to be up all night. Jillian would be baking at one in the morning while we talked on the phone. However, I am not bi-polar—just an insomniac with anxiety. Anyway, she stayed for twenty-four hours in the hospital and they sent her home. They said she did not belong there. She was fine.

While she was there I attempted to talk with a nurse or doctor. They were rigid about the privacy laws. Then I explained that I had information that I knew exacerbated Jillian's condition. Would they at least take that into consideration. The information I wanted to share was that her brother Mark's anniversary was this month and that was extremely difficult for Jillian, as well as for the rest of us. Even after twenty years, Jillian would have a memorial service for him, with some of her friends. I know this because Jillian told me and her friends told me. They all knew how much she missed Mark….It never stops hurting. You just learn to hone your coping skills. With this pertinent information, the staff said they would NOT take this into consideration. I was furious but couldn't do anything about it.

ANGELS IN THE ER JULY 6, 2008

Jillian was in the hospital for two days. Once again, she asked for help. Having gone without sleep, you begin to imagine things. I have also had that experience. Keep in mind the privacy policy. I was in touch with three different nurses on all three shifts. Emily, Monica and Julie, I believe with all my heart, were angels. I called about every two hours even through the middle of the night to see if Jillian had fallen asleep. I told them I was aware that they couldn't give me any medical information, but, as her mother, I had to keep calling.

All three of them, without any prompting from me, kept me informed about what was going on without divulging medical information They also mentioned praying for Jilllian and one even asked Jillian if she would like her to pray for her and with her. Jillian said yes. This was not a Catholic hospital. Of course, *I told them how comforting this had to be for Jillian as well as me.*

They were amazed that Jillian never slept or even seemed sleepy. She was alert and discussed her concerns at length, with these nurses. She had often told me how high her dosage was for her meds. She said that she honestly believed that her system was so desensitized, that *no amount* of medicine would harm her. It also did not seem to be therapeutic either. Her doctor would tell her to double the dose if she needed. I was appalled at the dosage for such a tiny girl.

When I questioned her nurses, they confirmed what Jillian had told me. Emily, Monica and Julie were so impressed with Jillian's knowledge about medications, side effects etc. They couldn't believe she hadn't had medical training. They cared for my baby girl lovingly and allowed me to speak about her talents and just how special she was. I did that all through the night. Jillian never slept a wink for forty-eight hours.

Thank you Jesus for providing these beautiful angels for a worried mother. Thank you, thank you, thank you for sending them to care for and comfort my baby girl when she needed it most. Jillian was discharged and she came home for a visit right after this incident.

SEPTEMBER 17, 2008

God help me to write this chapter. I know I must, yet the agony I'm feeling is overwhelming me. The tears seem endless. It's too soon. Yet, there never will be a right time. I know that because of Mark. My feelings are a collage of extremes. I never, ever thought I would have to endure losing another child. My baby girl has gone home to be with Jesus and her brother, Mark.

The pain is unrelenting, for long periods. Those periods come in waves—great tidal waves of anguish. When they are over, every ounce of energy I have is spent. I feel like a rag doll and wonder, how is it that I am still alive when my baby is not.

Jillian was home for a week in July. She looked wonderful, was happy and humorous though dealing with extremely difficult issues. Most of the time she hid her pain well and her effervescent personality would surface. Her diagnosis of bi-polar disorder, sleep deprivation and a combination of potent drugs prescribed by her doctor was alarming. She knew she needed help.

She was so knowledgeable about nutrition and exercise, was into eating healthy, mainly vegetarian, taking vitamins and also meditating. She remarked that she's prayed more now than ever before. A major problem, along with the bipolar disorder, was sleep deprivation, in the extreme. She was holding down a full time and a part time job. She averaged three hours of sleep over a 72 hr. period. That's brutal. I know, because I have experienced that first hand. You become confused, can't recall when you last took your medicine. When it appears that you're not getting sleepy, you rationalize that you must not have taken it. So you take more.

Still can't sleep. Get up, clean out kitchen cabinets, get a burst of energy then relax with a glass of wine. Then all of a sudden, everything kicks in. It's frightening. I know firsthand.

We had a family meeting about her staying in New Jersey and getting help for her to break the cycle of medication she was so dependent on. She wanted to be totally healthy. She referred to her psychiatrist as a licensed drug dealer. That probably is an accurate assessment. Though apprehensive about the treatment center she would go to, only because she couldn't see it beforehand, she agreed to go. She wanted to go back to Georgia just to make arrangements for her cat, "Little Girl" and for her mail to go to her best friend, Dan, for the months she would be in New Jersey. She was concerned about her credit and didn't want to miss any payments.

Jillian agreed that she had a stronger support system here in New Jersey with her family and her close friend, Jared. I reminded her that she had always taken risks in her life, whether jumping out of an airplane or climbing mountains. Though she was concerned, I reiterated that this decision to get help, though difficult, would mean the start of a new life. The good life she wanted. She responded, "You're right, mom." She hugged me and said "I can do this."

Jillian made it clear that she loved life so much and she wanted marriage and children, like her brother Ryan. She said that she would do whatever it took to get healthy, so she could have that normal life. She never got that chance. She went home Sunday night, called me to let me know that she got home safely and would be back soon. The call ended, as always, with "I love you mom." I love you too honey. Tuesday night, July 29, 2008, I got the call from Dan that Jillian had passed away....accidental overdose of prescription drugs.

The next moments were devastating. There was denial. "This can't be. I just talked with her as she flopped across my bed. I laughed with her, played Scrabble with her." Trudi just did a cannonball in her pool, surprising Jillian and upsetting her float. They both laughed so hard. My head pounded, my heart raced. I remember pulling my hair like I was trying to rip it out of my head. I wanted to wake up from this nightmare. "Please God, not again."

Herb held me and tried to comfort me but he was crying just as hard. I ran to Jillian's bedroom where she had slept. I hadn't changed the sheets yet. I crawled under the covers and could smell my baby girl's sweet scent.

Some things are clear, others are a blur. I called Ryan. I never will forget the anguished sounds and the repeated, "No, no, no.!" on the other end of the phone. I think Herb made all the other calls. I remember Bev and others in the bedroom. I think Bev was trying to get me out of the bed. I don't remember walking to the living room, but obviously, I did. George, David and Ryan were there.

I remember looking at Ryan, who sat quietly with tears streaming down his face. I told him that I had just finished making a novena (nine days of prayer for a special intention) for Jillian. He asked me what I had prayed for. I told him that I asked Jesus to hold Jillian close and let her feel His love, to give her peace and to take away her pain. Ryan looked at me and quietly said, "He's answered your prayers mom, maybe not in the way you wanted, but He has answered them."

LINDA...an unexpected link to Jillian

We met Linda at RCIA (Rite of Christian Initiation of Adults). She was a young single girl who came alone, unlike the rest of us. Claire and Bill were a couple, our age. The four of us took Linda under our wings. Later when she became a single parent of a daughter, she was stressed out about not having any Catholic men in her life, who could be godfather to Lila Mary.

It was shortly after Jillian had gone home to heaven. Linda would come to Mass and sit with us at times, or near us. Ryan, Jen, Kenzie and Jake usually sat with us. Linda loved Herb and the way he interacted with Jake and Kenzie. Suffice it to say, she yearned for that for her daughter. There was no room in our pew one Sunday so Linda sat behind us. Mass had not started yet. She stood up, gently lifting Lila over Herb's head and into his arms, whispering "Can you find room in your heart for another little girl?" She could think of nobody better and more loving than Herb to be Lila's godfather...and so he was.

She was aware we were still raw with grief and was sensitive to that. Linda was Jillian's age and, of course, the thought of someday holding my daughter's baby was bittersweet. Babies, however, bring their own joy. Lila is a beautiful little girl and we have become Uncle Herb and Aunt Roe.

Almost a year had passed before we found out that Linda has an exceptional gift. She was able to communicate with those who have passed on from this life. She didn't label herself a medium and assumed everyone had this gift. Her mother was aware of this from the time Linda was four years old. As she grew older, her mom cautioned her about talking to others about this, saying they wouldn't understand.

I have no doubt in my mind that Jillian's passing was purely accidental and Linda's account confirms this. You only had to know the zest for life Jillian had. This girl prayed to Jesus, acknowledging that this gift of hers was from God and not something she was doing on her own volition. Linda had never met Jillian, yet she was telling me that she was in contact with Jillian. I was furious at first, saying why wouldn't Jillian talk to me vs. this stranger. This person was so accurate about things that Jillian and I shared. She couldn't possibly know these things, these memories. Yet, she did.

Linda also knew I had breast cancer before I told anyone. I had just found out. She said Jillian told her and also told her I'd be okay. She called me one night and said that she needed to give me some information that Jillian was relaying to her. She spoke for a half hour describing in detail Jillian's apartment. At times, it seemed that Linda was oblivious to my presence on the other end of the phone. I was quiet, but Linda's descriptions and comments told me that she was taking a 'tour' of Jillian's apartment. She described pictures on the wall and placement of furniture. I remained quiet, in shock. Herb and I have been in Jillian's apartment and every detail that Linda shared was accurate. I could not deny Linda's gift.

Linda also switched gears after the apartment "tour" and told me she saw two men walking through Jillian's apartment. I asked her to describe them and she said that she couldn't because they had their backs to her. Also, she was initially seeing them from the waist down. Then she got a full view and said, "Oh my gosh! It's George." She knew George from seeing him at Mass. She didn't recognize the other man but offered a description He was George's height, had a great build and had dark hair with some gray.

She then gasped and said the other man had dropped to his knee and bent his head. I knew it was my brother Joe who had gone with George to pack up Jillian's belongings and bring them home to us. Joe is very spiritual so I assumed he knelt to pray. I talked with my sister-in-law Donna and asked if she could confirm what Linda was telling me. She talked with Joe and he said that he *did* drop to his knee and bend his head, but it was because he was having an attack. He has a history of atrial fibrillation. Once again, confirmation.

Linda said Jillian's suitcase was on the bed. She was packing to come back home. She walked into the bathroom, even describing Jillian's fluffy towels. Then she gasped because she knew what had happened. Linda tasted cold medicine. Jillian had taken her prescription meds as always. Without thinking Jillian took liquid cold medicine because she felt a cold coming on. She said that she had taken it in the past, just not so close to her other meds. She made it crystal clear to Linda, it was an accident. Since *I* never doubted that, I assume the message was to reassure someone else.

There have been dozens of messages through Linda. All are very comforting. Though I've talked about some of them to family members, it's a sensitive subject because not everyone believes. It was reassuring to me when Linda and I prayed together before she would relay these messages. I said that everything needs to be God centered.

One message I will share because I think it will be very comforting for all our family. I'm not concerned about convincing anyone of the validity of the message. It's there for the taking. Linda said she wrote down everything because it was a long one. She wanted it to be accurate. She did say, however, that she was confused about the ending but Jillian said I would understand.

"Mommy, I have seen more in this short life than people do in a hundred years. I have done things people only dream about. Everything I have seen and done in this life I have you to thank for. You gave me the wisdom and the courage and the love to live each day to the fullest! My life did not end, it goes on and it's truly awesome. Rest, knowing I'm very happy and at peace and, of course, having so much fun. I'm fulfilling dreams and most of all, I'm smiling at the world!! I love you mommy. Thank you for all I have..........Love "J"

Linda's confusion at the "J" was understandable. Linda asked me why Jillian would want her to use the letter "J". She was unaware that Jillian's nickname was "Jey", pronounced just like the letter "J." She had no way of knowing that. Only those closest to Jillian knew that.

FINAL PREPARATIONS

The following days were brutal. It was an effort just to place one foot in front of the other, make phone calls, making arrangements for Rachele to come home from Missouri, appointments with Jim, our friend and funeral director, who helped us so much with Mark. Now he had to bring Jillian home. He went to the Philadelphia airport to pick Jillian up…so different from all the happy times Herb would pick her up.

Herb, George, Rachele and I went to see Jillian before Jim had her dressed. Her long hair was billowed out behind her. She was as beautiful as ever. I kissed my baby then burrowed my face in her hair, which was so fragrant with Jillian's delicate scent. I remember thinking, "This isn't real. It couldn't be." In the next breath, asking Jesus to help us through this….asking Our Blessed Mother, who herself had gone through this, to help us and to hold my baby girl close to her until I could be there to do it myself. As I kissed her one more time, I heard and felt a soft breath from her, almost like a sigh. It felt as good as if Jillian had said, "I'm okay, mom". I told Herb, not knowing what his reaction would be. No need to worry. He had felt the same thing too.

The viewing was in the church, which we had found to be more comforting with Mark. Ryan's extended police family was there as were a continuous flow of family and friends. Our family, though devastated, remains strong. In the midst of the suffering, there is a sense of peace…peace and gratitude that we have each other to lean on. We are a strong family.

I stood by the casket and reached out to caress Jillian, brushing my fingers against her hair. But it wasn't the soft, silky tresses I had wound my fingers around earlier. It was stiff with spray. She didn't look the same as she had earlier. Ryan gave voice to my thoughts. He said, "Mom, Jillian is not in there." I told him that I knew that but I needed something tangible now.

We have each other and Jillian is with Mark and we will all be together again. I remember reading something, but can't recall the author. Like a ship sailing into the horizon until out of sight, the ship is not gone. It still exists, we just can't see it. Likewise, Jillian is not gone just because we can't see her and hold her. She just stepped from this life to a better one. I believe with all my heart that the moment her eyes closed on earth, they opened up in heaven.

My survival skills consist of focusing on all the positive memories of Jillian, talking about her, incessantly and showing her pictures to everyone. I've met some of the most caring people while standing in a long line at the store. Usually, they have a story of their own. I just want everyone to know how very special she is.

My memories…I treasure the phone calls—most were just "newsy" updates on Jillian and her friends. There were a lot of calls where Jillian would ask for prayers for her friends and herself. She'd sometimes put her friends on the phone so that I could "meet" them. Frequent late night calls came at 1:00am, 2:00am or later. Some were just pleasant loving calls, others were when she was experiencing deep depression. We'd talk for an hour and then she would calm down and say, "I'm okay mom (sometimes "mommy", which I loved). Then she would tell me that she felt like she could sleep now. She was so appreciative of the fact that she could call in the middle of the night.

Sometimes I'd call Jillian in the morning. I was a back-up to her alarm. She was not a morning person. Besides the lengthy phone calls lasting an hour or more, there were calls that lasted just seconds. She'd say, "I just called to tell you that I love you so much mom, but I'm at work and can't talk." I love you too, sweetheart, and she'd be gone.

MORE PRECIOUS MEMORIES

Jillian would share with me new words or new foods that she had sampled. Sometimes she would even send a menu or take pictures of a unique presentation. We shared our love of language and food. She'd try new recipes and ask for my old ones. She is a phenomenal cook, bordering on gourmet. She would often send flowers for no reason at all. She always made me feel special and appreciated. She loved getting my letters but strongly urged me to learn to use e-mail. When I did send her an e-mail, she was so excited that I was broadening my interests. However, she still wanted the letters to continue.

Jillian's favorite flowers are irises and tulips. Her friend Marta remembered that and sent a bouquet to the house. Jillian loved Marta and I have come to, also. We talk on the phone about all the special and loving things that Jillian was always doing for others. Marta's family is in Spain. She came to stay with us one time. It was so good having her here.

I planted about fifty irises outside Jillian's bedroom, which are visible from her window. She was thrilled when she came home to see them in full bloom. She was so excited, saying they were huge, like small trees. Of course, she grabbed her camera and would focus on one individual bloom. She loved everything in nature and took nothing for granted. I like to think that she got that from me. As a little girl, I would call her and Rachele outside to see a spider and its web, sparkling in the early morning dew.

Jillian's favorite color is green. Her favorite soup is Italian vegetable. One of her favorite snacks is cheese. We both love paper thin mozzarella, provolone, American. She'd microwave it for a few seconds so it was easier to separate the slices and nibble on, while we played scrabble. She loved Italian water ice and would take it back to Atlanta in an ice chest, before all the regulations were enforced. She loved sweet tea, green tea and Earl Grey. The scent of Earl Grey triggers so many memories of my little girl.

Jillian loved angel food cake and so did her cat, Miss Penn (Penny). They both would tear chunks off. We'd laugh til our sides hurt because Penny looked like she was foaming at the mouth with the angel food hanging out both sides of her mouth. Jillian would also go through dozens of miniature crème puffs while we'd play Scrabble.

Jillian was so thoughtful and pampered me. On one visit, Jillian gave me a massage. It was shortly after she was certified as a massage therapist. Herb and I flew to Atlanta to be there for Jillian's graduation. Jillian had asked Herb to co-sign on her tuition for the school. Of course, he said yes. I don't think Herb realized how involved and difficult the classes were. I would have to say that she was more knowledgeable than I am about the joints and how they function. She had to be in order to be effective in her work.

JILLIAN'S TREAT AND MORE MEMORIES

On another visit to Atlanta, Jillian treated Rachele and me to facials. It was so extravagant but felt so good. Chele and I had never experienced this before. Jillian was lying perfectly still, relaxing. Chele and I were getting restless, not used to being still. We ended up having a laughing fit as usual. Maybe we both have adult ADHD.

COUSINS

I have a beautiful memory of Jillian when she was a pre-teen. Jillian's cousins, Michele and Melanie were coming to visit. They were planning to skate around the lake at Archway School where I worked. She watched the weather report for days and was quite upset that rain was predicted for that Saturday. It had been raining Friday night and before she went to bed she listened one more time to the forecast--heavy rains all day Saturday.

We turned our statue of our Blessed Mother to face outside and Jillian asked if we could say a rosary for good weather. We did and she never doubted that the sun would be shining. The forecast on Saturday morning was still for heavy rains but my little girl rested easy, displaying the faith that, will indeed, move mountains. One hour before her cousins came, the sun came out and stayed out all day. A half hour after her cousins left, the skies opened up and the torrential rains started. Who can doubt the power of a child's prayer.

Jillian loved babies and toddlers and was truly altruistic. She wanted to get well so that she could be a good mother one day. She loved people, was compassionate and empathetic. I'm still finding newspaper clippings with her photo, when she was involved in the "Make a Wish Foundation". She also was involved in organizations that protected animals. I could go on and on. The list of the charities that Jillian gave to, in time and money, is endless. I try to honor Jillian by continuing her involvement with charities. It's disheartening though, how many use very little for their cause and a huge amounts for the CEOS of the charity. Make sure you check any charity out before donating. I've weeded out the bad ones.

As with Mark, I am often asked how I deal with the loss of my baby girl. I pray. I relive humorous memories. I pray some more. I look through the hundred or so photos I have of Jillian and focus on her smile. I anxiously look forward to being with her again. What a reunion that will be! I keep praying and talking to her. I know that she hears me. I also know that I'm not alone. I have my hubby and my children and grandchildren. I've been blessed with an abundance of friends.

I've always had a respect for Rose Kennedy and her amazing faith, in light of losing so many children. She lost her son Joe when his plane went down, defending our country. She lost a daughter, Rosemary. Her son John, our beloved president, was assassinated, as was her son Bobby who was running for president, then her son Teddy. She attended Mass every day. Her faith never wavered. She trusted God, as do I. I would have done things differently, but then I'm not God and can't see into the future. I cried rivers of tears but I can honestly say that I've never gotten angry with God. I still cry….often.

ROSE KENNEDY said something that impacted me deeply because she understands and expresses my feelings, also, when she said these profound words. I cried the first time I heard them.

"It has been said that time heals all wounds. I do not agree. The wounds remain. In time, the mind, protecting its sanity covers them with scar tissue. The pain lessens but it is never gone."

SISTERS

Jillian and Rachele, my two precious girls had a long-standing joke about "boobs". They blamed me for their small bustline. They exchanged the funniest cards and T-shirts for seventeen years, never letting me off the hook. One year, Jillian was thrilled to give Rachele her best birthday present ever. Her gift was in a container, similar to the kind you get at a Chinese restaurant. The item was nestled in pink tissue paper with an accompanying card that read, "You are now the proud owner of a pair of take outs—wear them proudly. In the box were two life-like breasts, which Chele immediately tucked into her bra. They were both elated when miracle bras became the fashion. For the first time in their adult lives, they both had cleavage. They didn't need the props, though. They are the two most beautiful girls in the world, inside and out.

They each had a collection of these silly but meaningful and humorous cards. Rachele's last card to her little sister was in a plain sealed envelope. She tucked it into Jillian's casket. George had no idea what it was, nor would anyone else. Yet, he got upset with Rachele and told her to take it out. I told her to leave it, but he insisted. She walked away in tears. Once again, appearances were so important to George. It brought back memories of Mark's viewing when George was upset that we were "junking" Mark's casket up. Mark had so many girls leaving notes and roses and mementos. I loved it but it was a thorn in George's side.

This incident reminded me of a question that Jillian had asked me just weeks before she went home to be with Mark and Jesus. "Why didn't you ever stand up to daddy?" I think she might have thought I was weak, in that instance and it pains me greatly. She was remembering a time when she and I were in my bedroom. Her father was angry about something and was pounding on the door with his fists. I had locked the door in an effort to avoid a confrontation. It wasn't until the door flew open, that I turned around and realized Jillian was hiding under the bed. The fact that I was able to stand up for myself now, didn't negate the previous. I told Rachele to put the card back for her sister but she was so hurt and she wouldn't defy her father. However, Jim, our friend and undertaker, made sure Rachele put her card in at the last minute.

I couldn't believe this was happening again, harsh words at our child's casket. The first time with Mark occurred when we were wording his obituary and I asked Jim to include Mark's daughter, Natalie Rose. George was livid. He knew Natalie was Mark's little girl but because Mark wasn't married at the time, he was worried about appearances. I was so angry. I said, "She's our granddaughter George!" He would not give in. Mark was lying in the next room and we're fighting. George said that he was paying for the funeral, so rather than continue fighting, I gave in. This exclusion caused a rift in what little contact I had with Kathy, Natalie's mother. She was in Florida at this time. George never did pay for the funeral. Thank God for Jim. It took me years to pay him and I probably owe him more in interest than I could ever think to repay. The kids and I chipped in to pay for Mark's gravestone.

I thank God that Natalie's mother, Kathy, in time was forgiving and understanding when I explained the situation. We don't see each other because she lives in Florida. When we do talk by phone, we make up for lost time. She's been a wonderful mother to Natalie and a blessing to me, keeping me posted all the years that Natalie was growing up. Kathy would send photos and notes. Now Natalie, who is an RN keeps in touch on her own. We had a wonderful visit for about ten days in the summer of 2011. She got to know the rest of the family and we had some serious all night conversations. She doesn't sleep much either. Insomnia seems to run in our family.

"WE KNOW THAT ALL THINGS WORK FOR GOOD FOR THOSE WHO LOVE GOD, WHO ARE CALLED ACCORDING TO HIS PURPOSE." Romans 8:28

Trust God and He will bring good out of bad. I've heard so many people say that their lives are forever changed because of the way Jillian lived hers. She had an appreciation of nature, evident in her activities such as rock climbing, skydiving, scuba diving, as well as her photography. Her photos of a single leaf floating in a stream, a single flower, sparkling with dew or crisp linens on a clothesline, gave evidence of her gift to make the ordinary, seem extraordinary. The music she wrote and played was another talent she nurtured. God must be so pleased with Jillian. He gave her much and she shared her gifts with everyone she came in contact with. Her radiant smile lingers in our hearts and every single photo that we have of her.

Dan and I knew of Jillian's wishes to be cremated if anything ever happened to her. She mentioned it to me years ago. As I mentioned before, most of our family has talked about our wishes, should we die. This isn't as ominous or morbid as it sounds. We've even discussed who will get what. I told the kids to let me know now what they want. Ry wants the hot tub. All the boys get a roll-away tool box and Trudi and Chele have their names on tags on the back of items they want. I think Jen thinks we are all crazy. I just think of how much easier it'll make things when I go. Our family has had some of the most humorous discussions on this topic. In 2012 I purchased two cemetery plots for Herb and me. We had talked about getting just one plot and having one of us cremated and the ashes placed in that plot. Herb said no to cremation, he couldn't take the heat.

I told the kids what I had done. They thought I was losing it. Kevin thought we should spend the money on a vacation. I thought this was a good idea, one less thing for the kids to worry about. Ryan said he wouldn't be visiting me at the cemetery because I wouldn't be there. I explained that I had chosen a spot near the woods where there were deer and turkey. I said that I didn't want flowers, but at least do a "drive by" and throw corn out for the animals. It's a beautiful area with park benches that are decorated for the season. Only my friend Maureen understood. When the weather turns warmer, we plan to take our lunch there.

Jillian wanted her ashes to be scattered on the ocean in California. What we didn't know, was she also wanted to be as close to Mark as possible. Considering that we didn't find this out until after the services, we did well. I'm sure it was Divine intervention.

There was one concern because as Catholics, human remains have to be in holy ground. We did both. We opened Mark's grave to place Jillian's urn with him. The other half of Jillian's ashes were taken by her best friend, Dan, to California to fulfill Jillian's last wish.

It's been almost two months since our tragedy. I wake every morning in pain and wish I could erase these months. I can't. Depression is debilitating. Yet, I know that I can't stay there. I say, "Good morning Jillian, good morning Mark, good morning Jesus, Mary and St. Joeseph. I have so many children and grandchildren still here. I am so grateful for them. I have my wonderful husband who helps me through each and every day. He gives me his strength. We have been blessed with an abundance of friends. We have our health, our vision, hearing (though somewhat compromised with age). Herb has a good job as do all our children. We all have beautiful homes and cars that run—most of the time. We have our faith, which without we could not survive.

I'm being repetitious but I think it bears repeating. Happiness is situational, joy is not. Joy can be present even in the midst of suffering. That can only come from God. My example of this is a simple one. I think Jillian and my girls would like me to share this story. We had to find an outfit for Jillian to wear for her viewing. I could not do it alone nor did I feel like I even had the strength to do it. Remember, all of Jillian's clothes were in Atlanta.

Bev and Jenny went with me to Jillian's favorite stores, "Marshalls" and "T.J. Max". I found out later that they were dreading this excursion, understandably so. There weren't many moments when I was dry eyed. They too, were mourning in their own way and having a difficult time. I prayed before walking into the store, asking Jesus to let something appropriate fall off the rack at our feet. Of course, it didn't.

We didn't find anything at Marshalls so we went to T.J. Max. The three of us headed in separate directions. Jenny found a top! It was Jillian's style and so pretty. We couldn't find pants or a skirt though, so, at Jenny's suggestion, we went to Joyce Leslie. We found a beautiful pencil skirt that Jillian would love. We all agreed that it was the perfect outfit.

No time for tears. We were frantic to get this last thing done for Jillian, and done right. We were ready to check out and I remembered we hadn't gotten underwear. I said that we had to find a pretty padded bra or Jillian would never let me hear the end of it. My girls did that in short order. Finding panties was not so easy. The three of us were looking and all we could find were thongs. Bev held one up. I started to protest and Bev said, "But mom, Jillian would….." I never gave her the chance to finish. I held up the thong, over my head, looked up to the heavens and said out loud, "It ain't happening Jillian!" Bev and Jenny laughed. So did I and, of course, so did Jillian.

Afterwards I suggested getting something to eat. Jenny said, "Where would Jillian have liked to go?" Each choice we made was with the thought of Jillian. I ordered my usual wine, then changed the order to vodka and tonic, Jillian's drink. We made a toast to their sister, my precious daughter. We talked, smiled and yes, even had a few laughs remembering fun times with Jillian.

When we got back to the house, I thanked Jenny and Bev. They started to say, "It was_____".I chimed in the missing word, nice. Maybe a better choice of words would be "comforting." Comforting to be with my girls, remembering all the laughter and smiles we all shared on Jillian's visits home. How could we feel that way? Only by the Grace of God. The joy that surpasses all understanding, and the knowledge that Jillian is happier than she's ever been. There's a rough road ahead of us, but we have a lot of support. We can do this, together, as long as we remember, "Trust thru sorrow brings triumph over sadness."

ANOTHER MEMORY OF JILLIAN

Jillian once told me that she was "becoming me." I asked if she meant that she was becoming *like* me. She said "No, I am becoming you mom." I asked if that was good or bad, bracing myself for the answer. She answered without hesitation that it was good. She pointed out that her vocabulary was extensive, her speaking articulate and that all the things I stressed to her while she was in school, like eye contact, no gum chewing or gum cracking helped her in so many ways especially in a professional setting.

Other obsessive habits caused laughter and sometimes, disbelief. Jillian and Chele shared stories with me. Chele, also, felt she was just like me in many areas. One of the chores the girls shared when they were still at home, was pulling weeds out from the walkway to the door and also in the cracks in the pavement. I'd actually be in the street, pulling weeds by the curb and dodging cars as they whizzed by.

Jillian told me about the time that she was coming home to her upscale apartment in Atlanta, a facility that boasted concierge service and several groundskeepers. The grounds were meticulously kept. However, one day when she was coming home from a date, she spotted a couple of small weeds on the path and stopped to pull them. Her date, incredulous at this unbecoming activity, told her that they pay people to do that.

Rachele was in the library and had asked the librarian for help in finding some books. She was standing at the counter when she noticed the dead leaves on large potted plants on the floor, at the end of the counter. She stooped down to pull them off and heard the librarian say "Rachele, where did you go?" She had turned her back to get the books and when she turned back, Rachele was gone. Kind of like when I disappeared in the ditch. When she stood up, she had both hands filled with dead leaves.

OCD gets the best of all of us at one time or another. Herb and I were in church and Mass had not started yet. Someone came into our pew and asked where I was. I heard him answer, "She's up by the Blessed Mother, weeding." There were dead leaves on the plants so I removed them.

MAMA VENTURAS Journal Entry

Herb made reservations for dinner on Mother's Day. Of course, I'm missing Jillian and Mark so I had their photo laying on the table by my plate. Our waiter picked up Jillian's photo and said that he had been Jillian's math teacher. Of course, he went on to talk about what a remarkable student she was. What were the chances of us getting a waiter who was moonlighting and knew Jillian. One more gift from God.

JILLIAN'S BIRTHDAY December 5, 2009 Journal Entry

I woke up at 7:27 this morning. That is the exact time Jillian was born. Thank you God. I'm sure this is just one more indication that my baby girl is right beside me. I slept with Jillian's doll, Baby Anne, that she kept for thirty years. I also slept with a tiny heart shaped pillow about the size of my hand, that Jillian had made for me. It's white with red lettering, saying "I love mommy and mommy loves me." She sewed it together in grade school.

I also have a baby pillow of Jillian's with a Winnie the Pooh pillowcase on it. She's had it since she slept in her first "big girl" bed. She was about two years old. Actually, she had the pillow in her crib even before that. That pillow went on the plane with her when she traveled. She loved it. She panicked one time when she was home for a visit, left to go home and realized on the plane that she left it behind. I had to send it to her and prayed it wouldn't get lost in the mail. Of course, the pillow is in bed with me. Herb knows when I'm having a difficult time because he can hardly move in the bed because of all Jillian's treasures in there.

Jillian and Rachele shared another treasure. They would take turns wearing Mark's bright pink tank top to bed. When Jillian was going through a rough time, Rachele would send the shirt to her. Their closeness to their brother never wavered all these years.

JANUARY 27, 2009 2:30 am

I wander through the rooms, thinking of my baby girl and our late night calls….willing the phone to ring. We'd both multi task during those calls. Jillian would be doing laundry or cleaning while talking about her friends or about something that happened at work. She had a lot of human interest stories because she cared so deeply about people. One of her co- workers had a handicapped child and she would give me some history and ask for advice or even, at times, would ask me to talk to them on the phone. Having worked with special needs children, she trusted my advice. I "met" many of her friends on the phone.

I miss you honey.…

ANGELIC VISITATION

A few days after Jillian's funeral Mass, Herb and I were in church waiting for the 9:30 Mass to begin. I was kneeling, praying and crying. I had trouble processing everything. It still seemed surreal. We had been with Jillian a week ago. Through my tears I looked up at the crucifix on the altar. The pain I was feeling was not just emotional but physical also. I was not even making sense in my prayers, rambling as always. As my eyes lowered from the crucifix, through my tears I saw Jillian kneeling on the altar, head bowed, with an angel beside her, his hand on her shoulder. I gasped, blinked my eyes and then she was gone.

Yet, I know I saw her. I did not imagine it. The amazing thing was that I felt a tremendous sense of peace. I also knew that that angel had escorted her home to heaven. I would venture to say that it was St. Michael because Jillian was always praying to him as well as Jesus. I also knew that Jillian was in her kitchen when Dan found her. Yet nobody had told me this. I knew this when I saw her with her angel. I later confirmed that that was where she was found.

We know the soul lives on. However, we are doubting Thomases when we hear stories like this. I used to be, not anymore. There have been too many unexplainable incidences, not coincidences, but Christ incidences.

ANGELS AMONG US PSALM 91: 11 FOR HE SHALL GIVE HIS ANGELS CHARGE OVER YOU, TO KEEP YOU IN ALL YOUR WAYS. IN THEIR HANDS, THEY SHALL BEAR YOU UP."

Herb and I had been in our home on Blue Anchor Road for about eight years when this next incident occurred. We would have to travel on Blue

Anchor, which is about a two mile stretch, to go into town, whether it was Berlin or Sicklerville. Several times a week, every week we would see a man walking. Even in hot weather, he'd be laden down with a belt full of tools, a helmet with a light, gloves etc. We thought it was strange and wondered about him. Keep in mind that this is for years.

Since our road is not the safest place to walk and has no sidewalk, I began to pray for him, for God to keep him safe. Herb was just curious. He wanted to know what the man did. He thought he looked like a lineman for the electric company. I also began to wave and smile at him when I saw him. He never seemed to walk as far as our house. We did decide that if he did come down our way, we would invite him for lunch. If I had to give a description of him, I would say that he was tall, slight of build and even scruffy and unkempt looking. He had long dark hair.

Shortly after Jillian had gone home to be with Jesus and her brother, Mark, I was driving down Cedarbrook Road and I felt the unmistakable prompting of the Holy Spirit. I felt strongly that Jesus was telling me to pull over to the side of the road. I did and then noticed that this man was walking on the other side of the road, still at a distance. I was told to get out of the car and talk to this stranger and give him my rosary. I'm still numb with grief but I do as I'm told.

I walked up to this man and introduced myself and said that I felt God was asking me to give him something. I also let him know that my husband and I prayed for him when we would see him walking on our busy road. He thanked me and I placed my rosary in his hand. He thanked me again. I, of course, asked him to keep our family in prayer and told him about Jillian. That was our first encounter.

When I told Herb about this, he was disappointed that I didn't even ask the man what he did for a living. He felt I missed my opportunity. The second time I saw this man, face to face, was a month later. I was coming out of a store and he was walking towards me. I smiled and said, "You probably don't remember me, but....". He smiled and said, "Yes I do, RoseMarie". Then he reached in his pocket and pulled out the rosary I had given him.

He said he takes it everywhere and prays for Jillian, me and our family. As he spoke, I was mesmerized by his gentle voice and his appearance. He was beautiful. His eyes and his smile lit up his face. I found myself staring.

Then I remembered Herb and asked this man what he did for a living. I told him my husband was curious. He worked in the sewers in New York and took the high speed line to work. That's why he carried all his equipment. Before we parted I apologized that I had not even asked his name. It was Julian....the male counterpart of Jillian.

Every week for eight years we saw this man. After this last encounter I never saw him again. Nor has Herb. Five years have passed since then. I realized early on, when I came home after that second "visitation" that this was no ordinary man. I believe I was in the presence of an angel.

JILLIAN'S SONG BY CHRIS NIXON

We found this song written by Jillian's friend Chris, on You Tube. God bless Chris for loving Jillian so much and having the talent to put into words what so many people felt about her. The words are beautiful but the music is hauntingly beautiful also.

"I heard the news this morning.
They told me you were taken from us yesterday.
So many things I had left to say.

The first time I met you
You smiled as though we'd been friends for so long.
Your voice was so gentle
As you strummed your guitar
And sang your songs.

I don't think you know the impact you made
On all of the people
You crossed paths with each day.

RoseMarie Dalbow

How can I explain to all the people
Who never got a chance to meet
The angel that we call Jey.

You loved to go dancing
And make sure everyone had a wonderful time
Your laugh was amazing
You laughed louder than anyone else in the place
So full of adventure
If you weren't soaring in planes,
You were scaling the face.

I still haven't gotten in touch with Chris but I intend to. His song touched me deeply. He touched on so many things that she loved, whether rock climbing, skydiving, or just looking out for everyone else. I missed a few words of the song. Also, "Jey" is Jillian's nickname that she used on her e-mails. What a gift this song is. Thank you, Chris.

Update: Thanks to Jillian's friend Stacy, I was able to get in touch with Chris and thank him personally.

BUTTERFLIES

Our family associates butterflies with Jillian. Trudi had actually compared Jillian to a beautiful butterfly when she was home on her last visit. Jillian loved that. We all have our stories, too numerous to mention all of them. On Jillian's anniversary there's always butterflies even though normally we don't see many of them. Last year my mother and sisters came down to spend the day with me. They brought my nieces and nephews. We were sitting by our pool watching the kids go off the diving board. My mom and my sister Mary dozed off. My sister Diane and I watched as a beautiful butterfly spent the next twenty minutes fluttering in front of each and every person. There wasn't a flower to be seen in the pool area.

One of my nieces was so enthralled that when the butterfly landed on some stones by the pool, she went over to "pet" it. Before I had a chance to caution her against this, because it can damage the butterfly's wings, she did indeed pet it. It became still. I felt badly, as did she. A minute passed and it flew away unharmed.

Everyday brings something else. I often wear a necklace of Jillian's. It is a blue dragonfly. Today I was outside and a half-dozen blue dragonflies kept flitting around me. There is no doubt in my mind that Jesus is allowing Jillian to speak to my heart, in more ways than one.

MORE BUTTERFLIES

Our neighbors Rosemarie and Alan are animal lovers like Herb and me. They really go to extremes, trapping feral cats on their property, then getting them spayed and neutered, then releasing back on their property. They must spend a fortune on them. They also have several indoor cats. They live right across the road from us, yet we seldom see them, except for waving at them when we drive by. However, Ro came several times a week with meals, when Jillian "went home". They are such good people.

When I walked down to return Ro's dishes from the meals, she asked me in for a cup of tea and just to talk. She is also a nurse so we have more than our name in common. She knows I like to read so she pulled a book off her shelf and gave it to me. I told her that I'd never be able to concentrate in my state of mind. The book, at 440 pages, looked overwhelming to me. She wasn't in a hurry to get it back so she insisted I take it and keep it until I could concentrate.

I wasn't going to take it, then I saw the author's name "Barbara Kingsolver". I got the chills. The excerpt that I would read to Jillian on her birthday every year was from Barbara Kingsolver's book "The Poisonwood Bible". I would also write the words and enclose it in her birthday card. Needless to say, I took the book home. It was titled "Prodigal Summer."

It was two days before I opened it. When I did, I gasped. The front and back inside covers (four pages) were covered with pictures of every butterfly imaginable. Ro had no idea of the significance and connection our family felt regarding Jillian's butterflies. The first Sunday without Jillian, we were coming from Mass and there seemed to be an abundance of butterflies in the small church garden. When we got home I went out on the back deck and their were dozens of butterflies even though all my flowers are out front. I read the book and took it as one more comforting sign from my baby girl.

UPDATE: DECEMBER 2014

Jillian has been in heaven for seven years now and still I get letters and calls from her friends. They have not forgotten my baby girl. Stacy is so faithful in keeping in touch and letting me know that Jillian is always on her mind. Her concern extends to the whole family. I love hearing from her and this year she asked Sham (another of Jillian's friends), at my request, if he could find out how to get in touch with Chris Nixon who wrote a song about Jillian. It's still on U Tube. I watched the video of Jillian laughing, singing and playing her guitar and it is so bittersweet. Yet, I am so grateful to have this, especially the song about "Jey", Jillian's sobriquet.

Trudi and Kevin always pay tribute to Jillian on her birthdays and anniversaries by posting memories and photos on Facebook. That touches me deeply. I never want those days for Jillian and Mark to go by unnoticed.

CHRISTMAS DAY

Mass hadn't started yet. I was looking at the altar with all the poinsettias and towering pine trees and the Manger. It was breathtaking and in my mind I said to Jillian and Mark that I wish they could see how beautiful it was. As clear as if she was whispering in my ear, she said "Mom, it's like that here everyday." What a Christmas gift! Then I told her that Stacy had written and she said "I know, mom."

UPDATE: JULY 29, 2015 JILLIAN'S ANNIVERSARY

I expect miracles on Mark's and Jillian's birthdays and anniversaries. I ask God to allow them to give me a sign, a blessing on those days. I must say that God has answered that prayer. Today, I went outside to find two huge, perfect white irises in full bloom. They bloom in early spring. We are in the middle of summer and among all the dried out stems, there are two perfect irises. I can hardly believe it, yet, I expected something. Besides being Jillian's favorite flower, Rachele informs me of the name of the white ones… "Immortality."

Jillian's and Mark's anniversary of when they went to heaven occurred in July. Their birthdays are two days apart in December. They seem to be in unison on many things. So, too, their surprises. I started the day with Mass. Afterwards, I was shopping at a thrift shop, just to keep busy. I practically bumped into my neighbor from across the street. We hardly ever see each other. I asked how she was doing and was surprised to see her home on a weekday. She said that she was on vacation. I suggested we go to the restaurant for lunch, that was right next door to the thrift shop. At first, she declined and then I said she had to eat so why not take some time. She agreed. We sat at the bar and had a drink and discussed her work. She's an RN and travels to Philadelphia every day. She wasn't thrilled with her job. I asked if she ever considered something closer. There's a number of hospitals and rehab facilities plus a psychiatric facility five minutes from her home. She had submitted an application there but they weren't hiring.

While we were talking, two good looking men came over to us. They were, obviously, twins. One of them began speaking to me. He said "RoseMarie, you don't remember me do you?" I did not although he looked vaguely familiar. Then he said it had been thirty-five years since he had seen me but he recognized me right away. He told me I hadn't changed much at all. He refreshed my memory. His name was Joe. He was in my nursing class. He introduced his brother to me and I introduced my friend Rosemarie to them. Then his brother told me that he had been a friend of my Mark's and actually shared a rental house with Mark and some other guys. Mark had me visit his home one time, however, I don't recall seeing Mike. This was beginning to become a reunion of sorts. Stories of Mark ensued and what had started out to be a difficult day turned into something uplifting. Having someone remember my Mark, twenty-eight years later was such a gift.

It seemed as if Jillian and Mark were working overtime to let me know that they were with me every step of the way. The recalled memories were great and the time spent with Ro meant so much. Even she was amazed at the turn of events. One more thing, Joe is a supervisor at the psychiatric hospital I mentioned earlier. Maybe that will come in handy later, for Ro....just hoping. Anyway it turned out to be a really good day for both Ro and me. Thanks Jillian and Mark.

"GRANDCHILDREN ARE THE CROWN OF THE AGED." Proverbs 17:6

MY GRANDSON DAVID, (David & Bev's son), came to Archway School, where I worked, to see me one day. He had been fishing and wanted to come see me. It was hectic at the school. People milling about preparing to dismiss the classes. David hugged me in front of all these people and told me he loved me. You made me feel so blessed, David. You were fourteen or fifteen—the age at which most boys don't want to be hugged. I felt so loved and so proud of you.

I also remember the lunch we had at Victory Lane. We just talked and laughed and you shared some deep feelings with me. He was blatantly honest with me about his difficulty in accepting authority. We talked at length about that. I appreciated the gift he gave me by trusting me, even though he knew there would be, not so much a lecture, but a counter to his views. I'll always treasure that time and hope that there are many more. I can't explain what it is, but there is a profound connection with David. I feel it every time I see him. I sense that he feels it too. I hope that he knows how much I love him....I know he does.

JULY 2011 DAVID's FAMILY GET TOGETHER

One of the most precious memories I have of this magical weekend was with my grandson, David, at his father's home in New York. We swam out to the far side of the "lake", then treaded water for about twenty minutes, just bobbing and talking about serious topics. I've always felt drawn to David even though we haven't spent a lot of time together. That seems to be changing now. Apparently, those sitting on the shore found it touching watching us so engaged in the moments that I'll always treasure. David eventually asked me if I was getting tired treading water. I wasn't, but he was and said, "Let's get out grandmom. I'll take you for a ride on the quad."

Later, David helped me gather rocks and stones from the creek for my garden at home. Great memory David!

I just had another flashback of David. We took David to our Pocono home one weekend. I remember Herb took him for breakfast at "Spanky's." Everyone got a kick out of this quaint restaurant where everyone knows everyone else. I didn't go that day, but was glad that David had a memory of doing something special with his grandpop.

Another time David was on our dock with a friend. They were catching frogs and snakes and he called me to come look. His friend was shocked when David put the little critters in my outstretched hands. His friend said that his mother would have screamed. David, grinning from ear to ear, said "That's my grandmom!"

UPDATE 2013

David called and wanted to spend the day with me. We had lunch, dinner and discussed heavy duty topics. It was a day that I will always treasure because my adult grandson made time to spend with me.

UPDATE October 2014

David, my grandson, my son David's only child is in Intensive Care. When will the pain end? Bev, his mother and Duane, his brother keep a constant vigil. Bev sleeps at the hospital. His brother Jason and his girlfriend as well as aunts, cousins, and me, of course, are in and out throughout the day and night.

David is unconscious and on life support but I know that he hears us. I cradle his head, tell him I love him and remind him of the fun times we've had together. At one point, Bev asked me to go to the chapel with her and Duane. We sat side by side and I asked God to help me to help them. There are no words that will comfort and console a parent or a brother at this time. I know that because of firsthand experience. We prayed the Our Father then I asked Jesus to please give the family, especially Bev, a sense of peace…the peace that defies our understanding, the peace that comes from God alone. Phillipians 4: verses 6 &7

I asked Bev if David was baptized. She said he wasn't but she would like that. I explained "Baptism of Desire" which anyone can administer in an emergency. I considered these circumstances dire. I took a small vial of holy water, made the sign of the cross on David and said "I baptize you in the Name of the Father, Son and Holy Spirit." It seemed to help Bev. However, I still felt the need to have a priest do it formally. The problem was that whenever we tried to get someone to come, wires were crossed, messaging got lost and Bev said that she thought she saw a priest in the hall, but when she went to get him, he was gone. She was beginning to stress even more. I told her to stay in the room. I prayed for help. It seems the priest was gone for the day. As I was rounding the corner I literally bumped into Father Hartman from another parish. Actually, I had been encountering this priest unexpectedly in several places this year…in my surgeon's office, in a pizza restaurant. I wasn't going to let him go.

He came into David's room, talked to Bev and asked if she wanted David to receive the Sacrament of Baptism. She replied "Yes!" adamantly. Father asked if David could hear him. I said that he could. I know this from all

I've seen when I was working in the hospital. Father leaned over David, introduced himself and proceeded to tell David what he was doing. I'll never forget when he said, "David, all your sins are forgiven. You have been baptized into the Catholic Church. Now I will anoint you and administer the last Sacrament, what we used to call the Last Rites. It is the Sacrament of the sick. It was beautiful and an almost tangible sense of peace was felt.

I felt very comfortable knowing that David would have wanted this. Often our talks would veer off into the spiritual topics. He asked a lot of questions and remarked on my faith. He remembered the Good Friday lunches at my home, with his cousins. We had grilled cheese sandwiches and I served grape juice in my best wine glasses, prayed, talked about Jesus on the cross then dyed eggs.

Bev received the peace we prayed for when one of the nurses, his name was Ian, asked if she would like to crawl into David's bed and hold her son for the last time. She did. She held him, talked to him about everything under the sun. She felt the most overwhelming peacefulness. The pain is still present, but her faith has shone through. Thank you Jesus!

David went home to be with Jesus on October 17, 2014. The last time we spent together was May 31, 2014. We sat together at his dad's wedding. We reminisced and laughed most of the time about days and years past. It was a wonderful day filled with smiles, laughter and hugs and I am so grateful for that gift.

OTHER MIRACLES

There were other miracles that occurred within the confines of the hospital. That does not surprise me. We have a generous God. One of the cardiologists in Lourdes Cardiac practice was extremely helpful to me, the day I found out that Herb was in heart failure. We had never met him prior to this emergency and have always had another doctor who had been very good. However, he was away at this time. This encounter may seem disconnected to David, it's not. Bear with me.

I was reeling with the bad news, trying to absorb what this new doctor was saying to me. Herb's surgery would be in the range of $350,000. He suggested I call my insurance company to see if they would cover it. I also had to make a choice between Lourdes Hospital and University of Pennsylvania. Overwhelmed, I went to the waiting room and called our children, asking for prayers and explaining the gravity of the situation. Then I tried to call the insurance company, with no success. The doctor came out, took the phone out of my hands and told me to go back to my husband. He would make all the calls. Trust me. I've worked with doctors. This was not normal. Again, amid the frenetic happenings, God was pulling strings as was this doctor.

After half an hour the doctor came looking for me. I was making more calls in the waiting room, on Herb's cell phone. I called the rectory to get Herb on the prayer list and to ask Father Jose to administer the Sacrament of Healing. The doctor said all the arrangements are made. I asked what the insurance company had said. He had tried for half an hour to get through to them, to no avail, so he made a decision without their input. He said "Your husband deserves the best! He's going to University of Pennsylvania, insurance be damned!" I can't begin to tell you the weight that was lifted from me. I gave him the biggest hug. Herb would be taken by ambulance.

So many times we've gone back to see Herb's regular cardiologist and always asked to see this other doctor. We kept missing him. Then in my grandson's hospital room as I was leaning over David and talking to him, I happen to glance up and see a doctor at the nurses' station. He had his back to me but was unmistakable. Not many men are 6'5". I literally ran out of the room. He remembered me and Herb and wanted to know if he was there in the hospital. I said that he'd be there in an hour. His rounds were up and he was leaving, disappointed that he couldn't see Herb.

Herb arrived an hour and a half later and regretted missing this doctor. After he visited with David we were walking in the hallway and we passed another nurses' station. Sitting at a desk writing notes I saw the doctor. I called him and when he saw Herb, he came over and grabbed both his hands. He was so happy that everything worked out so well. He also asked if the insurance company paid the bill. They paid every cent and it was over $400,000.00 just for the surgery alone.

This doctor was very compassionate and concerned when he heard about our grandson, David.

He also remarked that it meant so much for us to talk to him at this time. I honestly feel that David was already pulling strings for us.

JOURNAL

In the waiting room of the hospital was a white leather journal with black embossed words scattered on it. The words were many, such as "I wish you happiness when you are sad, I wish you wisdom, hope, etc." It was beautiful and took my breath away because years ago Jillian had given me the same words on a card. The card she gave me was blank inside. She told me that I'd know when to use it for someone special. I had the card for twelve years and thought I had misplaced it. However, when I was writing a letter to my son Kevin, who was going through a difficult time, I picked up a stack of paper, needing another blank page and Jillian's card fell out, landing on my letter to Kevin. I believe with all my heart, she chose the card for him. She loves him so much. I've never seen one like it since. I was ecstatic and comforted to know that my Jillian was there with me and David. Inside the journal were beautiful notes of thanks to the staff for caring for their loved ones.

As I was preparing to write in the journal, I noticed the note on the opposite page. It was a son thanking the hospital staff for the care they had given their father on his recent stay. It was signed with a name I recognized. I had been engaged to this son's father. Coincidence? Hundreds of letters and I happen to see this one. I thought it may have been God's way of letting me know that the family needed prayer. Of course, that's just what I did. I prayed.

I truly believe that all these happenings were an indication of Jillian's presence. She would be there for David. There was another small occurrence in the hospital waiting room. I have one tee shirt I bought because it reminded me of Jillian, with all the butterflies. I do not wear tees so this was unusual. I was in the waiting room talking with Bev's sister. She was hot and dressed in layers so she opened her blouse to reveal the same tee shirt I had.at home. It was enough to bring tears to my eyes. Others may brush this off as coincidental. I don't believe in coincidences. I believe in Christ incidences.

UNEXPECTED CONNECTION WITH DAVID

Herb and I have a favorite restaurant that we've gone to for close to fourteen years, Graziano's. We go weekly, sometimes more often. The owners Chrissy and Joe (brother and sister) have continued on with their parents' legacy, making this a gathering place that is so warm, you hate to leave. We usually sit at the bar and converse with everyone. Of course, I pass my little photo album around. I was showing the bartender my photos of David, including the one of me and Davey on the quad. Everything became quiet. I found out that Davey had worked for a short time in the kitchen at Graziano's. They were having a mechanical problem with something and someone who knew of David's expertise called him. It felt good to know that there was a connection, no matter how small. David was letting us know that he's still with us.

MY GRANDSON STEVEN, (Kevin & Trudi's son) Herb and I went to dinner on his birthday at Graziano's. Another time, I took Steven out to lunch, across from the Marine Supply place where he worked. Steven, you were so open and so motivated to do well, to succeed, yet to accept failure on the way to success. What a great attitude. It meant so much to me that you took the time to do these things with me. You seem to have made family a priority, as well it should be. Remember, too, to lean on God for help. You'd be amazed at what happens and how He helps in tangible ways.

Steven was spontaneous and had a sense of humor. There were several inches of snow on the ground when we were in the hot tub (104 degrees). Kevin and Trudi were with us when Steven said that he was too hot and bolted out of the tub to run around in the snow then lie down and make snow angels with his hot body melting the snow. Brrrr!

It's years later. I don't get to see much of Steven, but we did talk briefly about his prowess in online gambling. To date, he's won $40,000.00. I suggested Steven thank God for this. (I'm pushing now, Trudi). He just looked at me as if he was confused, until I offered an explanation. I agreed that Steven has a gift, a skill at numbers and yes, gambling. I believe that God gave him that gift, at least the ability to do what he does so well. He just smiled. Our talents are God's gift to us. What we do with them, is our gift to Him.

UPDATE; December 2, 2013

Steven wins 1st seat at New Jersey's Next Poker Millionaire Final

Steve is the first New Jerseyan with a chance to be New Jersey's Next Poker Millionaire after winning the first final table seat this past Sunday. Steven, at 28 is a telecommunications professional. He won out over a field of more than 1400 players for the chance to play for a $1 million guaranteed prize package at the "Borgata on February 1st.

Steven did play at the Borgata and he came in second. Congratulations Steven.

Update: Steven and his beautiful wife Amber live in Atco with their German Shepherd, Reese and are expecting a baby girl.

Update: February 28, 2015 Steven's Surprise 30th birthday party. As usual, Trudi and Kevin outdid themselves with the food and decorations. It was, of course, a "Poker" theme.

Update: It's the summer of 2015 and our great granddaughter Courtney Rose has arrived!!

Thank you Steven and Amber.

MY GRANDDAUGHTER, NIKKI, is so sweet and caring. I can still see her propped up on pillows in the bed, when she slept over. She loved being pampered as much as I loved doing the pampering. Nikki, you seemed to enjoy the hot chocolate with whipped cream and the fancy cookies brought to you on a tray. I like to think that we share our love of books. Never get too busy for the important things of life, your family, friends, books and always…God.

Nikki and I would get together for lunch occasionally. It was one of the special times in my life. I really look forward to time with my granddaughter. She's so open and unaffected. She is extraordinarily beautiful, has a captivating smile and eyes so brilliantly sparkling, that it's difficult to take your eyes away from her. The eyes are the windows to the soul. If so, Nikki's reveal an inner beauty, seldom seen.

She is extremely intelligent, excelling in academics, as well as common sense. She cares about the important issues in life, unlike a lot of young adults today. She had expressed a desire to join the Peace Corps one time when we are out to lunch. She's an adult but I still love focusing on childhood memories. I wanted some photos of her outside in the fall colors. I raked up a big pile of leaves and asked her to dive in. I think she thought I was a little bit eccentric.

I have memories of Nikki and me in the rowboat on Lake Wynooska and of overnight stays in the Poconos where we had a formal "tea" with one of the neighborhood girls. These are such simple memories but they make me wish I could go back in time and create more.

Nikki is also an animal lover. Her favorite cat, Trixie, is more than a pet to her. She's a companion of sorts and Nikki spoils her. She also has three other cats, but Trixie rules.

Recently she remarked that her mom was becoming me, embellishing details when we talk and talk and talk. You may not realize it, Nikki, but we both take that as a compliment.

Update: Nikki and her husband Bobby also live in Atco. They have two greyhounds that they rescued, Elizabeth and Frankie. We recently saw them at a 75th birthday party for Trudi's dad. As always, it's so great to see them. It seems the less we see each other, the more appreciative we are of our time together.

MY GRANDDAUGHTER, NATALIE ROSE, Mark's daughter, was born a year before he died. We have photos of Natalie and her daddy when she was about six months old. I saw her when she was a baby, then her mom, Kathy moved to Florida. We saw her rarely. Kathy brought her to visit when Natalie was about four years old.

Kathy was very good about answering letters and acknowledging cards and gifts that I sent to Natalie. Whether it was her birthday, Halloween, Valentines Day, etc. I wanted Natalie to know "Grandmom Rose". After all, Kathy made a point of telling me that Natalie was named after me. I was determined that the geographical distance wouldn't separate us. Kathy sent notes and drawings from Natalie. It was a comfort to me to see my Mark's little girl grow up, even if it was through letters and pictures. I give Kathy a lot of credit, raising Natalie as a single parent for many years before she married. Natalie is a beautiful, articulate woman now. It never ceases to amaze me, how much she looks like Mark. He would be so proud of her. She is now in the medical profession. She seems to possess the ambition her father had.

There were also some very unusual occurrences that indicate Mark is still with Natalie. Of course, I always knew that but it's neat to have things happen that may convince some who are "doubting Thomases". When

Kathy was contemplating helping Natalie buy her first car, she was appalled by the color Natalie chose—a bright yellow. Kathy had been in Florida when Mark told me that he wanted to get a brand new sports car—bright yellow. I tried to discourage him, to no avail. I can't remember the type of car as this happened so long ago. Yet, at the time Kathy told me, the memory was still fresh and I told Kathy what car Mark had wanted. She was very quiet, then told me that it was the same car Natalie wanted. As it turned out, Mark never got his yellow car. He settled for a red one, as did Natalie.

Kathy and Natalie came again to visit when Natalie was sixteen. Except for my letters and photos of the family, we were strangers. Yet, Natalie fit right in with her cousins and was so warm and loving to all her new aunts and uncles. It was beautiful to watch. She was so charismatic, so comfortable meeting her new family for the first time, as a young adult. I'll never forget that visit. She noticed all the balloons with ribbons and blank notes attached to them. Natalie knew of our ritual on Christmas Eve. We would sing Happy Birthday to Jesus, then write notes to Mark, go outside and wish Mark a Merry Christmas as we let the balloons rise up to meet him. She knew of this, because her mother made a point of telling her about it. Natalie took the initiative that night and asked me for pens to give out to everyone so we could write to her daddy. That was the first and only time, to date, that Natalie was here on Christmas Eve. It was such a gift to all of us. Kathy and Natalie are in my prayers, every day.

UPDATE: Natalie graduated from nursing school with honors. I like to think that she is following in my footsteps. However, she's gone even further. She is an RN.

UPDATE: December 2015 Natalie is now a Critical Care Nurse in Florida Natalie came to stay with us for over a week, one summer. We did not have our pool at that time. Natalie was on the swimming team at school. Her interests really do parallel that of her father, Mark and the rest of the family. Everyone loves the water.

MAKENZIE & JAKE - Ryan and Jenny's Children

MY GRANDDAUGHTER, MAKENZIE is four and is an absolute angel who has won the hearts of everyone who comes in contact with her. She is as intelligent as she is beautiful with her cascading blonde curls. At six months, she began signing single words. Sign language, considered to be a second language, enables babies to communicate their wants and needs, long before they can form the words. She picked this up so easily. By a year old, she could sign and recognize signs for about twenty words.

She is inquisitive beyond her years. Even toys are a challenge to her. It's not enough to play with them. She attempts to figure out how they work and usually succeeds. One small incident is a prime example. Kenzie spotted a new item on one of our shelves in our bedroom. It was a tortoiseshell clock. I picked it up at a yard sale because I loved the look of it. I didn't really care if it worked. However, I played around with it for about twenty minutes, to no avail. Kenzie asked if she could take it apart. I said she could but she had to put it back together. She was occupied with the clock for about ten minutes, put it back together and told me "It's fixed now Grandmom." I thanked her, shook my head at her unbridled confidence and placed it back on the shelf. The next morning, an unfamiliar alarm woke me up. It was several minutes before I realized that Kenzie had, indeed, fixed the clock!

Kenzie is loving, affectionate and the joy of our lives. Her favorite things are books, books and more books. Sometimes in the middle of a story, Kenzie will stop, turn my face towards her with her little hands on my cheeks, and say "I love you Grandmom". My heart feels as if it will burst at these times. Thank you, God.

Another favorite activity of Kenzie's is to have a tea party. "Let's do tea, Grandmom", is a frequently uttered phrase. Although Makenzie does drink the tea, I believe it's the ritual itself that she loves. She knows to preheat the teapot, fill the sugar bowl with sparkly cubes—and pop one or two in her mouth--, get out the tray and choose cloth napkins and have cookies or teacakes. She always pours her tea and mine, then stirs.

There was one time when all the men were invited to tea. Makenzie assigned seats and even chose differently colored teacups for each person. Can you even visualize her Dad and Uncle Dave, both over six feet tall, sipping daintily from tiny cups.

She likes to bake also. Aunt Jillian bought her real cookware, miniature sized. She has used the rolling pin when making cookies, ladled soup from her own pot and loves being the little homemaker.

Aunt Rachele made aprons for Kenzie, or as Rachele calls her, "Muffin Face". One of the aprons says "Grandmom's Helper" and has designs of a rolling pin, cookie sheet, spider and ladybug hot glued on it. Kenzie loves finding the real insects outside. The pockets of the apron are filled with seed packets and little gardening tools and tiny gardening gloves.

Another apron "Pop Pop's Helper" has birds, bird seed, a bird house, a mole (Kenzie's favorite storybook was "Who Came Out" about a mole) of "Pop Pop" cheese on it. All that is, is square cheese that Pop Pop buys fresh, just for Kenzie each time she comes to visit. She loves to assemble cheese and crackers for herself and everyone else. The pockets of this apron have a small scoop attached on a ribbon, so Kenzie can help Pop Pop by scooping the bird seed. She also helps him to feed the fish in our small pond. She's obsessive about switching aprons for the appropriate activities.

Makenzie is Pop Pop's "Angel Face", my angel, Uncle Dave's "Squirrely Feet", Aunt Rachele's "Muffin Face" and Mommy and Daddy's "Bug". She is a treasured gift to this whole family.

She also fishes and has had her picture in the newspaper several times for her big catches. This little girl is going places, thanks to her wonderful parents. One of the most touching things her daddy did with her, recently, was to wake her at 4:30 am to take her to the beach, an hour away, so they could watch the sunrise together. Afterwards, they went surf fishing.

When her daddy graduated from the Police Academy, Herb and I were with Jen and Kenzie in the audience. Kenzie was not yet two years old but very bright. Although you could not see them, you could hear the graduates singing as they marched down the halls, before entering the auditorium. Kenzie looked around and said very loudly, in a hushed audience, "Who's that singing?' Of course this prompted laughter from people around us.' There were more than a few smiles that broke out. As the graduates entered the auditorium, looking impressive in stature and uniform, that little voice piped up again and said "Hi! Daddy" as Ryan neared our row.

A NOTE OF LEVITY

Everyone knows the jokes about cops and donuts. However, I thought it was just that—a joke, until I heard three year old Kenzie ask her daddy to please bring home a donut from work for her.

Of course, Pop Pop is always armed with one liners. One day we were driving past Dunkin Donuts and, not seeing Ry's squad car, Herb said "Looks like Ry's not in the office today." ...Lame

SLEEP OVER

May 2009

We went to 4:00 pm Mass with Kenzie, then back home. Pop Pop made grilled cheese sandwiches, then we spent time on the rope swing—Kenzie's favorite. She was giggling and loving every minute of it. Then we got into our pajamas and went out on the back deck with just the cozy glow from a table lamp. It was so perfect. I love having time with Kenzie and although it's fun having Jake and Kenzie together, I treasure my individual time with them. It's easier to spoil them without them competing for my attention.

I decided to tell Kenzie her birth story, as I remember it, as she lay curled in my lap. She laughed when I told her that Aunt Chele and I drove to the hospital together when she was ready to be born. We yelled with joy at the people in each car we passed, or while we were waiting for the red lights to turn green. We're going to have a baby!!

At the hospital, your daddy came out to the waiting room with your little footprints on his shirt. He had tears in his eyes when he announced "We have a daughter!" How beautiful was that? There were probably at least, a dozen of us in the waiting room. Daddy said. Let's go and started down the hall towards Jenny's room. I heard a nurse say "Only two people at a time are allowed in the room." That was NOT happening. All of us piled into the room to see your mommy and you. Daddy introduced you for the first time to everyone and I got to hold you. Our precious angel, you were about to change our lives forever.

As I finished your story, you went limp in my arms, Kenzie, with a smile on your face. Goodnight sweetheart....

Sunday morning you woke up and went into Pop Pop's office. You love the computer. We had breakfast, then out on the swing again. Later you played with the black horses and the corral. You named them "Oreo" and "Beauty". I can hardly wait to give you your book, "Black Beauty" for your birthday.

You also wanted to sit out front on a blanket and count cars—something we did when you were a baby. It started to drizzle. We ended our day with lunch, popsicles and a trip to the library. I almost forgot. I taught you how to embroider. It would be several weeks later when you started embroidering in earnest. You were making Christmas presents by embroidering "Mommy", "Daddy" and "Jake" on pillowcases. It was so time consuming and tedious but you completed the project beautifuly and you are only seven years old.

OCTOBER 25, 2011 2:30pm Journal Entry

It's sunny and breezy, about 70 degrees. I'm lying on the chaise lounge entranced by the breeze creating ripples in the pool. It sparkles like hundreds of tiny diamond facets. Kenzie and I were out here the day after our Halloween party. She said that it looked so tropical and beautiful, with all the palms, that anybody seeing this would be jealous. She's only eight and amazes me with her abstract thinking. She obviously appreciates this pool as much as I do.

We were lying down in the haystack and she explained the difference between hay and straw to me, straw being hollow. Then she beat the husks against a rock until you could see a fine powder. I then used this opportunity to talk to her about my grandmother who used to live in Poland and had to bake everything from scratch, after they pounded the wheat into a fine flour. Kenzie is just a wealth of information because she's so inquisitive and reads every chance she gets. She actually taught me something I did not know. I love it!

UPDATE: 2013

Kenzie is now ten years old. Where did the time go? She is more beautiful than ever and has a matching intellect. She is consistently on the honor roll and is inquisitive beyond her years. She is reading on a high school level. However, her vocabulary is even more advanced. She peppers her speech with words such as lugubrious, coerce, sated and too many more to mention. She is cognizant of their meanings. She's been using these words since she was in second grade. She recently read the adult version of "Heaven Is For Real" by Todd Burpo, which is an amazing true story. She absorbs information like a sponge.

She is an avid softball player who takes the sport seriously. She's tall but very slim. It's difficult to reconcile her slightly built physique with the power in her arm. She loves surfing and is open to trying anything, whether it's jumping off cliffs into water or doing flips off the diving board. She's a strong swimmer and thinks nothing of jumping into the pool when the water temperature is 54 degrees. We open our pool early. One of the most uplifting things to me, is seeing Kenzie with a book in her hands, which is almost always. She loves books as much as I do. What a gift she is in every way.

At the risk of being redundant, Kenzie excels at everything she undertakes. She's avid about fishing, surfing, softball, soccer, swimming and recently, track. She runs with her dad and has been on hunting trips with him. Her artistic expertise is detail oriented and well beyond her years. She is also an altar server in our church. Herb and I are overwhelmed with pride when we see her in her white robe on the altar. As "Pop-Pop" says, "She is our angel."

One more feather in Kenzie's cap. Ryan took her for her bow and arrow test so she could get her hunting license. She passed, which is no surprise. However, looking at Kenzie's slight build, I'm amazed she had the strength to pull back on the bow. It gets better. Ryan took her hunting as soon as the ink dried on her license. First time out, she shot a deer!

UPDATE 2015

Kenzie turns twelve next month. She grows more beautiful each year. She's as tall as me and the epitome of femininity with her grace and her long, blonde flowing tresses. Stand back though and brace yourself when she's on the pitcher's mound or at bat. She's a dynamo! To date, she pitches a ball at 60 miles an hour. She remains an avid reader of, not only fiction, but history, recently reading Bill O'Reilly's "Killing Lincoln." She's consistently on the Honor Roll. She is the only girl on the hockey team. Go Kenzie! The men in our family do not have a monopoly on strength or guts. She also went bow hunting for deer and got a ten-pointer. She provided food for her family and has a beautiful trophy.

This year Kenzie's teacher was doing a review for a chapter test in 7th grade Enrichment Science. The game was "Last man standing." She went around the room asking questions until all but one student was eliminated. Not surprisingly, Kenzie answered all the questions correctly. She was the last "man" standing. The teacher asked if she wanted to continue with the rest of the questions, even though she had already won. Always up for a challenge, Kenzie continued on. She answered all of the remaining questions correctly. Her teacher said that in her fifteen years of teaching, Kenzie was one of only four students to complete this challenge. You make me proud Kenzie!

JAKE RYAN

Watching Kenzie with her little brother, Jake is beautiful. She loves him so much and wants everyone to see how cute he is. There's no jealousy, just love. Jake, or "Little Man", as his daddy calls him, is three months old and beautiful in so many ways. He's got the biggest, most expressive eyes and the most pleasant disposition, smiling that shy, flirty, crooked smile. Holding him, looking into his eyes and hearing his gurgling and seeing his almost constant smile, is actually soothing. I look forward to spending as much time with him as I have with Kenzie. What a blessing he is to our family.

Jake is a year old now. He is a precious little boy. Pop Pop describes him as the "smilingest little boy," smiling from ear to ear all the time. No matter how often I see him, each time my heart skips a beat. He has a shy, playful, almost flirting manner about him. He is a bundle of energy, almost non-stop. Yet, there are times, usually when he is tired, that he will cuddle and hum as I sing to him. I cherish those moments. How blessed we are to have little Jake in our lives.

SLEEP OVER; JAKE IS THREE YEARS OLD

Jake's smile lights up the room and my day. He loves to help me in the kitchen, whether its making mac and cheese or baking. He's become very adept at breaking eggs into a bowl, using one hand. As with Kenzie, he loves the ritual of making tea—the little teapot, the sugar cubes etc. Unlike Kenzie, though, he will drink cup after cup.

Our walks through the woods are special with Jake observing every little miracle of nature. He never tires of gently running his hands over the beautiful mossy areas and spotting lichen on the trees. We've taken our shoes off to feel the cool softness of the moss. Sometimes, we'll even lie down on it. He doesn't miss a mole hole or tunnel or insect of any kind. Feeding the neighbor's chickens and guinea hens as they venture into our yard, is a treat for Jake.

He is such an easy going, happy child. Whether we have a picnic on a blanket in our yard or go under the sprinkler, he is so appreciative. His manners are impeccable, even thanking me for reading a story to him. Even naptime is an enjoyable experience with Jake. He'll tell me when he's tired and go to the bed after brushing his teeth. I'll lie down with him and we'll read a book that he's picked out. As his eyelids get heavy, he'll roll over and wrap his arms around me. I can't adequately describe how this makes me feel. The only word that comes to mind is "ineffable", Jillian's favorite word. After a two hour nap, Jake wakes up with a luminous smile, ready to play with his trucks. I am truly blessed to have Jake in my life.

Jake is also our little patriot. We took him with us when we voted in the last election. We showed him the diagram of the voting machine, that the township sends us so he would be familiar with it. He watched intently as we signed in, then came in with me first. He very quietly asked if he had the right buttons. He remembered every single one correctly. He punched them in. looked at me for the approval to push the last red button that would register all the other choices. I nodded and he pushed the last button.

I don't know what the rules are regarding taking children into the booth but nobody seemed to have any objections. My daughter Rachele always took her boys with her when they were younger. Now they vote on their own. Pop Pop asked if Jake wanted to go in with him to vote. Of course he did. On exiting the booth, a man sitting nearby asked Jake if he liked to vote and why. Jake said "Yes, I'm a patriot." The man said "Do you even know what a patriot is?" Jake said, "It's someone who loves their country." I was so proud of him.

FEBRUARY 27, 2011

This is a very special day in my memory bank. I was so emotionally moved at Mass this morning. The sanctuary candle was burning for Jillian and Mark. Their photos were visible to us from our pew. Jen, Ry, Kenzie and Jake were there with us. During the Our Father we all held hands, then Jake let go and raised both his little hands, palms up, to heaven. When we went up to receive Communion, he got between me and Pop Pop and held our hands. Tears of joy trickled down while I prayed after Communion. I had an overwhelming sense of peace that my baby girl and Markie are happy and safe. Also very touching, was Jake with his head bowed on the pew, as he knelt after Communion, just like his dad…beautiful!

UPDATE 2013: Jake is now six years old. The years have wings!

Jake loves to come over for a sleepover. He orchestrates the whole day. If "Pop Pop" isn't there when he comes over, he'll call him at work and ask him to hurry home. The teasing starts as soon as Herb gets home. Jake tells him that he'll have to sleep in the garage with "Ginger", our outdoor cat because Jake's sleeping with me in the big bed. Then "Pop Pop" starts telling corny jokes to Jake. Jake rolls his eyes and shakes his head because "Your jokes aren't funny "Pop Pop". I'll attest to that. So will everyone else.

Jake will say grace at mealtime and pray for his entire family, naming each one, including pets. He does the same thing when we say bedtime prayers. He's such an easygoing little boy. He's always gone to bed without a fuss. In fact, most times he'll tell me when he's ready for bed. We'll read several books, then all of a sudden he'll say "I'm tired Grandmon. We'll finish the book tomorrow." A good night kiss, an "I love you" and within seconds, he's sound asleep.

The next morning Jake awakes with a smile and a "Good morning grandmom! Let's make eggs for breakfast." Since he was four, he had a knack for breaking the eggs against the side of the bowl, with one hand. He'll break a half dozen eggs and has never gotten any shells in the bowl. I can't even say that for myself. Scrambled eggs, sausage, toast and orange juice. He also insists on making "Pop Pop's" coffee all by himself. He's so adept in the kitchen that he may be a chef someday.

Jake also loves football and is a virtual encyclopedia of football facts and stats. Today we watched him play a game and he got three touchdowns!. He, also, excels at soccer and baseball. He loves the ocean and pool and could spend the entire day swimming. He starts first grade this year but is already reading books much more advanced. Ryan and Jenny are doing a wonderful job with their children.

Herb and I enjoy our time with Jake as well as Kenzie, but there seems to be a special bond between Jake and "Pop-Pop." No matter what they do together, whether it's in the garage, fixing a leaky faucet, feeding our cats, or ordering the same thing at Dunkin Donuts they end up laughing, sometimes uncontrollably. They love to scare each other and play tricks on each other.

I'm looking forward to teaching Jake's CCD class this year, at his request. I was Kenzie's teacher one year so Jake said it was his turn now. He already has an obvious love for Jesus. This should be very rewarding.

Jake is six now and has decided he wants to be a paleontologist when he grows up. You should have seen Herb's face when he came out with that. Jake explained that even though dinosaurs are now extinct, we can pretend. We dug up "bones" (tree roots), brushed them lightly with brushes, then marked the sites with colored caps from Pop Pop's garage.

Jen, Kenzie and I went to a party for Autumn, Kenzie's cousin. Jake and Ry had a baseball game. Afterwards, Ryan had to work and Pop-Pop was in charge. When we came home that night, I noticed the small teacups were in the sink. I knew Herb had no idea where I kept them but Jake did. Not only that, but there weren't any pop tarts left in the kid's snack cabinet. Jake told Pop Pop where to check for a new box. Herb didn't have a clue. I love to watch the two of them together. When we came home they were on the sofa laughing at a Duck Dynasty show.

December 2015

Jake is playing hockey this year and he is so good. How about scoring eight goals in one game! That is his average. Way to go Jake!

Note: I still feel guilty because I seldom bought Mark pop tarts. He loved them but money was tight and it wasn't a necessity so it was crossed off the shopping list. I'm sure Mark is laughing about this but it's a sensitive memory for me. Every time I buy them, I think of Mark as well as Jake.

UPDATE 2015

Jake is now eight and growing by leaps and bounds. He's on the Honor Roll at school and also enjoys reading. He's reading books several years ahead of his age group. He's great at soccer, hockey and baseball and will be adding basketball to his agenda next season. He has been preparing this year, to receive his First Holy Communion on May 2. He's excited, we're ecstatic and planning to have a celebration at our home. The pool will be open April 29. I'm sure it will be ice cold but that won't stop our diehard family from going in. Of course, Herb will fire up the hot tub to counteract the hypothermic guests. Jake loves the hot tub! We love Jake.

JAMIE, TYLER AND BRANDON RACHELE AND EL'S SONS

JAMIE is tall, handsome and intelligent, with a serious nature. As a young boy he was always interested in science books, well beyond his years. I think that he's probably the most inquisitive of the three boys. Last time I saw him was about a year ago, shortly after they moved to Missouri. He was 18 then.

When Jamie was younger and I was working at Archway School, he spent the day there with me. He was going to receive the sacrament of Confirmation and one of the requirements was for him to serve in his community in a capacity that he chose. I had the honor of being his sponsor and couldn't be happier that he opted to be of service, working with special needs children. I'll always remember that day. Jamie is an exceptionally talented artist.

What I think of most when I think of TYLER is a shyness and a ready smile. He wasn't very talkative as I found out when Herb and I took him to MacDonald's for his birthday. I remember also that he, as well as his brothers, take after their mom, in that they all love the water and are great swimmers.

Tyler, like most of the members of our family, has an incredibly high tolerance of pain. He gets that from his mom. Rachele never "babied" her sons. She's fond of saying that complaining of pain or discomfort won't make it better, so just "suck it up." There's one incidence that occurred when Ty was about ten years old that still evokes cringing and sympathy. Rachele's sons would learn from their mom how to be tough and not to panic.

Jamie and Ty were riding their bicycles when Ty spotted a weed in his chain. He reached down to pull it out while the bike was still moving catching his fingertips between the sprocket and the chain. It was not a pretty sight. They ran home to show mom Ty's injury. As Rachele was tending to Tyler, she told Jamie to "go back and get your brother's fingertips." Jamie looked at her with disbelief and asked how he was supposed to do that. She said to follow the trail of blood. Of course, there was nothing to be found but it diverted Jamie's attention for a few minutes. There was a trip to the emergency room, where a male nurse explained that he had to debride the wound and it would be painful but he wanted to numb the area. Tyler, was more afraid of the needle, and told the nurse to do it without the shot. He grimaced and bit his lip but toughed it out. He received nothing but praise from the nurse.

NOVEMBER 12, 2009

Tyler was chosen by state officials in South Central Missouri to represent the youth in a jobs initiative program. He was the only one chosen out of 330 participants to attend a dinner at Governor Jay Nixon's mansion. The program was an initiative to connect Missouri's youth with cutting edge businesses across the state. Tyler was recognized for his expertise in web development and graphic design.

Jamie and Tyler have always been risk takers, adrenaline driven. When they moved to Missouri they would swim in the river and do back flips off of a twenty-five foot bridge. Sounds like they have a lot of their great grandfather in their genes and some of Aunt Jillian and their mom, both of whom loved rock climbing, swimming and diving. Some of their genes that are obviously from my grandfather, their great, great grandfather, show up in their height. Jamie is 6'3" and Brandon is 6'5". Tyler is 5'10".

BRANDON is one of those children every parent would love to have. He's funny, caring and sensitive, does well in school, consistently making the honor roll and wouldn't think of disobeying his mother. He's also an avid reader.

I regret to say that I didn't spend as much time with them when they were little. Part of it was because I was a single parent, working full time, going through a divorce and in a persistent state of depression. I am not making excuses. I guess I'm attempting an explanation.

I remember picking Tyler up from pre-school a couple of times. I didn't babysit, though, because Rachele's marriage was, in some ways, like mine had been. We didn't need babysitters because we never went out—no lunches, no movies, no shopping trips, no entertainment whatsoever. I know that sounds far fetched but it's true. The only social life we had was when there was a family wedding or other celebration. Oops! I stand corrected. George and I did see two movies in twenty one years, "Mash" and "Jaws".

Now I can spend quality time with my adult grandchildren, maybe an occasional lunch. I don't have those opportunities with Rachele's children because they're so far away in Missouri. If we could only use our wisdom, acquired by years of experience, to relive our youth and correct or prevent mistakes. I would have, could have, should have....God bless Jamie, Tyler and Brandon and keep them safe always.

UPDATE – 2013

Jamie is twenty-five years old and works at Mountain View Nursing Home. Tyler is twenty-one and an associate at WalMart. Brandon is sixteen years old and and has taken on some new endeavors. He is playing piano and sax. He recently has won a trophy for a three day chess tournament. Brandon is also tutoring elementary school children in algebra. His plate is really full. I've often said that I believe we're all put on this earth to be of service to others. Brandon takes that to heart. We are looking forward to seeing them in September.

UPDATE 2015

Brandon graduates from Mountain View High School with honors!! Great job Brandon!

Tyler has recently been diagnosed with juvenile rheumatoid arthritis. Doctor told Rachele that he has the arthritic joints of a sixty year old. More prayers needed.

Rachele's sons, thanks to her, are proud of their Polish heritage. It shows. Jamie recently got a very large tattoo of the Polish Falcon on his arm. Brandon still calls me "Babci" which is Polish for grandmother. Rachele has even taught her boys how to make pierogies from scratch in order to keep Polish tradition alive in her family. I'm sure their great grandparents must be pleased. I am.

COURTNEY ROSE

Steven & Amber presented us with a beautiful great-granddaughter this past summer. We are truly blessed to have her in our lives. Courtney was center of attention at her first birthday, pool party in August. Two weeks later, at a surprise 50 th birthday party for Trudi, Courtney was still center stage on the dance floor. She is as precious as they come.

HERB, MY WONDERFUL HUBBY

"Love, if you have it you don't need to have anything else and if you don't have it, it doesn't matter what else you have." Sir James Barrie

Where do I begin? I met Herb at a "Parents Without Partners" dance. He was wearing dress pants and dress shirt and a sweater vest and tie. His appearance was so neat. So many guys were in jeans. To me, it seemed that they put so little effort into looking presentable. If this was the way that they tried to attract women, I wasn't impressed. Needless to say, my first impression of Herb was a good one.

He invited me to dinner at "Pufferbelly" in Lindenwold, N.J., then a show in Atlantic City. We enjoyed each other's company and kept dating. I was beginning to sense that Herb was getting serious, rather quickly. I thought of him, more as a friend. I told him how I felt and he was okay with this. Hopefully, he said, my feelings would change in time. If not, I'd have a friend for life. He took Ryan, Jillian and me to see the Globetrotters. It meant a lot to me when he included my children on dates.

Eventually, I broke up with Herb. He was having difficulty in knowing how to deal with my bouts of depression. Mark had died that past summer and I would break down and cry frequently. He didn't understand why I wasn't getting better. Better?? I was furious that he was so insensitive. I guess I was an emotional wreck. Herb was devastated when I thought we should go our separate ways. We did agree to see each other occasionally, as friends. He was very concerned that I would meet someone else. The last thing I needed was someone else in my life. I did, however, go out with my friends RoseAnn and Florence. Florence was a widow and Rose Ann had been divorced years before.

Rose Ann was a dance instructor. Dancing became the common denominator for us when we would go out. We all loved swing dancing. I actually met them through a man who was a father image to me. Vince was my bus driver when I worked at Archway School and we would pick up the children in wheelchairs and on oxygen. He was in his seventies then and was an amazing man with a wealth of information. He became protective of me. He was the one who gave me Florence's phone number and suggested I go out with her. She loved to dance.

Florence mentioned Rose Ann who happened to be the sister of friends and neighbors. All our children went to school with their children. We had such a good time the first time we went out. It was something we tried to do on a regular basis. I've seen Florence from time to time, but we drifted. Rose Ann and Al and Herb and I are still close. We go out together occasionally but talk on the phone regularly. They are both very spiritual and we can count on them for prayers, always. They, also, have had more than their share of medical crises. Needless to say, they are always on our prayer list.

Ironically, that first night out with the girls, I met someone who could empathize with me about Mark. I seemed to need to talk about Mark incessantly. The man I met had lost a son, Mark's age, to a serious illness. We were able to comfort each other, laugh at good memories and cry because of the loss of our sons. It was as if the floodgates were opened and I could talk and cry about Mark without having to explain. It helped to ease the ever-present pain.

Although, it would seem that our families should be the ones to give solace at this time, we were discovering that each person handles grief in their own way. Some of our family members couldn't talk or didn't want to. This relationship with Ed soon turned serious. We became engaged and were together for two years.

Periodically, during this time, Herb would call or show up unannounced just to see how I was. I would get upset and remind him that I was engaged. He would say, "But you're not married. I'm not giving up until you are." He would profess his love for me over and over. I would tell him not to call or come over again. His tenacity was driving me nuts! I ached for Herb, though he never knew it. I remember how it felt to love someone so much and have them tell you that they didn't love you anymore. Herb hung in there for two years, never losing heart. Thank God!

You wake up each day thinking, "How can I still be alive when I'm in so much pain. Herb seemed to handle it the way that I handled my breakup with George. We both lost over twenty pounds. Herb looked great. I didn't. I was in nursing school at the time and my instructors expressed concern because they thought I was anorexic. It wasn't deliberate on my part. I was just so depressed, that food held no interest for me. This will be a shock to everyone who knows me, because I savor every new eating experience.

I felt Herb's pain. I had been there. Even years later, though healing had begun, I had painful flashbacks of my own breakup with George.

This time, though, I had to deal with the realization that I was the cause of the pain, not the recipient. Of course, I prayed for Herb. Yet, I also remembered what came to mind years before when friends would tell me that they were praying for me, for strength. I didn't want to be strong. I wanted to be happy.

For reasons I will get into later (because there's a great spiritual aspect to this story), I broke my engagement to Ed, six weeks before the wedding. Guess who showed up on my doorstep. I have a strong feeling that one of my children must have called Herb. Rachele?? Of course, I was, in no way, ready to start dating again. Besides, I could not reciprocate his love.

SECOND CHANCE FOR ME

In time, I remember asking God, why I couldn't just fall in love with this gentle, caring man. He was good to me and my children, morally strong, never had an unkind word about anyone, was always available to help anyone and everyone and had the patience of a saint. Months went by and there came a day when I was actually surprised to realize that my feelings were beginning to change. I was falling in love with Herb. I still doubted that God would want me with Herb because of his lack of faith. It always helps to have support in that area as well as others.

I found out, many years later, that Herb had gone to the cemetery where Mark was. He promised Mark that he would always take care of me and make me happy for as long as he lived, if Mark would help him to win me back. The rest is history.

It's October 2015 and we have been married twenty-one years...good years, filled with an abundance of love and laughter. There are episodes of sheer joy even when everything seems to go wrong. Happiness is situational and we have that, but we also have joy, which can overshadow the difficult times. Joy is possible because of the third party in our marriage...Jesus.

Our day starts early. Herb gets up at 4:30 am for work at the Philadelphia Airport. He's been there for forty years. At 5:30 am he brings me a steaming mug of tea and gives me a good morning kiss before he leaves. There are times that I'm difficult to rouse from sleep because I may not have fallen asleep until 3:00 am. However, we have an agreement that he will wake me because we don't ever want to chance missing out on what could be our last kiss and "I love you", should anything happen to either one of us. You never know. Negative thinking? Not hardly. Positive, because no matter what happens or when, we'll have that last good memory.

I have evolved, with the help of God, from a pessimist into an optimist. Do I ever have negative thoughts? Of course I do, I'm human. Usually though, as quickly as they surface, I redirect myself by turning my doubts or fears over to Jesus. This may happen several times a day. Just as it has taken years to establish bad habits, it will take time to forge good and positive habits. I'm a work in progress. God's not done with me yet.

I don't think that there's anyone more positive than Herb. I mentioned one breakup with him. There was another. Anyone else would have given up on me. Herb didn't. One of our issues, for lack of a better word, was that I wanted it all—relationship wise. I wanted communication, romance, friendship, more communication, discovery of each other's likes and dislikes, dreams, etc. Herb was willing to settle for anything I had to offer. He asked nothing. He was content just to be in my company. He was very passive. I was very demanding in our relationship. Having been in a marriage where the word "communication" caused arguments, I would not settle for anything less than ongoing communication.

For all my girls who think that Herb is perfect...he's not. He's a wonderful husband but not perfect. Besides, I always thought that perfect might be boring. So please, understand, I don't want perfection. Maybe I want more participation. I remember one occasion vividly that was the onset of some problems, early on. Herb and I had been seeing each other for about six months. I felt as if I was doing most of the 'work' in the relationship. I've always believed that a good relationship needs nurturing and fine tuning. Just as you wouldn't run a car for thousands of miles without a tune-up and oil change, how much more important is a relationship. It requires effort. Herb thought the opposite, that a good relationship just happens and requires absolutely no effort. That was a red flag waving, if ever there was one.

I didn't need to know everything but I did want to know what Herb's feelings were about different things. Maybe if he had really listened to what I was feeling about Mark, it would have helped him to understand me better and maybe prevented our breakup.

We were at a restaurant and I was looking around at the other couples talking animatedly. I wanted that for us. Herb barely said anything. How would we get to know each other.

Don't misunderstand, it's not that I feel we have to talk all the time. I can be comfortable, quietly reading a book or listening to music in the same room as my husband. In fact, we do that quite often since we're both avid readers. It gives me a warm, cozy feeling. We may take a break. I'll make coffee or Herb may bring me a cup of tea. We'll give each other a hug or kiss, then go right back to reading. However, there are times when words are necessary or desirable. I do have to say that the most important words, "I love you" are uttered many times a day by both of us. There are other times, however, when words are warranted.

For instance, I could break down and cry or I could be angry, audibly so, and Herb won't even ask what's wrong. He'll act as if he doesn't notice and hope it will all go away in a few hours. I find this maddening!! I always say that problems are like wounds. You have to scrape away the infection, which is painful, before the healing process can begin. I liken Herb to putting on a band aid on top of the infection and hoping it will clear up. It never does. Whether it's a physical or emotional wound, it needs tending... that is, if you don't want a superficial relationship.

Anyway, while I was observing the other couples, I mentioned it to Herb, saying I'd like for both of us to put more effort into getting to know each other. Herb said that we didn't need to talk. He said that after dating me for six months, he knew all there was to know about me. I was LIVID!!! I told him that if he was with me for twenty years, he still wouldn't know everything there was to know about me. He hadn't even scratched the surface. Then I got up and walked away from him. Not a good day.

Herb vowed that he would never take that attitude again. He eventually agreed that a good relationship would require effort, claiming to understand my rationale. Time would tell. Lest you think that problem was resolved so easily, think again. It still requires work to maintain a good relationship, but it's a labor of love.

I love Herb's sense of dry humor. I talk about growing older (not old) together. He says we're already old. I keep telling him to speak for himself. I feel young. I don't ever intend to be old. I may age and turn gray and my wrinkles may increase, but I refuse "to get old". I don't plan to allow him to do that either. We laugh about that a lot.

One of the most touching things Herb did for me was in the middle of the night. I had gone to bed late, as usual, but I just couldn't get warm. He had turned over to hug me and felt my ice cold feet. He got out of bed, got a pair of his socks, warmed them with the blow dryer, then put them on me. How sweet is that!

"A MERRY HEART DOETH GOOD LIKE A MEDICINE."
Proverbs 17:22

Herb's sense of humor is unique and at times eccentric. He has been known to follow me into ladies restrooms, asking if I need any help. Keep in mind, this occurred decades before transgender bathrooms. He could care less if someone sees him. He has started dancing with me in Fashion Bug, when our song came on. I have to say that he makes me laugh every day. He's attentive and funny and I love being around him. Even after twenty-one years, my heart skips a beat when I hear his car pull in the driveway. We both feel blessed to enjoy the time we have together. Thank you, God.

Our grandson Jake laughs so hard at Pop Pop's silly jokes. When he stays overnight, we ask Pop Pop to help turn down the bed. He responds "Why? Is it too loud?" We play a lot of Scrabble and I've had to deal with

"Herbonics". Herb makes up words such as "knue". and waits for me to figure it out. Canoe. There's a lot of laughter and challenging going on. Despite his silly antics, he has become very competitive. We take our Scrabble games seriously, as do Kevin, Trudi, Jake and Kenzie. Jake has said that Kenzie is more tenacious than he is. Yes, that was Jake's word for Kenzie. Keep in mind that he is only eight years old. Love it! On Jillian's last visit home, she played Scrabble with Herb and me. She couldn't believe the words he came up with and the "new" rules he made that applied to him only. I couldn't stop laughing because he was driving her crazy. Jillian wiped us both out. She takes this game very seriously. She even had a travel size magnetic Scrabble to take with her. There was no winning for anyone else when she played.

Rachele and Herb have a close bond and a unique method of communicating by text messages. It has to take longer to do this but they both are so used to it, it comes naturally. It's bizarre and it involves "Herbonics." Here is an example.

Herb to Rachele: Use rites good. Use shud bee an Anglaish teach.

Rachele's reply: Use is gud nuf two rite fer Fox Nus.

HERB'S FAMILY

Herb is one of eight children. He has one brother and six sisters, two of whom are in heaven.

He worked hard from the time he was nine years old. There was no time for dances or sports or school activities. He would earn money and hand over every cent to his father. He packed tomatoes, cut asparagus, made the crates for shipping the asparagus, picked eggplant, loaded everything on the trucks. He did all the hoeing and fed the pigs. As he got older he would even inoculate turkeys.

He was working on cars by the time he was a teenager. He also was interested in electricity. Everything he did, he did exceptionally well. He was self-taught in so many different areas. He tells of one time when he was about eleven years old, he was putting a new end on an extension cord. As he plugged it into the outlet, there was a huge explosion outside. His father screamed "What did you do?!!" Herb had done nothing wrong. The extension cord worked. It seems that at the exact moment he plugged it in, a transformer on a electric pole at the neighbor's house had exploded. However, for those few seconds, he also thought he had done something wrong. He took the extension cord and threw it under the stairs so his father wouldn't see it.

When Herb was eighteen he joined the volunteer fire company and ambulance crew. Back then it wasn't as regimented as it is today. You didn't need to be certified. He served in that capacity until he was twenty and then drafted into the Army. He served six months in Vietnam after doing sheet metal work (airframe repair) in Fort Eustis, Virginia. Military service was a big plus in my eyes. Just about every man in my dad's family was in the military. My father, all my uncles, my brother Ed, my cousin Cliff. My cousin David also served as a police officer, as does my son Ryan. God bless them all.

Herb was close to his Uncle Fred and I, also, took a great liking to him. While others in the family played cards, I sat with Uncle Fred as he played the piano and organ, both in his little music room. We sang the old songs from the forties. I spent a little time with his mom, helping her once with her respiratory treatment. I was alarmed because she was on oxygen and still smoking!! Shortly after that Herb's mom passed away. Then so did Uncle Fred. I was glad for the short time I knew them. Much to my shock, Uncle Fred left his piano to me in his will. Herb and I weren't even engaged at the time. I will always treasure the player piano he left me. He obviously knew I loved music. I played it every chance I got and kept a photo of Uncle Fred on the piano. His favorite hymn was "How Great Thou Art." To this day when I hear that hymn, it takes me back to Uncle Fred's music room. He was a very special man.

MARRIAGE ENCOUNTER

I do know because of a very intense Marriage Encounter weekend that my husband's love for me runs deeper than I ever realized before. Marriage Encounter is an enrichment weekend for couples with good marriages. It is not counseling. It involves written and verbal communication, which Herb insists he cannot do. Yet, his communication on this weekend was nothing short of a miraculous gift.

An announcement about Marriage Encounter was made at our church on Sunday after Mass. Herb said, "I guess you'd like to go." I was surprised that he even mentioned it. I hadn't. Of course, he knew that I was all for communication. I responded, very low key. "It would be nice." Herb looked at it as a weekend getaway. Little did he know of the work it would entail.

We arrived early on a Friday afternoon in Avalon, N.J. for our encounter weekend. We sat at the bar in the upscale hotel, had a drink and ordered shrimp cocktail. It was during Lent and no meat on Fridays still applied, although shrimp is not what I would call a sacrifice.

When people started arriving, we went to the conference room. There were about thirty couples, all ages. We had a snack, coffee and soda while the presenters explained the format. The presenters, who would role model for us, were two married couples and a Catholic priest. The program is sponsored by the Catholic Church but open to everyone no matter what their religion. The priest would explain how Jesus is a third partner in our marriage, which I had always been aware of, and how it also played out in his vocation.

I was more interested in looking around at the other couples, checking out what they were wearing and being observant of their body language. It was the first and last time that I would notice them. The weekend was so intense there was no time to focus on anyone, other than your spouse. We began with a "ten and ten", which was ten minutes of writing, then ten minutes of dialoguing on what we wrote. The presenting couple, after a half hour sharing session of their own life, would give us a question to answer. We'd separate, men stayed in the conference room, women would go back to their hotel room. We were to focus on each other. At no time did we ever share with the group or presenters. No one would ever know what we had written to each other.

One of the guidelines was to be sensitive to each other. No throwing barbs about past grievances were allowed. We were to share feelings, not just state facts. Also, they stressed that feelings are neither right nor wrong, they just are. The first "love letter" from Herb was good. He basically came on the weekend to please me. However, he said that we had a great marriage and couldn't see this weekend making a difference.

Next session was different. Herb came back to the room with his book and said that he had such a difficult time expressing his thoughts. I reassured him that no matter what he wrote, it would be fine, because his "feelings were neither right nor wrong" and I would accept them, whatever they were. It was then that he said, "You don't understand! I couldn't write anything."

Was I upset, that after nine years of marriage, my husband, who said that he loved me more than when he married me, couldn't think of anything to say to me. Inside, I was in shock,. crushed. I wanted to scream at him and at God to Whom I'd already thanked for this opportunity. I also had asked Jesus to be in the middle of this weekend. Where are You now? Why did You bring us to this point, just to be disappointed, hurt, angry, etc. Anyway, I didn't scream. I was beyond words. I quietly asked Jesus to help me handle this situation without the anger that was beginning to bubble up in me.

Herb just said, "I thought that I could do this, but I can't. I love you more than ever, but I can't do this." A calmness settled over me and I asked him if he wanted to leave then. Since it was after 10:00 pm, he suggested that we wait until after breakfast, in the morning.

Next day we assembled for Mass in the conference room. Father Skip gave a beautiful homily. Herb remarked that he really liked Father Skip. He had a sense of humor, like Herb. I just remember feeling very sad that we'd be leaving. I was envious of all the couples that were staying. I remained quiet. Herb spoke with the other couples at breakfast. That was the only time that socializing was encouraged.

We went back to our room and I started packing. Herb hugged me and said that he'd like to give it another try. I was at a loss for words, but tears of joy flowed freely. Thank You, Jesus.

All day long we wrote and dialogued. It was exhausting. We took breaks for meals, which were exceptionally good, and we even went outside to look at the ocean to refresh our spirits.

There was one couple who was married forty years. He was griping halfway through Saturday, that "these people couldn't show him anything that he and his wife didn't already know." He wanted out, but he stayed. Everyone stayed.

Father asked if anyone wanted to receive the sacrament of Reconciliation (confession), that night, he was available. I wrote my name down on a slip of paper and an hour later he knocked on our door. Herb answered and Skip jokingly said that he needed time alone with me. Herb left and found something else to do. I was a little nervous until Father Skip plopped down on the bed, after turning down my offer of the only chair in the room. He just made conversation about anything and everything. I was so comfortable that I almost forgot why he was there. Then he heard my confession, answered a few questions for me, gave me absolution and a hug, then left.

Not to get off track here, but I think that the Catholic Church is way ahead on this sacrament. We can receive this sacrament everyday, if we so choose. Therapy and counseling at no cost versus $100.00 an hour in the secular world. Actually, this isn't even the church's idea. This sacrament was instituted by Jesus when He told his apostles to "forgive men's sins and they are forgiven." Of course, the priests don't do the actual forgiving. Jesus does. The priests are just instruments acting on His behalf. Only God can forgive sins.

We continued with our ten and ten all day long and all night too. No TV or other sensory input. Just us, our meals and the presenters, baring their souls to teach us this profound method of communication. Twenty minutes doesn't sound like much time, yet they cautioned us that it would not be easy finding the time at home. Daily routines and unexpected events would interfere. They were right. Yet, these couples with young children, jobs, sports for their children and other obligations, made time every single day to dialogue. I admire them so much for their commitment. Weekends weren't even theirs. They were volunteering their time to teach us. One couple said that for awhile there, the only time and place that they could do their ten and ten, with a houseful of kids, was in the bathroom. He sat on the "throne" while his wife soaked in a bubble bath. He said that the view was a bonus. They encouraged us to be creative.

Last day, Sunday, Mass again, breakfast then back to the ten and ten. Finally, our last session. The question they posed was "What would you like your spouse to know if he or she were to die tomorrow?" Then they forewarned us that we might be upset at what they were going to ask us to do next. This was not a ten and ten. We were to write for one hour, then dialogue for one hour. Everyone moaned. I was almost afraid to look at Herb. The general consensus was, Herb included, was that we couldn't do this. Yet, we had come this far. We had to try.

About this time in the weekend, I was aware that something unexplainable was happening. There was definitely a spiritual force at work. Jesus was in the center of this. I don't think that Herb even realized it yet. His "love letters" were so revealing, sensitive and enlightening. During our exchanges when we read each others letters, we became very emotional I hadn't seen this side of my husband before and he was better able to understand me. Still, writing for an hour......

After the above question, there were other questions just in case the first one was answered before the hour was up. We separated and began to write. Herb came bounding into the room, seemingly upset. I asked him what he was doing back so early. What was wrong? The hour was up. I couldn't believe it. It was the quickest hour I've ever experienced. Apparently Herb too. He was upset because he wanted more time to write. He hadn't even finished answering the first question, after an hour of writing. There was so much more to say. I couldn't believe it.

We dialogued for the entire hour, after exchanging the most beautiful, heart wrenching letters we'll ever receive. We were an emotional wreck, crying, hugging, more crying, laughing at times and crying some more. We went through two boxes of tissues and sat there with a roll of toilet paper between us, blowing our noses and wiping away tear after tear..... good, healing tears.

We were physically and emotionally drained, as was everyone else, even the couple who was married for forty years. We met back in the conference room for the last time. Our presenters looked tired too. Keep in mind, that the couples and Father Skip were available all night for questions or any help they could give.

There is no sharing except for the presenters. However, they found that some people were on such a "high" that they wanted to talk, so they gave them an opportunity, if they wanted to share a part of their experience, or just their thoughts. A few people spoke up and tried to share parts of their experience. When I saw Herb's hand go up, I was stunned. My very private husband, who had difficulty sharing thoughts with me, was speaking in front of a crowd of strangers. With tears coursing down his face and his voice cracking, he told of how much he had loved me before, and though he wouldn't have thought it possible, now loved me even more. He thanked the couples and Father Skip for this precious weekend.

This method of communication works for parents and children too. It's nothing short of amazing. Now, the big question. Do we continue to do our ten and ten? Not daily and infrequently, but we are drawn back to it from time to time, usually about important things like, "How do I feel about (HDIFA) Herb's heart surgery or our new grandchild. Rereading our letters makes me want to try to do it more often.

Our pleasures are simple...nature, animals, food, a soft breeze that rustles the leaves, thunder and lightning that remind us of God's awesome power. More than anything, our love for each other, our children and grandchildren are our greatest joy. We can't ask for much more. God has blessed us richly.

Oh yes, a little footnote. I hear so many negative things about the Catholic Church asking for money. This weekend, which takes place worldwide, cost us $50.00 for a beautiful room in an upscale hotel, five meals, coffee and snacks all through the night and a view of the ocean. You could donate more if you wanted, which we gladly did. On the other hand, if you couldn't afford the $50.00 the church would pick up the tab. Nice.

PET PEEVE: INCORRECT SPELLING

Herb and I also communicate occasionally by notes, usually left in the morning. I might leave one when I make his lunch the night before. Sometimes, he'll leave notes that he knows will agitate me. I have a love of language and usage and one of my pet peeves is incorrect spelling. Herb is extremely intelligent, yet seems to make a game of disproving that. The following notes were written, obviously, to elicit laughs.

"U arr soe goode two me. I could knot fine a beter person fore my wife."

Luv u, Hubby

"Hon, Take it eazy twoday. Your dewing weigh two much. It ain't no goode four your hip. I no. They don't call me Dr. Dalbow for nothing."

I found out inadvertently that Herb graduated second in his high school class at the age of sixteen. He would never have volunteered this information. When I asked him about this, he'd make a joke of it and say that there were only five in the class. I, however, found his yearbook. There were one hundred and sixty-five graduates. He's so humble, to a fault.

Over the years, we would encounter men that he worked with, or who worked for him. Some of these people hadn't seen him in ten years. Yet, every single one had something positive to tell me about him. They would mention something that he had taught them, that wasn't in any book.

They talked about his inventive ways of repairing things and of how he imparted knowledge that could not be found in any manual. It would not be an exaggeration to say that he has had a positive impact on everyone he's met. Do I sound just a little bit proud!

MY DAUGHTERS-IN-LAW

BEVERLY,

Though David and Bev never married, they were together twenty-plus years. She and David have one son, David. Bev has two sons, Duane and Jason from a previous marriage. I have always considered Bev one of my girls.

My son David, Bev, Herb and I went to Union Lake on a very warm Sunday. David had a fishing tournament, if my memory serves me right. Bev and I were dressed in long, flowered, softly flowing dresses, as was the style. We were the epitome of femininity.

The sun on the lake made a golden glow with soft ripples, enticing us. I kicked my shoes off, waded waist deep, then began swimming away from shore. Disbelief on Bev's face turned into a question mark, then "why not". Off came Bev's shoes and she swam out to meet me. Sheer joy! A moment that indeed, did draw us closer. David was annoyed and couldn't believe Bev would do this. Of course, she made it clear that it was my idea. Herb laughed. He's used to the unconventional occurrences.

Another touching moment took place in Shop Rite, where Bev works. Bev was working at one of the registers. I just wanted to let her know that I was thinking of her, so I gave her a quick hug. As I walked away, she shouted "Mom". I and everyone else turned. Simply stated, yet loudly enough for everyone to hear, she said, "I love you mom". Tears welled and I returned the "I love you, too, Bev." It had started out to be a very difficult day for me—too much to do, in too little time. Bev made my day so rich with a memory that won't fade. Whenever I see her, no matter how often, we declare our love to each other. Thank you Lord for more memories to sustain me in my twilight years. Thank you for Bev.

UPDATE

David's dream to build a home in New York was shared with enthusiasm by Bev, at least initially. It took several years to complete because David would work in NJ all week and go to New York on weekends. He built a reading nook for Bev in the loft, so she could read and look out on the mountain. I remember her being really excited about it. She seemed to love it up there. It was an entirely different lifestyle.

Years go by and Bev's son Jason presents Bev with her first grandchild, a little girl. She chose to stay in NJ. It was a difficult time for both Bev and David. I see Bev when I shop at Shop Rite where she works. Decisions affect everyone, but the relationship between Bev and me remains intact. I'm still her "mom".

TRUDI, my son Kevin's wife is so generous to others, whether family or friends. She is one of eight children. One of my earliest memories of Trudi is when their son, Steven, was sick with a high fever. I said I'd be over, but to quickly get Steven into a tub of lukewarm water. When I arrived, Trudi was sitting in the tub in her jeans and blouse, holding Stevie. You didn't waste time, Trudi, when I said "quickly". What a good mother you've been.

Your wry sense of humor is a blessing too. We've had many difficult and even serious situations occur from time to time in our family. Although, lately, it seems like it's ongoing. Trudi, you can take the edge off in an instant, and put things in perspective and suddenly things don't seem so dire. You have a real gift. Thank you, God, for Trudi.

I smile when I think of how you rely on me for medical advice. I know so little, yet you make me feel as if I know everything. You also gave me a compliment years ago, that touched me deeply. You felt that my faith was unshakeable, yet I don't push it on anyone. There's a part of me, though, that wonders if that's really a good thing. I feel so strongly about my faith that I want to share it. I truly believe God can do anything in our lives, but because He gave us free will, He is limited in our life if we're not praying. I heard someone else put it another way. "Every failure is a prayer failure and every success is because of prayer"…food for thought.

TRUDI'S PRAYER IS ANSWERED: THE PURPLE SWIMMING POOL

Trudi claims that her faith is not as strong as mine. Therefore, she doesn't feel the peace I feel when I talk about Jillian. She wanted to know that Jillian was okay but nothing I said could satisfy her. That comes from within. She said that she wanted to hear from Jillian. I told her she'd have to ask Jesus to allow Jillian to give her what she needed. Jillian couldn't do anything on her own.

I'll never forget the Saturday that Trudi called, almost hysterical, saying "Mom, you need to come over right now". I explained that we were in the middle of doing yard work and couldn't come. She said that I *had* to come. I asked if she and Kevin and the kids were okay and she said yes. I couldn't imagine what was so important. She did tell me that Kevin was on the roof taking pictures???

When I walked through the gate to their yard, I gasped in disbelief. The water in their in ground pool was a deep iris colored purple. They then told us their story. They had been sitting outside having their morning coffee, when Trudi noticed that the pool, starting at the deep end, began turning purple. It slowly came towards them like a wave until the whole pool was purple. Trudi had had a breakdown years ago due to a high stress job. When she saw the water turning, she didn't say anything to Kevin, thinking that maybe she's losing it again because of the trauma of losing Jillian. However, it was Kevin who spoke first and asked Trudi if she saw what he saw. She said "What do you see Kevin?" He said, "Our pool is turning purple." She was relieved.

Cameras were going off like the paparazzi on Oscar night. Trudi's brother who works for Budd Pools came over and took a pool sample. He had never seen or heard about anything like this happening. I remember telling Trudi that no matter what the results are on the pool sample, she should take this as a gift from Jillian and God. The last place that Trudi was with Jillian was in her pool. Jillian also knew that Trudi's favorite color is purple. Seeing is believing. Oh, the test results on the pool sample were normal. There was no explanation. It went back to its original color two days later.

We were over Trudi's and Kevin's home for Jillian's first anniversary. We had balloons and all kinds of goodies that Jillian liked. We were all standing around the pool getting ready to send our balloons up with lots of love when the strangest thing happened. Without saying a word, Trudi and I looked at each other, held hands and jumped in the deep end of the pool fully clothed. It was almost like a push from Jillian who would not think twice about doing something spontaneous. Jake and Kenzie were only six and two years old and wanted to go in the pool too. Ryan said that they didn't have their bathing suits. Kenzie said "Grandmom and Aunt Trudi don't either." I guess we weren't the best example to them.

AUGUST 2008

Our family is still reeling with grief over Jillian. Trudi wanted to get me out of the house so she drove me to their home in Lake Wynooska. We stopped at a very nice restaurant for dinner. Our emotions are still raw. We did have a drink and a good meal. Early on, I had said it was my treat. She insisted she was paying. We talked about Jillian, had another drink then left.

We're standing in the parking lot, still talking when the waiter comes running out. We forgot to pay the bill. Our minds were elsewhere. Then we hear sirens and a police car is headed for the restaurant's parking lot. We assumed it was for us. It wasn't. I explained to the waiter about Jillian, using her as an excuse for our lapse and I even took out my pictures of Jillian to show him. In the midst of our sorrow, we found ourselves laughing. I can just imagine that Jillian and Mark were both laughing with us.

JENNY, Ryan's wife, is such a significant member of our family. Since she comes from a large family, she's used to the chaos, positive and negative, and dealing with so many diverse personalities. She's warm, caring and sensitive to others needs and desires. Jen has a degree in criminal justice.

I've seen her at bridal showers for other people and she's as bubbly, enthusiastic and excited as she would be for herself. She exudes sheer enjoyment of even simple pleasures. It's uplifting to be around her. She's a great listener, a trait too many of us lack. More than anything, she shines as a wife and mother. I have only to look at my son, Ryan, to see how happy he is. They're devoted to each other and their precious daughter Makenzie.... our "Angel Face". In another month, they will have a son. How beautiful and touching it is to see Makenzie say goodbye to her family, when Jenny and Ryan leave her with me for a few hours. She kisses her mom and her dad, tells them she loves them, then lifts up her mommy's blouse to kiss her baby brother goodbye. Her little hands seem to be gently caressing her brother inside Jenny. How beautiful the world would be if all little ones were taught to love, as Kenzie has been taught.

Since my daughter, Rachele, has gone to live in Missouri, I feel a tangible loss. We would talk everyday, sometimes for a few minutes, mostly for an hour or more. Both my daughters live in other states. It is difficult being so far away from them. Letters and phone calls are a blessing, however, it's still not the same as knowing that I can hop in the car and see them in ten minutes.

Jenny probably feels the brunt of my loss. She's patient with me when I ramble on about what's happening, whether it's important or insignificant. I hope that she knows how much I appreciate the time she affords me, never cutting me short. I really do think of Jenny, Bev and Trudi as daughters. My friend in the Poconos appeared to be confused when we first met and were in the beginning of establishing our relationship. She couldn't keep all the names of our children straight and at one point was trying to clarify them. She remembered me saying that I had four sons and two daughters, yet as we talked, a puzzled look crossed her face. To add to that, Trudi came over while we were talking, apologized for interrupting, then said "Come on Mom, you're coming with us on the boat—better known as the "Booze Cruise". Later, my friend remarked that I seemed to have more daughters than sons. I smiled and said, "That's the way it's supposed to be, isn't it?" They all meld into one big happy family.

JAYNE

David's wife Jayne was born in Norwich, N. Y. She has one sister, Karen. Her dad Jim worked at Norwich Pharmaceutical doing drug research for several years then moved to Delaware to teach. Jayne was six years old when her mother died of a brain tumor. Jim and Eleanor had been married for eighteen years. Years pass and Jim remarries. He and Pat have been married forty-eight years.

Jayne attended SUNY Cortland for Therapeutic Recreation/Education and graduated in 1981. She worked in Binghamton following graduation, did field work at Children's Home of Wyoming Conference and worked there until she got her job at Broome Developmental Services in 1982. She was a Senior Recreation Therapist and worked there until retirement in 2014, loving every minute of it. She bought a house in Chenango Bridge and called a friend in construction to help her with a problem. Her pipes had frozen. Her friend sent David out to her house and that is how they met. David and Jayne became engaged in November 2013. They married in May of 2014.

Jayne has a love of history and has done some extensive traveling to Ireland, England, California and the Caribbean. She even got David to travel to Alaska. That is nothing short of a miracle. It is so obvious that Jayne has a profound love of people. I had the opportunity to witness this firsthand at David and Jayne's wedding receptions, yes that's plural. She is obviously loved by so many. Though Jayne is retired now, we had a chance to meet, not only family members, but her co workers, friends and clients, young adults with Down Syndrome. It seems we have something else in common. At Archway School I worked with children who were developmentally delayed, many of whom were Down Syndrome children.

We are blessed to have Jayne in our family.

MARLTON LAKES HOME Our Dream Home

Marlton Lakes was our dream home. It was our first home in N. J. and quite a drastic change from living in a row home in Philly. We had a builder from Marlton Lakes do the construction. George helped on the weekends. Even my mother and dad came to help us paint as our move in date approached.

It was exciting to see the kids run around our half acre and up and down the gravel road. At this time, we only had four children, David, Kevin, Rachele and Mark. We thought our family was complete. Did I mention that God has a unique sense of humor. There were only a few houses on Peach Road at that time. They'd go down to the lake and find all sorts of treasures that they never saw in Philly. At the end of our road was a field where we'd pick wild roses, berries and grapes. It was what I thought heaven would be like.

It wasn't all fun and games though. Carl, the builder, was behind schedule. We were to move into the house the first week of October. There had already been many unseasonably cold nights and our heating system wasn't even installed. We had no working toilets or running water for baths and showers. We used an outside pump for water. One of our neighbors heard about our situation and brought a kerosene heater over for us to use.

Roughing it made me irritable. It also made us all appreciative of our modern conveniences. Every few days we'd go to mom and dad's to get a shower and baths for everyone, then have a hot meal. That hot water sluicing over my body was a luxury I've never taken for granted, ever again. I had sent out invitations for an Interior Decorator's party weeks before we knew the house would not be completed. All our friends from Philly were so excited to see our new home. That's what my friend Lorraine had said. I was frantic but Carl said that I would have my kitchen countertops installed in time for the party, so I didn't cancel.

Carl came through with his promise. One hour before the party he and his men carried in the countertop. However, there was no cutout for the sink. My friend Lorraine, with her crazy sense of humor, told our neighbors and friends when they arrived that we had so overextended our budget, we didn't have enough money to finish the kitchen. We would have to wash dishes in the bathroom sink. There was actually one person who believed that.

My mother was concerned and even worried that the move to the country would be difficult It was not. I did have one scare when I couldn't find Rachele who was only five at the time. I kept calling her and could only hear a faint response. We found her twenty feet up in a tree. Thus begins her escapades as a tomboy. This is only day one in our home.

David and Kevin focused on exploring the woods, lake and swamp. Mark tagged along at times and other times just amused himself in the woods. It was all new to them. David's collection of reptiles became the talk of the small community. He had a molded plastic swimming pool in the yard, filled with turtles, snakes and frogs. He focused so much on learning about these creatures and became very knowledgeable about them. Rachele was in Brownies and when they started to discuss reptiles, she told her troop leader about David. Her leader was also one of our neighbors on the other side of the lake. She called me to ask if David would be open to giving a class to her group. He did and I still can see him in my memory as clear as if it was yesterday, explaining confidently to these awestruck girls, the ways to recognize poisonous vs. nonpoisonous snakes. He was patient with answering their questions. Their leader was impressed at his knowledge.

Watching TV was a rarity because they had a whole new world opening up to them. David caught his first fish by the dam. Some of the things they did were probably downright dangerous, yet there was a sense of calm I felt then, that I didn't in later years. They all wore their Brown Carmelite Scapulars around their neck and I believed with all my heart that Our Blessed Mother was protecting them. Of course, there were the fish hook incidents, cuts, scrapes and even snake bites. There was an incident where Kevin was injured when Tommy Wynn threw a rock at his head. Quick thinking David stanched the flow of blood by applying pressure from his backpak. There was also a trip to the Emergency Room when Mark was acting like a frog sticking his tongue out to scoop up a marble, and swallowed it. Everything came out fine in the end. Despite these and other incidents, our children survived and even thrived.

Neighbors were closer then. Kids were in and out of each other's houses and integrated into other families. Parents looked out for all the kids. A prime example of this is one memory that our friends, the Conleys and I have never forgotten. We reminisced about this on our last visit to Missouri. Our Rachele and their Michele came home on the school bus together. It was an icy day and when they got off the bus, they watched the older kids hang on to the back of the bus as it pulled away and they were gliding on the ice.

Rachele was in first grade and Michele was in kindergarten. The ice remained and the next day the girls decided to mimic the older boys. They didn't know that Jerry, Michele's dad happened to look out and see them hanging on to the bus. He came out bellowing "What the hell are you girls doing!!!" He grabbed both of them by the back of their coat collar and marched them inside and told them to take off their coats. After explaining the dangers of what they had done, he took off his belt and let Michele have it. Rachele started laughing out of nervousness. Jerry turned to her and said "What are you laughing at girl. You're next." She got the belt too. Then Jerry told Rachele to go home and tell your mom what you did. She did.

Today, that would probably land someone in jail. We were grateful that someone cared enough to teach a lesson that would never be forgotten. The girls remain close and Jerry is like a father to Rachele even now. She's 49 years old and still appreciates the lessons he taught.

There are humorous memories, too many to write about but a few stand out. The Conley's five kids and our four hung out together. They built treehouses that were the envy of all the kids in Marlton Lakes. I didn't find out about how they had acquired the wood for their great treehouses, until we had moved from there. It seems that the nine of them would go to construction sites since there were new homes going up in our area.

They would sit and watch the construction workers and in a sing song voice would chant "We want a two by four, we want a two by four", over and over and over until the workers were so sick of hearing them that they gave them a two by four. Next day it was the same tune, different words. "We need a box of nails, we need a box of nails."

They got all their materials that way. When the homes were completed, the workers left all the scrap wood for our kids.

There was one neighbor who lived next to the clubhouse that was obsessive compulsive about his home and his property. His lawn was like a carpet. He mowed it twice a week so it was always the same length. He had flower beds galore and a koi pond. Mr. Furster hated when the kids would get too close to his property. He was at work one day and Michele came running to tell Rachele that "Your brother's going to be in trouble!" It seems that David caught a fish in Mr. Furster's pond.

NOT ALL DREAMS LAST FOREVER

The days and years we spent in Marlton Lakes were tranquil most of the time. I wanted to stay there forever. Most of the women were stay at home moms, so we took turns having lunches at our homes. Those were the years I honed my cooking and baking skills and made everything from scratch, even bread. Those lunches were my social times and I savored them. I remember sitting at Bev Thompson's house in the screened in porch and listening to the stream on her property. She had lilacs from her yard on her table. I had never seen or smelled lilacs before. I don't remember the food served, but the scent of lilacs remains intact as if it was yesterday.

The one constant stressor through all our years, whether in Philly or Marlton Lakes was financial problems. Of course, even being stressed out, was infinitely better in nature's setting. And the lake...our beautiful lake was soothing for my soul. I immersed myself in the frigid waters in April when the kids were in school and was still swimming in October when they went back to school. Water is healing to me, mentally as well as physically.

Our warm, comforting lifestyle started to change right before George wanted to move again. He had been promoted to service manager at Xerox. He worked later hours and after work went out with his co-workers for drinks, dinner and even dancing (I found out about the dancing years later when George freely admitted it.) I was concerned but not worried at that time because we had a good relationship. At least I thought we did. Anyway, we only had one car at the time and I needed it at home for shopping or picking up the kids if need be, from school.

I would drive George to Lindenwold high speed line in the morning and pick him up at night. However, the calls to pick him up came later and later. It was winter and I had to wake the kids up, take them out of a warm bed and put them in the car because I didn't want to leave them alone. It was always on a school night. When George would call at 11:00 pm to pick him up, I dreaded it. The kids were asleep in the car, no seatbelts back then, and I was coming down Jackson Rd. to the intersection at White Horse Pike when the light turned red just as I was going through it. I didn't want to stop the car too fast and have the kids jarred in the back. There was no other traffic at that time. A cop gave me my first ticket that night.

Just a bit of trivia for those who are familiar with the intersection at Jackson Road and Route 73—can you imagine trying to get across there with no traffic lights? Well, there were none and even back then it was tricky. Maybe that's why I have an aversion to driving in heavy traffic.

I talked to George and told him that he would have to come home after work from now on because I wasn't going to drag the kids out of bed anymore. Besides, we needed the money that he was spending in bars and restaurants. I told him I was serious and he laughed. He called after 11:00 pm the next night and I told him to take the bus home. There was bus service at the high speed line but he didn't have enough money for it. That is an indication of just how bad our financial situation was. Several hours later the doorbell rang. I opened the door to find George holding out a Dunkin Donut bag with a peace offering. He had walked from Lindenwold to Marlton Lakes. He had just enough money for a coffee and one donut. After that he came home at a reasonable hour....for a while.

GOING BACK AGAIN

We moved from our Marlton Lakes home to Dock Road where we had two acres, were close to our friends, the Conleys. It was just across the road from Marlton Lakes, but we missed having the lake a stone's throw from our back door. We again moved from Dock Road because of high taxes. We moved to Franklin Avenue in West Berlin. I hated the moving. We were like Nomads. Not surprisingly, our financial problems continued to be an issue.

Years later Herb and I went to a yard sale in Marlton Lakes and there was a lot for sale, waterfront property, next to the yard sale. I couldn't believe that God was bringing me back here. I was ecstatic. Herb loved the area. Emotions ran high, we were a combination of naivety and reckless abandon. We placed a $1,000.00 deposit on the lot, cash. This was all we had in our savings. We were so excited, we didn't ask for a receipt.

The lot was two miles from where I worked, at Archway School. I would go over after work each day and just sit in my car, looking out at the lake, picturing our home and morning swims like I had before. It was a dream come true. One day while I was sitting there daydreaming, thoughts and words began to run wild in my mind. I attempted to write some of those thoughts down but there were too many, coming too fast. I drove home, hoping I could retain these thoughts long enough to type them. That was not a problem. I sat at the typewriter typing with barely a fore thought of what I was typing. The words just flowed effortlessly. Over an hour later, I had written a very lengthy poem.

I knew I could not have done this on my own. What poetry I had written in my teen years and early twenties, came with difficulty and struggle, trying to force my thoughts to meld with the words. My daughter Rachele and my son Kevin are the poets in the family. They both have a rare gift of expression through their words. I did not. Therefore, after typing for over an hour without even thinking about what I was typing, I was shocked when I read the finished poem. I recall that my first thought was "I didn't write this." It was inspired and cathartic. As Rachele said, it was as if the

Holy Spirit was painting a vision for me with words and thoughts. I have no doubt that that is exactly what happened. Why? I have no idea.

THE DREAM......AGAIN

Long ago I had this dream
In a place You touched with special grace.
The pristine lake so sparkling clear,
Could it be filled with angels' tears?

Each day an adventure, a continuous lark,
For my children, David, Kevin, Rachele and Mark.

The treasures they found,
The lessons they learned
From Your abundant gifts of nature
Are memories I yearn....to relive.

Our home on Peach
Once seemed so out of reach.
It was a simple house built with a
Plentiful supply of
Hope, dreams, prayers and love.

A simple house transformed
By Your resplendent cathedral in the woods.
In ever changing garb adorned,
For each new season.

I recall the feel and scent
Of kaleidoscope leaves crunching underfoot,
And of naked branches bent
From the weight of softly falling snow.

I stood barefoot in Your snow at night
And listened to the whispering flakes in flight.
They melted on my tongue and nose
And numbed my fingers and my toes.

We reveled in newly discovered treasures.
For David, his first fish by the dam
Instilled in him a lifelong plan
To be the best and catch the biggest that he can.
He is, he has, he loves this gift You gave him.

His love of nature persists.
The turtles and snakes were just the start
Of a lifelong love that fills his heart.

Your sunrise and sunset in the woods,
The owls and fox and deer.
Even the storms that whipped the waves
And caused him fear,
Are all gifts to be treasured.

I remember Kevin with his sidekick Sheba
And little Penny bringing up the rear
And your little brother Mark by your side.

I can still see so vividly
My two little boys…
Your heads bobbing as you walked and talked,
My face wet with tears of joy.

Rachele discovered trees,
Thirty foot trees…
So high for a six year old.
And inchworms brought in from the cold
To decorate her room.

I can see Mark sailing through the air
Landing with a voluminous splash,
With the help of a grandpop who dared
To wring the joyous offerings from our lake.

Quiet thoughts evoke memories of a bucolic life.
A soft breeze rippling the water's edge,
An exhilarating swim in icy water
That sucks the breath from me.

I recall daddy chopping wood
For our first mesmerizing fire.
I can feel our spirits
Soaring higher.

Never to take for granted
A fluffy rabbit or a comical chipmunk,
Home baked bread, crackling fires…
A feast for all the senses.

That was a dream come true
Way back when.
Times change, people change.
God, can I go back again?
For a little while…
My losses have been overwhelming at times.
I remember Mark finding a tiny, lifeless bird.
He cried, buried it and placed a cross of sticks
Over the grave, and then we prayed.

He was so heartbroken, as I am now
With the loss of him.
Did You draw me back to immerse me
In the same waters my Mark loved?
Is this Your soothing balm for my pain?

149

Now today I sit on the road by the empty lot
Reminiscent of a time long past.
Can it really be over twenty years,
I don't feel that old.

Did I say "empty lot", not so
Crystal waters by the edge do flow.
Sparkling diamonds jostled as the ducks swim by.
And several azure jays swoop down and fly
Through the red and orange brilliance of
Sunlight glancing off the fluttering leaves
That land gently, carpeting the earth for tiny creatures.

I experience a collage of emotions,
Elation at the thought of a second chance in paradise,
A surge of hope and thankfulness.

Ambivalent creature that I am,
I also fear that my dream
Won't come to fruition.
My yearning is so intense.

Forgive me God, for my lack of faith,
Increase it if You will.
I know that You alone know best.
I'll try patiently to wait…
To be still.

Two weeks after I wrote this poem, we lost our deposit when we found out that we could never build on that lot. The seller was aware and never told us. He said that he spent the money on a new roof. I even said we were willing to take a loss and accept $500.00. He refused and said that we couldn't do anything without a contract or receipt. He was right, technically. Yet, I think that we all hope that people are honest. It's a huge letdown when you find out otherwise. It used to be that a man's word was contract enough. How sad that that is not the case now.

Back to Scripture, Jeremiah 29:11

"For I know the plans I have for you, declares the Lord, plans to prosper you and not to harm you, plans to give you hope and a future."

DOCK ROAD HOME

We moved from Marlton Lakes to Dock Rd, in Atco. It was literally across the road from Marlton Lakes. Jerry Conley, our friend and builder, and George built a smaller house even though I was pregnant with our fifth baby, Ryan. We did have two acres which was a big plus. Although the house was smaller, I loved the layout of it. It was a three bedroom two bath rancher with a massive living room and kitchen divided by a huge brick, see through fireplace separating the rooms. There were built in bookcases on both sides and having dinner by the fireside was a bonus I hadn't expected. Both rooms were in the back of the house and looked out on the two acres. It was beautiful when it snowed because there was no traffic to mar the pristine fall of fresh snow.

We had a large garden for the first time and loved growing our own vegetables. Each day when George would come home, he'd go out to the garden and lift the huge leaves of the plants to check for ripe vegetables. One day the kids played a trick on him. I was hanging out clothes earlier in the day and low and behold there was a snake near my clothes basket. David got his BB gun and killed it. Then the kids carried it over to the plants and shoved it under the leaves. It was completely concealed. When George came home, he routinely made his rounds with the kids close behind him. Keep in mind that he is afraid of snakes to begin with. He lifted up the leaves, saw the snake, screamed and spread his arms out as if to protect us, yelling "Snake! We couldn't stop laughing for the longest time.

This triggered another memory of something that happened in Marlton Lakes. David had an aquarium in his room, for a snake. The snake was getting so big that George got a bigger aquarium for David's birthday. He put the gravel and the branches in and set it all up to surprise David. When it came time for George to move the snake to his larger home, he backed away. I thought he was kidding. He wasn't. He had a real phobia about snakes. I moved the snake to his new home.

This in turn triggered another memory of David with another snake…a massive one. I don't know what kind it was but I'm sure David's intent was to scare the heck out of me. I was sitting in a chair, reading when David placed this huge snake around my neck. It was so heavy that my head fell forward with the weight of it. I appreciated the beautiful markings and even the feel of it. No, I did not scream. I can't recall where he "borrowed" it from. He worked at the Berlin Farmer's Market and they used to have a truck outside with snakes as the attraction. I'm making an assumption but it's probably a good one.

There are memories of driving the kids to Assumption School, over the railroad tracks every day. No matter how slowly I went, the muffler always came off at one point and David in his navy dress pants and white dress shirt would get out of the car to fix it. There were trips to "Annings" store which was a grocery, hardware and automotive store. We'd take bowls from home and have them scoop out ice cream. It never tasted so good as it did back then. They had an orange ice (not orange sherbert) that was to die for. All the dozens of flavors we have now, yet no one has ever duplicated it. What used to be "Annings" is now "Leo's Ice Cream Co." Sometimes after the summer softball games, Kenzie and Jake's teams go there for a treat.

Mark made his First Communion in our living room where Father Bober celebrated Mass. My family came and even George's parents came for a rare visit. The Newmans lived down the road and since I worked with Evelyn Newman, I became close with the family. They had three children, David, Debbie and Diana. Diana was the same age as our David. However, she and Rachele spent more time together riding Diana's dirt bike. Diana had a serious accident on the bike and sustained a critical head injury. Miraculously, she survived.

The Newmans were a military family. Though Norm served in the Army, his three children served in the Navy. Diana was a helicopter mechanic. She lives in Missouri with her two sons and keeps in touch. The Newman's farm was seventeen acres and they were always bringing over fresh vegetables and berries. We are so blessed to have this family in our lives. Evelyn has since gone "home", Norm is 94 and recovering from a fractured hip. His memory of some things is faltering but he seems to recall the times when we lived on Dock Rd.

He talked about George as if it was yesterday. He remembered the go cart track the kids had on part of our property. He actually stirred memories that I had forgotten. He never complains. He always makes me laugh.

Ryan and Jillian were born while we lived on Dock Road. I was so tired of moving, when George started talking about moving again. The catalyst for this move was financial. Taxes went up and we just couldn't afford to stay. He said the move would help our situation. I couldn't see how. It never seemed any better on paper but I trusted him. I vowed that the next time I moved would be in a pine box. We did move to West Berlin to a four bedroom bi level on a very busy street with a small yard.

Maybe I never liked the house because we were having problems at this time. The kids and I also had to give up Sheba, our German Shepherd who had been with us for eight years. She was family. I had no idea we would have to do this. George told us after we moved that because we didn't have a fence, she had to go to the pound. I begged him to let us keep her. He was adamant about this and when I said I wouldn't do this, he did it.

There were some good things about the move, our neighbors Pat and Dave. Their children Mark and Laura, and our children grew up together, played and went to school together. We remained close even after we moved. George, once again, was cordial but didn't seem interested in anyone outside of work except for Lorraine and Paul. By now, he was even avoiding the Conleys. I found out why, twenty years later. So much for communication skills. We were failing miserably.

Life is difficult. That's to be expected. I believe that everything that happens to us whether good, bad or downright tragic can be a learning experience. Trusting God through it all, allows Him to use every experience for our benefit….to bring good out of it. That being said, doesn't make it any easier when you're going through it. I think that I'm getting better with the trusting in all circumstances, as I get older. I hope I am. It's just so darn hard.

OUR FIRST HOME ON LAKE WYNOOSKA IN THE POCOONOS

Herb and I had gone to a friend's wedding in Hawley, PA in the Poconos. We stayed over in an historic hotel, where the reception was held. It was like going back in time. We had hours before the wedding took place in a beautiful Catholic Church that sat high above the town. We walked through the town visiting all the little shops. We fell in love with the area, the people and the slow pace of everything. It was refreshing.

The hotel we stayed in fit right in with the unique way people up here did things. When we came in late, we sat in the "living room" and decided we wanted to get a drink before retiring to our room. The setting was inviting, the fire was lit in the massive fireplace. When we went to the bar, there was a note from the bartender saying "Help yourself, left early." There was a tip jar to leave money in. Can you even imagine doing that anywhere else?

Next day we drove around trying to familiarize ourselves with the area. We saw other unusual things which spoke to the trust and integrity of the community. We saw an expensive camera on the front seat of a convertible. Yes, the top was down. Keys left in expensive cars. Who does this? We so wanted to be a part of this different lifestyle.

We returned home only to make a decision that we'd like to buy a vacation home there. It was a crazy, impossible dream because we had no savings and were in debt. We had good credit but no other assets. That didn't stop us. We made the three hour trip up, three hours back in one day, every Saturday for a month. We couldn't even afford a hotel to stay over. The realtor took us to dozens of houses and then one that was on a small lake. We loved it. The kitchen was massive with two sets of sliding doors and a fireplace. The living room was huge and had four sets of sliding French doors and a stone fireplace. There were two small bedrooms on this floor as well as a full bath. The second floor was a dream come true master suite.

This, also, was amazing with two sets of sliding doors, a separate sitting area with a sofa in front of yet, another fireplace and an outside deck overlooking the lake. This was heaven on earth.

The house was in foreclosure. A neighbor came over to talk to us to tell us that the second floor was a recent thirty thousand dollar addition. She seemed to know everything about everyone. The bank was asking $139,000.00. We went home and crunched the numbers and no matter what we did, we couldn't afford it, even though it was a great deal. It had been assessed at $189,000.00. Why it didn't sell long before we saw it, was a mystery. Then we saw the tiny basement which you accessed by lifting up a part of the deck on the front porch. There were wires and broken pipes all over. It probably scared everyone off, but not Herb and not David who came up to look at it. They agreed it wasn't anything major, at least for them.

We had the realtor, Lenny, out to show us the place about five times. We took him to lunch because we felt so bad about our indecisiveness. I remember walking out on the dock to look at the crystal clear lake and imagined what it would be like with the family there. I wanted to dive in right then and there. We prayed for God to be in the middle of our situation. As badly as I wanted it, I was fearful of making a huge financial mistake. I figured God could see further ahead whether this was in our best interest or not.

Herb and I decided to make an offer but it had to be low. I asked Herb to let me handle this. He was only too happy to absolve himself of what I was about to do. It was almost embarrassing. I told Lenny that we wanted to make an offer of $75,000. He laughed and looked at Herb since he was used to Herb kidding around and making jokes. Then he looked at me and said with disbelief, "You're serious?" I said "Yes, we're serious. That's all we can afford." Lenny said he'd take our offer to the bank but they'd probably laugh. They came back with a counter offer of $79,000.00. We took it. Then we had to borrow the down payment.

We made settlement in mid-December. It was snowing. Some of the paperwork was incomplete, things that would hold up a settlement in N.J. Not here in this quaint town. Your word was good here in the Promised Land which is the name of the area we were in. That first night we curled up with blankets and pillows in front of a roaring fire in the bedroom. We slept on the floor. I even had a dream about a black bear. Later, that dream would come to fruition when we had a bear and two cubs on our deck. We did have some surprises. When Herb took a shower, I thought I heard water elsewhere. Sure enough, we had some pipes that must have frozen. The water was "raining" down in the downstairs bathroom. Herb's first repair job.

I'll never forget the first time I was in the kitchen, cooking, and Herb was in the basement. There was about a foot of snow on the ground and more coming down. I had the only radio station we could get, Froggy 101, which played country music. I was singing at the top of my lungs and dancing around. When I spun around, I stopped dead in my tracks, looking out the sliding doors at seven deer just standing there looking at me. The only other live deer I had ever seen was outside my hospital room when I had David, in Maine. Usually, I saw them in the back of David's truck, and then years later, in back of Ryan's, when they came to Archway where I worked to show me when they got a deer during hunting season. I loved that. Even though, I love animals, I know that nothing was wasted. We all love venison. They were providing sustenance for the family.

It was a rule of thumb, though, no hunting on our property. There was one deer we eventually could feed by hand. What an unbelievable thrill when "Pretty Girl" came up to me. We had turkey, raccoons, fox, opossum and bear. Chipmunks would crawl up our leg to be hand fed. Beavers would glide by along our canoe. There were also snakes and a cacophony of bullfrogs at night. I remember the first time our grandsons came up and asked where the TV was. There was none. What will we do, they echoed. That was the one and only time they asked.

We had family gatherings that I'm sure no one will forget. There was ice skating on the lake in winter and skiing and sledding down our steep road. Summer brought swimming, fishing, snorkeling, berry picking and walks down to the end of the road and in the woods where there were rushing streams and waterfalls to bathe under when the bathrooms were all occupied because we had thirty people over. It seemed that no one ever slept. The huge bonfire was kept blazing round the clock so that the boulders surrounding it would be warm at night, when the temperature dropped.

We had so many skunks come and even bring their babies. They never sprayed. One night David was leaning against a tree, night fishing, when I heard him say "Oh, sh__". I followed his gaze and there at his feet was a skunk. We had some that were all white and looked like Persian cats. Now, we'd get in trouble, but back then, we fed the animals. Neighbors had pictures of themselves, hand feeding a family of raccoons.

Our neighbors were great. Larue and Herman were in their eighties but young at heart. They'd call us over even before we made settlement to have a "cocktail". Cocktail hour was big up there. Herb never drank but I had my first Manhattan and loved it. One time Bev came up with us and she stayed behind to relax and read her book, while Herb and I took a walk. When we came back, Bev was nowhere in sight. The car, the boat were still there. We're calling her and here she's up at Larue's having a "cocktail". They drew everyone in like family.

I was swimming one day. There wasn't another soul in the lake. I swam towards the dam and heard a voice from up high (Larue's house sat up higher than all the others). I heard big band music playing and Herman calling me to come have a drink. I shouted back that I'd swim home and change. They said just to swim to their dock. They met me with a big fluffy bath towel and a Manhattan. As Glen Miller's playing in the background, I'm thinking, this is like being at a resort with a swim up bar.

We knew that Herman and Larue went to bed early because they were early risers, so when we first moved there, in the snow, and wanted to sled and ski down our road (it was treacherous), we told everyone to try to be quiet. We had to pass their house and didn't want to wake them. Of course, I was so scared going down the hill that I was the first one to scream. Herman comes walking over and I thought he's probably upset we woke them. It was 10:00 pm. I apologized and he said "What for?". Just then Larue comes out with her skis. She wanted in on the fun.

Our other neighbors Dick and Snookie welcomed us also and we became good friends and keep in touch to this day. They travel between their Pocono home and their Florida home. The four of us had plans to go out for New Years Eve and got snowed in and ended up having a big party at our home with all of the neighbors bringing food. It was one of the best times we had.

Ryan loved the Pocono home as much as we did and would often come on weekends with friends or even drive up alone just to spend time there. I remember when we made the decision to sell our home after seven and a half years, because Herb and I both had been laid off from work within a two week period. We didn't want to risk losing the house and we had two mortgages, so we sold it. The house was almost empty and Ryan and Jen were in the kitchen embracing each other. I overheard him say, "Where will we take our kids?", even though they didn't have any at this time. It was a heartbreaking moment for me.

Jillian came to our Pocono home with her friends from Atlanta. At our request, she sent us at list of things she wanted to have there so she would not have to go out for them when they arrived.

Herb made up a list of restaurants and points of interest along with directions as we were not going to be there. This was her vacation. Jillian said they had such a wonderful time they didn't want to leave the house. When we arrived the next weekend she and her friends had bought us a cd player for the house.

MAKING NEW FRIENDS

We hired someone to do brick work on our Pocono home. Up there, people move at a slow pace. It was one of the things we loved about it. We would leave the rat race in New Jersey and travel three hours every Friday to our beautiful retreat. We needed brick work done quickly. We prayed about it, then hired someone recommended by a friend. We pray about everything. At least I do. My husband would go along with this method of choosing people, however, I know he was doing it just to please me. In time though, his prayer came as naturally as mine. Think about it. How do you know that you're getting someone honest, capable and reliable? Sometimes a friend will direct you but even that hasn't always worked out. So I'd rather leave it in God's hands. Especially, when it comes to choosing doctors.

Anyway, before I get too far off track, my husband found Randy. He was dependable, honest, capable and worked quickly. He did his work, did it well, then would stand outside looking at "our" lake and saying that we had a slice of heaven here on earth. He echoed our feelings exactly.

I ended up talking with Randy too. He shared how he was so close to his Dad and worked side by side with him, learning the trade, as he went along. Then his Dad died. He didn't feel qualified to continue alone in this business because he didn't know enough yet. Then Randy said he prayed and asked God to help him make the right decision. When he was able to make a decision and feel a sense of peace about it. he had his answer. He continued on with the business, establishing his own name and reputation. He always felt his dad's presence.

Randy and I discussed my job also. I worked at a private school for special needs children. It opened up a topic dear to his heart. He related some stories about his encounters with handicapped children. He was so sensitive to them and very comfortable with them. He had such a deep respect for anyone working with them.

My trusting husband opened our beautiful home to this stranger. At this point, we had only talked to him twice. Herb gave him the keys to our home because we were only there on weekends, and most of the work would have to be done during the week. We didn't go up one weekend and Herb told Randy to bring his family and stay at our place for the weekend.

He told him to enjoy our slice of heaven and swim, fish and watch the endless array of animals that came to feed and visit.

Herb found out that Randy loved taking pictures. My generous husband left one of his cameras, a Nikon, for Randy. It was a gift, not a loan.

My neighbor and friend across the road saw Randy leaving that first day we met. Randy thanked me for sharing stories and I did the same. Then he gave me the biggest hug and sunniest smile. We waved goodbye. My eyes teared up. It never ceases to amaze me how uplifting it is when Christians get together and share their gifts...their stories....their love in Christ.

My neighbor came over later and asked "Who was that?" I told her and she said, "I thought you didn't know anyone here." I said, "That's true." She remarked, with a confused look, that he had hugged me as if I was a close friend. How long have you known him, she asked. I said, "A couple of hours". She shook her head and mumbled something like "It must be great".....It is.

SWIMMING WITH GRANDCHILDREN

One of my sweetest memories was the first swim across the lake to the dam with my grandchildren. The water was icy cold and most of the adults chose to forego this swim. I was in my glory in the water. When Jamie saw me he asked if I would swim with him across the lake. All the children knew not to go in the water without an adult. Jamie was a strong swimmer and made the trip across and back effortlessly.

We were both climbing the ladder out of the lake when Nikki came over and asked if I would swim with her across the lake. Of course I did. We were making new memories. I was so proud of her, as this was a daunting undertaking for one so young. When we were going up the ladder my grandson David came over and asked if I would swim with him across the lake. I began to wonder why they didn't all just come down together. I was beginning to tire but once again I swam with David. By this time,

Rachele decided to come in and we both swam with the rest of the kids. A good time was had by all.

We were in our home for seven years when Herb and I were both laid off from work within a two week period. Rather than risk losing our beautiful home, we chose to sell it. It didn't sell right away so we had many more months to make memories. Making that decision was extremely difficult. Little did we know that this would not be the end of our ties with Lake Wynooska. In a crazy roundabout way, God brought us full circle back to the Promised Land almost ten years later.

PACKING UP OUR LAKE HOUSE

This was an emotionally charged task for everyone. Trudi, Bev and I went up to the house on a Friday night. Trudi drove and I promised we'd stop at one of Trudi's favorite places—the penny candy store. We pulled up to the store after a two and a half hour drive, just as they were placing the "Closed" sign on the door. Trudi even knocked on the door to see if they would open up. No such luck. She was so disappointed.

Next stop would be a restaurant that Herb and I had gone to. The food and ambience were five star, prices were low. I promised the good meal would make up for missing out on the candy. We pulled up to the restaurant to another sign "Gone Fishing". I'm batting zero here. We finally did find another restaurant, had a great meal and a few drinks and left when they began sweeping the floor. They close early in the Poconos.

We were on the last stretch of our trip, going up and around the mountain in a spiral. The road was barely wide enough for two cars. Thank God Trudi was driving. I couldn't do it. It's dark and there in the middle of the road, apparently stunned by our headlights was a fawn. He would not move even when the horn was sounded. Bev and I got out of the car to chase him off the road. Looking back, that was a reckless move. If a car had come in the other direction, it would have been too late to get out of the way. On one side was the mountain and the other was a sheer drop, there was no shoulder. The angels were with us that night.

We finally arrive at our lake home and it was so depressing because a lot of the furniture had already been moved. Trudi and Kevin had been helping us the week before,. as well as Ryan and David. Our massive kitchen with the hardwood floors and the stone fireplace was empty. There was a bedroom off the kitchen that still had a queen bed. Bev and Trudi wanted to "camp out" in the kitchen right in front of the two sets of sliding doors. Trudi took charge, opened the frig and threw everything (and I do mean everything) out in the back yard. This would insure we got to see all our animals one last time.

I was going to sleep upstairs in our master bedroom which also had a fireplace. That lasted five minutes because it just wasn't the same without my hubby. I came down and suggested we get a fire going but that was nixed. I don't remember whose idea it was but we got sticks together in the middle of the floor and put a candle to illuminate our "campfire". We also had goose feathers in our hair. I honestly don't think we drank that much, yet, writing this I have to wonder. I never knew wine coolers to pack such a punch.

None of us wanted to sleep. We were used to staying up until two or three am to watch the parade of animals. They did not disappoint. I was in the bed off the kitchen and had a perfect view of Trudi and Bev lying on blankets on the floor. Our skunks came about midnight and were joined by "Opie" our opossum. By 1:00 am I started to doze until Bev yelled that there was a red fox. All this time the deer were the one constant presence. I remember seeing Trudi sitting on a small milking type stool with her face almost touching the sliding door. She was trying to stay awake and was startled when she opened her eyes to a raccoon looking in at her. We saw a flying squirrel and what I thought was an owl, but by this time, sleep deprivation was making us all squirrely. I guess Trudi and I fell asleep and were awakened by Bev who was watching a strange furry animal. She couldn't imagine what it could be. We got out the binoculars. Trudi said "It's a cat!" We all had a laughing fit. We were so used to our exotic menagerie, we didn't recognize a domestic animal.

Next day we finished packing, Bev sat on her gazebo and Trudi and I went for one last swim in the icy water. God how I'm going to miss this. What are Your plans for us now? The guys came up and we all went to "Old Rangers" restaurant for our prime rib dinner. On the way to the restaurant, Bev said she was so disappointed because she never got to see our bear. We only saw her twice in seven years. I was kidding around (sort of) and said that the chances of her seeing one now were slim. If she wanted to see one so badly, she should ask Jesus. She did and we *did* see a bear at close range, meandering through the woods minutes after we left the restaurant. Thank you Jesus. Next day the guys came up and we finished packing.

The men and Trudi did all the heavy lifting and it was brutal. The lift on the u-haul was not functioning. The piano, washer, dryer and other furniture had to be lifted up and over obstacles. I'm amazed that everyone was still upright after that move. A tearful goodbye and a palpable emptiness was felt by all of us. We thought that this was the last of Lake Wynooska but God had other plans which would come to fruition years later.

Rachele proceeded to start her own book about our home and the emotions it evoked. Of course, the home is not a house, but the people who inhabit it. She wrote as an outsider, looking in at our family. The following is from her writings and pretty much shows the impact our home had on everyone.

"It's as if I stepped into another dimension. I no longer run from the demons that haunt me. Here, it is different, no hurry, truly the Promised Land. I recall a distant memory I once learned at the Promised Land, but only a ghost of the memory comes forth.

I hear the thin layer of snow crunch beneath my invasive boots and I feel out of place. I stop, close my eyes and listen. Nothing. Beautiful silence, but not for long. Suddenly, a symphony of sounds. The tat, tat, tat of millions of tiny snowflakes on browned leaves and winter pines. The rustle of a squirrel hoping for one last acorn for his store. A cardinal's flamboyant feathers appear as he calls to his mate. In the distance, I hear a brook hollow as it runs through a tunnel of thin ice. From behind, the sporadic crunch of a winter hare hopping along the forest edge. The lone cry of a wolf searching—for what, I do not know.

I stand in the glorious cold, feeling the chill of a setting sun. Slowly, I open my eyes and a family of deer saunter across my path. I do not move, lest I break the spell. They turn momentarily to look at me. Our eyes meet and for a moment there is understanding of whose home I am in. They dart, white tails waving and I jump, startled by their sudden departure.

I turn my collar up to the cold. The snow is falling faster now and I walk on. The wind picks up. I happen upon a small lane near the lake and my curiosity gets the better of me. Deciding I'll take a quick look. The lane has a slight curve, slow and winding like the pace of all else around here. A house comes into view. There is something different here...peaceful, almost surreal. The inside is bathed in a warm, golden glow that casts long gold shadows in the snow. Snow swirls about, surrounding it like a vigilant guard, challenging all who enter.

Through the darkness, I make out a thin wisp of smoke, lazily trailing from the chimney, and the smell of burning pine. I hear them and see them through the glass, their smiling faces basking in firelight. A crackling fire, laughter seeping through the cracks in the foundation, children's laughter, a family's laughter. A woman comes through the kitchen doorway and I am mesmerized by her. I see the sparkling reflection of the now risen moon on the lake behind her. It surrounds her in bluish glitter. She smiles the smile of a mother's love and is very much at peace. She holds a tray of mugs as they all take one. Such a gentle face, yet the look of a strong woman. What pain and suffering has brought her through to this place?

I see another woman—younger, take the empty tray from her hands and replace it with a hug. Mother and daughter, sons and children. I feel almost as if I am invading their privacy, yet, I cannot pull my eyes away from the scene. So much love and happiness, so many smiles.

A pillow fight breaks out among the children and the "over thirty" children. The laughter grows louder. I expect, at any moment, the wall will explode with all the emotion. A man stands to poke the fire. A few stray sparks escape the chimney, only to be lost amongst the falling snow. Overwhelmed, I subjugate the urge to knock on the door and become a part of the scene which continues to play out in front of me.

It feels like minutes, but I have been here for hours. The majority have retired for the night. Four indiscernible adults decide to walk. Bundled up, laughing and joking like school children, they head for the lake.

The lights dim, leaving only the glow from the fireplace. The man...the woman, their silhouette in front of the dying fire. They reach for each other, they kiss. My feet are numb, my hands are cold. I look away, ashamed that I have watched for too long. I turn to leave, my footsteps filled in by the falling snow, vanishing like the last fiery embers in the house, that sits on the lake....in the Promised Land."

Obviously, our first Pocono home, activities and our experiences there left an indelible impression on Rachele.

KEVIN & TRUDI'S HOME ON LAKE WYNOOSKA

I'll never forget the phone call from Trudi, asking to stop by on their way home from David's house in upstate New York. They had something they wanted to tell us. It was a four-and-a-half hour drive from David's so I knew they must be tired. Whatever they had to discuss must be important. They loved David's house and his seventeen acres of woods, mountains, streams and solitude. Kevin and Trudi had decided they wanted a place of their own that would be a retreat from the "rat race".

Of course, I assumed they wanted a place in N.Y. I was wrong. They had checked out a house for sale on Lake Wynooska. It was two doors away from our first lake house. They had never been in it but we had. They were so excited and decided to make an offer on a house, sight unseen. I said, "Trudi, you can't do that. You have to at least see it." She said, "No we don't. We love the area, the town, the people" and she did indeed call and put in an offer over the phone. The house was no small undertaking since it was $249,000.00.

Herb and I went with them the first time they went to see the house. I was so nervous because we had told them it was a great house and in good repair. I felt some responsibility and actually held my breath as we walked in. Trudi spun around in the huge kitchen with wrap around windows with a view to the back lawn and lake and said she loved it. Kevin was out in the backyard having a similar reaction. Relief flooded through Herb and me.

Herb and I were thrilled to be back in the Promised Land twelve years after we had sold our first home there. Trudi and Kevin made a generous offer to build a mother-in-law suite for us. Thank you God for our caring · and generous children. We did consider that option but our regrets about selling our first home on the lake had intensified. Herb didn't think it would be the same. He wanted our own home there. Of course that wasn't going to happen. There were too many variables against us and we knew that. It's a tiny community and houses would rarely go up for sale. Also, the cost of houses had skyrocketed. Twelve years before, we had paid $79,000.00 for our three bedroom, two bath, three fireplaces, lakefront home. Two doors away, Kevin and Trudi's home was triple that amount.

It's as if we passed the torch to Trudi and Kevin. Family gatherings are at their place now. Kevin built a huge fire pit and traditions continue. New memories are added to our family. Kenzie's first swim across the lake, family dinners, fireworks, you name it. Kevin even took up fishing with their dog Zoey as his sidekick. I remember the excitement in Kevin's voice as he called to us to look up and see the eagle soaring over the lake. At the risk of being redundant, this truly is a magical place.

One of the funniest memories I have is of Kevin when they first moved. They wanted so much to see a bear. Herb, Trudi and I were at their kitchen table. They had two walls of windows looking out on the lake so we had a perfect view even though it was dark, because they had floodlights on. Also the ground was white with a fresh layer of snow. Kevin was outside, bundled up with one of those hats with the ear flaps. He had a bucket and a large paintbrush. He was painting a tree?? We asked Trudi what was in the bucket. Molasses. He had heard that bears liked it.

Kevin came inside and we played cards. Within a half hour there was a black bear rolling around in the snow. Herb went outside with the camera because he couldn't get a clear shot inside as the screens were still in the windows and the camera wouldn't focus. The following week Trudi called, sounding terrified. She and Kevin were backed up against the refrigerator and Kevin had his shotgun. There was a bear right outside their windows and he was huge. He was several times the size of the one we saw the week before. No more painting trees.

We played a lot of Scrabble and did a lot of rocking on the porch. We tried to read but the surrounding view was so breathtaking, it was distracting. I have another memory of Kevin and my nephew Josh taking the canoe out at 1:00 am on a night when there was a full moon. Josh and Julie were staying with Herb and me next door (explanation follows). The girls turned in early that night. It was chilly. I walked out on Kevin's dock and gasped with delight. The moon shone a silvery path on the water, illuminating everything with its reflection. The canoe just glided on this path. It was almost surreal.

I have another memory of my mother, orchestrated by Trudi. Trudi, mom and I went up to our Pocono homes early. Remember, our homes are now side by side. Trudi helped us unload our belongings and told mom that we were having a pajama party—a girls' night. This did not go over well with mom. She's more of an introvert compared to the rest of our family. Mom wanted to go right to bed when she got in her pajamas. Trudi opened her house up then came back with a deck of pinochle cards. I made drinks, probably highballs and mom told us she'd watch us play because it had been twenty plus years since she had played. Trudi was persistent and insistent. My mother had met her match.

I drew up a "pony", a list of what constituted meld. We all needed a refresher course. It didn't take mom long before she was shuffling cards like a pro. All her years of playing, came back and she whipped our butts. It was so obvious that she was enjoying this night immensely. After a good night's rest she enjoyed all the gifts of nature this magical place has to offer. Kevin and Herb came up that morning also.

AUGUST 2007 OUR SECOND HOME ON LAKE WYNOOSKA

After eight months of looking in New York and finding nothing, we found out that the house next to Kevin and Trudi was being renovated. They became friendly with the owners, Wayne and Patti, as did we. They wanted to rent the house to a retired couple, long term. I didn't want to rent but Herb was relentless in convincing me it would be a good idea. We wouldn't have to come up with a huge down payment, pay taxes, do repairs or mow the grass and shovel snow. We also wouldn't have the large monthly payment. Instead, we would pay about what we would for a small apartment in New Jersey, $1,000.00 a month. And we're right on the lake.

Our home is a rancher with three bedrooms and two full baths, full basement, garage and two covered porches so we can sit outside during a storm—one of our favorite things to do. This house was made to order for us and it's on Lake Wynooska, three houses away from our first one and right next door to Kevin and Trudi. Herb is ecstatic, as am I. The fears of renting have evaporated. It feels so comfortable, so peaceful....so right.

It just goes to show you that if you ask God to help you with anything and you are prepared to say yes to whatever He has planned, even if you veer off in the wrong direction, He will get you back on course. We prayed for eight months and did the footwork, looking in New York because we honestly felt, because of David's offer to build us a house and because of the beautiful towns and churches that we fell in love with, that we were being divinely guided there.

We knew there was no way to go back to the Poconos because of the prohibitive cost. However, when God is in control, at our request, He worked out the details. Ask and you shall receive.

Just for the record, I find it amazing that we found our retirement home here. Consider that this is not a large community so the chances of a home being available were minimal. There's about a dozen homes on a gravel road. We think that we got the best, along with Kevin and Trudi.

I would like to convey why this place is so special, although the reasons could fill a book. I'll try to be succinct. We've had three day family reunions which included friends as well as family. These gatherings took place on the fourth of July for the seven and a half years we lived there. We made friends whom we've kept in touch with even though we were away from here for five years, after we sold the house. We've entertained animals galore. We hand fed a doe, "Pretty Girl". We've had about eight different skunks come visit and bring their babies, despite all the activity in our yard. They were mostly white, resembling Persian cats and were so docile. They ate everything except mushrooms and never once sprayed. Not even when my young grandson was running towards one and jumped over him.

We've had a mother bear and two cubs on our back deck. We glided in our canoe with beaver escorts, had a fox and opossums. We had chipmunks that would climb on our lap and shoulders for attention and a peanut. We cared for two orphaned raccoons. My daughter, Rachele orchestrated a mini play about Native Americans who had lived there, long before us. She researched the history of this place. "Wynooska" means beautiful river. None of the residents had known this.

WE'RE BACK !

We're home! It's almost surreal that we are back on Lake Wynooska, that we've been given a second chance. God's so good. We left our choice of a retirement home in His hands. We also assumed that it would be in New York, considering my son David's generous offer of building us a house and only charging for materials. We also fell in love with the beauty of upstate New York, the people and the laid back lifestyle. We even had a favorite bar/restaurant in Norwich. Everyone would talk to you at length and the food was great. One night while sitting at the bar, we began talking with the bartender and a few other guys who had rode in on Harleys. We talked about kids and somehow got around to faith and prayer...in a bar. God will make openings. You just have to be ready to jump in.

Eight months of looking and praying turned up properties and sometimes a house that we liked, but they were situated in proximity to homes that were rundown or littered with refuse. David's home was in a beautiful area. We wanted nothing less.

At one point, Herb said he didn't think he'd be completely happy unless he was on Lake Wynooska in the Poconos. We didn't look in the Poconos because we knew that we couldn't afford anything there.

Regrets surfaced again and again about selling our first home on Lake Wynooska. It was supposed to be our retirement home. It was so beautiful, with three bedrooms, two baths and three fireplaces—one in the massive kitchen, one in the living room and one in the master bedroom. We had bought the house for $79,000.00 in a foreclosure.

So how come we had to sell it? At the time, we had two mortgages and lots of bills. Now, the $800.00 a month mortgage payment seems so small. Yet, when we were both laid off from our jobs within a two week period, we were afraid of losing the house, so we sold it rather than take the risk. Retirement seemed so far in the future at that time.

UPDATE 2013 Moving away from Lake Wynooska...again

Since Jillian went home to be with Jesus and Mark, Herb and I haven't been back. That was the last place we were with her. We had a wonderful dinner at "Raintree" Restaurant, came back to the house and played Scrabble. When the weekend was over we headed back to our home in New Jersey. All the joy seemed to dissipate. We did not have the desire to go back. Trudi and Kevin decided to rent their home for the last several years. They go up occasionally to check on the house. Hopefully, they will be able to retire there when the time comes. For now, they're enjoying their beautiful N.J. home. They also have an in ground pool and with Kevin's recent outdoor addition, a luxurious cabana, their backyard feels like a summer resort.

OUR BLUE ANCHOR, N.J. HOME

Herb and I had our Pocono home up for sale. We were also contemplating selling our home in West Berlin, N. J. Herb had never liked the house and although I did have some good memories in that house, I was not emotionally attached to it because of all the problems George and I had in that home.

We started looking at homes with the help of our friend MaryAnn. We also looked at "over 55" developments. It seemed clear that we would have to stay put. We couldn't afford what we wanted. We wanted a rancher. I had a diagnosis of congenital hip dysplasia, deformity of the ball joint and diminished femoral hip space. I was not ready to have a hip replacement yet and the stairs in our home wreaked havoc on me.

We also wanted some acreage with mature trees and windows that afforded us a view of all this. I also wanted hard wood floors. The cost of ground in New Jersey is prohibitive. Once again we left matters in God's Hands. We stopped looking at houses because it was frustrating. Then we let go of the thought of moving.

In a turn of events that only God could orchestrate, He found us a home when we had decided to stop looking. Funny how that saying "Let go and let God..." comes into play so often. I was still working at Archway School. Carol, our director of nursing, and I shared a large office. One of the teachers, Mike, would come down regularly to make phone calls on my phone. Teachers' phones were just available to call the principal's office, not for outgoing calls. While he was at my desk, I would continue working at a table in the office.

I wasn't really paying much attention to him, but Carol heard him talking to a realtor about selling his house. She thought I should ask him about it. It was a rancher, ten miles from our current house but the same distance from work, from the opposite direction.—just more rural. The house had hardwood floors, massive windows in the living room and dining room, three average sized bedrooms, two full baths, two car garage and a full basement. Windows, siding, roof and porch were brand new even though

171

the house was forty years old. Kitchen was small and dated but in good repair. Almost too good to be true, it was on 8.2 acres.

We loved the house and surroundings but Mike would not quote us a price. He just wanted to wait until we looked at it. Also, eight acres was a bit much for us. He then said that he would pay to have it subdivided and asked how 3.2 acres sounded. That was ideal. However, still no price.

We decided to have our friend MaryAnn do a drive by. She said that the house with the land was probably around $140,000 even if it wasn't in great shape, the land being the most valuable asset. The house was in good repair and actually looked like a newer home. After hearing her ballpark assessment we talked about shelving the whole idea because we knew that we would not be able to afford it. Our absolute limit was $130,000.00. We did, however, look at the home one more time and pressed Mike for a price. We let him know outright that we couldn't afford it. He said "How do you know? I haven't even given you a price." We told him that we knew what the house was worth.

Mike then asked what we could afford and we told him $130,000.00. He said "Okay." I said "Okay what??" He said he'd sell it for that price. I asked him how he could do that when he knew it was worth so much more. He reiterated that it was his house and he could do whatever he wanted.

Mike loved the animals on his property—deer, turkey, raccoons, hawks, opossums and skunks and even the buzzards. He also knew that we were animal lovers because I was always bringing pictures in to show everyone all the animals we had on our Pocono property. Mike did say that he didn't want anyone hunting on the property which was rich with wildlife.

Also, his neighbor was a disabled veteran and Mike looked out for him. As a nurse and a patriot, Mike already knew that I would do the same\and that meant a lot to him.

The rest is history. We've been here fourteen years and treasure everyday that we spend in our own private heaven on earth. The veteran whom I was looking forward to meeting, moved away before we moved in.

One of my most precious memories here is of my girls, Rachele, Trudi, Bev and Jen sitting at dusk on the front porch, shortly after we moved in. I believe it was Trudi who said "Mom, this is so much like the Poconos. All we're missing is the lake." The calm and serenity it evokes is almost palpable. As for the lake, there is one "Oak Pond" less than half a mile from our home. Rachele loved fishing there.

One of the funniest memories here occurred shortly after moving in. Our neighbor Gregory raised chicken, goats and guinea hens. He knew we had no problem with them meandering over to our yard. Herb and I were in the kitchen having lunch when we heard loud, unfamiliar noises coming from our garage. We had left the large garage doors open. I opened the kitchen door to the garage and couldn't believe my eyes and ears. There were twenty guinea hens in the garage, on Herb's motorcycle, on his workbench and just everywhere you looked. They are the noisiest creatures. We laughed so hard at our raucous welcome to the neighborhood.

Our home and forest have been the stage for family parties, Halloween parties where we spent weeks decorating even the path through the woods. We've had gatherings for church families and my CCD students and their families and in the last few years, pool parties. We are so blessed to be able to share our home with so many.

Thank you Mike…thank you God for finding us our own personal retreat in the most unexpected circumstances.

UPLIFTING THOUGHTS ON OUR ETERNAL HOME

Naturally, having two children and a grandchild in heaven, along with many friends and relatives, death is something I think about, pray about and deal with in an ongoing way. Bear with me. This is not going to be morbid. I have read, at different times in my life, views on this subject. Sometimes, questions were answered and comfort was felt in an almost tangible way. Always, my faith was reinforced.

I feel that my faith is strong, yet, I cry often when I'm looking at the moon and talking to Mark and Jillian. I can be having a great time with family and friends, then all of a sudden, there's those empty seats at the table. I rationalize that I'm human but it's not enough. I realized after reading Scripture, John 11:35 *"Jesus wept."* that my tears are not a lack of faith. It just means I miss my kids. Even Jesus cried at the loss of his friend Lazarus.

"Your life is like a mist. You can see it for a short time, but then it goes away." James 4:14

I know this to be painfully true. Mark and Jillian were laughing one day, teasing, having fun and the next day they were gone. Gone from this earth but very much alive in heaven with Jesus. I've read so many accounts of NDE (near death experiences). They all have the same thread running through them. No one wanted to come back here. The beauty, the nature, the overwhelming love described in heaven, was ineffable. I especially treasured the descriptions of doctors who have experienced this, doctors who said it was impossible or it was a result of anesthesia, doubting Thomases. One such case was a neuro surgeon who showed no brain activity for a week, while battling meningitis. He said we lack the vocabulary, the colors, the scents to even describe what he experienced.

Knowing this gives me comfort. Jillian and Mark are basking in pure love and joy…and recently my grandson David. It's almost selfish of me to wish them back.

Remember, "No eye has seen, nor ear has heard, no mind has conceived what God has prepared for those who love Him" (1 Corinthians 2:9)

"The day you die is better than the day you are born." (Eccl. 7:1) Wow! Think about how we celebrate the birth of a baby and yet, the day we die is even better. I can just imagine the celebrating when my beautiful children entered heaven.

Isaiah 57:1-2 "Good people are taken away, but no one understands. Those who do right are being taken away from evil and are given peace. Those who live as God wants, find rest in death. Death is God's way of taking people away from evil." Though I believe that, my feelings don't always reflect that. I have friends and family members who have suffered loss. Some have a simmering anger, some outright rage. especially when it's the loss of a young person. We rationalize that it's not always a bad thing when the person is in their eighties or nineties and suffering. But a child, a teen, a young adult....that is so hard to fathom. The longer they are gone from us, the harder it is. Most people don't understand that grief doesn't fade when you lose a child. The passing years don't make it any easier. We just learn to hone our coping skills. At least that is how it is with me. That is why I love talking about my kids and appreciate it so much when others do.They are always on my mind and in my heart and I am looking forward to the day that we are together again.

DECEMBER 6, 2006 Journal Entry

What an amazing day! Don't ever think that Jesus isn't interested in our little problems too. I went to Mass, then St.Vincent de Paul's to donate some items and, of course, I found a few treasures, as always. I got two beautiful baby journals, a pair of shoes for me and flannel sleep pants (Dockers) for Kevin, all for six dollars. It was half price day. Then I went to Boscov's to return some items.

Last night I was going to throw out a bagful of plastic zippered bags, the kind that pillowcases come in. I needed one of them for a tablecover I was taking to St. Vincents. When I pulled it out, it had a new curtain in it. I pulled the rest of the bags out and found two more curtains that had never been opened. The receipt, from eight months ago, was still in one of the bags. So much for my organizational skills that allowed me to find the receipt and lose the curtains for eight months.

Money's tight so I'm looking for and, of course, praying for bargains. Herb and I volunteered to buy two gifts for two girls in our parish. They suggested toys or games but I wanted to include an article of clothing. This is for a needy family. I'm sure they could use it. My dilemma is what to get, what size, something pretty without a big price tag. As I entered the store, I prayed for Jesus to help me. This has become second nature.

While waiting to return the curtains, an older woman and a young nun came up behind me. I told them to go ahead of me. They just wanted to have something scanned. The nun put a beautiful girls sweater with matching scarf on the counter. The price tag read $20.00 but it scanned at $5.99. I asked where they had gotten it. The older woman said it was in linens where someone must have thrown it, after changing their mind. The cashier said that there was a whole rack in the girl's department. I was ecstatic. I had found my beautiful and inexpensive gifts. Coincidence? One might think so, however, after hundreds of these "coincidences", I like to think of them as "Christ incidences". After all, I did pray for help.

The cashier rang up the nun's purchase and I discreetly motioned for her to charge it to my account. The nun pushed a $10.00 bill towards the salesgirl. I gave it back to her. She was so confused. She was from India and just learning the English language. The older woman explained everything to her. You would have thought that I had handed her a hundred dollar bill, by her reaction. She grabbed me, hugged me, kissed me and promised to pray for me every day, stressing "every", twice. Such a small amount of money, so much appreciation.

I experienced something intangible in this little exchange—pure, unadulterated joy. My feelings were so out of proportion to this small event, it didn't make sense. I was tearing up with "happy tears" and felt like singing. All I could think of was, this is the joy of the Lord. By the way, even though I didn't expect to get any money back because of the lapse of time involved (8 months), I got $50.00. Thank you Lord.

One of the men that Herb works with always remembers Herb's birthday. Herb gave up asking him to please refrain from gifts. That's a sore spot with Herb. Even the vendors that come to the airport and want to do business over lunch (everyone does it) have been turned down by Herb. He just doesn't think it's right even though they all have business accounts for that purpose. Anyway, his co-worker gave him a $100.00 gift card to Macy's. He gave it to me. I don't shop at Macy's. I shop at thrift stores and Kohls. I usually give it to someone else. One time Herb said he'd like to see me get something nice. Just go see what they have. We walked through the front door of Macy's and I saw two nuns there. I couldn't imagine what they would get there. I asked Herb if he'd be upset if I gave it to them. He already figured I would do that before I even said anything.

AUGUST 24, 2000, Thursday, 7:00am, Sea Isle, N.J. (journal entry)

I'm on the back deck of the shore home that George rented. It was very generous of him to invite us. George, my first husband and the father of our six children, and my husband Herb have become close friends. It's a relationship that some scoff at, but it works for them and makes it so nice for everyone. No one is ever excluded from a family affair.

Anyway, it's overcast, slightly breezy and warm. I'm standing at the rail with a steaming mug of tea and a piece of raisin toast. The deck overlooks the marshes. To the left, is the bay. A heavy flutter of wings and I have a visitor, a beautiful seagull, two feet to the left of me. I gladly share my toast, he gratefully accepts. In short order there are a half dozen more gulls with their high pitched, ear piercing squeals. I'm sure that the neighbors are not happy with me. Hopefully, God is, for appreciating His beautiful, however, raucous creatures. I also heard and saw a new bird, charcoal gray. He sounds like a slowly moving roulette wheel, click, click, click. How appropriate since we're so close to the gambling mecca in Atlantic City.

Yesterday we had breakfast outside by the water, at "Carmen's". Ryan and Jenny were with Herb, George and me. It was so peaceful. It's times like these that I think I could make the transition from our mountain home to the shore. Herb and I were both feeling that way until yesterday. We were on the beach. It was warm, sunny and windy. Within minutes, blankets, books and bodies were covered with a layer of sand. It was in our hair, eyelashes, mouth etc., not pleasant. Herb opts for the mountains. He likes the serenity and lack of crowds, and the endless array of animals at Lake Wynooska. We are so immensely blessed to be able to experience both the shore and the mountains.

JUNE 20, 2001 (journal entry)

God has given me a strong push this morning, to write. I'm on the deck of our Franklin Ave. home, the sheltered part of the deck, just outside our bedroom door. A deck that our son David built for us. It really is a sanctuary. The morning is warm and dry. The sun feels hot on my back. As the steam drifts off my mug of tea, I watch and listen to "Reds" and "Ruby", our cardinals. "Blue", our jay is warbling melodically instead of his usual screech. He helps himself to a peanut. Miss Penn, our cat, lies on the deck absorbing the heat and the show. Several other birdsongs fill the air and little house finches argue noisily about which perch to occupy on the thistle feeder.

A slight breeze ruffles the leaves and brings with it the scent of sassafras. Our next door neighbor had his trees trimmed. The fresh cut in his sassafras tree is redolent with memories for me. After moving from a tiny row home in Philadelphia, our first home in New Jersey was on Peach Road in Marlton Lakes. It was a dream come true. We used to dig up sassafras roots, to boil to make tea. The enticing licorice aroma and taste have long been a favorite of mine and my daughter, Rachele. Rachele thrives on childhood memories and recalls them with the accuracy of a Polaroid camera. She truly does have an eidetic memory.

The jays are now squawking. They want more peanuts. Ruby is looking for safflower seeds. The crows, my gentle giants, are dunking bread in the birdbath. I've seen tiny birds bully them into moving over. Our doves seem to be ever present. They barely move when I come out.

I'm on vacation from Archway School, for two weeks. It helps to be an early riser to get things done. But today, my wash is calling me, the dust settles anew and yet I feel that God has called me this morning, to write, even before I say my morning prayers. I know that He works through other people and two of those people have recently reminded me of my writing… my wonderful husband, Herb and my supportive friend, Lorraine.

Lorraine has been my friend since my firstborn, David, was a baby. I was pregnant with Kevin and we moved to a little row house on Scattergood

Street in Philadelphia. Our only nights out were across the street to play cards at Lorraine and Paul's or Frank and Miriam's, or our home. We played Pinochle and the guys took turns running to the houses to check on our sleeping children. We snacked on cheese and crackers, chips and pretzels. The guys drank coffee, the girls drank soda. On very special occasions, such as a birthday, we had mixed drinks. We always had something sweet at the end of the evening, usually around 11:00pm. Lorraine would have honey buns. I would bake something from scratch. My banana bread became such a staple that Paul swore I had them stacked up like bricks in the freezer. They all loved the homemade goodies. Frank thought I should start baking extras so he could take them to work and sell. He worked at a very upscale salon. I didn't listen. To this day, I regret that I didn't.

I'll never forget the night that I had my first taste of, what was then, exotic food. Frank was a hair stylist and worked with a predominantly Jewish clientele. He brought home the gourmet treat from one of his clients— bagels, cream cheese, onion and slivers of lox. I begin to salivate just at the memory. I loved it! Forty years later, it is still a favorite of mine.

I am writing this book as a legacy, of sorts. I know very little about my grandparents and even my parents. Our family tree has branches that remain bare. I was raised at a time when children were to "be seen but not heard". My questions to my mother about her childhood and teenage years remain unanswered. "I don't remember", was a repetitive response. My maternal grandmom "Babci", was born in Poland, though my mother does not know the name of the town or city. My grandmother seemed willing to talk when I asked questions. However, I needed my mother's help in understanding grandmom's broken English, laced with Polish expletives. My mother brushed me off time and again, saying, "You don't need to know that." I knew enough not to push. Now I regret not having pushed.

UPDATE

The previous paragraphs were written several years ago. Since then I have overcome my fears of insisting that my mother share some of her past history with me. Mom is 80 at the time I am writing this, a very young

80. We celebrated her 80th birthday at our home on Franklin Ave., West Berlin, N.J., in February. We had 63 people help us celebrate. We kept the Christmas tree up for Mom's party and decorated it with hearts (since it was in February) that had old sepia photos of Mom and Dad, and of course, all us children. I dreaded taking the tree down.

We even had a reunion, of sorts, with my Aunt Rita and my cousins Cliff and Loretta. I hadn't seen Cliff for almost twenty years. He looked the same, except for the gray hair. His smile would warm a room. He gave mom a gift to be treasured—a videotape of her and Dad and all of us when we were children. Cliff and Nancy's daughter, Holly is a grown woman and so beautiful, inside and out. Their son, Eric and his wife Tracy have a daughter, Serene, born on our Mark's birthday.

LORETTA

Loretta was my closest cousin, while growing up. There were sixteen cousins on my dad's side of the family. I was the oldest and Loretta was nine months younger. We still get a lot of mileage from the "I'm older than you" phrase, which I played to the hilt. Aunt Rita used it also when explaining why I was allowed to wear makeup and Loretta wasn't. She assured Loretta that one day she would be glad that I was older. That day has come. Even in our fifties, I am still introduced as Loretta's older cousin.

Anyway, after the long separation of eighteen years, it was as if we never parted. I can't believe how close I feel to Loretta. She and her husband Edgar live in Florida. Her daughter and granddaughters live there also. We do keep in touch.

UPDATE 2014

It has been many years since Loretta and I have seen each other, yet, the bond between us strengthens. We talk regularly on the phone, but this last year was so special. With Herb's cardiac surgery and my three cancer diagnoses, Loretta was my "rock". I could call her anytime no matter what my mood. However, she made it crystal clear to me that I could handle anything. She reminded me of how she looked up to me...still, and I couldn't let her down. She was adamant about me being able to handle anything. Her vociferous statement, "RoseMarie, make me proud girl!", still brings a smile to my face.

Listening to Loretta talk...going back in time with our memories, amazes me because I really did not have any idea that I was such a role model for her. She was beautiful with her natural blond hair, lilting voice and warm personality. I was the "wallflower" with my drab brown hair and glasses. To hear her talk, lifts my spirits even now. I just think my favorite cousin has such a generous spirit that she sees the best in everyone.

Loretta brought up a memory that I had completely forgotten about. During my last year in high school I would take the bus after school to go to Port Richmond for my part-time job as a receptionist for an optometrist, Dr. Ralph Miller. I was able to utilize my typing and shorthand skills. However, my insecurity surfaced again. It was Saturday and Dr. Miller told me to take a lunch break and go next door to get something to eat. It was a small store with only a counter. I was out of my element and felt conspicuous sitting at the counter. This is such a small thing but one that I had never done before. I actually had palpitations. I hated to be noticed. I wanted to fall between the cracks. Anyway, I ordered a tuna sandwich and all I remember is that it was the best one I ever had....baby steps.

Loretta saw me as self-assured and I was scared to death of everything. I became engaged at age sixteen! At seventeen, just three months shy of my eighteenth birthday, I would be graduating from Little Flower Catholic High School for Girls. Two weeks later on June 23 I would be getting married to George and then moving to Brunswick, Maine where he was stationed at the Brunswick Naval Air Base. I talked to Loretta about taking over my job. Dr. Miller interviewed her and she got the job. Loretta typed but did not do shorthand. She said she devised her own shorthand, then had trouble reading it back. Once again, she sang my praises, saying that Dr. Miller was always bringing my name up in a positive light.

Loretta's parents, my Aunt Rita and Uncle Earl have a beautiful story of how they met. Uncle Stan (Rita and my father's brother) was in the Merchant Marines and used to write to his sister. Because it was wartime, the mail had to be censored to insure locations were not revealed. Uncle Earl, in the Army, was doing the censoring. He was on the island of Curacao, off the coast of Venezuela.

The content of Uncle Stan's letter was about Rita, asking why a beautiful girl like her wasn't married. Uncle Earl took this opportunity to start corresponding with Aunt Rita. Rita's first letter never reached Earl. Had she not written again, who knows what would have happened to change the course of events. But she did and they corresponded for over a year. Uncle Earl proposed to Aunt Rita before he had met her. Aunt Rita said that she'd reserve her answer until she met him. They met for the first time at the train station and were married soon after. It was obvious to anyone who was in their company, how very much in love they were.

Herb and I went to visit my Aunt Rita when she was sick. She was staying with her son Cliff and his wife Nancy. We talked about so many things. I thought maybe Aunt Rita would have remembered how to make grandmom's meatballs and sauce. She said that her mom didn't use recipes. No matter what changes I make in my meatballs, I can't duplicate that taste. After sixty years I still remember that incredible flavor.

On the heavier side, we talked about grandmom and when she was admitted to the hospital for depression. Jillian had been asking questions about our family, trying to gain insight on her bipolar disorder and whether she inherited it. Also, she wanted to know what measures were taken, if any. I hadn't thought of any of these things in years.

As children, we were kept in the dark about serious issues. I vaguely remember whispering among my parents and aunts and uncles, but knew better than to ask questions—until Jillian started asking questions. Aunt Rita remembered the time I was talking about but couldn't shed much light on the issue. She remembers being afraid and standing outside the hospital while her sisters Florence and Josephine went in. She did know that shock therapy was part of grandmom's treatment.

It wasn't enough information to really help Jillian but we knew more about our family after that day. My sister Mary also struggles with bipolar disorder. She and Jillian talked about it openly. Mary has since adopted Jillian's description of the low times, as "being in a very dark place", as a very apt description. They both have trouble egressing out of those difficult periods.

Aunt Rita went home to heaven to be with Uncle Earl several weeks after our visit. It was bittersweet because she would be missed so much, yet, I felt comfort from knowing that my aunt and uncle were together again.

One of my most treasured items is a quilt that Loretta gave me when her mom went to be with her father in heaven. It is so special because her mother and father made it together. Lying under that beautiful quilt I feel warm and cozy for more than one reason.

MY PARENTS

MY MOTHER.

I talk by phone to my mother, every week. She is eighty-six and still walks to Mass every day. She's in good health, but tired, wanting to go home and be with my dad.

Some of the most special times we have are when she comes to visit and stays overnight. It gives me great pleasure to pamper her, to make her feel special. I don't know whether it was real or just my perception, but I sometimes didn't feel my mother's love growing up, probably, because she was such a strict disciplinarian. I'm not saying that she didn't love me, just that I didn't always feel it.

There was one time that my negative feelings were confirmed. I had just graduated from nursing school. It had been a struggle since I was a single parent at this time. I got through it though, and at the risk of sounding vain, I was proud of my accomplishment. So were my children. My mother never mentioned it. Yet, at a family gathering, she was bragging to me about my sister-in-law who had just gotten her teaching degree. Mom actually said "Can you believe it! She has six children and got her degree in teaching. Isn't that amazing?"

I agreed with mom. It really was amazing. Yet, I wondered why she never mentioned *my* accomplishment. I also had six children and no husband supporting me at the time. It hurt. I never questioned her because I didn't want to be the cause of a disagreement. Still the passive one, I remained quiet.

Time lapses, things change and there is no doubt in my mind that my mother loves me. When did that change? I have no idea. It was so insidious, I can't pinpoint it. It doesn't matter anyway.

My mom was always there for me each time I went to the hospital to have a baby. During those years, it was a four-to-five day stay. She generously cared for our other children, the whole time I was in the hospital.

My mom also is solely responsible for me being able to walk normally. When I was just a few months old, she noticed that I was kicking with only one leg. She addressed her concerns to the doctor, who brushed them aside and said, "Let's wait." She was angry. By the time she found a doctor who said, "If Mike and Ike aren't alike, something's wrong." Both legs and hips were encased in plaster for over a year. I was diagnosed with congenital hip dysplasia.

My grandparents were unsupportive, thinking that mom should have waited until my father had seen me. I was eighteen months old before he had seen me for the first time. That would have been precious time lost and more damage incurred. Dad was in the Army Air Corps. It was during World War II. My mother stood her ground against all the opposition and I thank God that she did.

During the time she was going back and forth to the hospital, she met a wonderful Jewish couple who had a little boy who had the same diagnosis as I did. They were a wealthy family and had a custom-made highchair designed for their little boy, to accommodate the splayed legs. Since they were done using the chair, they offered to loan it to my mother, for me, requesting only that she pass it on to someone else in need. My mother, who is a wonderful seamstress wanted to thank this couple in a tangible way. Without measurements, she looked at their little boy, went home and made a fully lined suit for him. His parents were thrilled. The suit fit him perfectly.

Mom would make matching outfits for my children when they were babies. She would also make clothes for me and my sisters, always in the current style. I never had any interest in sewing when I was a teenager. Now, of course, I regret it. I can, however, embroider simple things like monograms on pillowcases.

My sisters and I have been getting together regularly with mom. Mary will bring mom and Diane over to my house. Sometimes we'll have lunch here. Other times, our brother, Eddie will treat us all to lunch at a nice restaurant. I can't explain how or why or even what keeps us laughing, but by the time mom is out of the car and not even through the front door, we are all laughing—belly laughing. By the time the day is over, we ache from laughing so much. This, too, must be the joy of the Lord.

UPDATE; 2013 Mom is now ninety-one. She moves much more slowly and though she has some health issues, she's grateful that she's still ambulatory and free from pain. Her memory fails her more often (so does mine) but she is still able to enjoy an occasional visit. Just recently, my sister Mary brought mom, my sister Diane, five of her grandchildren and her son Paul to visit. Jen and Ry came over with Jake and Kenzie and all the cousins had a wonderful time in the pool. Mom just enjoyed watching them. She said that it was great entertainment.

Diane recently moved in with mom and Eddie and will help with mom's care, although even when she was living in her own home, she did a lot for mom, taking her to the hairdresser, to Mass, even on a bus trip with the people she worked with.

UPDATE 2015

Mom is ninety three and in St. John Newman Nursing Home. She seems to have adapted to her new surroundings. Then again, she's in the throes of dementia. Sometimes there's recognition when we visit, sometimes not. My brothers and sisters still reside in Philadelphia so mom has frequent visits from them. Herb and I visit every month, usually attending the 11:00 Mass in the Chapel with mom. Despite her forgetfulness, she has never forgotten to genuflect on her arthritic knees when she's in the Chapel. She's probably most at home there.

Sometimes we'll take mom out for lunch. Other times she may not want to go. This affords time for Mary and Mike and Herb and I to get together. We usually meet them when we go to see mom. Mom used to love to sit by me on the piano bench when I played songs from the forties. On one visit I asked if she wanted to do that since there was a piano in one of the rooms. She said "No." However, when I started to play a few of her favorite tunes, she came over and sat beside me, even singing. It was a beautiful moment.

UPDATE 2015

My brother Ed brought my mom and my sister, Diane to our home for a visit. Trudi and Kevin also came. It was a really good, uneventful visit. Mom has dementia and I don't think she knew who I was. She gravitated towards Trudi and thought she was at her house. She did, however, perk up when I played some songs from the forties, even recognizing them. She also remembered my Kevin even though it had been years since she had seen him. Her favorite phrase from when Kevin was a toddler, was "hurry up honey." How precious it was to hear that phrase trigger a memory.

DECEMBER 2015

Mom falls and sustains injuries to her neck and nose. She has to wear a neck collar for the rest of her life, which she is not happy about. She is recovering remarkably, considering she will be 94 years old in two months.

JANUARY 2015

Herb and I visited mom at the nursing home. My brother Ed was sitting with her in the piano room. I brought some music so I could play a few songs for mom, hoping she'd remember the times she sat on the piano bench with me, while I played. She didn't really know who I was but Herb said when I started to play, she closed her eyes and smiled, as if remembering. I love you mom…

UPDATE 2016 Mom passed away in February at age 94. I am sure that she's enjoying being reunited with my dad.

MY FATHER

Daddy was a warm, gentle, loving man who loved God, my mom and his children. He was patient with anyone and everyone. He was an avid reader of books of the saints and anything of a spiritual nature. Though quiet and even shy it never kept him from talking with people.

My brothers and sisters and I loved the water, whether it was in a pool, lake or the ocean. We definitely got that from our dad. He was a strong swimmer and would execute a perfect swan dive or jackknife (pike) from a thirty foot platform at Clementon Lake Park. He wasn't one to exaggerate so we know the story I'll tell next was true. Though the platforms at that time were ten, twenty, thirty and forty feet high, the water was only ten feet deep. Pretty shallow considering the height of the platforms. Dad dove in and didn't come up as usual. Uncle Stan dove down to find him stuck in the mud. It's a miracle that he didn't break his neck. God had other plans for him. It was only one of many close calls.

Dad's brothers Stanley and Billy (Henry) were also adept at diving. Uncle Stan was in the Merchant Marines for most of his life and was always diving off ships. Dad's sisters, Josephine (Aunt Jo), Florence (Aunt Flossie) and Rita were all excellent swimmers. Their mom, my grandmom Sophie had been a lifeguard. Grandpop couldn't swim a stroke.

When my children were little, my dad and mom would take us on Mondays to Margate for the day. Mom would make lunch and her famous orange lemonade, from freshly squeezed fruit. It was always in a red and white gallon jug. For hours we'd all be in the waves, except mom. She was afraid of the water.

Daddy taught David, Kevin, Rachele and Mark how to swim and dive. They would dive off of his shoulders into the waves. Most of the time my dad was completely submerged as the waves washed over him. He loved swimming with the kids in Marlton Lakes too. Even Sheba, our German Shepherd would go swimming with us.

At the end of our day at the beach, daddy would carry the little ones back to the blanket so they wouldn't get their feet sandy. We'd powder them with baby powder to take away the stickiness. They each had a plastic drawstring "Good and Plenty" bag, with their clothes in it. Then with towels draped over the windows of the car, it became our dressing room.

On the way home we'd stop at "Burger Chef" and get burgers and fries and slushies, a special treat for all of us. It is a beautiful memory for me as well as the children. Even David remembers those days. If it wasn't for my dad, we wouldn't have ever gone to the shore or even had fast food. Those little things were huge to us. As young as they were, our children were so appreciative.

My dad and his entire family were warm, loving and so much fun to be with. I treasured my times with them. Dad and Uncle Stan decided to build a boat in Uncle Stan's single car garage. It was a row house in Wissinoming, on Charles St. Someone called the fire company when the fumes from the fiberglass became overwhelming, affecting the neighbors also.

When completed, we launched the boat on the Delaware River near Tacony. We set up camp on a sandy beach. A large beach umbrella with a blanket over it became our changing room thanks to Aunt Rita. We built a big bonfire and threw potatoes in the hot coals to bake. We had hot dogs on sticks. Most of our cousins were there. Aunt Rita, Uncle Earl, Loretta and Cliff as well as Uncle Stan, Aunt Gene, Bobby and Jeannie, Uncle Billy and of course, my mom, dad, brothers and sisters were there also.

This would be our first attempt at water skiing. The boys were so sure they could do this and even though Loretta and I were a little older (13 and 14) they were making fun of us. The boys tried so many times to get up without success. Loretta and I got up the first time and stayed up. Within weeks we were able to kick one ski off and remain upright, zig zagging across the wake. It was a great experience to see the sun setting on the water and feel like you were skiing into the sunset.

Dad had an idea to get the boys up but it didn't pan out. He had Eddie on his shoulders and as the boat took off, Eddie looked like he was skiing but once again, my father was submerged. The combined weight was too much.

Uncle Bill was a little more reckless than dad and Uncle Stan. He was also younger. He was a brilliant man and had a basement full of intricate electronic equipment. I remember dad telling us that Uncle Bill would sometimes be in a hospital operating room, because of all the hi tech equipment he had to monitor. He was also an alcoholic, which I didn't realize until I was an adult.

When Uncle Bill drove the boat, he'd get very close to the larger boats in the channel. We knew we had to stay up on those skis. In hindsight, it was probably downright dangerous. Uncle Bill died in his thirties of a drug overdose. I don't know all the details because so much was kept hidden from us. We all loved and missed Uncle Billy.

Daddy loved having children around him. It didn't matter how many. Whether playing ball, swimming or rolling down hills at Burholme Park, he'd always keep us busy.

Dad was in the Army Air Corp during World War II when I was born. He told us that after he got bit by so many spiders or snakes that were in his boots when he was in the jungles of New Guinea, he'd check his shoes and boots every single time, always expecting something lurking there. He did that for the rest of his life. That story stuck with me because I still do the same.

He was a paratrooper. I guess Jillian inherited her love of jumping out of planes from him. He was also in the Philippines. At one point he was on a ship, anchored for several hours. He and his friend spotted another friendly ship almost a mile away. They decided to go for a swim. They reached the other ship and were pulled up by some sailors who said, "Are you crazy? These are shark infested waters!" Their guardian angels were working overtime.

Another time dad got stung by a Portuguese Man o' War and was in the hospital for days. They didn't think he would survive. Once again, God had other plans. He also was hit in the head with a hardball and ended up in the hospital for several days. Prognosis was not good, however, he recovered.

My father didn't see me for the first year and a half of my life but mom would send him photos with notes from me on the back. He dedicated me to the care of our Blessed Mother. That's probably why I have a strong devotion to her.

Dad was a conductor for the Reading Railroad. He took David and Kevin on the train one time just to show them everything. He loved having kids around him. When we lived in a little row house in Philly, dad did some cement work for us. He broke up our sidewalk which was all uneven. It was back breaking work, especially since he was working alone. He had to cart all the chunks of cement to the dump. With each trip he made, and there were many, the number of kids in the car for the ride along, would increase. He had David, Kevin, Paul and many other of the neighborhood kids. They loved my father.

Fridays were payday for dad and he would give each of the kids a silver dollar. He did that for years. There is one story told by dad and Uncle Stan that is atypical of my father. As I said before, he was a quiet, gentle man. However, as my brother Ed recently said, he had a breaking point. He was in line at the Girard Corn Exchange Bank, a very long line, waiting to cash his paycheck. A man much bigger than daddy pushed ahead of everyone in the line, including a woman. My father went up and punched the guy in the jaw. My father's hat flew off his head in the effort. The man, who was a head taller than my dad, stooped down to pick up my father's hat, brushed it off, then handed it to him with an apology. Think about the consequences of something happening like that, today, in this litigious society.

My father had told me that his father had taught him and Uncle Stan to box. Dad was Stan's sparring partner. Uncle Stan, at one time, was so good at boxing that he made more money on the side than he did on the ship. He was strongly encouraged to do this.

One time my dad was throwing a switch on the railroad track and his finger got stuck. He could not get it out and no one was within calling distance. He felt the vibrations of an oncoming train, got out his red bandana handkerchief, turned his head as the train severed his finger. He placed the finger in the handkerchief, stanched the flow of blood and drove himself to the hospital. It's amazing that so long ago they were able to re attach the finger successfully without benefit of a specialist.

I remember he told me of the day Mary and Joe were born. It was December 21. The doctor came out and said, "Ed, what did you want? A boy or girl?" Dad said he didn't care. The doctor said, "Well Ed, you have one of each."

I remember when daddy would go to the gas station, he would say "Riley sent me." There was a TV show called the Life of Riley, starring William Bendix. During the commercial they would tell people that when they filled their tank, they should say "Riley sent me." They would give out little dolls from around the world. Chele, of course, benefited from this promotion.

I also remember getting Green Stamps from the gas station, which we could later redeem for an item out of a catalog. There was another time that for each full tank of gas, you would receive a dish. They were white with a gold wheat pattern. I ended up getting an entire set of dishes.

Dad was diagnosed with Lymphoma when he was fifty-eight. He died at fifty-nine, way too young. Mom and he had planned to travel in the United States by train when he retired. They could go anywhere for free, but the only trip I remember them taking was to Niagara Falls when mom was pregnant with the twins and one trip to an island, Tenerife. We have pictures of my mother holding a lion cub and also holding a cape while bullfighting. She also loved animals.

My Jillian, as an adult felt cheated because she never got to know her grandfather and have the beautiful memories that her sister and brothers have of time with him. She was only a baby when he died. I'm sure she's basking in his love now....in heaven. As for me, everything changed drastically after daddy was gone. Nothing was as much fun from then on.

As he was succumbing to the cancer in his body and becoming weaker, he had one last thing he was intent on doing. Kevin had been diagnosed with Keratoconus bilateral and needed special contact lenses to stabilize his eyes. Otherwise, he could lose his vision. Daddy wanted to pay for those lenses even though we had the money from an income tax return. He insisted and with an amazing show of strength, pulled himself up in bed and was adamant about this. Almost shouting, he said, "I want to do this for Kevin!"

A few months after daddy had gone to heaven, one of the lenses popped out of Kevin s eye while he was mowing the grass. I said let's pray and ask grandpop to help you find it, knowing that it was almost an impossibility. Yet, he found it. Maybe I should say grandpop found it.

Typically, dad had envelopes for each of us kids with $200.00 in them, to be given to us on the day of his funeral. He didn't want anyone to lose a day's pay if he died on a weekday. He remained altruistic to the end and gave his car to the priest since mom didn't drive.

I look forward to being with my dad again…I love you daddy.

SISTERS

There was such a big age gap between my sisters and me but I always loved them and knew that they loved me. I was engaged at age sixteen and married just before I turned eighteen. When I left home, Mary was seven and Diane was eleven. I do remember spending a lot of time with the twins, Mary and Joe, because my mother needed help. I mostly took care of Joey, because mom would make a game of it, and take Mary. We'd have races to see who could bathe and diaper and dress the fastest. Joey and I came out ahead a lot.

DIANE

Today my relationship with my sisters is stronger than I could ever have imagined. Diane is still a gentle, loving compassionate and, at times, shy woman. She possesses a spiritual strength that few people will ever know. She works at a medical facility for retired nuns. She probably has brought more souls closer to Jesus and His mother by her example alone. I admire her for so many reasons it's hard to know where to start. I look at her and see a saint. She's patient and always sees the best in people. Most of us can do that sometimes. Diane does it all the time. She is involved in the Holy Souls Ministry and her home phone is a hotline for anyone needing prayers. She attends daily Mass.

Diane has four sons and one daughter. She also has fifteen grandchildren and one great grandchild. Miraculously, she works full time and still makes time for all the grandchildren. She even takes the older ones to Confession when she has them over. I've felt especially close to her sons Josh and Eddie and their wives, Julie and Renee over the years. Diane has raised wonderful children, now adults. More than anything, Diane exudes the Joy of the Lord.

I am closest to my nephew Josh. I often thank Diane for sharing him with me. He is such a caring person and always keeps in touch no matter how busy he is. He's like another son to me. His wife Julie (she's an RN) and their children Haley and Bear are also very caring. Haley and Bear send me drawings from time to time, and they never forget Uncle Herb. He had artwork from them as well as our Kenzie and Jake adorning his hospital room.

Diane's son Eddie and his wife Renee and their three children, Jackson, Olivia and Mason are also close to our hearts even though we don't see them often. When I had a hip replacement, they were here with gourmet meals that Renee made. They lived over an hour away at the time so that wasn't an easy task. Olivia has Herb entranced. All their children are beautiful.

There have been so many touching moments and hours with Diane. She'll lift my spirits sky high, even over the phone. I love to hear her laugh. She's had a difficult life and raised her five children as a single parent. Again, she doesn't dwell on the negative. She would probably deny all these positive attributes, because she also possesses humility. I am blessed to have you for a sister, Diane.

UPDATE

It's October 1, 2013 and I just finished talking with Diane for almost an hour. I sometimes am overwhelmed with gratitude that I have her to confide in. We talk several times a week and she's always so happy to hear from me. (I would be getting on anyone else's nerves by now). Just when I think I couldn't possibly love her anymore….I do.

UPDATE 2014

Diane and I have shared so many of the same fears, not only in childhood, but throughout a large part of our adult lives. Now I believe that we're stronger for overcoming them. Yet, our sons have a difficult time seeing us that way. Diane's son John Paul is a psychologist and encourages his mom to "step outside of her comfort zone." She flippantly said "I've been out of my comfort zone since you were born John." I laugh out loud every time I think of that remark because it's so out of character for Diane.

Diane was staying in Washington, DC with John, Lauren and baby Elizabeth Rose, while Herb was in the hospital for cardiac surgery. Diane and I talked every day. She kept John updated. She said that he was very concerned for me and Herb. He stressed having someone with me at the hospital at all times. I had just completed radiation treatments for breast cancer. I kept telling Diane to tell him I'm fine. He probably thought I was in denial.

My Ryan never used the phrase "comfort zone" yet it was implied. If I dared to utter a sound getting up from a chair, because of my arthritic knees and back, he immediately tells me I'm not getting enough exercise. Though I know that he's kidding, I also know there's a very large grain of truth in what he says. He believes I should push myself to do more. Hey, Ryan, does washing the siding on the house with a bucket and rag and climbing up and down the ladder count as exercise?

As for my comfort zone, in a few days we're having our Polar Plunge Party. It's October, the weather is cool, the pool is cold. I am now seventy years old. My oncologist tells me that my immune system is severely compromised. I know how I feel. I am not about to 'baby' myself now. Can't wait!

UPDATE 2015

Diane now has seventeen grandchildren and one great grandchild!

MARY

My sister, Mary has been such a help to me in recent years, emotionally, spiritually and any other way you can think of. I see Mary as extremely strong, though I'd bet anything that she would argue with that assessment. Mary, at age fifty two is physically beautiful and looks like a model. She and her husband Mike have six children, three sons, three daughters. Her day also starts with Mass. Their youngest boys, Timmy and Paul, were born when Mary was in her forties. They are a year apart. She also spends a lot of time with her five young grandchildren. I don't know where she gets her energy from.

On top of all that, Mary finds time to visit or help friends in need, whether it's taking someone to the doctor or just spending time with them. One of the most touching things she had done for me was to show up at the hospital when Herb had his first cardiac surgery. She came laden down with a small ice chest filled with drinks and chicken and other goodies. She stayed with me all day. She just sat and kept me company...all day.

I wish I could impart to anyone who reads this, how profoundly this impacted me. As I write this, the page is blurring because I can't stop crying...just remembering. Mary came just to be there to offer comfort at a time I needed it most. I was at the hospital for twelve hours a day because I was too afraid to drive or even take public transportation. Trudi or George would drop me off in the morning, about 7:00 am, and I would stay until someone would take me home at night. When I couldn't get a ride, I'd stay overnight.

Mary insisted that I go home with her the next night and stay over and she would bring me back to the hospital in the morning. We went to a restaurant. I think it was Ruby Tuesdays, had dinner, a drink and a lot of sharing of feelings. I felt myself beginning to relax for the first time in days. Then Mary said something I will never forget. She said that she wished she had been there for me years ago. The floodgates opened and hot, salty, healing tears flowed on both sides. A tremendous weight lifted. I cannot even hope to explain the feeling of unconditional love I experienced. Jesus truly was in the middle of our dinner. I even knew at that moment, that Herb would be fine.

We went home, I soaked in a hot tub and then literally collapsed on the cozy sofa bed that Mary had set up for me. The next morning, I awoke to the cheerful voices of my nephews, Timmy and Paul. They looked like cherubs and I felt like I was having a taste of heaven at my sister Mary's home. Things can change dramatically in an instant when God is in the center of things.

UPDATE 2013

Mary continues to stay strong though she's dealing with a lot on her plate. Since she also suffers from insomnia, she called one night at midnight. I heard water sloshing and asked if she was in the bathtub. She said, "No, I'm in my kitchen." We had had heavy rains and her home is in a flood zone. Everything was destroyed. Furniture, cabinets, carpets, tile etc. not to mention the problem with mold afterwards. It was about eight months until everything was back to normal. However, every time it rains, the fear sets in. Not too long after that we had more rain. It never reached the house, but my nephew Timmy was in a canoe in the street in front of their house—not funny.

Mary was extremely sensitive to my Jillian because she suffers from the same bi-polar disorder. She works full time at Fox Chase Cancer Center and loves being a grandmother to her grandchildren, taking all five of them overnight at times. Keeping with the spiritual upbringing we've all had, faith is a crucial part of her life. She attends daily Mass before going to work and has a Rosary meeting once a week for friends and co-workers. She amazes me. She also is involved in peaceful and prayerful protests against abortion clinics. Our family is pro-life and knows that life begins at conception. All those babies that were aborted are now growing up in heaven. Not my words... but the words of Colton Burpo who died on the operating table, then was resuscitated.

In his book "Heaven is For Real" he tells how he met his older sister in heaven. He was only four at the time. Even now, many years later, he recounted his story in an interview. He had no idea about having another sibling because his mom miscarried when she was just a few months along.

His parents never thought there was a reason to tell him. Imagine their shock when little Colton told them. This is another example of getting involved in the pro- life movement to change things for the better. Many believe as we do, but then do nothing. One person *can* change things. It's happened at this clinic. There are other ways to get involved also without leaving your home. Calls to our state representatives, letters. Petitions. We all have to do our part. Mary does.. I am blessed to have her for a sister.

UPDATE 2015

Mary and Mike have just had their seventh grandchild, Scarlett Rose, thanks to Missy and Jay.

RED, WHITE & BLUE THRIFT STORE ADVENTURE

My sisters Diane and Mary came for an impromptu visit. Mary had been through a lengthy episode of severe depression, part of her bi-polar disorder. Now she was on a high and it was great to see her relishing life once again. There's no telling how long the manic stage will endure. Hopefully, as in the past, it may be months.

She came bounding in the front door with a hug and telling me to get my things. We were going to go to "Red, White & Blue", my favorite thrift store. Diane shrugged and laughed. I told her we'd go after they stretched their legs, after riding for an hour. I had cut up fresh fruit and used that as an excuse to delay our outing. We were in the car in fifteen minutes. When we got to the store I was about to ask whether we should take just one cart. Too late! Mary was off and running ahead of us. Diane and I each took our own carts.

After a half hour, Diane and I checked out and waited outside....and waited. Mary finally came out dragging two lawn and leaf sized bags filled with "treasures." We got in the car and Mary said that she wanted to drive by our old home in Marlton Lakes. She loves to fish and complains that there are so few good lakes in her town. So we drove to Marlton Lakes and talked about the good times we had had there.

She then decided she wanted to look for "For Sale" signs on ranchers. We found one and called the realtor. She insisted on making an appointment for that afternoon. We did. Then we drove by Archway's lake and she got so excited, pulling into the parking lot. She asked if she could fish there. I told her she needed a permit. When I worked there, I got them for free for my sons and grandson. She parked the car and went into the administration building. Diane and I were at a loss. How were we going to stop Mary from buying a house. In her state of mind, we had no doubt she would do just that. She came out with her permit, less thirty-five dollars.

Then we head home for lunch and rum and cokes for Mary and me. Diane doesn't imbibe. When Herb came home, Mary said "Let's go see the house." Herb looked at me with a question in his eyes. I said to get in the car, we'll explain on the way. Just then, Mary's cell phone rang. The people changed their mind about showing the house. Thank you, Jesus! Instead we went back to Archway's lake. Mary fished off the dock. It had an instant calming effect on all her frenetic energy.

Diane and I walked around the lake. I took her on a tour to all the different buildings, the outdoor pool and indoor pool. We even got to go in one building. The memories surfaced of my twenty years there. Most were good. Yet, this was the lake I looked at every day since Mark's diving accident. Painful memories also. The teacher in the pre school had finished putting up summer decorations. She spent a lot of time on the theme that included a lifeguard stand and the beach. When I returned to work the next week (I couldn't afford to take extra time off), Janine had taken all the decorations down. Mark's diving accident had its beginning on a lifeguard stand. I was so grateful to her. She also insisted on staying overnight with me. She wanted to be there. She even gave me a beautiful Rosary for Mark that had been blessed by Pope John Paul. I haven't seen her in decades but will always be grateful for her.

As Diane and I continued to walk, talk and drink in the natural habitat, the walking trails, the birdsong, turtles and so on, I realized how God had blessed me abundantly to provide such a haven for me through those troubled times. I was overwhelmed with gratitude. We arrived back at the dock to see Mary and a duck keeping her company. Suffice it to say, it is a day we'll never forget.

BROTHERS, ED AND JOE

I am the oldest of five children. **My brother ED** is next in line. He is single and has lived with my mother since my father died. Mom is able to do most things for herself. However, she never learned to drive so she's dependent on Eddie and my sisters for trips to the doctor and food shopping. All my siblings still live in Philadelphia or nearby.

Eddie served in the Navy. I also remember him having a motorcycle. He's very spiritual and altruistic. He takes after my dad, in that he's an avid reader of all things spiritual, in particular, Catholicism. He is patient, gentle and very caring. When my children were little, I always remember him down on the floor playing with them.

He's helped so many people whether it's at his job on the railroad, Amtrak, where he works as a signal technician, or the family. Observing him for years, it becomes obvious that his aim in life is to serve others. We know that we're in his prayers. Yet, the only time I get to spend time with him, are the times that he brings my mother to our home in N.J. Mom will stay overnight then Ed will pick her up again. He usually comes laden down with Dunkin Donuts coffee or Christian Brothers port wine. He reminds me so much of my dad—not in appearance but in the things that he does.

One particular incident comes to mind that meant so much to me. He brought my mom to the hospital in Philadelphia when Herb had open heart surgery. I didn't expect that. Five days later, on Herb's first day home, Ed arrived that night with a gift for Herb, a Rigid cordless drill. Herb absolutely loves this tool. Eddie only stayed long enough to give us both a hug, then left to make the hour trip back to Philly.

HUMOROUS CATHOLIC SCHOOL STORY

Recently Ed and I were reminiscing about our grammar school days in St. Martin of Tours Catholic School. I had so many fears about Sister Cyril throwing the boys out of the second story window. Also, about what constituted the difference between a mortal and venial sin, firm purpose of amendment and such.... big words for a seven year old. I've heard dozens of stories over the years but never one to match Eddie's. In our classrooms we had old fashioned radiators with a metal cover and a bleeder valve. Of course, we didn't know what it was back then. Eddie said he was terrified because when the kids acted up, Sister threatened to remove the cover and turn the valve that would hiss loudly and "open the gate to hell"....or was it purgatory? It didn't matter because he and every one of the students were terrified of both and visualized flames engulfing them. How else could you keep order with sixty students and no aide.? The nuns were creative, I'll give them that.

UPDATE In recent years we have seen more of Ed, which is a blessing. Kevin and Trudi especially enjoy talking with him.

My brother JOE is ten years younger than me. He and my sister Mary are twins. Joe and his wife Donna are an amazing couple. They have six children, five boys, one girl and are now raising their oldest granddaughter, Alyssa. They felt it important to raise Alyssa in the Catholic church. She is now attending Catholic school... Three of their sons are married to three sisters.

Joe works as a supervisor for the Philadelphia Water Department. He also renovates houses that he buys as an investment. At this writing, they have sixteen grandchildren. I'm sure that there will be many more to come. As with all our families, there is a very strong, faith-based ethic.

When Joe was in high school he volunteered his summer time to work in New Mexico digging wells for the indigent population. He lived in the same primitive surroundings as the people. He remarked how generous they were with how little they had. Sounds like you're pretty generous too, Joe.

My sister-in-law Donna is a pre-school teacher. How blessed those children are to have such a great influence so early in life. Donna's passion is children. I've always felt close to Donna although we don't see each other as often as we did in earlier years. We do get together at weddings and baby showers.

Just recently Donna and I were talking about our grandchildren and all things related to babies. One of our favorite topics is breastfeeding and all the benefits. It jarred a memory of our girls when they were infants, and also gives an indication of just how close we were and how much we think alike. It's a beautiful memory.

I can't remember the exact occasion, though we didn't need excuses to get together. I'm usually running around like a chicken without a head when I have a party, barbecue or whatever. I used to be obsessive compulsive about organizing everything and getting the food and drinks out. Donna, on the other hand, is so relaxed about entertaining or anything else.

While I was stressing about getting everything ready, Donna saw no reason to bother me about my Jillian waking up needing to be nursed. She just sat down and did it. She had what Jillian needed and gave it to her. She was also nursing her little girl, Regina. I thought to myself, how generous and loving Aunt Donna was. Jillian loved hearing that story.

Donna and I both had stories to tell of being a "wet nurse" long before I even knew what the term meant. Donna helped out a friend to give her an overnight break when, of course, no one else could. I helped out a friend whose baby refused to nurse from her mother. We were in a cabin, forty miles from the nearest store. We had to pump our water to wash our cloth diapers. We had no supplement bottles. David was only three months old. So was the other baby. I was totally exhausted after that weekend.

In recent years I've felt a closeness to Joe, not previously there. I can't explain why not, just as I can't explain why it changed, although, I do remember when it did. Joe and Mary's children gave them a fiftieth birthday party. At that party, Joe asked me to dance. Questions arise as to what happened to change things. I don't really care nor do I need to know. I do know that prayer changes things. I'm content with the results of prayer and don't need God to reveal how He goes about making improvements, whether they're physical or spiritual. I just thank Him.

MATERNAL GRANDPARENTS

My grandparents Albert and Clementine Swica (mom's parents) were born in Poland. They had two daughters, my mother Rose Helen and her only sibling, Helen. My mother said that her mother had "a lot of brothers and sisters", but she has no idea how many. When I asked my mother about my birth, she said the labor was not bad at all. She and her mother walked several miles to Northeastern Hospital in Philadelphia. It was during World War II and my dad was overseas. My mom said that she was one of six women in a ward. All of their husbands were at war. Dad didn't see me until I was a year and a half. Mom sent him pictures with little notes from me to him on the back. She said that he dedicated me to the care of our Blessed Mother. Maybe that's why I have a strong devotion to her.

In order to make phone calls, mom would have to go to the corner grocery store. Likewise, if a call came in for mom, the grocer would send someone to get her. She talked about taking bowls from their kitchen, to the store, where the grocer would fill them with ice cream, a real treat. Think of all the trash that would eliminate. That's really conserving. This reminds me of when we lived on Dock Road in Atco. We would go to "Annings" which was a combination grocery store and five & ten (this is a reference that's giving away my age). You could buy food, curtain rods and we even took bowls for them to fill with ice cream…just like long ago. Sometimes progress seems to result in regression.

Grandmom came to America when she was fifteen. Two years later she was on a ship to return to Poland, but halfway there, the ship reversed course to return to America's shore because World War I had exploded in Europe.

She then took a job working at a thread company. Her home was a room in a boarding house. It was there that she met my grandfather.

My grandfather worked at a textile mill, as a weaver. He also got my grandmother a job there. They didn't have much money. Grandmom taught my mother to cook, plain fare. They ate a lot of kielbasa, stews, chicken soup, babka and other Polish dishes. They all belonged to St. Adalbert's parish. My grandmother did not go to Catholic school but she did receive her Communion at another parish, with very little instruction. The family did not attend Mass regularly. My grandfather played the violin. He was also a phenomenal gardener. He would bring plants from his tiny garden in Philadelphia, to plant in our N. J. gardens. I recall my grandparents as being very stern, my grandmother as being the sternest.

Grandpop had a motorcycle with a side car, that my grandmother would ride in. He rolled his own cigarettes and even taught David and Kevin how to roll them. Grandmom used to ice skate in Poland in her bare feet. She also recalled that her mother baked bread every other day and shared with the neighbors. They likewise did the same. This is how they had fresh bread everyday without baking everyday. Remember, there were no preservatives then. Since there were no screens for the windows, they used to drizzle honey on the windowsills to contain the flies there instead of in the house—ingenuity.

My Aunt Helen, my mother's only sibling told me a story about Grandmom and Grandpop's wedding day. Apparently, Grandpop had an old girlfriend who didn't want to let go of him. She was determined to break up the wedding. She got close enough to my grandmother to grab her bouquet, pulling off all the petals, leaving nothing but stems. When the bride and groom and family went to Grandpop's house for the reception, the tap on the keg of beer which was on the front porch, had been deliberately left open. It was near empty. They found out that the brother of the girl was the culprit. I don't have any details about how it ended. I just know that my grandparents were together for life. I actually have the newspaper clipping that this story was in.

GRANDPOP'S SWING

Grandpop built us a swing in the yard of his little row house in Port Richmond, Philadelphia. Why the address, 2958 Gaul St., sticks in my mind after all these years, I'll never understand, especially since I forget so many other details these days. Anyway, he took it all apart after building it so he could transport it to our home in Marlton Lakes, where he reassembled it. It had double bench seats facing each other, with a floor to rest our feet on.

The kids loved it, as did I. Some of our fondest memories involve that swing. My father used to hold Rachele and swing for the longest time. She loved those times and still talks about them even though forty years have passed. Years later when we were moving once again, I pleaded with George to take the swing to our new house which was just a mile away. He said that he didn't want to be bothered with it, so we left it behind, but the memories of it remain intact.

My grandmother's maiden name was Laskowska. She had a brother Chester who lived next door to her on Gaul Street in Philadelphia. I can't remember the whole family but I do remember my cousins Lillian, Esther and MaryAnne. Lillian and I kept in touch for many years after we married but lost touch after she moved away to New England.

PATERNAL GRANDPARENTS

My father's parents, Stanley and Sophie Wawrzyniak, were the opposite in temperament. I loved going over my grandparents' house, even if my many cousins weren't there. Grandmom would take us in her tiny kitchen. The kitchen table had a drawer for silverware but it was filled with bubblegum and other treats. I still remember their house on 4506 Shelmire Ave. in Philadelphia, as if it was yesterday. I can hear my grandmom telling me that if I ate the sliced, fresh peaches that she had sprinkled with sugar and poured fresh cream on, my complexion would be as smooth as "peaches and cream". I, of course, believed her. I still love the taste of fresh peaches with cream and a sprinkling of sugar. It's a summertime treat that stirs up memories of a grandmother who always had time to spoil me. I felt so loved in that home.

My cousin Loretta and I recently shared another memory of Grandmom. She used to take hankies and wrap loose change in them and tie it in a knot. I don't know if that has anything to do with me collecting old hankies at yard sales and thrift shops. I love them. You can never have too many hankies. Jillian and Rachele always carry them and I've enclosed them in birthday cards for just about everyone I care about. I usually enclose a little story about them. There was an old saying that the "Plain hankies are for blowing and fancy ones are for showing."

I can still taste my grandmother's spaghetti and meatballs. She and my grandfather were Polish too. However, I have never tasted meatballs to equal grandmom's. They had a slightly sweet taste. There was no recipe to copy. I would love to taste them again. My grandmother was also a lifeguard. She loved the water, as did all her children, including my dad. They're all strong swimmers and the men were excellent divers. They used to draw attention at Clementon Park, N.J. when they had ten, twenty, thirty and forty foot high diving platforms.

My grandmother was in her sixties when she swam way beyond the breakers in Wildwood. The lifeguards would blow that whistle and she would just keep swimming further out. She was in her glory in the water. The entire family, children, grandchildren and great grandchildren take after her, in that respect. Grandpop couldn't swim, but he was a boxer and a baseball player. He excelled at both. He tried to act stern, but it was just a veneer that couldn't hide the love and pride he had for his family.

Grandpop also was a college graduate. He told us of a trick that he played on the brothers who taught him. It was a Catholic college. At night the brothers and priests would leave their shoes outside their doors. Certain students would polish them, then return them. One night my grandpop and some of his friends replaced the priests shoes with the students shoes. They never did find out who did it.

Grandpop also got recognition for batting a ball over the "Jack Frost" sugar building in Philadelphia, down by the docks. I have a photo of the building and as best I can tell, it was ten stories high. As tough as he was, he was also sensitive. My cousin Cliff recalls how grandpop hugged him and cried when Cliff came home from Vietnam.

Grandmom was in her eighties when she died. My grandfather was healthy, but a month later he was lying in a hospital bed, dying. We believe he died from a broken heart. My last time with him was quiet and uneventful. It was in the hospital. My aunts were there and my uncles. I had always loved my grandfathers beautiful, silver hair that fell in waves, even in his eighties. I told him that I loved him and ran my fingers through his silky hair. I remember Aunt Floss saying that he had yelled at them for doing that and suggested I not do that. He got upset with her and said that it felt good. It's so comforting to know that I will see them again in heaven.

CCD ANECDOTES

Rachele and I have taught CCD classes for years in separate parishes. I taught at Our Lady of Mt. Carmel and she taught at St. Edwards in Pine Hill. We shared stories and tips on reaching the students who didn't want to be there.

Her teaching style is a bit unorthodox, to say the least. She related a story which was later confirmed by someone I know. They were walking through the halls and heard a commotion outside of Rachele's classroom. Looking in, they saw Rachele in stocking feet standing on top of the teacher's desk, throwing candy to anyone who had a correct answer. This was mentioned to her pastor who was aware of this. He said, "Whatever she's doing, let her continue. She has the highest rate of attendance, parent participation and the most knowledgeable students".

I, on the other hand, have been, until recently, more conservative. Of course, this year (2008) I would not be teaching. We had just had Jillian's funeral Mass last month. I couldn't even think clearly.

I remember sitting on the step of our back deck, looking at the woods and the flowers and trees. It was a beautiful day, but as I told God, I couldn't appreciate it. Everything hurt too much. I had driven Jillian through our woods on our golf cart and we had talked and laughed just weeks before. She thought it was so creative that Kenzie pretended that the fallen trees were crocodiles and we'd have to race to avoid them.

I forced myself to get in the car and go to the store to get a few things I needed. As I was driving, the Scripture, "Rejoice always. Pray without ceasing. In ALL circumstances give thanks, for this is the will of God for you in Christ Jesus." I Thessalonians 5: 16-18, came to me. By now, I was sobbing. How can I possibly thank God for taking Jillian home. I had to pull over to the side of the road. I knew I had to trust God with Jillian but I was gritting my teeth, telling Him that I couldn't do this. I remember telling Him that if He wanted me to do this, He would have to help me. He put the words on my heart, but it went against everything I felt. Once again, feelings can get you into trouble. By the time I was exhausted from crying, I did thank God for taking care of Jillian even though it wasn't the way I wanted Him to. You might say I half-heartedly acquiesced.

I finally reached my destination, the dollar store and someone I know had come up to me and gave me a hug. She told me she had "taken" Jillian to a baby shower and passed her photos around, telling them about all the adventurous things she had done. Then this woman asked me to wait. She came back with the manager of the store. He proceeded to tell me about losing his nine year old daughter. He said that he and I were left here on earth because God still had a job for us to do and it was up to us to find out what that job was. Then he hugged me, promising to keep my family in prayer.

I drove home and talked to Jesus all the way. I told Him if He had a job for me to do, He would have to be crystal clear about it, because my mind was so fogged up with pain, that I'd never be able to figure it out by myself.

I tried to keep busy by unpacking boxes we had brought home from the Poconos. Since Jillian had been there with us on her last visit, I just couldn't go back. I didn't want to go back without her. I was in my kitchen, boxes on the table when the phone rang. It was my friend Bea, who was also the Director of Religious Education. She apologized before she told me of her dilemma and asked if I would consider teaching a CCD class, come September.

Initially, I emphatically said "No!" Then someone interrupted her and she excused herself. She was going to call back but I said I'd wait. I figured I could be productive while waiting, and unpack a few boxes. I was surprised that she would even consider asking me at this time. How effective could I possibly be in my state of mind.

She had explained that she had been praying about her situation, needing another teacher. She prayed through the night and my name and face kept coming to her, even though she did not want to ask me. She was left with no choice because she felt God was guiding her. While waiting for her to come back on the phone, I opened the first box and viewing the contents, I moaned. "Please God, I can't do this." The box was filled with CCD materials—books, stickers, rosaries etc. I had bought it at a yard sale and forgotten all about it. Was this crystal clear or what? Be careful what you pray for.

Bea came back on the phone and said she was sorry that she put me on the spot. She said she'd give me some time to think about it and pray about it and call back in a few days. I told her I had gotten my answer while waiting. I'd take the class. Of course, I told God that when I asked what He wanted me to do, I didn't expect this, nor did I want this. However, I don't run the show. As my bumper sticker states, "Stop giving God instructions and just show up for work."

Mom, Dad & Me

Mom holding Kevin, Dad holding David & Rachele

Kevin

Tom, Rachele, Herb and me

Mark with daughter Natalie Rose

Jillian and mom

Family picnic at Washington Crossing Park

Herb and me when we first started dating

Grandmom, Rachele & Ed

Left to right me, Mary, mom & Diane

Left to right Gene Ryan & Mark is holding Nikki & Steven

Rachele skydiving, note Jillian's picture in her hands

Natalie's visit: Front row L to R: Steven, Amber, Jen, Kenzie, Natalie, me, Nikki & Bobby Back row L to R: Kevin, Ryan (holding Jake & Herb)

David & mom

Kevin & mom

Jillian's magazine cover (Courtesy of Newcomer Magazine, Atlanta, Ga.)

cover

HOLIDAY SHOPPING AND BEYOND
by Debbie Humphrey

Atlanta has grown to become a city of culture and class, mixing varied influences from around the world. When it comes to shopping, the city offers everything from upscale malls to neighborhood boutiques and from outlets to consignment shops. Whether you are looking for the chic of Rodeo Drive or the artsy influence of SoHo, you are sure to find it in Atlanta. The following are some of Atlanta's best places to shop for the holidays and well beyond.

Jillian's magazine cover story (Courtesy of Newcomer Magazine, Atlanta, Ga.)

Jillian, my beautiful baby girl

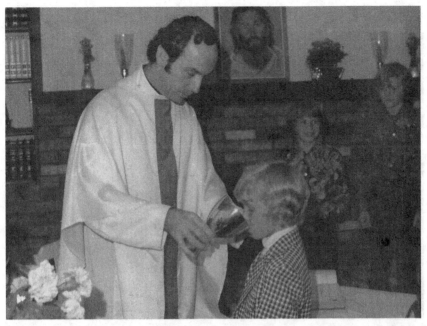

Father Bober administering First Holy Communion to Mark in our home

Ryan and Jake (cousins)

Herb & me with grandsons Brandon, Jamie & Tyler

L-R Rachele, David, Ryan , Jillian & Kevin (Ryan & Jen's wedding)

Nephew Josh & wife Julie with "Bear" & Haley

Left to Right Daddy, cousin, Uncle Stan, cousin
& Uncle Bill (3 bros. & Mary)

Ryan & Jen with Makenzie & Jake

Back row L to R Me, Jillian, mom, Rachele, Jen
& Bev; Front Nikki, Natalie & Trudi

Mark, me & Kevin

Makenzie, Me & Jake

Rachele proponent of Second Amendment

Me & my cousin Loretta

Mark supporting little brother Ryan

L-R Ryan, Jillian, cousin Michael & Rachele

Mark's Confirmation with Uncle Ed & Grandmom

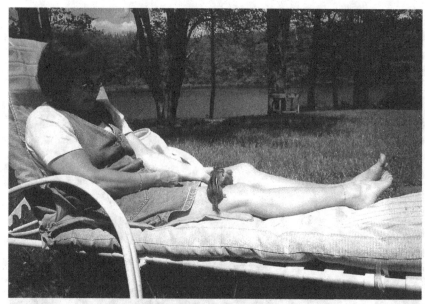
Me & "Chippie" in backyard Pocono home

Grandmom & Kenzie

David and Jillian

Rachele, Mark & Kevin belting out "Jeremiah was
a Bullfrog" at Aunt Mary's wedding

Grandpop with cousin Loretta & me (I'm on the right)

Pop Pop & Kenzie at the library

Dad working on the railroad

Kenzie & grandmom, continuing the tradition

L-R Mary, Joe, Me, Ed, Diane

Herb & me, now engaged

David & Jayne's Wedding with Ryan, Jen, Kenzie & Jake

Herb in Vietnam

Herb & me heading to Peddler's Village

Mark dressed for work at Lucien's

My beautiful grandpop & me

Ryan & Jillian

Jillian, me & Rachele, my gorgeous daughters

Grandpop Stanley & Grandmom Sophie (paternal grandparents)

Grandpop Albert & Grandmom Clementine (maternal
grandparents) with Eddie, me & Diane

Ryan & me

L-R Joe, DJ and Ryan (at Ry's police academy graduation)

Me & George with David, Kevin, Rachele & Mark

Steven, Amber and Courtney

Jake & Kenzie with "Lily"

Rachele with Kenzie & Jake

Wild ride with my grandson David

Pop Pop & Jake's version of Duck Dynasty

Rachele, Herb & Bev

Me & my granddaughter Nikki

Me & my grandson Steven

Herb & "Becky" in the Poconos

Grandson Steven & Amber

Polar Plunge! L-R Michele, Jen, Sam & me

Kenzie & Jake with cousins

Mom & Dad

Rachele & me with Sister Agnes, Sister Theresa and Sister Carmel

Rachele's First Holy Communion with her brothers

Mark & me

Me & Mrs. Temple (I think it was mandatory for
every Polish kid to play the accordion)

Kenzie and Grandmom with baby goat

Jake & Kenzie enjoying God's aromatherapy

Grandson David and me

4th of July in the Poconos

Enjoying my piano in our Pocono home

Herb & Jillian (Marching Band)

Daddy & me (age 17)

Josh & me

Cousins L-R, Kenzie, Samantha, Makayla, Gabby, Brooklyn & Alyssa

Melanie & me

Herb in Vietnam

David & David, father & son

Pop Pop & Jake

Rachele & me with Davey & Steven

Graduating from Nursing School

L-R Jillian, me & Rachele

David & Jayne

Ryan, Jen, Kenzie & Jake

Mom holding Diane, Grandmom, Daddy, Aunt Helen
(mom's only sibling) Eddie & me in front

Kenzie & Jillian

Grandson Brandon & me

Me & grandson Jamie at Archway Programs where I worked. Jamie volunteered his time to be of service to me & the students.

Front row Amber, Steven, Nikki & Bobby; Back row Kevin & Trudi

Kenzie

Mark left, Kevin right

L-R Mark, Kevin, Rachele

Jillian & David

Jake

Kenzie

L-R Brooklyn, Kenzie, Makayla, Gabby

Mermaids – L to R Gabby, Makayla, Kenzie

George & Rachele

George and me with Mark

L-R George, David, Ryan, Steven, Kevin, Herb at
Ryan's corrections officer graduation.

Aunt Floss (Daddy's sister) & Uncle Stan's Wedding,
Left; Flower Girl me, Right; Loretta

Me and Natalie Rose

L-R Aunt Rita, Uncle Earl, Aunt Jo (Daddy's two sisters)

Aunt Rita & Uncle Earl

L-R Mark, Kevin, David & Rachele in Margate, NJ

Jillian & mommy (Jillian's favorite photo)

Jillian caught wedding bouquet at Rachele's wedding, Mark caught
garter (this was taken two weeks before his diving accident.)

L to R Jillian, Mark & Ryan

Mountain View Standard News Wednesday, December 9, 2009

Mountain View youth, Tyler Rulon, who attended dinner at the Governor's Mansion with Governor Jay Nixon because of his success in the Next-Generation Jobs Team summer youth employment program. (Photo submitted to the Standard)

Tyler 2nd from right in Newspaper article (courtesy
of Mountain View Newspaper)

Jillian & Herb

Rachele & Josh on Appalachian Trail

Jake and me

Kevin & Trudi with granddaughter Courtney

Kenzie & Jake raising the flag with hands on hearts

David & me

Me & Granddaughter Nikki

Bobby & Nikki

Herb & me on our wedding day with our beautiful family: Back Row, L to R: Ryan, David, Elwood (Rachele's first husband) and Kevin; Middle Row: Bev, Jillian, me, Herb, Rachele & Trudi; Front Row: Nikki & Steven

Mary & Mike & their family: Front row L to R, Brooklyn, Ryan, Mike, Mike's mom Gertrude, Mary, Makayla & Gabby Back row: Michele, Arthur, Collin, Melanie, Brian, Michael (in stripes), Tim, Paul, Scarlett, Jay & Missy

Diane's family, Pennypack Park: L to R, Peter, Jen, Debbie, Brittany, Diane,
Jimmy, Jacob (partially hidden) John (with clock) Jackson, Renee, Olivia,
Ed & Mason, Julie, Bear; front: Jonathon, Josh, Haley &
(some family members are missing)

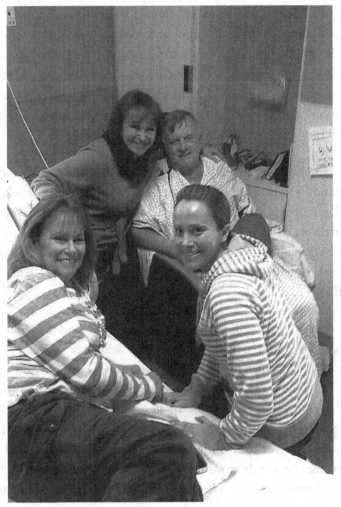

Front: Mary & Missy, Herb & me (note Photo of Jillian & Herb on shelf);
Though not a flattering photo of Herb, it was one of our happiest times.
We had come so close to losing him. This was five days after cardiac
surgery & we were all so grateful to God for this miracle.

HELP!!

I was unusually nervous about this class. I arrived early, prayed, told God I'd do my best but needed His help. Keep in mind that help comes from strange places when you are God centered. I was reading Bill O'Reilly's book "A Bold Fresh Piece of Humanity, a title given him by one of the nuns who taught him. The very last paragraph I read before going into the classroom was about how Bill handled the students he taught, because they weren't much younger than him. The very last sentence I read was "Even in my callow youth, I knew boundaries would have to be quickly established or chaos would ensue."

Considering how distraught I was and ill prepared (I did pray and study beforehand but my mind kept wandering) I felt sure Jesus would see to it that I got an easy class. My first student and parent arrived. The parent introduced her child and said "He has no respect for anyone or anything, especially the church. Good luck!" I felt like walking out but I didn't. I asked Jesus to guide me with His Holy Spirit. It was then I remembered what Bill O' Reilly had said.

I asked the students to take a seat, introduced myself and then asked them to introduce themselves. My problem student would not sit and was getting the rest of the class riled up. I asked him one more time to sit down and do me the courtesy of remaining quiet. He stood (literally) his ground. Bill O'Reilly's words were echoing in my head. It's now or never to establish who's in charge. I walked up to this boy, my face just inches from his and loudly said "PARK IT!" I think he was so shocked to hear a teacher talk this way, that he just dropped to his seat. He also was respectful, helpful and considerate after that. He turned out to be one of my best students. All I did was set the parameters.

Another class I had was younger, third grade. My granddaughter Makenzie was in it which was really a fun experience. The class was one of my best. The children were so conscientious and wanting to learn more about Jesus and their faith. They absorbed information like a sponge. Our routine was to say a prayer before we started. We would hold hands and thank Jesus for anything and everything, and I do mean that literally. Many would be thankful for family, friends, and as Kenzie would often say, freedom. They were thankful for their homes, bicycles, video games and toilets. Did I just say "toilets?" I did. We even discussed that at length, how years ago their great grandparents would have to go outside in the snow to the outhouse. They were truly an appreciative group.

LET GO AND LET GOD

One day we got a new student who refused to hold hands, said he had nothing at all to thank Jesus for and was not going to pray with us. I was dumbfounded. I encouraged him to think of something. Surely, his family. Nope. He had no intention of going to church either. I asked him how he had gotten to my room. He walked in. So I said that he could thank Jesus for his healthy legs. I told him that I worked with children who couldn't walk and were in wheelchairs. He was recalcitrant. He was not going to pray.

At first I was annoyed with this child. Then I had to ask myself, what kind of family problems did he have. Probing a little farther, revealed many problems. I just prayed and continued to ask for Divine Help. It came, but not the way I expected. I asked my Ryan if he would speak to the class. I had told them how he prayed for seven years to become a police officer. I had shown the kids his picture and some recognized him. This stubborn child was so impressed that I had a son and Kenzie had a father who was a police officer. Ryan, of course, would not do this.

A couple of weeks later Ryan brought Kenzie up to my class. One of the other teachers had asked me to go downstairs and collect two of my students who were awol, so to speak. I couldn't leave the class alone so I asked Ry if he would stay with them while I got my other two students. He said he would. As I was leaving, I heard my student (the one who refused to pray) ask Ryan if he had really prayed seven years. Ryan, of course, confirmed it. This boy was full of questions, when do you pray, how often. I smiled as I ran down the stairs. I couldn't orchestrate Ryan's help, yet God did. By the time I got back it was time for our prayer. I had no intention of asking Ry to stay for the prayer, yet it came out of my mouth when he leaned down to kiss me goodbye. Ryan stayed, everyone including this boy, held hands. Ryan and everyone else thanked Jesus for something…even my very stubborn child. Thanks Ry.

DOES GOD ANSWER EVERY PRAYER?

When teaching fourth graders in CCD (Confraternity of Christian Doctrine) class, they often remarked that God didn't answer their prayers. I told them that He answers ALL prayers. Some, He answers "yes", some He answers "no" and some He answers "wait". One little boy was asking God for a bicycle for his little brother. That was commendable and selfless. Why would such a generous prayer go unanswered? I don't profess to know what God's reasons were but this little boy needed an answer. Since I've lived in excess of sixty years, there are some things that come to me, at times, recalling experiences I've had. Again, remember that I pray all day long. So when this boy posed this question to me, my immediate thought was "Jesus, please send Your Holy Spirit to guide me". I explained that even though the bicycle seemed like a good thing, maybe God saw that your brother was too young to handle that responsibility. Maybe, God was preventing an accident. Maybe, He was saying "Wait. In a year or too, your brother will be able to handle it better."

I also like to give the example of a small child reaching for the pretty blue flame on the stove, or the orange flame in the fireplace. The child sees something pretty and desirable. They reach for it and the parent slaps their little hand and says "No!" The child cries. The slap hurts and they think that their parent is mean. The child is too immature to sense the danger in the situation and doesn't realize that the "No!" was a loving no. We do the same thing with God. We think that we know what's best for us and become upset if our prayers aren't answered the way we want them to be. I know from experience that we, too, are like that child. We're too immature spiritually and can't see that far into the future. But God can. Trust Him. There's a country singer who also confirms this with his song "Thank God for Unanswered Prayers."

CCD CLASS (Confraternity of Christian Doctrine): Also known as Faith Formation

I taught the fourth grade class of twelve boys and loved it. Eventually one girl came to class. The boys were not happy. They said "This will spoil things Mrs. Rose". I thought so too, but, of course, would not voice that thought. Rachel was the daughter of Michele, my son Mark's first love. Since I was close to Michele, her daughter would be welcomed. Rachel had so many questions, so many doubts about Jesus' personal interest in us, in her. She had a way of challenging me every week. She was beautiful and so intelligent and inquisitive. She reminded me of my Jillian.

I had to answer her questions. God had a way of providing answers to my students by ways of humbling experiences for me. Some of them I wasn't too happy about. However, I always did recognize His Hand in it and thanked Him.

One afternoon when class was over, Rachel needed a ride home. Since she lived two blocks from me, I said I'd gladly take her home. Keep in mind that I had just ended my class the way I do every week. I told my class to rely on Jesus for everything. Always ask Him to be a part of whatever you're doing—playing, taking a test, shopping, riding your bike, etc. He'll never let you down.

On the way home, my car died. I coasted to the side of the road and moaned. It was a narrow road with heavy traffic, Rt. 561 near Nardi's deli, not a very safe place to be. Rachel was upset because she was afraid that she'd be late for her dance class. She said, "Call someone on your cell phone." She couldn't believe that I didn't have one. I still don't have one and it's November 2013. I tried to start the engine several times, unsuccessfully. "What are we going to do?" she asked. I took her hand and said that we were going to pray and ask Jesus for help.

I talked to Jesus as if He was in the car with us. Jesus we thank You for all the gifts you give us everyday...life, family, friends, food. But right now we need You to help us with this car. Rachel needs to go to dance class and I need to get home. It's not very safe on this road with all the traffic zipping by. You said, "Anything two or more ask for in My Name, I will give you." Please start the car. I turned the key and it started right up. Rachel was so excited. She remarked that Jesus answers quickly. The car went about fifty yards then died again. Jesus gave me exactly what I asked for. He started the car.

At this point, I felt so frustrated. Now, Rachel was really confused. In my mind, I kept saying to Jesus, "You can't let Rachel down—forget me, but show her You care. I know that you do, but she doesn't....not yet. After all these years, I still find myself giving instructions to God. I need to practice what I preach.

Rachel said, "Now what do we do?" I took her little hand again and said, "We pray again. Dear Jesus, please get us some help so that Rachel can get home in time for class and that I can just get home. Thank You." I told Rachel to get out of the car and we'd go to a nearby house and ask to use the phone. She listened well to her mom's caution about strangers. She said that we couldn't go to a stranger's house and refused to move. I explained that we weren't going to go in the house but would hand the person the paper with her mom's phone number and ask them to call her. She still did not feel comfortable.

I was becoming exasperated. I said, "Rachel, we have to do something. God helps those who help themselves." Just then a car sounding its horn pulled up behind my car. The sun was in my eyes so I couldn't even tell who it was. I heard a car door slam and a tall figure walked toward us. A familiar voice said, "Miss Rose, do you need help?" As my eyes focused, I saw that it was George, the Maintenance Supervisor from Archway School where I worked. He handed me his phone since he knew I didn't have a cell phone. I called and reassured Rachel's mother. While on the phone with her, another car pulled up. Rachel was beside herself with excitement. It was her friend on the way to her dance class. I relayed this information to her mom, who told me to let Rachel go with her.

Before she left I asked Rachel if she understood what had happened here. There were no doubts in her eyes anymore. She knew that Jesus cared about her, personally. Not only did she not challenge me at the next class, she witnessed to the others how Jesus started the car, found us a cell phone and got her a ride to dance class, right on time.

2012 NEW JOB!

I thought that I was retired. God had other plans. The summer of 2012 brought new surprises. We were having our annual CCD family picnic. My friend, Bea and Herb and I were talking when Bea told me that my name had come up, as a replacement for Sister Rose, who had moved from our parish. If I took the job, I would become the next "Pastoral Associate of the Sick". I wasn't interested. I'd rather teach CCD.

I have no sense of direction and the job entailed visiting the sick and dying, and people who just couldn't leave their homes due to physical disabilities. It covered several towns. I could visualize myself getting lost and having panic attacks. Herb jumped into the conversation and said that he thought I'd be great. In fact, when he saw a notice in the church bulletin, he immediately thought of me. He forgot to mention it to me. I guess this was my first confirmation, my husband's approval and support.

I still wanted time to think and pray about it. I, of course, wanted more confirmation also. I wanted to change the subject. I saw Lou coming towards us and asked him to sit down. He and his wife Karen have become close friends. I was their son's CCD teacher for several years. Anyway, I asked Lou what was new with him. He proceeded to tell me that he had been busy volunteering with the Multiple Sclerosis community, making phone calls and determining if anyone needed any help in any area. He was a liaison of sorts. This really impressed me because Lou also has a diagnosis of MS and has difficult times to say the least. He discovered that volunteering to help others was the best thing for him, and very rewarding. Is this my second confirmation Lord, that I should be helping others?

I took the job after talking with our pastor. I also continued to teach CCD or Faith Formation as it's called now. I was given a car and a list of people to visit. I'd drive to church in my car for the 8:00 am Mass. Father would place the Consecrated Hosts in my pyx (a small container for carrying the Consecrated Hosts to the sick). By 8:45 I'd be on my way to visit, pray with and distribute Communion to "my people" as I began calling them.

On my first day, I felt so ill prepared for this ministry. I asked Father Jose to please give me a blessing before I left. His words calmed me and brought tears to my eyes. I felt the enormity of what I was being asked to do. I felt honored. This was a privilege. I need to make it clear that this was NOT a depressing job. I spent an average of thirty minutes with each person, some even longer. They were hungry for company.

I've mentioned that I don't believe in coincidences. I believe they are Christ incidences because He is at the center of everything. My first few days of visiting people for the first time was a prime example. I had been so nervous and by the end of the day, I was laughing, feeling comfortable and also feeling like I had entered the Twilight Zone. The first women I met were Josephine, Florence, Genevieve and Rita and Helen. Unusual names for sure. How about those being the names of all my aunts. I was close to all my aunts, all of whom were already in heaven. However, I felt their presence that day. I couldn't help but think that God had orchestrated this.

I had up to thirty-eight people to visit over several days. I felt like I was on a treadmill. I also found myself getting very close to certain people...many people. I'm human, I have favorites. I found myself talking about them, how uplifting they were to me. I'd also ask others to keep them in prayer. My daughter-in-law Trudi told Herb not to be surprised if he came home one day and the wheelchairs and walkers were lined up around the pool.

There was Bette who loved to read. I started out taking a book each week, for her to read, then two a week. Finally, I took a whole shopping bag of books. She had an insatiable appetite for reading. Her son-in-law said that she reads, day and night. I met her family. Her daughter, Maria is also battling cancer and is one of the strongest woman *I'll ever meet and has a matching faith.*

I had another mother and son to visit. Mary also is an avid reader and we'd spend time discussing authors, families and doctors. I'd walk in the house and shout, "I'm home! She loved that. Mary was in her eighties, on oxygen and walked with a walker, yet she made her son Frank's meals. Frank was sixty and bedridden and he worked via computer at home. He was extremely intelligent, pleasant and interesting. He had recently had his second leg amputated. Yet, his outlook was positive. Both of them were so appreciative of the visit and especially being able to receive our Lord in Communion.

About four months into my ministry, my Ryan said that he noticed a change in me. My energy level had changed and he thought I was showing signs of stress. He also saw my list of names and addresses and the police officer in him surfaced. He was adamant about me not going to two of the locations because they were in dangerous areas. I heeded his advice on that. Even in difficult situations, God was watching over me. This next incident will clarify that. I showed up at Frank and Mary's house unexpectedly. It was not my usual day. I just felt strongly that I should go.

When I arrived at the house there was a police car outside. Frank's male nurse was also outside. I assumed there was a problem with Frank since his medical issues were more severe. I ran up the ramp and was shocked and pleased to see that the police officer was my son Ryan. He hugged me then I ran to see Frank, who was crying. I asked if he was in pain. He looked confused and said "Roe, how did you know to come? Who called you?" He explained that his mother had just died. He realized something was wrong when she didn't bring him breakfast. As for my answer, it's obvious that the Holy Spirit imparted that urgency in this unplanned visit.

I ran into the other room and found Mary, looking very peaceful. I laid hands on her and prayed over her. I then called the rectory for a priest to administer the last Sacrament to Mary. Frank was so grateful. He said his mom would love that. Father Jose was there in ten minutes, hugged me then asked me to take him to Mary. He left and our good friend, Jim, our funeral director arrived. He hugged me and said, "What are you doing here Rose?" I said this is my work, Jim.

I was fine until everyone left, then I broke down. Ryan hugged me again and said "Mom, you have to quit. Look what this is doing to you." I saw it a different way. Yes, it was upsetting but in reality I knew that Mary was well and happy now. The tears were a release. And look what God did for me in this situation. He sent three people I love, to comfort me!

As it turned out, I only worked for another two months. I had been having a lot of pain in my knees, back and wrists—so much so that I was limping and couldn't even turn a door knob without pain. I do have osteoarthritis, but it was never this severe. I couldn't figure out what I had done that caused it to get to this point. I was looking forward to the break at Christmas. Within a week, the pain was gone. Apparently, getting in and out of the car so many times a day and turning the steering wheel had exacerbated my joints. I gave a month's notice to Fr. Jim. The six months that I had worked as a Pastoral Associate for the Sick, provided me with a lifetime of memories.

I had made so many friends that I still visit some of the people, regularly, but at my own pace or when I'm in the area. Other people, I'll call. Becoming close to these people, I was aware, was setting me up for heartache. I've been to more funerals this year than in all my adult life. Then again, it's not always sad. I look at older people and at times, envy that they are "closer to the finish line." as author Nick Vujicic would say, and he's decades younger than me.

My daughter-in-law Trudi predicted that somehow, some way, I'd get Herb involved with these people. We both denied that. Yet, that's exactly what happened. After I stopped working, Herb and I would visit a few people, sit and talk with them, have coffee and pray with them. My wonderful husband was perfectly comfortable with this.

I'll never forget the first person he visited. Agnes was well into her nineties, bedridden, frail but cognizant of everything. She was also blind but could make out shadows. She had loved reading and now her daughter supplied her with audio books. She took her privilege to vote, very seriously. Her daughter got her an absentee ballot, after she took her mother in a wheelchair, to vote and they wouldn't let her go in the booth with her mom to help her find the right buttons. What an example to all the people who don't even bother to vote. Agnes was still beautiful with her delicate features. I learned that she loved to square dance when she was younger.

Of course, I mentioned Herb and through normal conversation and she felt like she was getting to know him. One of the first things Agnes would say to me was "How's Herb?" She wanted to meet him and she was afraid that it wasn't going to happen. She knew she didn't have much time. I told Herb. That Saturday I called her daughter Ceal and asked if we could stop by. I asked her not to tell her mother that I was bringing Herb. I wanted to surprise her. I held Agnes's hand and like clockwork, she started to ask how Herb was…..then stopped and looked towards the doorway. She could see shadows and there was a very tall shadow and she smiled and said "You brought Herb!" My eyes misted up as he kissed her and held her hand the entire time.

I feel so blessed to have been offered the opportunity to take part in this ministry and to meet so many people that have been an inspiration to me. I have so many stories about "My people", but that would be an entire book in itself.

Thank you Jesus…..

NOVEMBER 25, 2013

Today was the Thanksgiving dinner for the seniors, at our church. We've gone the last few years and it has been a real treat. Our friend Bea Raiker orchestrates everything and all the teens are the waiters and waitresses. They also provide entertainment, usually a pianist and singers. Herb and I thoroughly enjoy this occasion and spending time with our church family.

This year was especially meaningful. God had some more surprises for me. I'm still recuperating from my breast surgery, but am feeling well. When we walked in, the first one to rush over to us was Abbie. I am so drawn to this beautiful, thoughtful teenager who gives the brightest smiles and best hugs. Herb feels the same connection too. She was concerned about me and had been praying for me, as was her whole family. I even got a hug from her brother Colin, which surprised me. I saw her mom, Ann Marie also. The only ones missing were Emma and their dad, Jim. They all are so loving and warm. We usually see them at Mass.

Then my friend Dennis Chang came over to greet us and we sat together for dinner. It gave us a chance to catch up on a few things, although I do see Dennis from time to time at Mass or at St. Vlincent De Paul Thrift Shop, which I've been known to frequent.

I got an even bigger surprise when Cecelia, whom I haven't seen since her mother went home to heaven, came over to talk to Herb and me. This was more than a coincidence since I had just written in my book about Agnes, Ceal's's mother, a few nights ago. I think of her often and when I go to take flowers to Jillian and Mark's grave, I "visit" Agnes who is in close proximity to them.

Cecelia had brought something with her, hoping to see me. She went to her car to get it. I was so emotionally moved to see her mother's cobalt blue glass crucifix and two plaques of Jesus and our Blessed Mother. They are from the 1940's and exquisite. I had admired them when I used to visit with Ceal and Agnes, and pray with them and give Communion to Agnes. I feel so blessed and grateful and honored to receive such a treasure.

I've missed seeing Cecelia, Agnes, John, her husband and Maggie, their golden Lab. John has a green thumb and his plants and flowers are magnificent. He's made a mini Longwood Gardens at his home. I've been the recipient of several of his plants. The philodendrum he gave me is literally taking over the living room it's so big. Maggie has cancer too but is comfortable. Cecelia suggested we get together for lunch. I plan to do that soon. I can't pass up the blessing of another friend…Thank you Jesus for providing so much support for me.

UPDATE

It's November 2013. Our parish has a new family member, Sister Anne who visits parishoners who can't get to church. She is an amazing woman with a beautiful sense of humor. The people love her. I know because I continue to talk to some of them. There are two women that I still visit twice a month, and one that I take Communion to. I treasure their friendship and one of them, Amy, I talk to frequently. She is an extremely strong woman. She had cancer, one of her daughters has cancer, and her grandson died in a construction accident. She's been through so much and her faith just keeps getting stronger. No matter what negative things are going on, she is able to interject humor and make me laugh. I love her so much.

The other woman I visit is Gladys. She's beautiful, in her early eighties and has a dynamite personality and sense of humor. She is on dialysis and her son Steve takes care of her, which in itself is a feat because Steve is in constant pain from back injuries, despite surgery and medical intervention. There are also days he cares for his little grandson. I've become emotionally close to Steve and Gladys.

Even Steve's son John is an amazing, selfless young man. He was on break from college when I began radiation treatments for breast cancer. He wanted to take me for my treatments since he was home. I assured him that it was no big deal because side effects were minimal. I thanked him for his offer and was deeply touched by his concern.

Gladys is beautiful inside and striking physically with her long flowing silver hair held back by a black headband. She has six sons, one of whom is in heaven, so we share even that. She has innumerable stories of her childhood, her husband who died very young, and her children. There are even Dr. Berger stories because she lived on the same street his office was on. There are so many parallels in our lives. She also has started garnering stories to write a book as a legacy for her children.

She made a remark the other day, that put voice to my thoughts. "Why couldn't we have met years ago. We'd have been such close friends. We would have…however, we are grateful for our friendship now.

It really is true that the more you open your hands to give to others, God is able to fill those open hands with His gifts. They are too numerous to mention all of them, but one stands out in my mind because it came at a difficult time for me. I had gotten to know another family on my visits. Bert is a retired teacher and was caring for his aunt who was in the last stages of cancer. I would also see him at daily Mass. Sometimes I'd see his gorgeous wife who also had cancer. When his aunt died, I'd see him and his wife at Sunday Mass. There would be hugs and promises of continued prayer.

One visit with Bert's aunt was so memorable because of "Danny Boy" and "Murphy", the family's two Boxers. I had just reached out to take his aunt's hand and said "Let's pray." Danny Boy who had been sitting by me placed his big paw right on top of our clasped hands, as if he understood. The three of us prayed together.

I hadn't seen this family for a few weeks. I was in the checkout line in Shop Rite. I stopped on the way home from my radiation treatment. I was feeling hopeful but also was concerned. I was depressed. There was another lady in line after me, when all of a sudden, Bert slides past her to hand me a rose. He knew I had cancer and just wanted to lift my spirits with a rose and a promise of prayer. His brilliant smile made my day. It happened so quickly and I was moved to tears, happy tears, that the clerk asked "What just happened?" God blessing me with yet another friend. With all the tears I shed, I find the statement "Tears can be healing" to be true. I just can't recall who said it.

UPDATE

Bert's beautiful wife Donna, has since succumbed to her cancer. Bert still attends Mass, daily. His faith, through all his heartache, shines through as an example to all who know him.

THOUGHTS ON AGING

I'm sure that you've heard the old adage "You're only as old as you feel." Don't believe it, at least not entirely. Herb and I are both 62. I still feel like I did in my forties. That's good, believe me. I was able to dance for hours in spiked heels. Now, I can barely walk in them.

Herb, on the other hand, says he feels like he's ninety on some days. However, that doesn't slow him down. Probably the biggest part of his problem, not discounting aches and pains, is sleep deprivation. He averages five hours of sleep a night, sometimes less. He's always so busy at the computer or puttering around in the garage or inventing things. This is at the end of a full day at the Philadelphia Airport. He's on call 24/7 and yes, he's received calls at 2:00 am and 3:00 am on a Saturday or Sunday.

Despite the fact that I feel younger, my body refuses to cooperate. There is a huge disparity between how I feel and how I look when I see my image in the mirror. I'll just leave it at that. I'm young at heart. Let me preface this chapter with a very heartfelt thank you to God for all the years my body has worked without incident. Of course, parts are going to wear down. I am not complaining but stating facts, forewarning all my girls— it's coming!

My mother used to tell me that a woman's weight will shift around the age of forty. I was feeling pretty confident when I was able to wear a two-piece bathing suit well into my forties. I had defied gravity. Then it happened.... overnight. I kid you not. I happened to look in the mirror while drying myself off after my bath. I did a double take. I couldn't take my eyes off of my butt. What happened to it???? It had dropped, the firmness was gone. If it had been any lower, it would be behind my knees.

Next thing I noticed was that my, almost nonexistent, hips had bloomed and were covered with "ugh" rolls, like gigantic marshmallows on each side. I've looked at the charts and I am not considered overweight, so why did this happen? Then I started noticing dimpling all over my thighs— cellulite. I've had six children, weighing eight and nine pounds and I have no stretch marks. I escaped that but, obviously, can't escape the ravages of time.

I've always been told that my legs are my best feature. When I get dressed in a short dress (down to the knees) the legs still look good, from halfway across the room. I wear pantyhose even when the temperature is in the nineties. They do much to improve the look of my legs. Now if only someone would design a pair to be worn under bathing suits. I'm all for the old fashioned bloomer bathing suits to make a comeback.

Our little granddaughter, 'Kenzie, was cuddling with me one day and began tracing her tiny fingers along my very pronounced blue veins on the top of my hands and asked, "What are these grandmom?" They are just one more indication, along with age spots, that I am aging faster than I want to.

I now need a first-aid kit when I go out and I'm healthy. I haven't even had a cold in over two years. I need drops for my eyes. As you get older they start to dry out. I carry extra panties and liners in case I laugh or cough (stress incontinence). At least I'm not alone in this. When I worked at Archway I used to buy panties at the dollar store and keep a supply of them in the nurses' office. I can't count the times that one of the staff would come down and take advantage of my emergency supply. What a perk. Most of the women who came down were much younger than me, which made me feel infinitely better.

I need medicine, since my gallbladder was removed, before I can even eat in the morning. Then although I've never had a problem for fifty-five years with any food, I now find that if I eat too much fruit or sweets, I need another medicine. I don't want to get too graphic here, so you can figure it out for yourself. It's just over-the-counter meds. I do have lactose intolerance so that means lactaid tablets and, of course, gas x when I'm all done eating.

My skin turgor has changed too. Pinch the skin on your forearm. In a younger person, it springs right back to its original state. In someone older, you pinch it and it stays, like little mountain ridges. I never used moisturizer on my face until I reached my fifties. I didn't need it. I started using it, not realizing how desperately my skin was sucking it up until one time when we were staying with friends in Missouri. I had showered and realized that I hadn't packed my moisturizer. Oh well, no problem. I was reading my book in bed. It was late and everyone was already asleep. I had this new sensation, stiffness and a tingling in my face. I couldn't smile and could barely talk, except through clenched lips because my face was so taut. I looked in the bathroom drawers and closet—nothing. I went into a second bathroom. There had to be something, hand cream, Preparation H (models use it), anything. I finally found some vaseline. My next stop would have been the refrigerator. I just know that I'll never forget my moisturizer again.

There are so many products to help us look younger. They don't work no matter how much they cost. One of the most highly rated creams to decrease cellulite is made by Avon. You can't get more reputable than that. It was a costly expenditure for me but if it worked, it would be well worth it. When my Avon lady handed me the bag, I looked, with disbelief, at the tiny tube. This is not going to work I told her. I need to take a bath in the stuff.

Herb says nothing about his aches and pains. He is definitely not a complainer. He has two torn rotator cuffs that are beyond repair. It hurts him to lift a mug of coffee. Yet, he'll dig and plant and paint and just bear the pain. I guess misery loves company and one time I asked him why he doesn't tell me when something hurts. He remarked that it would be much quicker to tell me what doesn't hurt, his hair. He also has an aortic aneurysm.

Today I had a cervical spine X-ray because the nerve extending from my neck to my hand is causing me pain. I also have several herniated discs. It hurts when I play the piano or type. I play anyway. I love to and I won't stop. It hurts when I lift my grandchildren. At times, I improvise because I can only lift a certain way. That's okay. I will not stop lifting them. The joy I experience with them far exceeds any discomfort.

My neck hurts when I turn a certain way so I make sure to find two parking spots together so I can pull straight through and avoid turning my head when backing out. There's always a solution.

My knees crackle like Rice Krispies when I walk up and down steps (arthritis), but my new hip implant is working great. That eliminated so much pain. I have very few limitations, though there are a few. Keeping all this in mind along with Herb's disabilities with his shoulders, my shoulder and neck, Rachele asked if this was causing any problems in the bedroom. I laughed and said that we still manage very well. However, with all the joint problems, she said that it must be like playing "Twister" and having sex at the same time. Creativity and a sense of humor are crucial. Of course, we're also very thankful to God for the beautiful gift of sex. Does that shock you? It shouldn't. He's the One that designed us this way. As Duck Dynasty's Phil Robertson tells his grandchildren, sex is a gift for married people.

This week has been filled with doctor's appointments. Again, I'm very grateful that we're both healthy. These are "maintenance" visits. In the last week I've had appointments with my dentist and family doctor. Herb had a podiatrist appointment. He's been limping for over a month (arthritis and bursitis). He also had an eye exam. Thank you God that we both have healthy eyes.

Today, June 12, 2007 I went for a scheduled, routine gyn exam and Pap test. I had tried to get my mammogram the same day. There were no openings until the end of July. I really wanted to get all the visits over with but no such luck. Just an inconvenience, nothing major. I've been struggling with mild depression and couldn't even be specific in my morning prayers. It's too much of an effort. Of course, there is some concern about the results of all my tests so I draw on one of my favorite Bible verses: Philippians 4:6 "Be anxious for nothing, but in everything by prayer and supplication, with thanksgiving, let your requests be known to God." This always eases my mind. My request was just for God to be in my day. Well, this day ran so smoothly, like a well-oiled machine.

I was given a 10:00 appointment that had just opened up, for the cervical spine Xray. As I was leaving the building, that inner voice, the Holy Spirit, told me to go back and ask about a cancellation for a mammogram. They sent me to the next building where I asked the receptionist if there were any cancellations for mammograms that day. She laughed and said, "I doubt it." We're booked solid. I explained that I had other appointments that day and I would appreciate it if she would double check. A look of surprise crossed her face as she checked on her computer, and then said that someone cancelled their appointment. "How's 12:20?" I was as dumbfounded as she was and took a few seconds before answering that it was perfect. I never expected an opening, but I also never ignore my inner voice. Ask and you shall receive.

I arrived half an hour early for my first two appointments and I was taken early, no waiting. That left me with an hour to kill before the mammogram. Since I had forgotten my book, I decided to treat myself to lunch, a Caesar salad, at the building next to the hospital. It's a combination of doctor's offices and a health center. I had an enjoyable lunch then went for my mammogram. They took me immediately and I was on my way home by 12:40. It pays to start your day with prayer.

UPDATE; Herb and I have recently celebrated our 70th birthday! A lot has changed, healthwise and otherwise, but we're still here. Our swimming pool is a lifesaver for me. I've been swimming at least forty laps a day. Herb is still working at the Philadelphia airport and toying with the idea of retirement. Only thing holding him back is the fact that we still have a mortgage and he does not get a pension. Big decisions ahead…more prayer needed.

APRIL 23, 2013 @ 9:30 pm DREADED DIAGNOSIS

"Troubles are often the tools by which God fashions us for better things."

The phone rings and I see Dr. Baker's name come up. I know already that it's not good news. I listen as he tells me that the biopsy from the lesion on my back is melanoma. That dreaded word that I feared all my life, cancer, is now a reality. I need a surgeon. It looks like it was caught early but there's no way to tell for sure until the margins are extended. "Be anxious for nothing and in everything through prayer and supplication, with a grateful heart, make your requests known to God." Phillipians 4:6

Our friend Linda is a person who talks to people that have "crossed over". In other words, a medium although she has never used that word to describe herself. Linda called and said that she had a message from Jillian. She (Jillian) knew I had cancer but I'd be fine in the end. These messages from the other side are comforting but take some getting used to. I asked a priest one time about this. He believes that certain people have gifts just as the saints did and they were ordinary people also. As long as everything is God centered there should be no fear.

Herb is quiet. He doesn't know what to say. I call Ryan. He has so much faith and also has faith in me that I can handle this "test". Jen and Rachele ask questions and offer prayers. Right now I feel numb. Initially, I felt nauseous and shaky. I talked to Jillian and Mark. I thought of all the people I visit in our parish, who have cancer.

I need to finish my book. Herb changed the dressing on my back and the back of my leg (my leg is fine), after my shower. It could have been worse. The lesion on my leg was not cancerous. We knelt, as always, by the bed for prayers. Then he just wanted to hold me in his arms. I have cancer but I am still blessed. I'm tired and on the verge of tears. I don't know why. I want to see Kenzie and Jake graduate and dance at their weddings. I need to hold my great grandchildren. Jesus, what are your plans for me? Help me to be strong for my family.

I woke up early. It was not a nightmare. I have cancer. I had tea, did laundry, ironing, hung Herb's shirts on the line. The sun feels so good on my face. The same sun that can damage our skin. The breeze is cool, the trees are greening up and the birds are singing. The laundry is blowing and I have my vision to enjoy it all. I'm not sick, not in pain, just busy making appointments. I am so blessed with friends and family.

I call to the rectory to put my name on the prayer list. I'll take all the prayers I can get. Soon word gets around and the phone calls start. Steve called and confirmed what Ryan said, it's a test, you'll pass it. Then another friend, also named Steve called. First thing he said was "It's a test Roe". I visit Steve's mom Gladys, who is on dialysis. Steve is dealing with severe back. injuries. They have it so much worse than me. Pat offered to go to appointments with me. My friend Donna has so many medical problems, but continues to work. I'm retired. I'm blessed again. Donna is coming over for lunch next week. Some friends, no matter how busy their schedule, their lives, make time to get together regularly....another blessing.

Clare called and asked if I got my results back. I told her and she was reassuring because she also, had melanoma. Bill will be able to walk Herb through the process of caring for the wound after surgery. It was a long process.

May 13, living ten days with cancer. Then again, maybe not. Hopefully, Dr. Sollitto removed all the cancer on May 7. Since I have 27 sutures on my back (the lesion was flat and half the size of a pencil eraser), he obviously did some digging. I don't care. I don't have to look at it. Mom, Mary and Diane came down. It was so good to see them and have a normal day. It helps so much.

Jake's T ball game tonight, Kenzie's softball game tomorrow. More shades of normalcy.

MAY 12 MOTHER'S DAY

Jillian's irises are in full bloom, another sign of God's grace. She loved that I planted them outside her bedroom window. It's like a rainbow, mostly deep purples, but there are light purple, yellow and white—a feast for the eyes.

May 15 Still waiting for the results of my surgery.

May 24 Margins are clear. Thank you Jesus!

My good news is tempered with Clare's bad news. She needs a partial mastectomy. We can't let up on the prayers. Clare and Bill are such an inspiration, so upbeat and quick to affirm. Bill says that he and Herb have a job to do...taking care of their girls. He's so positive and warm. On Sundays he'll come over before Mass starts, just to give me a hug. He and Clare usually sit on the opposite side of the church with their grandchildren. If their grandchildren don't come, they come and sit with us.

UDATE: Clare is doing well. Thank you Jesus!

STRANGE DREAM OR PORTENT?

In November of 2012 I went to our Nurse Practitioner, Heather, for a refill on my Tussionex that I would take for a persistent, unproductive cough. I would only take the medicine on Sundays or when I had a CCD class to teach, because the coughing episodes were so disruptive during Mass.

Even though I had been coughing for five and a half months, I didn't think that anything serious was wrong because my lungs were clear and I felt fine. I'd get these episodes as far back as I can remember. Heather refilled the prescription then strongly suggested that I see a Pulmonologist even though she confirmed my lungs were clear. She gave me the name of one. I assured her that I would follow through. However, when I got home and looked at the name of the doctor, I told Herb that I didn't want to go to him. He asked why and I was unable to give him a plausible answer. I didn't know the doctor but I trusted Heather completely. It was a gut feeling or maybe the Holy Spirit guiding me.

He then asked me whom I wanted to go to. I said I didn't know anyone and asked if he could pull some names up on the computer (I'm computer illiterate). He found several and I picked out Dr. Morowitz, no rhyme or reason. I made my appointment and the night before I was to see him, I had a dream. I couldn't see the doctor's face in my dream, but I thought I heard him say that I had a few years to live. I asked him to confirm it and he said, "Not a few years, just two." That dream disturbed me. I started out not having any concerns about my cough but by the time I pulled up in the parking lot of the doctor's office, I was prepared for the worse.

Before I left for the appointment, I called Rachele and shared my dream with her and asked for prayers. She usually makes light of things like that. This time, her silence reinforced my ominous feeling. I guess I was thinking lung cancer from secondary smoke. George had smoked three packs a day for as long as I could remember.

The doctor was wonderful. He even took my medical history himself which I found unusual. I was tested for about an hour. I waited for the diagnosis as he pored over the results. He said that he couldn't find anything wrong. He then asked if I had either a post nasal drip or a reflux. I had both. He said to take Zyrtec for two weeks and call him back with the results. I laughed. How will allergy medicine help? He said that it might not but he felt it was worth a try. If it didn't resolve the problem then he would do additional testing.

By now you know that if an opportunity presents itself, I will interject Mark and Jillian into the conversation and whip out my photos of them and all my children. Well, there was no opportunity or opening for me to bring them up. Yet, for some reason, I did it anyway. Dr. Morowitz looked upset and sat down. He asked me how I get through this. Of course, my faith, my God get me through it, but I never get over it.

Christmas was coming up and he expressed a sympathy and compassion that was obvious. I started to tell him about the balloons with notes that we send up on Christmas Eve and he raised his hand and asked me to please stop. He was visibly moved. He then shared with me a tragic experience that he was witness to when he was young. His friend's sister had died and he said that the family was never the same after that.

It was obvious that this long ago incident remained fresh on his mind and heart and troubled him. It even played a part in his choosing to become a doctor. He stood and thanked me for sharing my story with him. I thanked him for allowing me to. I was keeping him from his other patients. I told him that he was a blessing to me. He hugged me and said, "No, it's me who is blessed to have met you."

I cried most of the way home, tears of release, tears of joy. I was healthy. I also was aware of the gift of God arranging for me to meet this extraordinary man. Yes, I was a patient, but I was also a stranger to him yet it didn't feel like that. He spent so much time with me when he had a waiting room full of people. I continue to pray for this doctor, daily.

I arrived home to a message from Rachele. She said that she had been praying for me, but felt strongly that nothing was wrong with me. She said "You'll probably have another human interest story to tell me. Maybe you were there for someone in the waiting room. I just know that this doctor's appointment wasn't for you alone." I called Rachele back and told her my story.

Did something I say help the doctor? I don't know. Next day was the tragic massacre of the children at Sandy Hook. I don't dare try to surmise how God uses these situations. I did think that, possibly, my words would help the doctor when feeling the pain that we all did when we heard about these innocent children and the ensuing agony for the parents. I remember telling Dr. Morowitz that even though I only had twenty years with my Mark and thirty-one years with Jillian, I am so grateful that He chose me to be their mother for that time. Those years are precious. I'm hoping that through all the pain of the parents, the gift of the time that they *did* have with their children, will sustain them, even though the pain *never* subsides.

After writing about the tragedy in Sandy Hook, I felt that Philip Yancey's words, as follows, are appropriate:

"For a good portion of my life, I shared the perspective of those who rail against God for allowing pain I could find no way to rationalize in a world as toxic as this one. As I visited people whose pain far exceeded my own, I was surprised by its effects. Suffering seemed as likely to reinforce faith as to sow doubt." I would hope that my faith is so solid that no amount of suffering can erode it....I'm trying.

Dr. Morowitz called me personally in two weeks to see how I was. I wasn't home to take his call, but he left a message. When I called him back, he was out so I left a message…telephone tag. Miraculously, the cough was gone. I can't believe all the years I suffered with these debilitating episodes of coughing, and the secondary problem of stress incontinence and sore ribs.

UPDATE; It's been ten months since that visit and I haven't had a recurrence of the cough even though I only took the Zyrtec for two weeks. When my cough returns twice a year, I immediately start the two week regimen over. However, I had another disturbing thought. I've since had surgery for Melanoma and I'm also scheduled for a biopsy of my breast tomorrow, October 24, 2013. I wonder if maybe the dream was fortuitous and does that two year time frame still exist. If so, I would have another fourteen months. Just a thought. Don't mean to be morbid…..Pray, pray, pray.

HERE WE GO AGAIN…..

SEPTEMBER 30, 2013

We're just back from Rachele's wedding and the doctors appointments start again. It feels like they're never ending. I had four appointments today, Pap test, Mammogram, Dexa-scan and Lumbar spine X ray. Pap test was normal. Dexa-scan reveals osteopenia plus it appears that I've shrunk two inches. I used to be 5'4". Lumbar spine test reveals moderate to severe osteoarthritis, three herniated discs and significant narrowing and degeneration of the spine. I believe that these are mostly age related. Also, lifting children out of wheelchairs for years may have been a contributing factor.

OCTOBER 9, 2013 Our 19th Wedding Anniversary

I received a call regarding my mammogram. I need to have another diagnostic mammogram and an ultrasound. The mammogram showed a mass in my left breast. While going through this routine again a conversation took place between me and one of the nurses who asked me who my doctors were. She was so young and had had melanoma in her early twenties. We had a lengthy discussion in which she confirmed that two of my doctors and my surgeon were the best I could possibly choose. She, also, believed that prayer is a significant factor in choosing doctors. I am literally surrounded by faith-filled people.

Emily, one of the girls at the Women's Center, went through the same thing last year. She is a woman of faith and so she did what came naturally—held my hands and prayed. We both talked to Jesus right there in the waiting room. She lifted my spirits. Even though my news wasn't great, God was still letting me know that He was right beside me. His love, this time, came through Emily.

Now I had to see a specialist. I have no idea who to go to. Jesus help me find someone and give me confirmation....please. I was speaking with my friend Maryann and told her what was happening. She asked if I knew of a good breast specialist. I said, "no". She told me that she had just had her mother to Dr. Diane Gillum, who is supposed to be one of the best. She said that her office was in Voorhees, but she didn't have her phone number. We talked a few minutes and then Maryann started laughing. She said I wouldn't believe what just happened. She accidentally bumped her Rolodex (aren't they obsolete?) and Dr. Gillum's card fell out. First confirmation. Now Maryann can't say that these spirit led incidents don't happen to her. She used to think they just happened to me.

I called to make the appointment. There were several doctors there and the girl I spoke with said that they were all good, but since Dr. Gillum was their most requested doctor, there would probably be a wait. Normally, I'd go with any of them but I told the girl that I prayed about this and felt that I was given Dr. Gillum's name in answer to prayer. She said "How's October 24 sound?"

In the meantime, I went to the rectory to arrange for candles for Jillian and Mark. While I was there I saw Bernie, who is a volunteer there. She had given me a beautiful figurine of an angel and a poem she wrote about my angel, when she heard I had melanoma. I don't see her often because she only works one day a week. She is such a positive, spiritual and humorous person. You can't help but smile in her presence. I asked her for prayers and told her why. She said that she had the best doctor ever do her mastectomy....Dr. Gillum. Second confirmation. Bernie related what she thought was a humorous story. When she was on the operating table, they stretched her arms out to the side and tied her down so she couldn't move. She said to the doctor "I feel like I'm being crucified." Dr. Gillum leaned down just inches from Bernie's face and responded "Then you're in good company."

I was scheduled for an ultra sound of my carotid artery. I called the day before to make sure that my primary doctor had received my referral and doctor's order. He had. I went the next day and my insurance company had minutes before, denied the test. I would have to go to a hospital for the test. Forget it, I said. I'm so overwhelmed now, I'm just not going to bother. I told them to have a blessed day and started to leave. One of the girls that I hadn't ever met, called me back and took me to an examining room. She did the ultra sound and told me the results were normal. Actually, she said my arteries looked like those of someone half my age. I didn't want her to get in trouble. She didn't seem concerned. She was so glad to give me good news. I cried I was so relieved. I hugged her and told her that she was an angel. Her name was Jen. Who gets a free ultra sound! It's amazing what God can do if we leave things in His Hands. I called a few days later to ask if Jen was working. I was going to drop off some soft pretzels and dips for the girls. They said they didn't have a Jen there.....I guess she really was an angel.

Next I had to go back to the Women's Center in Voorhees to pick up all my X rays from three previous years. I saw Emily again and she asked where I was going to have my biopsy done and by whom. I told her and she told me that she had had Diane Gillum for her surgery and said that she was wonderful. Third confirmation.

Back to our Nurse Practitioner, Heather. This time it's for Herb. He's got his yearly allergy related cough and needs Prednisone. While there, Heather asked if I had all my tests done. She hadn't gotten the results yet. I told her about my breast and she asked who I was going to. She had a strong recommendation for me—Diane Gillum had done her surgery when she was twenty years old! I was shocked. Fourth confirmation. I'm good to go.

HALLOWEEN 2013

Dr. Gillum calls. There *is* a problem. It is cancer but in the early stages and she doesn't think I'll need chemo. Thank God for that. Herb and I are going to see her tomorrow morning. She'll tell me my options. How do I feel? Surprisingly calm, no tears. I told the kids and a few of my closest friends. Ry, of course, said I'd be fine and that I'm strong. He actually said that I'm the strongest person he knows, given all I've been through. What a great compliment. I will be fine, no matter what happens.

My surgery is scheduled for November 18. It's a lumpectomy, which, in my case, is a misnomer since there is no lump, just abnormal cells. Outlook is positive. Thank you Jesus for that and for the calm I feel. It can only come from You. Rachele tells me "Mom, you are strong and true to our bloodline—strong Polish stock. We fight like a girl and more than most, we prefer to fight from our knees."

Dr. Gillum was reassuring me that cosmetically, there wouldn't be much change in my breast. I said that I didn't care about that. I placed my hands on my breasts and said that they had been working breasts, having nursed my six children. I'm done with them now. A loud voice pipes in "I'm not done with them." Herb and his timely sense of humor again. Dr. Gillum and I both laughed at my lovable husband.

NOVEMBER 18, 2013

Surgery went well. First nurse I saw was Iris (Jillian's favorite flower), second nurse was Julie. I'm beginning to feel comfortable. Julie is Josh's wife. I'm hearing familiar names. I took Jillian and Mark's photos in the operating room. The nurse placed them so I could see them. Other than nausea on the second day, I did well. I came home that day to a gorgeous arrangement of flowers from Kevin and Trudi. Trudi told me that Kevin had chosen them on his own. That meant so much to me.

NOVEMBER 22, 2013

Follow up visit and results of the tissue that was taken on the 18th. We're in the waiting room and Herb is still making me laugh, as well as the other people in the room. I got up to look at something and on the way back to my seat, I bumped into the corner of a chair. I knew I'd have a nasty bruise, it hurt so bad. Herb expressed concern then said, "I guess the next stop we make will be the eye doctor since I hadn't seen the chair."

When I was leaving the house earlier, Herb grabbed both our books. We don't go anywhere without a book. I happened to see another book "The Shack" in my bookcase. I actually have three of them. I'll buy extras at the thrift store so I can pass them on. I felt like I was being told to take one of the books, Holy Spirit working overtime. I glanced at all the people in the waiting room but wasn't getting any indication to give the book to anyone.

Now we're waiting in the examining room, waiting for Dr. Gillum. Herb asked why I brought "The Shack". I said that I had no idea, other than I felt I was being guided to. He looked down at the three books in his hands, his book, mine and "The Shack", and remembered something Dr. Gillum had said to him after the surgery was over. After telling him I was fine, she saw that he was reading a book by Bill O'Reilly and remarked that she had just finished reading his book "Killing Jesus". Herb told her that I had read it also, as well as his books "Killing Lincoln" and "Killing Kennedy", all excellent reading, by the way. Then she noticed my book by Anita Shreve. She also told Herb that she loves her books too. I asked him why he hadn't told me before and he said that he didn't think of it. Anyway, when Dr. Gillum walked in, I handed her "The Shack". Now I knew why I brought the book. She was visibly surprised because she had been wanting to read it. I told her to enjoy it and pass it on.

My results are good, margins are clear, however, we're not done yet. I may need radiation. That can best be determined by genetic testing. Dr. Gillum will send some tissue to the lab. Results will be forthcoming in about three weeks. I called to make an appointment with Dr. Ari, Chief of Staff. I will see him on December 2 for a consultation. As per usual, I look for my confirmation from on High. Before I chose Dr. Ari, I happened to see two separate articles in the Courier Post newspaper, extolling him. Once again, ask and you shall receive.

My friend Maureen called, insisting that she will go with me for the treatments. I told her it wasn't necessary. There are no side effects so I'll be able to drive. Once again, I am grateful that God has seen fit to bless me with such extraordinary, loyal friends. My friend Karen was sorry to hear about this next bout with cancer but told me, that for me, "it was just another blip in the radar. You're strong Roe. Take one for the rest of us." Believe it or not, this confidence in my ability to handle this was just what I needed.

Our days seem to revolve around doctor's appointments. I'm not complaining, just stating facts. I'm grateful to God for the good physicians in our lives. We had a much needed break in appointments and went to "Oceanos" for breakfast. Afterwards, we went to St. Andrew's for noon Mass because it's a holy day. Our church had an evening Mass but we didn't want to wait until then.

The priest at St. Andrew's was one that I hadn't seen in over ten years, Fr. Howard. He had been the pastor at Assumption Church in Atco. It was close to Archway School where I worked, so I'd often attend Mass before work. Ironically, I had just written about him in my book a few days ago. He's aged quite a bit and walking with a walker. I spoke with him before Mass and we promised to pray for each other.

Then, Victoria, one of Leslie and Michael's girls, came up to me and hugged me and sat with us. They are one of our 'church families.' After Mass, Tom and Gloria came over and hugged us. They also are friends from our church. Considering that none of us were from this parish, I found it interesting that we all showed up at a time when those hugs and support were needed. We went from there to our family doctor to get blood work done and make an appointment for an EKG. It was a productive day...I'm tired.

RADIATION

Radiation treatments began after Christmas and ended on January 28, 2014. I went every day, five days a week. Herb went with me for the first treatment and Jenny also came with me once. However, I was fine and not experiencing any side effects so I chose to go to treatments alone. I also treated myself to lunch and shopping at "Red, White & Blue" thrift store. I actually found myself looking forward to the day. It's ironic that for so many years I was terrified of getting cancer and now that I had it, the anxiety and fear was gone...lifted from me.

The environment was not the cold, white, sterile room that I had envisioned. There was dim, cozy lighting, illuminated beach scenes on the walls and ceilings and music. When asked what kind of music I preferred, I said that I'd come prepared next time and bring my Kevin's cds. Then, of course, I showed them my Kevin's picture, as well as those of all my children. At one point, I brought Jen and Herb in the room before my treatment started. I wanted them to see how beautiful and serene the setting was. Herb was focused on the equipment and was amazed at the massive size of it.

The women I met in the dressing room were amazing. Most of them were also undergoing chemotherapy. I was so thankful that I didn't need chemo. The strength and fortitude of these women, made me proud to be in their midst. No vestige of self pity in this group. Some were younger than me, many were my age. There was a 90 yr. old Italian woman who was spunky and comedic. Cancer took a back seat here to the determination and positive outlook of these women. Some were working full time and even picking up grandchildren between treatments.

Normally, I would see the same women every day. However, one day the equipment wasn't functioning. I hung around for over an hour hoping it would be repaired. Finally, I left at the nurse's suggestion. She said to call back in two hours. It was too far to go home so I visited a woman from our parish, who lived near the hospital. Then I went to Marshall's to kill some time. This was Jillian's favorite store. It was January and there were bathing suits on the racks. I had no intention of buying anything, least of all a bathing suit. Then I saw a navy suit with ruching which is great for hiding flaws. I had always wanted a navy suit and never found one to my liking. I tried it on and fell in love with it. I never looked at the tag until I came out of the dressing room. I balked at the price of $60.00 and was going to return it to the rack when I noticed the brand name "Juicy Couture". I got the chills. That was Jillian's favorite designer. I knew my Jillian had something to do with this so I decided to buy it. When I went to pull my charge card out of my wallet, a "Marshalls" gift card fell out. I was shocked because I could not recall anyone giving me a card. Anyway, I used it and ended up paying a mere $10.00 for it.

The manager, Karen, checked me out and specifically asked about Jillian. She wanted to know if I had her pictures all over the house for Christmas. Of course I did. It just seemed that no matter where I turned, Jillian made her presence known. Two hours later I called my doctor to see if the radiation equipment was working. It was not. I was told to call the next morning. I did and again was told it still was not working. I was upset because I was concerned this would delay my treatment deadline. One more call and I was told to come in late that afternoon. I then asked Jesus what was He orchestrating for me, with this delay. I needed to stop complaining and accept that there is a reason for everything.

I went in for my treatment early that evening. The waiting room, which was usually full, was empty except for one new patient, Colleen. She was my age and was visibly shaken. We talked as I was getting changed in the dressing room. She began to tell me about her husband who had died of cancer five years before. She believed that they would have had a better quality of life those last years, had he not undergone treatment.

Colleen was thinking of giving up. She told me how scared she was during her first treatment and that all she wanted to do was say the rosary and she couldn't remember the prayers. There was no way that she knew I was Catholic. Now I knew why I was there. I opened the dressing room door, reached into my purse and handed Colleen my beautiful rosary. She didn't want to accept it at first but I insisted or should I say the Holy Spirit insisted. She hugged me and kept thanking me.

The next day I was told by my radiologists that Colleen's spirits were sky high. She felt that God had sent her an angel when she needed one. She held the rosary each day when she underwent her treatments. I also brought in a pamphlet with all the prayers and mysteries of the rosary for her, which the radiologist passed on to her. One radiologist was moved to tears when Colleen explained why this little act of compassion had such a profound effect on her. God had planned our meeting. I only saw her one other time when she almost bowled me over in the hallway, with a bear hug.

LAST RADIATION TREATMENT

I took cookies in for the staff, banana breads the week before. One doctor, not even my doctor, hugged me and thanked me for the treats and said he'd miss me. I said my goodbyes, then my nurse and Dr. Ari met me in the waiting room. The receptionist gave me a flower and a hug, then, as is the tradition on completion of the treatments, I rang the bell three times and read a poem that was very significant. Everyone applauded, Dr. Ari hugged me and I cried, tears of joy for me, tears for the patients who still sat in that waiting room. Jenny and Herb were with me. Ryan had planned to be there but an unexpected snow day delayed the opening of Jake and Kenzie's schools. We went back to Ryan and Jen's and they treated us to lunch at a quaint Italian restaurant in Medford. Food and company were exceptional and the day was great. Once again, I'm cancer free!

CHIROPRACTOR

In between all the other doctor's visits, I made an appointment with Dr. Nicoletto. Confirmations came, unsolicited, in passing conversations. Angela, the owner of our favorite restaurant, said that Dr. Nicoletto actually saved her life. Another friend brought his name up when she heard that I had breast cancer. She's had a double mastectomy and goes to Dr. Nicoletto regularly. I strongly believe in alternative medicine, especially, since Herb had miraculous results with acupuncture.

I made a trip to South Jersey Radiology to pick up my x rays of my spine and also the reports. I wanted to be prepared. Dr. Nicoletto was amazing, gentle and very effective in his manipulations. I actually felt my spirits soar when he told me that he thought I hid my defects well. He was trying to reconcile the x rays and reports, which spoke to the deterioration in my spine, scoliosis, and herniated discs with my normal posture. The only discrepancy he could see was one shoulder was slightly lower than the other. I felt pretty good about myself.

Of course, I was still having considerable pain in my lower left back. I felt wonderful for three days, then screwed everything up by raking. I plan to go regularly to see him and find out what activities I shouldn't be doing. Raking, obviously, is one of them. As for the cost which I've heard people say runs about a hundred a visit. My insurance won't cover this so they told me they would accept what I usually pay for a copay to a specialist, $40.00! How good is that?

HERB'S HEART FAILURE

February 14, 2014 VALENTINE'S DAY

"Armed with faith, people are capable of doing things that would otherwise seem unimaginable." By Malcolm Gladwell

Herb and I went to Oceano's and had a wonderful dinner complete with champagne. We even dressed up for the occasion. We had the special which was a combo of lobster tail, filet mignon, shrimp skewers and bacon wrapped scallops. It was wonderful. Angela, the owner, took our picture. That is a photo I've looked at dozens of times to see what I missed in Herb. He looked great and his color was good. Nothing in his demeanor spoke to me of an impending problem. He was very romantic and humorous as always. I remember thinking that this was the best Valentine's Day ever. We fell asleep in each other's arms that night.

At 5:00 am Herb woke me and said "I think we need to go to the hospital." The following two weeks was an ordeal I wouldn't wish on anyone. Yet, that 5:00 am wakeup call was the worst moment for me. It was a sickening feeling in the pit of my stomach, my heart racing and wondering if the outcome would be good. It felt paralyzing yet I did everything quickly, by rote, getting dressed and getting the car keys because Herb refused to go in an ambulance. He said that he just felt a little short of breath. He had taken his aspirins that I insisted he keep on him at all times. Herb does not wear our Blessed Mother's brown scapular, but I put one on him before we left the house and cautioned him not to remove it. So many miracles have been attributed to it, not the scapular itself, but our Mother's intervention.

It was dark and my night vision is terrible. My doctor told me years ago not to drive at night. Herb actually wanted to drive. I said "You've got to be kidding." It seems God cleared the way for me. Due to the early hour there was no traffic, hence no glare from oncoming traffic. I was going about 70 mph and even went through a red light. I actually hoped there would be a cop to stop me then ride ahead to clear any traffic. God obliged and cleared the way. We prayed all the way to Virtua Hospital ER in Voorhees.

Initially, doctors determined Herb's problem was pulmonary related even though his lungs were clear. I was confused even more when they suggested pneumonia. He was not sick, not even a cold. Two days later after much testing the diagnosis was heart failure. How could this happen when I was right there with him? It seems the only symptom he had was shortness of breath when he navigated the stairs in work, several times a day. We live in a rancher so he wasn't climbing stairs at home—no sob (shortness of breath). I was furious that he didn't tell me sooner. He claimed it had just started the day before and he really didn't think it was anything to worry about.

Herb had had an aortic valve replacement ten years prior to this incident. They weren't kidding when they said that the life span of the valve was ten to twelve years. Time was up. I never took Herb or his health for granted, after almost losing him once. He didn't like me to fuss over him. It irked him if I heard him cough and got out my stethoscope. Each night when he was asleep, I'd make the sign of the cross with holy water on his forehead....still do. Though his valve was nearing expiration, hindsight tells me that he might have gotten a strong push from all the sodium he ingested in that Valentine's meal.

Herb was actually enjoying his stay at this super luxurious hospital. The staff was attentive and when one of the nurses saw that he was wearing his brown scapular, she pulled hers out of her uniform to show him. She took very good care of him. He could order from the extensive menu anytime he wanted, even if he wanted a midnight snack. I know Herb and he was not worried. I did that for both of us. He would be happy no matter what happened. He even thought about being with Jillian again. He just didn't want to leave me alone.

Last rites now called the Sacrament of the Sick, were administered by Fr. Jose. Family was notified and discussions ensued about where, when and who would do the surgery. I wanted Dr. Joseph Bavaria. The cardiologist said, "You may want him but may not be able to get him. He's the best in the country"...more prayer.

Arrangements were made by the cardiologist, even making calls to the insurance company that I should have done. He shouldered more responsibility than most doctors would have. Herb was transferred by ambulance to one of the Philadelphia Hospitals. Ryan drove me to the hospital. My first impression of the facility was that it was old and dingy. I soon found out that the care and attention and infection control measures were phenomenal.

Dr. Bavaria came in (another prayer answered) with several of his staff. Herb's blood pressure was 68/42 yet he still insisted that he felt fine, just tired. The word "weak" doesn't register with my husband who will push himself until he drops. All the staff were taking notes and instructions from Dr. Bavaria at such a rapid rate, it would have challenged my shorthand skills. He was only there for about seven minutes. He explained everything to us and said that if we wanted the surgery within 24 hours, the length of time to complete pre-op testing, one of his associates would be able to perform the surgery. If we wanted him to do the surgery we had to wait several days as he was on his way to the airport to do surgery in Atlanta.

I had one question, then one request. Herbs blood pressure was dangerously low and he was in A fib (atrial fibrillation) intermittently. This is a very fast electrical discharge pattern which results in blood not being pumped effectively to the ventricles. It's more involved than that but I don't want to get too technical. Would Herb survive the next few days of waiting? Dr. Bavaria was confident that his staff would be able to stabilize Herb. He said "your husband will be fine." He also said that, if necessary, he could take an early plane back. His staff would keep him updated. Decision made. Now my request…I asked if they would all pray before starting Herb's surgery. They smiled and said that they always do that.

Those few days felt never ending. I just wanted to be his wife but the nurse in me wouldn't allow me to rest. When the alarms would signal a problem I barely made it out the door and a nurse was there running by me. Efficiency prevailed. There was a recliner in the room and we had two large picture windows overlooking the city which was beautiful at night. We also had a birds eye view of the helicopter landing pad.

I stayed overnight but couldn't sleep so I decided to go home one night and try to catch up. That was a disaster. We always knelt by Herb's side of the bed to pray. I couldn't do it so I knelt by my side and wept. I was so afraid, at the same time telling myself that fear is not trusting God. I did trust him and left Herb in His Hands. The next morning Trudi took me back to the hospital. I walked into the room and Herb got up from his chair and gave me the biggest bear hug and he wouldn't let go of me. He said that he was actually "shaking with joy". We were only apart for twelve hours. He said it seemed like days. He held my hand all day and I felt like a teenager falling in love all over again. I felt cherished.

Herb had visitors every day, my brothers Ed and Joe and Joe's wife Donna, David and Jayne came from N. Y., Mary and Mike came and while Mike stayed with Herb, Mary and I took a walk and got something to eat. It felt good to get away from the hospital. At the same time I wanted to get back. Surgery was the next morning. I would not see the surgeon beforehand. I would attempt to sleep in the chair again. Mary planned ahead and brought me an ice chest with a salad, all kinds of goodies and what I thought was blue Gatorade. She said "Don't let anyone see it." It was blue vodka mixed with soda, very little soda. That would help me sleep. I did drink it but didn't sleep. I was sleep deprived and not thinking clearly. I just wanted a few hours of sleep. I took my Xanax, forgetting that I had a drink an hour before. Even then, I still couldn't sleep. I thought of my baby girl and wondered how many times she had gone through this.

Herb had a visit the day before from another priest and received the Sacrament of the Sick again. We both received Communion. He was good to go. As they were wheeling him down to the elevator, my sister Diane called. She was calling from the Chapel in work and had been praying for Herb. Other than me, she was the last one to talk to him, literally minutes before he went into surgery. She just wanted to tell him she loved him. I heard him say, "I love you too, Diane". He obviously was touched. His voice was wavering.

The waiting room had a digital board similar to those at the airports. It listed the doctor, patient and how far along they were, whether they were prepping, closing etc. Mary came at 7:30 am and sat with me until 11:45. Diane's son John who is a psychologist, was right when he said that I should have someone with me at all times. This was life or death and I'm frantic between periods of calm when I pray and when I can't. I thought I could do this alone. I was wrong.

The following are actual notes I wrote in the waiting room.

Six and a half hours since they took you to the OR. Praying, crying, brain is all scrambled from worry and sleep deprivation. I even forgot Dr. Bavaria's name. I'm scared. Nurse took us on a tour of the Cardiac Intensive Care Unit so we'd know what to expect. It's helpful but doesn't take away the fear. You'll have tubes from every orifice, will be on a ventilator, unable to talk for 48 hours. You were terrified of that last time and the tube was only in for a few hours.

Rachele, Mary and Diane are texting updates to family and friends. I couldn't handle going home to fifteen messages a night and repeating everything. They've been such a godsend. The upside of all this is looking forward to the next twenty years. I love you so much Herb, but you already know that.

Mary has to leave for work but Mike will be coming to stay with me until you get out of surgery. Kevin and Trudi will come tonight. Mike will pick me up again tomorrow then Melanie will come visit and then take me home. It's such a long trip for them and I didn't even ask. They just said that they would be there. I was so grateful to them.

I had to take a bathroom break. I was gone only ten minutes and when I got back I checked the digital board and your name had been dropped! I panicked, thinking the worst. The nurse called the OR and allayed my fears. Surgery was going well. Eight hours since I kissed you goodbye in the elevator honey. I'm praying that you're surrounded by angels and they guide Dr. Bavaria's hands.

I brought books to read but can't concentrate. I feel like I need to walk and get out in the sun but I'm afraid to leave the surgical waiting room for fear of missing the nurse who comes down periodically with updates. Mike is here and has been such a support for me. He's in constant pain with his bad knees and can barely walk and yet, he does. He's my favorite brother although he's actually my brother-in-law. We talk about everything. He keeps my mind busy and gives me a break from worrying. The surgery was supposed to last around eight hours. It's now twelve. Mike has not left my side and is with me when Dr. Bavaria calls us into a private room. He is visibly exhausted. He looks at me and says "Your husband has been a very sick man for a very long time." Mike and I look at each other with disbelief. Mike said, "Nobody told Herb that." Dr. Bavaria is confused trying to reconcile what he found when he opened Herb up with what we were telling him.

Herb had been working full time. He shoveled snow three times in the last two weeks. He said Herb's heart was functioning at only 25%. On completion of the surgery it was already up to 40%. He had calcifications around the valve which could have caused a stroke. He had to remove scar tissue from the last surgery, repair an aortic aneurysm and repair the aortic arch. He said that if Herb had gone to work on Monday, he would not have come home. He would not have survived.

Looking at Dr. Bavaria I understood what the nurse meant when she said that he didn't consider what he does a job, but a calling. How comforting to know that God indeed is guiding this amazing doctor and that Herb was blessed to have him. I'm numb but a release of tears feels good. Herb's not out of the woods yet. Thank God Mike was there to ask questions. My writing is becoming fragmented. I hug Dr. Bavaria and promise to pray for him and his staff every night…Eight months later and that promise continues to be fulfilled.

CARDIAC INTENSIVE CARE

Herb is in his room. The vision before me is overwhelming, even though I've cared for people in intensive care. There were numerous monitors, pumps, ventilator and intravenous medications keeping him alive. There were tubes from every orifice and when they ran out of openings, new ones were made. I stopped counting at eight IV bags. He was still under the effects of the anesthesia but I talked to him and caressed him. The only spot I was able to touch without disturbing tubes, was his hair. He always liked when I did that. Kevin and Trudi came shortly after.

Next day Herb was starting to respond. He wanted the tube out of his throat. He was pleading with his eyes. I had promised him before the surgery that I would do my best to make the staff aware of how much he hated that. In turn, his blood pressure would be exacerbated. The tube was in for three whole days. The longer he was dependent on that, the more concern there was for complications.

ANGELS IN AND AROUND THE HOSPITAL

Obviously we were blessed with an amazing staff but there were others whom I believed were also ministering to both Herb and me in the most amazing ways. I would spend all day at the hospital and whomever would come that evening or afternoon would take me home. One afternoon I went outside to wait for Ryan to pick me up. I must have looked worried because one of the parking attendants came over to me to ask if I was okay. I told him I was waiting for my son to pick me up. He said, "How about I wait with you?" He took me by the arm and guided me to a wall where we could sit in the sun and wait.

His name was Joseph. He asked me to tell him about my husband. I never even thought to ask how he knew that I was there for my husband and not someone else. Can you understand why I believe this was Divine intervention? We talked at length, he squeezed my hand and said that he would be praying for Herb and me. He asked me all about our children. I in turn, asked about his family but he always turned the conversation right back to me.

Joseph was there every day when I came to the hospital. He would see me and come running over to give me a hug before I went in to see Herb. I got a hug when I left too. He was always reassuring and if he didn't have a car to park, he would even walk me inside the hospital. Trudi teases me about talking to everyone in my path and when she and Kevin drove me to the hospital the day Herb was being discharged, she just shook her head when she saw Joseph hug me. Even here, mom? Especially here Trudi.

JULIE

Julie, my nephew Josh's wife worked in the NICU (neonatal intensive care unit). She was on duty and came up to check on Herb. She also took me down to see the newborns that she cared for. There were over a dozen and I was speechless at the enormity of the responsibility Julie carries. Most of the babies were under three pounds, some weren't even two pounds, yet they were perfectly formed. How precious and fragile these little ones are.

How sad it made me to think of a large part of our society that does not value life….all life. How proud I am of Julie and the calling she takes so seriously. How pleased God must be with Julie.

Herb was blessed by Julie even though he was unaware she would check on him in the middle of the night while he was sleeping. The nurses would tell me she came to see him. He really was surrounded by angels.

Herb's nephew Joe came to visit the next day. He actually came close to making Herb laugh. He knows what an avid Fox News fan Herb is and said he was going to put CNN on. That almost got him moving. While I was there, the lab reports came back positive for a lung infection. That is a major threat to his recovery, even to his survival at this crucial time. I was devastated. Staff once again expressed the need to remove the tube, but because of his status, they couldn't.

Next day my daughter-in-law Jen took me to the hospital. We reached the double doors to the Cardiac Intensive Care Unit and I stopped dead in my tracks. I literally could not move. I was terrified to go in, even though I had called throughout the night every three hours. Each time I spoke with the nurse, nothing had changed. Jen looked at me and knew that I was scared. She said, "How about we pray before we go in, mom." We did and once again, gratitude surfaced for Jen, who knew just what was needed at this time.

We walked through the doors and into Herb's room. I immediately lost my composure, crying tears of joy, laughing and actually clapping my hands. My hubby was sitting up in bed and the dreaded tube was gone! Antibiotics had started to work on his infection. Things were looking up. More answered prayers. Thank you Jesus!

Next day Mike is back and my nephew Michael is with him. It's been over a year since I've seen Michael. Since only two people at a time were allowed in the room, Mike and I went down to the cafeteria to eat the lunch that Michael had brought us. We came back to a very warm, emotional scene. I stood outside Herb's room and just watched as Michael was feeding Herb ice chips from a spoon. He was talking to him, leaned over and kissed him on the forehead and said "I love you Uncle Herb". How blessed Herb and I are to have so much love. Thank you Michael for a memory I'll have forever...

CARDIAC CARE UNIT

Herb is leaving intensive care. The nurses and doctors on this floor were nothing short of amazing. It's been five days since surgery. Herb is out of bed, in a chair and taking short walks with a walker. His nurses are amazed because he refuses all pain medication. Aside from the discomfort of his "zipper" of fifty staples down his chest and many puncture wounds from tubes, he says he has no pain. Staff doesn't understand. I do. Herb is in so much constant pain with his two torn rotator cuffs, he's just acclimated to it.

Ryan, Jen and Kenzie and Jake visited Herb as well as others in our family. There was one day that we actually had a lot of laughs. My niece, Missy and her husband Jay came with Mary and Mike. Herb was in a chair and Mary hadn't slept all night (another insomniac) so she was curled up in the bed. I actually took a picture of that scene. Though it's not a very flattering picture of Herb, it is a reminder of a very difficult time, when he was surrounded by so much love. Rachele always said that the reason she and her brothers and sister had to wear contact lenses or glasses was a direct result of the flashes from my camera always going off in their face. I did take a lot of pictures.

ANOTHER MIRACLE

Herb had a roommate next to him. I asked him how he was doing and what exactly did he have done. He was up and around and it was only four days since his surgery. That was amazing. He had also had an aortic valve replacement and an aneurysm repair. His doctor was also Dr. Bavaria. He was operated on the same day as Herb. I thought Jim got his days mixed up but he did not. By the time Mike and I spoke with Dr. Bavaria after

Herb's surgery, it was 7:00 pm. There was no way Dr. Bavaria could have done Jim's surgery.

Jim assured me that it was Dr. Bavaria himself who did his surgery. He explained that his surgery was in the evening because Dr. Bavaria had had a very difficult surgery lasting much longer than expected. Of course, that difficult surgery was Herb's. How could this surgeon be on his feet all day and into the night and do his job with such accuracy. When I questioned the nurses shortly after Herb's surgery, I expressed concern for Dr. Bavaria who was in there for twelve hours with my husband. Surely, he had to have a break at some point. The nurse smiled and said" Dr. Bavaria never left your husband's side." Again, it was clear what they had meant earlier when they said Dr. Bavaria does not look at what he does as a job, but a calling.

Dr. Bavaria is a humble yet awe inspiring man that employs a sense of humor which seems paradoxical in his calling. He obviously is working side by side with God. There is no other explanation.

HOME RECOVERY

I could hardly wait to get Herb home. Within two weeks we were living a nightmare. He thought he was the perfect patient. I thought he was the worst. He was content to sit in the recliner and read book after book after book. That I didn't mind. We both have an insatiable appetite for books. But…That's all he wanted to do. He was supposed to do breathing exercises on his spirometer, twenty times an hour. He didn't even do twenty times a day.

His legs were grossly swollen, with pitting edema, yet every time I reminded him to raise his legs, I was nagging. Fluid intake was another cause of my "nagging." We had a visiting nurse come three times a week even though I kept a running log of his blood pressure, weight, temperature and heart rate, daily. She would echo everything I would tell him. He'd ignore her also. He just wanted to be "comfortable".

I would tell him now is not the time to be comfortable. Now is the time to heal and recover. You can be comfortable afterwards. I was afraid of the potential for pneumonia and for blood clots. No matter how I explained my concerns to him and the rationale for them, he would not do his breathing exercises or keep his feet up. All we did was argue. I told him that he had a hell of a nerve, jeopardizing all the good that Dr. Bavaria had accomplished, standing on his feet for twelve hours, saving your life and you're too lazy to do your lousy exercises. One afternoon I was so angry that I stood in front of him and raised my voice so that even I was sick of hearing myself. I told him I was leaving the house for an hour. If anything happens, call someone else. I'm out of here! I didn't have a cell phone at that time.

Herb didn't know it but I was on my way to confession at Assumption Church. I wouldn't even go to our parish because I know both priests so well. On the way, there was an accident on Route 73 so I pulled over to see if anyone needed help. Everyone was fine and the ambulance had just pulled up so I left. By the time I got to the church, confessions were over. I went home and vowed to be more patient with Herb. It didn't work. Next Saturday, same thing, only this time I gave myself extra time. Still when I got there, the priest was talking to his parishioners, Mass would be starting in fifteen minutes and I was not leaving without going to confession. I went up to the priest and asked if he would be hearing confessions. He said he was done. I brazenly said, "No, you're not!" He smiled and said "I'm not?" I confirmed and he said he'd get his vestments on. He heard my confession, gave me absolution and I went home to a fresh start. This coming week would be better....and it was.

NURSING SCHOOL

I went to nursing school at Camden County Vocational Technical School in Berlin. George was supportive of this endeavor because he had already told me he didn't know how long he'd be able to help me with child support. He said that I needed to be able to handle things on my own. He was already sporadically missing child support payments.

I graduated from Camden County Vocational Technical School in a year with an LPN license. The first two months were in the classroom. After that we still spent a few hours in class then the rest of the day was spent in the hospitals or nursing home. The children were all in school, so that helped. We all got out about the same time. Mark would cook dinner often and tell me to go study. I was the oldest in the class of thirty five. I did well in the written tests but my retention was poor. I'd have to read something several times before it stuck with me. However, if I had a patient on my rotation with a specific diagnosis, it was much easier than reading about it. I did better relating to people, not cases. In other words, I am a kinetic learner. I learn by doing.

My first day in a nursing home was humiliating. I was naïve despite my age. I had on my white uniform and cap (they still wore caps then) and someone called "Nurse, nurse!" It was a few seconds before it registered that this man was calling me. He was in a wheelchair and needed to use the urinal so I got it from his bedside, closed the curtain I and handed it to him. His hands just lay limp in his lap. He said, "Honey, I can't move my arms." My first instinct was to call a nurse. Now I *was* the nurse. After I assisted him, he laughed, thanked me and went to shake my hand. There was nothing wrong with his arms. I ran from the room crying, ready to quit.

Then I got a woman with dementia. She was capable of washing herself, but refused to do it. We always encouraged patients to do as much as possible for themselves. At her insistence, I began her bath, only to be slapped in the face and told "All you men are alike! Get out of here."

I picked myself up the next day and went back, a little wiser. Several weeks later I met a beautiful woman in her fifties. She was dying and knew it and was okay with it. It upset her that her family was in denial and wouldn't listen to her last wishes. Even the doctors pushed her to have more tests that she didn't want. She told me everything was copacetic. I even learned a new word from her. She would say, I don't need to know where the cancer started. It didn't matter to her. She claimed that the continuous testing was the worst part. I told her that the doctors worked for her and she should call the shots.

It was one of the many times that I got in trouble for saying the wrong thing (or right thing, depending on how you looked at it.) As yet another staff person came to take her down for more tests, she loudly protested and said "I'm not going! I don't want to go and RoseMarie told me I don't have to go." She was very appreciative. My instructors were not. Are we not supposed to be an advocate for the patient?

I had another incident that occurred in an ICU unit. I was the only student nurse from my school and there were two others from a four year school. They were in their third year. Obviously, I felt intimidated. They knew so much more than me. The patient had a trach and had numerous tubes from every orifice of his body and was unconscious. It was overwhelming. The girls and I were checking the monitors when the patient appeared to be choking on copious amounts of mucous. I looked to the girls with more experience to do something. They stepped back so I gloved up and turned the suction catheter on and suctioned him through his trach. It was one of the few things I felt comfortable with. By the time the nurse got to his room, he was fine. Afterwards, I asked the girls why they hadn't done anything. They explained that they've had three years of book work and this was their first hands on experience. I was becoming a nurse.

Two months to go until graduation and I end up with a couple of fractured ribs, due to forceful coughing. If I couldn't lift patients, and I couldn't because of the pain, I would have to repeat the whole year. I knew I didn't have the stamina to do that. Dr. Berger to the rescue! Though taping ribs had become obsolete as a remedy, there was no other choice. I kept my injury from my instructors, knowing they would have to let me go if they found out. Doctor Berger insisted I lift as little as possible and only with someone else helping me. I got by those two months thanks to God and Dr. Berger.

My favorite rotation was the psychiatric ward. I was the only one who liked it, even though a patient did try to strangle me the first day. We had been taught basic measures of self defense before going on the floor so I was able to break the hold. I don't know who was more scared, me or the patient. We had been warned, however, never to show fear, which would exacerbate the patient's behavior.

My nursing instructors encouraged me to go on with my education and get my RN. They felt I had a gift with psych patients. (Is that good or bad? Only kidding) yet, as a single parent with so many young children at home and my unstable life, I knew my limitations. I could not do it. Two weeks after graduation, I started work at Archway School for special needs children. The first eight years, the pre-school children I cared for had so many anomalies. I had several children who had had tracheostomies and gastrostomy tubes. I also had a little boy with Prader-Willi Syndrome and several other disorders that I had never heard of in nursing school. I had a beautiful, bright little boy who had severe burns and scarring over his entire body, from the neck down. His parent immersed him in a tub filled with hot water.

One of the most devastating diseases I ever encountered was Epidermolysis Bullosa. I had a five year old, very bright child who suffered from this brutal affliction. He was a handsome boy, had a trach and was covered with blisters all over his body. It also affected internal organs with an accumulation of scar tissue. It was heartbreaking. Years later, I had heard that his mother had another little boy with the same diagnosis. Life expectancy is not long.

One of the most upsetting things for me was the lack of infection control measures. There were no gloves and no allowance to buy them. I bought my own. I also called Children's Hospital asking them to send me their protocol for infection control, for caring for children with trachs, g-tubes and respiratory issues. Gloves were at the top of the list. After submitting that information to the nurse in charge, I made my case and they paid for the gloves. They weren't very happy with me. I was making waves... imagine that. I'm slowly coming out of my shell.

The later years were much different. Though I still had a lot of children who had respiratory problems, the majority were behavioral, ADHD (Attention Deficit Hyperactivity Disorder) and ODD (Oppositional

Defiant Disorder). It was an amazing place to work. I was one of several nurses. There were speech therapists, occupational therapists and physical therapists as well as a child psychologist. There were indoor and outdoor pools for therapy, as well as horseback riding and paddle boats on the lake. There was a music therapist and an art teacher on staff. I loved my job although there were some aspects of it I didn't like.

I eventually left the pre-school after several years and was sent to work at another building on the campus, The Lower School. My boss, the Medical Director, Carol was wonderful. We shared an office, friendship and even our faith. She would attend Mass sometimes before work, as would I. I actually realized a dream of working, to some extent, with the psychological needs of staff. Carol and I were kidding about hanging out a shingle, because we seemed to do so much counseling. Our principal Sue, called our office "The Holy Land", because we were always praying for someone or counseling them.

Ironically, I had worked at Archway before I became a nurse. I was a receptionist. I had worked for nine months then summer vacation for the kids would be starting. I was given an offer I couldn't refuse. It was very expensive to pay for Archway's summer camp but my boss was willing to pay for all four of my kids, if I would just stay on. This really boosted my self confidence. They would have a great experience, so I thought. They had horses to ride, paddle boats on the lake, swimming pools, fishing and a petting zoo. George said absolutely no!. He had wanted me to work and now that I was enjoying it and feeling good about myself, he was adamantly opposed. I couldn't figure him out. Of course, once again, I did what he told me to do and handed in my resignation. What a wimp I was.

GOD PROVIDES ANOTHER NURSING OPPORTUNITY

God seemed to provide me with so many unusual opportunities to be of service. I often would tell my kids and CCD students that, as Christians, we're supposed to be of service to others. I had been dating someone for a few months. He was Catholic and strong in his faith and echoed some of my views about service to others. He had a friend, whose mother was dying with cancer. The disease had eaten away parts of her face, lips, nose etc. He had difficulty keeping nurses for her. They would come once or twice and not return. He also had a struggle caring for her and felt guilty about it. He didn't know what to do. My friend told him that he thought I would be able to handle this.

I don't think I'm anywhere as strong as people think I am, but I believe that God immerses me in these situations and I have no choice but to live up to their expectations. Or should I say God's expectations. Anyway, I prayed that God would help me through this. Nothing prepared me for what I encountered with that first meeting. The deformity of facial features (what was left) was shocking. As a nurse, I did not let that register on my face. She really didn't need much medical care from me. She did have a gastrostomy tube for feedings and medication since she couldn't ingest anything orally. Yet, she didn't want me to help her with that. She was very capable of doing it by herself. She was lonely. That's why I was there.

We talked about everything and though her voice was not clear, I was able to discern her words. I can honestly say that once we started talking, I never gave her appearance another thought. She was truly a beautiful woman, faith-filled and accepting of this disease. I looked forward to visits with her twice a week. Those visits lasted about a month. On our last visit, she took my hand and squeezed it and thanked me. She told me that she loved me, in slow, measured speech. I, also, had come to feel the same for her. I admired her so much. She was strength personified.

Her son, Ed, was so grateful for my visits. Afterwards, when his mom would fall asleep, we'd talk. See, God's providing more opportunities for me to counsel or walk Ed through this trial, and hopefully to let go of some of the guilt he felt. He just couldn't bear to see his mother go through this. That's natural. Ed played guitar and was a very talented country singer. One night after mom was tucked in, we walked to a neighborhood bar/restaurant to get something to eat. He played his guitar and asked me to sing along. I have a horrible voice but always wanted to sing. Another gift from God. He played Patsy Cline's "Crazy" and I sang. His voice covered mine, so my mistakes weren't so obvious. It was fun. It had been a good visit, a relaxed ending to the night. Before my next visit Ed's mom went home to heaven.

LAUNDRY My daughter Rachele coined the phrase "God's Aromatherapy"

Laundry! I love it. I love the ritual of washing, hanging clothes on the line, watching them blow in the breeze, folding them and inhaling the scent of them. Most people think I'm crazy. I can't explain why but doing laundry is almost therapeutic for me. I started when I was eighteen years old and a Navy wife in Brunswick, Maine. At one point I didn't have a washer in our apartment and I actually filled the bathtub and washed sheets, then hung them out. I didn't do that often. That was backbreaking. When I did have use of a washing machine and dryer, I never used the dryer. I remember dipping my husband's Navy white uniform in the liquid starch, wringing them out, drying them, then sprinkling them with water, rolling them and a few hours later they were ready for ironing.

Years later, with four young children, two in cloth diapers, I had an abundance of laundry that was never ending. We didn't have a dryer then. I would have liked it for rainy days. With a family of six and all the diapers, I was averaging three loads a day. That's not counting the days I did sheets. If it rained for more than a day I had to hang the clothes on lines in the basement. The basement smelled so fresh, better than any linen scented candle you can buy today. We didn't have softeners back then so fresh air it was.

When we moved to New Jersey and David, Kevin, Rachele and Mark attended Assumption Catholic School, there were twenty white dress shirts a week, plus George's dress shirts that he wore when he worked for Xerox. I was still dipping the collars and cuffs in liquid starch. I continued ironing their twenty-five shirts plus my blouses every week, even after Gene Ryan and Jillian came along. Jillian was the first to wear disposable diapers. I still found the routine comforting. It gave me a great sense of accomplishment to see all those crisp white shirts on hangers.

On a windy day, if my laundry basket is empty, I'll take the curtains down, strip the bed just to take advantage of God's breezes. Sometimes I get carried away. This winter the temperature was below freezing, which doesn't usually stop me because if it's sunny and breezy, the clothes will eventually dry. On this morning, though, I didn't check the temperature. I hung out the sheets, took one look at them flapping in the wind, then came back in to warm up. I got busy and a couple hours had passed. I went out to take the sheets down. They were frozen solid. I had to bring them in because it was clouding up. I could not fold them. I carried one at a time and had to open the large garage door because it was like carrying a billboard. The temperature had been in the teens.

"I LIFT UP MY EYES TO YOU, TO YOU WHOSE THRONE IS IN HEAVEN" PSALM 123:1

There are other benefits to "solar" drying. It is more economical and for those who favor "green" energy, it's a must. Yet new housing developments these days restrict residents from having a clothesline. They say it's an eyesore. You've got to be kidding! I pray that there are clotheslines in heaven or else I may go into withdrawal. When I reach up to hang my clothes I can't help but notice the clouds, the swaying tree branches and butterflies, thanking God for these precious gifts of vision, scent and the rustling sounds of the wind snapping the sheets and towels.

Truth be told, I prefer a sun baked towel even if it is a bit scratchy. It absorbs better than one infused with fabric softener.

I remember when we first moved to our home on Blue Anchor Road. We had sold a home in West Berlin and one in the Poconos, both within two weeks. Moving two huge homes at the same time was extremely stressful. I was so thankful that we were going to be living in a beautiful rancher with three acres of woods, filled with deer and fox and other precious creatures. I thanked God every day, then would break down and cry when I would see the never-ending boxes to be filled. It was overwhelming. Not only that, but the temperatures were in the high nineties when we moved. We moved ourselves. Our children helped or we couldn't have done it.

I remember one incident that occurred in Clementon, N.J. where we rented a storage garage for furniture, until we could move into our new home. As I said before, Herb keeps going, like the "Eveready" bunny. We had to unload this truck and although some of our children were coming to help us, they weren't home from work yet. We had gotten there early. The sky was getting darker by the minute and Herb didn't want to wait. He insisted that we move everything before the rain started. I don't have the strength he does, but I was used to lifting heavy children in and out of wheelchairs, so I was holding my own, until.....We were nearly finished when a crack of thunder and a streak of lightning opened up the skies. Keep in mind we're in a U-Haul, holding on to an aluminum canoe, coming down an aluminum ramp. I did not want to do this. I told Herb, as lightning streaked across the sky yet again, that we were going to look like two crisp pieces of bacon when the kids found us. He didn't give me a choice. Keep moving he said. I just prayed for protection. We finished without incident.

Our washer and dryer weren't hooked up yet so I would drive over to Trudi and Kevin's house to do our laundry. One day I reached my breaking point. It was 98 degrees out and I was in our car, with no air conditioning. I had a small cooler with cold water in it. Road work was slowing traffic on the White Horse Pike, almost to a standstill. I had half dozen errands to run. Start the laundry, go to the Post Office, to the bank etc.I was so hot that I took my bottle of ice water, drank half and poured the rest down my blouse. I didn't even care what I looked like. It gave me some relief.

My errands were almost done, except for going back to Kevin and Trudi's to pick up my laundry. When I got there, my grandson David was in the pool. He said, "Grandmom, come on in." I told him that I couldn't. I had too many things to do. I placed my laundry baskets in the car and stopped short of turning the key in the ignition. I thought I couldn't let this opportunity pass me by. How many teenage grandsons would ask their grandmom to go swimming with them. David was still in the pool with his friend. I told him I had changed my mind. I took off my watch, my glasses and my shoes, dove in, clothes and all. David was laughing so hard, saying "That's my grandmom." I didn't stay long but long enough for it to be a memorable moment. I got back into my car, dripping wet, on the cloth seats. I didn't care. There's some advantage to having an old car, besides no car payment.

My day was improving. That night my daughter, Rachele, came over. I was still unpacking and didn't realize what she was doing until she took me out back and showed me the clothesline she had strung between two trees for me. I actually cried. She understood what I had needed, what would give me some comfort. She knew because she also loves to hang out her wash. It turned my whole day around. She is so sensitive and caring. I miss her so much. Even though we talk on the phone every day, Missouri is so far away.

Herb and I love the crows that come to visit in our yard. One day I was hanging out clothes on a very long clothesline. I was at one end when I felt the line sag under my fingertips, as if someone had tied a weight on it. I glanced down the far end of the line to see a large crow perched on the line. Another gift, to be able to get so close to nature.

I would like to end this chapter with a poem that resonates with truth, at least it was this way years ago.

I REMEMBER CLOTHESLINES

The clothesline
A clothesline was a news forecast
To neighbors passing by.
There were no secrets you could keep
When clothes were hung to dry.

It also was a friendly link,
For neighbors always knew
If company had stopped on by
To spend a night or two.

For then you'd see the fancy sheets
And towels upon the line;
You'd see the company tablecloths

With intricate design.

The line announced a baby's birth
To folks who lived inside,
As brand new infant clothes were hung
So carefully with pride.

The ages of the children could
So readily be known,
By watching how the sizes changed,
You'd know how much they'd grown.

It also told when illness struck,
As extra sheets were hung;
Then nightclothes, and a bathrobe, too,
Haphazardly were strung.

It said, "Gone on vacation now."
When lines hung limp and bare.
It told, "We're back!" when full lines sagged,
With not an inch to spare.

But clotheslines now are of the past,
For dryers make work less.
Now what goes on inside a home
Is anybody's guess.

I really miss that way of life.
It was a friendly sign,
When neighbors knew each other best.
By what hung on the line!

(Author Unknown)

"I Remember Clotheslines" poem was provided courtesy of "Country" magazine. Find more great stories at www.country-magazine.com

UPDATE 2014

My grandchildren Jake and Kenzie have recently started doing laundry. They are seven and eleven years old. I think it's great that their parents are teaching them. Jake enjoys it so much that he has taken it to another level. He actually sits and watches the clothes spin in the dryer, until they're done. Sounds like I've passed on my OCD about laundry.

CATHOLICISM

I was raised a Catholic and went to twelve years of Catholic School. St. Martin of Tours was my school from grades one through eight and we were taught by nuns averaging sixty students in a class, one nun and no aides. You didn't dare step out of line. Our parish was a large one and I remember it felt cold. We went to church and came home, no congregating afterwards, no priest shaking hands. We went every single Sunday and holyday. Every two weeks we'd go to confession. We never, ever missed Mass.

Across the street from St. Martin's was a Protestant Church. I was so curious and tried to sneak a peek when the doors were open. I wanted so much to see inside but it seemed to be an unspoken taboo. Everyone's heard the horror stories of the nuns and their rulers, clickers and their rosaries clicking as they swished down the halls. If you had gum, you had to spit it out right in their hand. My girlfriend Gerry had teased hair so high she gained four inches in height, until Sister marched her down to the bathroom and put her head under the sink.

Cruel? Not if you listen to all the kids who endured it. They have lasting anecdotes that will survive a lifetime. My biggest complaint was the uniform, burgundy with a dull tan blouse. I couldn't wait to go to St. Hubert's High School where my cousin Loretta would be going, a year after me. Instead I went to Little Flower Catholic High School for Girls. I had the same color uniform for another four years, boring burgundy with tan blouses. Loretta had a medium blue with light blue blouse.

My first day in high school was fodder for another Catholic School tale. Most of the nuns were St. Joe nuns. I swore that they were all at least six foot tall. They seemed to loom over us. There were a few nuns from the Holy Family order which I thought would work in my favor. They were Polish. My maiden name was Wawrzyniak. Sister called me to the front of the room, addressing me by my last name, using the Polish pronunciation. She then asked me to recite the Our Father. I started, Our Father who art in heaven, hallowed be Thy….when a whack on the back of my head stopped me cold in my tracks. What just happened??? Sister said "Say it in Polish, Wawrzyniak." She could not believe that with a name like mine, I didn't know any Polish. My parents spoke in Polish when they didn't want us to know what or whom they were talking about. How sad, not to have learned the language.

For the first six years in New Jersey we were members of a small church "Assumption of the Blessed Virgin Mary" in Atco. Everyone talked after Mass and the priest shook hands and made it a point to get to know everyone by name. I attributed that to the size of the parish. Then we moved to a very large parish "Our Lady of Mt. Carmel" in Berlin. It was no different from the small parish.

Herb loved the camaraderie among the people and called them our "church family". At the time we married, he was not Catholic, nor anything else. Yet, he went to Mass faithfully for fifteen years before deciding to convert to Catholicism. We have made so many friends, not just aquaintances, it truly is an extended family.

When Mass starts, silence reigns. After Mass I've heard some people complain about the noise level and the clapping when the last hymn has been sung. When it gets noisy, I thank God for my hearing, impaired as it is. As for the applauding, I believe it's a show of appreciation for our choir and pianist, vocalist, guitar and sax musicians. They are amazing and uplifting. They work so hard and long, they should be applauded. Call it the Joy of the Lord.

THE PRIESTS IN OUR LIFE

We've been blessed with the friendship of many priests in our lives. This was unheard of in Philadelphia, where I grew up. Even in the large parishes in N. J. most of our priest and pastors have made it a point to get to know their parish family personally.

This was very foreign to me when George and I and David, Kevin, Rachele and Mark moved to N.J. I had called the rectory, to register in a small parish in Atco and was told that I could stop by at any time. A few days later, a red-headed young Irish priest stopped by and introduced himself to me. He thought he'd save me a trip and came by with the paperwork.

I was so nervous. I didn't know how to treat a priest in my own home. My family, especially my dad, had always held them in awe. To have a priest in my kitchen was disarming, to say the least. What do I talk about? What are my children going to do? They all respected the priests but they were treating this priest like their Uncle Ed. My nerves! He's Irish. Make him tea. He was all for that. My hands were shaking as I put the kettle on.

Oh, did I mention that since we lived in Marlton Lakes, we lived in our bathing suits. I'd clean the house, rush down to the lake for a lengthy swim, come back and change into a dry bathing suit, then start dinner. I had a cover up over my very small black bikini. I was in my twenties at this time.

We lived in a split level and the kitchen was four steps above the family room. I had my back to the children while making the tea, and heard this racket. I raised my voice for the kids to settle down and didn't know what to respond when they said, "Father Meaney started it, mom." There was Father with a pillow, poised to throw it. Now what do I do. I have a priest and four kids having a pillow fight in our family room. Time for tea! I poured, we sipped and talked about everything. It was so much easier than I thought it would be. Listening to FATHER MEANEY with his lilting Irish brogue was actually soothing.

He remarked on our beautiful lake and how we must enjoy it. We were all in bathing suits. I suggested that he come over some time and bring his bathing suit. (Dear God, what was I thinking). He said, "What about now?" "Now?" I asked, increduously. He just happened to have his suit and a towel in the trunk of his car. The kids and Father raced down to the lake and barreled into the water. I sat on the beach. Father came out and said, "RoseMarie, if ye be hiding from me because ye have on a bikini, it's not necessary, lass. I've seen them before. Come on in. The water's fine." I took off my cover up, ran and dove in. We had a wonderful, carefree time, laughing and swimming with this endearing, sometimes comical priest.

Another priest, FATHER BOBER was from Poland and would visit us and play the organ I had in the living room. He was a more serious type but very warm. My dad and mom, who spoke Polish, thoroughly enjoyed his company. I remember Daddy giving him an envelope with money. It was something that people did then, out of respect. Most priests didn't have much spending money, unless it came from their family. Father refused several times to take it. He was obviously uncomfortable with this. I took him aside and explained that my dad really wanted him to have this small gift, so please take it.

George and I were in a financial bind at this time because I had dental work done. I wanted to wait because it wasn't urgent. There was a small space between my top front teeth. Appearances were important to George and he assured me that the medical insurance would cover 80% of the cost. However, what he didn't realize was that it didn't take effect right away and we were hit with a $1000.00 bill. We had no savings and I knew that Father was looking for an organ for the rectory. I asked him if he would want to buy mine. He became upset because he knew how much I loved it. He said that the price was great but he couldn't take mine. I explained that I would have to put an ad in the paper and sell it to a stranger. I'd rather it go to someone who loved it as much as I did.

He finally agreed to buy it but made me promise not to watch him take it out of the house. He said that he couldn't bear to see my face and the tears that were sure to surface. He knew me well. I did cry but not in front of him. That was really the only material possession that I loved.

I remember he threw the keys to his truck to one of the boys and told them to back the truck up to the front porch. I gasped. I can't remember which one of the boys it was (David or Kevin) but they were both years away from being old enough to drive. Father assured me that they knew how to drive. Whoever it was backed the truck up quickly and expertly as if they'd been doing it for years. Father never answered me about when he taught them to drive. He just laughed.

Father offered Mass in our home and Mark received his First Communion at home. It was such an honor and privilege to have Mass celebrated in our home. Both Kevin and Mark were altar boys at this time. We lost touch after moving to West Berlin. Many years later, when Mark had his diving accident, Father Bober showed up at the hospital. He was the one who helped me in making a decision to donate Mark's organs. Had it not been for his support and encouragement, I don't think I could have done that. As it was, six people are alive because of Mark. Rachele received three letters from three of the recipients. Contact was made through the Delaware Kidney Foundation. Besides his kidneys, they were able to use valves from Mark's heart.

Then there was FATHER SMITH who had a stern facade but was so caring. They didn't have youth clubs then and Father tried so hard to keep all the boys busy with odd jobs like gardening, planting etc. The gigantic Christmas tree on the church grounds had to be strung with lights each year and David was elected to climb it. That tree had to be over twenty foot tall. I wonder how many other risky things I didn't know about.

Father Smith would take a group of rambunctious boys out for pizza, after they did their jobs. They really loved him. He did have a wealth of patience. Sometimes he'd take a few boys down to the shore to his parents' house, when they needed painting done. It enabled them to earn some pocket money.

One summer he took David and a few of David's friends down the shore. This time they rode their bicycles. David said they'd stop at the bars and get sodas and Father would get a beer. They made the trip uneventfully.

One night when we had a big snowstorm, Father Smith got stuck near our house on Franklin Ave. He knocked on our door and asked George if he could help him out. George bundled up and they got Father's car out of the snowdrift. George invited him in for hot chocolate. Father said, "You can have hot chocolate George, but Rose and I will have Scotch!" I also remember discussing books that we read since we had similar tastes. One of those authors was Father Andrew Greeley. He was one of my favorite authors and I have read over twenty of his books.

Father Smith gave Mark's eulogy at the Mass. He praised Mark for always being there to help others. Mark would volunteer his time on Memorial Day to serve as altar boy for the Mass that was celebrated at the cemetery. Father talked about Mark loving excitement and taking risks. He made it clear that Mark was very much alive, just in his new life, enjoying what God had prepared for him. I cried tears of anguish for missing my Mark, but I also felt comforted by visions of Mark in his best venture of all.

Then there was FATHER BOURKE, gentle, devout, compassionate and always there for me, whether it was 10:00 p.m. or early in the morning. He counseled me for over a year when George and I were in the process of ending our marriage. Most people don't realize that priests do this as routine for their parishoners. I couldn't afford therapy otherwise.

One of my pet peeves is people who make derogatory remarks about the church always asking for money. I haven't had that experience. In fact, when I worked as a bank teller, I still gave what I could in the collection basket on Sunday, even though it wasn't easy. I don't believe in giving "leftovers" but writing a check as I would for any bill. God has blessed me so abundantly, I want to give. I don't give to get back tenfold or a hundredfold, but a lot of times it really works that way, just like it says in the Bible.

Anyway, it was during the Catholic Charities Appeal and I wrote a check— probably considered generous, since I was on food stamps at the time. Next day at the bank, another Irish priest, FATHER CAREY, who was considered very brusque, was in my line. I might add that this was not a priest that I was close with. He hands me the bag of money and checks from Sunday's collection, then hands me a personal check ripped in half. It was my check. He said, "RoseMarie, don't you dare write anymore checks to the church. You're having a rough time and we should be there to help you." So much for the money hungry church that people refer to. Father Carey was also the priest that encouraged me to seek an annulment.

This next story about Jillian and Ryan giving to the collection basket occurred when they were teenagers and had part time jobs. Both had been laid off from their jobs and were having difficulty finding a new job. A couple weeks had gone by with no response for any of the applications they had filled out. A lay person at Mass that day had asked if people would consider increasing their donations. Ryan took out two one dollar bills and made sure I saw him put it in the basket.

Jillian was more discreet, trying to hide what she put in the basket. However, Ryan was determined to see what his sister gave. When he got outside he said "Mom, did you see what Jillian did. I can't believe it. She gave her last $10.00". Talk about generous! Oh yes, as for getting back tenfold—they both had jobs within the week.

FATHER PETE was a friend of our pastor, Father Carmen. Pete wasn't actually in our parish, but helped out regularly. He was young and gorgeous. He had an efferescence about him and a way of tying the gospel in with today's world. He was so interesting and had a timely sense of humor, as well as a vivid description of the gospels. You'd feel like you were in the boat with the apostles during the storm. You could almost feel the spray on your face and taste the salt. Even Herb stayed awake during his homilies.

Father Pete would always ask about Jillian and pray for her. He was so reassuring of all things positive. If I received an upsetting call from Jillian, who was going through so much at that time, I would feel so helpless. It hurt so much to know that my baby girl was in so much pain. Father Pete would look at it in a positive way, always. He would tell me that I didn't have to do or say anything, just be there. I would do that but I never felt that it was enough. He told me to be grateful that Jillian called when she was upset. He told me that she felt safe with me and knew that I loved her and would be there any time of the day or night. We have also lost touch but I will always be grateful for all the times Father Pete was there for me.

FATHER CARMEN was our pastor for only a year before he was transferred. He was unique, good looking, charismatic and he used self-deprecating humor to get a laugh or make a point. I initially misjudged him because he had three very expensive cars, an SUV, a Mercedes and another one which I can't recall what make it was. I couldn't conceive of a priest having such luxuries. Weren't they supposed to take a vow of poverty? I spoke with someone who told me that Father Carmen's family had money and Carmen also had made some very good investments in property. They told me that all priests do not have to take a vow of poverty, but always, chastity and obedience.

Herb really liked Carmen more than any other priest he had met (until Father Renee came along). I soon realized, through Herb, that Carmen could not be driving all three cars at the same time. Yet, most of the time, all three cars were not in their parking spaces. He, obviously, was allowing others to use them. He would go into Camden to minister to the aids patients every week. He could have sent someone else to do this, however, he was committed to this cause. He loved to socialize and would have dinners for the parishioners, just to foster his idea that the parish was one large family. When Herb attended RCIA (Rite of Christian Initiation for Adults), I went to all the classes with him. I was thrilled that he had chosen to convert to Catholicism. To welcome everyone, Carmen had a big dinner party in the rectory, complete with wine.

I just had a flashback of one of Herb's RCIA classes in the rectory basement. Father had told everyone to silence their cell phones. Sister Theresa came in a few minutes late and sat down.

Her phone rang. She was so embarrassed and even more so, when Herb said "That better be God calling, Sister." Of course, everyone laughed.

There was one Sunday night that we went to Mass and it was snowing hard. Only about thirty people showed up. Father Carmen commended everyone for braving the storm and giving up the Sunday night football game. He also asked everyone to come up on the altar during the Consecration, the most sacred part of the Mass, when the bread and wine are changed into the body and blood of Jesus. He wanted everyone to come to the Lord's table. We were crowded around him and he grabbed an older woman and said, "Mary, stay by my side." He told us that this is the way it should be, but with so many hundreds of people, it's impossible. I had never been so close to the priest during the Consecration. My eyes brimmed with tears as he held up the Host and said, "This is the Body of Christ."

I do believe that Father Carmen had a profound effect on Herb, and, in part, that may be why he decided to convert to Catholicism. After all, Herb had been going to Mass with me for over fifteen years and never expressed a desire to convert—until Carmen's watch.

Many in the parish were upset when Carmen was transferred after such a brief stay with us. Trying to explain the vow of obedience to Herb, failed to make him feel any better. Father Carmen has been gone for over a year and Herb still talks about him. We're actually thinking of showing up at his new parish, with friends of ours who also miss him.

Herb has become so comfortable with so many priests over the years and has so much respect for them. It's so sad, that with all the scandals, the bad priests have given all the priests a bad name, at least in many people's eyes. What has happened was absolutely egregious and horrific. It has affected everyone. I just hope that people realize that there's good and bad in every group. That's why I'm focusing on the good ones.

Now we have two new priests. FATHER JOE, our pastor, encourages the young children to come up to the altar. More than once, he's had them—dozens of them, sitting on the floor around him, during the Mass. Our pianist has his two year old son on his lap while he's playing the piano.

Likewise, if he goes up on the altar to do a reading, his little boy goes with him. Father Joe used to be Methodist and he has quite a few humorous stories stemming from that. His grandmother was not accepting at first, but that soon changed.

Our second priest is from El Salvador. His name is FATHER RENEE. He's newly ordained and such an asset to our parish. Herb loves what he does after he baptizes a baby. He goes to the middle of the altar and raises the baby over his head and asks the congregation to welcome this little baby into our Christian family. Everyone applauds.

My granddaughter, Nikki, and I were out to lunch and Father Rene was there also. He came over and hugged me then took Nikki's hand and hugged her. He talked with her a little while, then when he was leaving, he came back and asked Nikki about school. He eventually asked her to have grandmom bring her to church some Sunday. He hugged us again then left. I could tell that Nikki was surprised that this was a priest. She really liked him. Father Rene is charming, sincere and lovable with a sense of humor. I'm so glad that Nikki got to see a side of priests, that isn't in the newspapers.

UPDATE JULY 7, 2013

We were at Mass with Jen and Jake, Clare and Bill and got a wonderful surprise. Fr. Renee would be celebrating Mass and baptizing a baby. It's been years since we've seen him. His homily was empowering. The baptism, of course, was personalized. He had baptized Jake almost six years ago, took him on the altar and held him up in the air and asked the congregation to welcome their newest member. Everyone cheered. When Jake saw Father Renee lift the baby up, I told him that that's what he had done with Jake a long time ago. As we were leaving church, Father hugged Kenzie and Jake in a group hug and planted several kisses on the top of Jake's head, telling him he had baptized him years ago.

Ryan was working but we were able to tell him about Father when he joined us at Dunkin Donuts to give Jake a hug. Then Jen and Kenzie walked in.

Kenzie was an altar server for Father Renee's Mass. He remembered her too. Ry only stayed a few minutes because he was on duty. Yet, it was long enough for another gift. A man with his children was at another table and as Ry hugged us all to say goodbye, this man thanked him for his service. I love, love, love anyone who appreciates what our policemen do, and of course, our military. Thank those in uniform for serving our country, our towns, our cities. As we were leaving, I thanked this man for his appreciation. He also is a police officer. He said "We all need each other."

FATHER MIKE is not in our parish, but I go to his parish for Mass during the week because it's closer in proximity to where we live. He became a priest late in life (in his 40's). He had been in the Navy and also had been doing quite well for himself in business when he got out of the Navy. He then decided to change courses and go in the seminary.

Herb would be confirmed at Easter Vigil Mass in our parish, 2006. It was an emotionally charged night. Even our friends Joann and Jerry came from Missouri for the occasion. My sisters, Diane and Mary, my mother and Diane's son Eddie and his wife Renee came too.

Anyway, there had been a difference of opinion from the priests and deacons about whether or not Herb and the other candidates should receive the sacrament of Reconciliation first, before his Confirmation. Father Mike, again, not from our parish, felt strongly that it was best to go to Confession (Reconciliation). He offered to come into the church to hear Herb's first confession, if he decided to do that. He said that he'd be at the church 7:00 pm on Wednesday night. This was not scheduled for everyone. He was going out of his way.

I left it up to Herb. He hadn't quite decided what he wanted to do. George was here too.

Herb didn't think he had any sins. I jokingly said, that that was the sin of pride. George chimed in and said that he'd give Herb some of his sins to confess. We laughed and I didn't push Herb. He had come this far on his own. This was his decision. It was Holy Week, two days before Good Friday. Herb said that he wanted to go to confession. He was, however, concerned about what to say, how to say it, remembering the act of contrition and so on. I told him that he didn't have to think of any of those things. Just focus on Jesus and the Holy Spirit will give you the words. Relax.

We got to the church and it was dark except for a few vigil candles. We knelt in the pew for awhile and then the green light came on over the confessional door. George went in first and was out in a few minutes. He said that he had confessed missing Mass once. Ex Navy man that he was, Father Mike cut right to the point. He asked George if he missed Mass because he was sick. George said, "No." Then he asked if he missed because of the big snowstorm we had had. George said, "No" again and Father responded, "Enough said." and gave him absolution. After hearing how brusque he was, I began to regret suggesting Father Mike to Herb. I didn't want his first experience to be a negative one.

No need to worry. Herb was in there for fifteen minutes or more. He came out with tears in his eyes and bowed his head and prayed. When we left church I was curious as to what he had said but I would never have asked. Kidding around, George did ask. I told Herb that he did not have to tell us, but he said that he wanted to.

He told Father Mike that he was so sorry that he had waited so long before allowing Jesus into his life. How absolutely beautiful! Father Mike and Herb talked for awhile and there was no penance. Father Mike just asked Herb to look around and appreciate family, friends and nature, all the gifts that God gives us.

FATHER PAWEL (PAUL) a wonderful priest from Poland became a good friend. His broken English reminded me of my grandparents. He was only at our parish for a year and a half, but won the hearts of the people. He was in the process of trying to teach me to speak Polish—not an easy task. My grandparents and George's grandparents and George spoke fluent Polish. My parents never taught us the language.

Anyway, I have memories of our young friend, Linda, also from the RCIA class, and Herb and I in the rectory kitchen, talking while Father Pawel was the perfect host, making coffee, tea and setting out treats to eat.

We have kept in touch with this priest. He's in a parish down by the shore. Another couple from RCIA class, Clare and Bill, Linda and Herb and I all visited Father at his new home then took him out to dinner. Afterwards, Father took Herb for a ride in his hybrid car since Herb was so interested in it. Then time to say goodbye to our dear friend. In true Polish form, 'bear' hugs were forthcoming all around.

FATHER JOSE

Father Jose has become a part of our family. He is from India and is so warm and caring. He has been such a strong support for me during the time I was visiting the people in the parish. If I pulled into the church parking lot at the end of the day and he was out in his little garden, he would always come over, hug me and ask how my day went. He would also want to know how the people were. There were difficult days when that hug and concern helped me tremendously.

Again, during CCD or Faith Formation classes, he was there again to come into the church where I taught my classes, and hear confessions. No request was ever refused. He was there for George when he was in the hospital, and it was literally at a moment's notice when I called him. He is the epitome of what a good priest should be.

We were invited to Father's twenty-fifth anniversary in the priesthood celebration. The Mass was so beautiful and the dinner afterwards was a real treat as was the entertainment. When I couldn't do visitations anymore, Father took over for me until Sister Anne came. I still visit one of the people who got very attached to Father. Gladys is eighty years old, beautiful inside and out and has a great sense of humor. After meeting Father Jose for the first time, she told me she thought he was so handsome (he is). She said that if the church ever allows priests to marry, our church would be packed with young available women because of Father Jose. He got a kick out of that.

We are so blessed to have these wonderful, selfless caretakers in our lives.

GIVING TO THE CHURCH

I just wanted to touch on this because I think it's important. There are so many Catholics who resent giving money to the church. I can't help but think of all the times our priests have been there for us. Most of them are on call 24/7 (God's business hours). Father Bober sat with me when Mark was in the hospital, dying. I couldn't handle the doctors and nurses talking about organ donation. Father Bober helped me to see, that as generous as Mark always was, with others, he would want me to do this. Father Bober was not in our parish at this time.

Father Smith was there for Mark's funeral and gave a heartfelt eulogy that comforted me greatly. He wasn't even in our parish at the time....but he came.

These priests visit the sick in their homes and in the hospitals. They go out of their way for so many special occasions. Fathers Bober and Smith celebrated Mass in our home. They're available for confession not only at scheduled times, but late at night. I know. On top of that, they have the upkeep and bills of several buildings, the church, the rectory, the convent and the school.

I had a year of counseling, every single week....no cost. Why would anyone have a problem giving to the church. In this day and age we pay for everything—parking, going over a bridge, even missed doctor's appointments. Why exclude these loyal servants of God.

Herb considers charitable giving, not only to the church, but in other ways. I agree with him on this. He often picks up the tab, discreetly, at a restaurant for an older couple or someone dining alone. He knows of someone in work who has financial problems. He has many times given a hundred dollar bill to him. He's very generous. It's also fun to catch a glimpse of someone when they go to pay their bill and find out it's paid. Giving *is* more fun than receiving.

You also never know how much one little act of kindness will have a big impact on someone. I was recently in Panera's waiting for my friend Pat. It's one of our favorite places to have lunch. Several police officers came in and got in line. I discreetly went to one of the girls behind the counter. I handed her some bills and asked her to pay for the officers' lunches. I specifically said not to tell them. However, afterwards, she came over to me with tears in her eyes telling me how much it meant to *her* because her brother was a police officer and more often than not, had been treated disrespectfully. She hugged me and couldn't wait to tell her brother. I gave her a St. Michael holy card for her brother. St Michael is the patron saint of policeman.

OUR SISTERS

I would be remiss if I didn't mention the nuns too. Our sisters are from Ireland and most of them are up in years now, but still teaching. They taught our children, nurtured them, disciplined them and have stories about Mark to match mine. Herb has an especially warm spot for Sister Carmel. He wanted to be sure I included her in the book. She's so tiny, walks with a cane and has battled cancer. She is warm, loving and caring. She is dwarfed in Herb's arms when he hugs her. She and all the sisters pray daily for our children.

We were blessed to have Sister Agnes, Sister Theresa and Sister Carmel for dinner before they returned to Ireland. They had served our parish for over fifty years. We showed them videos of Jillian skydiving, mountain climbing, white water rafting, scuba diving and she was even in a "Chili's" commercial. The sisters mentioned that there wasn't much Jillian had not done while here on earth. Sister Agnes said there was nothing left for her to do here on earth so God took her home.

Our dinner was so enjoyable, the company that is. The food wasn't bad but at one point I looked at the sisters' plates and said "Have some more" because their plates were empty. Sister Agnes, with her timely sense of humor, cut right to the bone. She said "RoseMarie, our plates are empty because we've been eating. Yours is still full because you haven't stopped talking!" I said that I should have worn the tee shirt Rachele sent me that said "If you think I talk too much, tell me. We can talk about it."

UPDATE: Sister Carmel is with Jesus now. I can only imagine my Mark, who used to drive her crazy in class with his funny antics, is doing the same up in heaven.

SISTER ACT

Herb and I bought tickets for the play "Sister Act" that was held in the church hall. I wasn't sure he would enjoy it because he had not gone to Catholic School. At this time, he's not even Catholic. However, they had snacks which is right up Herb's alley. I had a glass of wine and we settled in. He recommends that every one see this play. He laughed so hard he cried and said his sides hurt.

SPIRITUAL ERRANDS

For lack of another title, this one will have to suffice. When I start my day asking Jesus to guide me in everything I do or say, or to use me to help someone, and to help me recognize when I should speak up or shut up, He takes me literally. I believe that my thoughts are often inspired by the Holy Spirit. I used to agonize over little things that I believe He wanted me to do. I'd wonder if it was of God or was I imagining it and doing it on my own. Then I heard a preacher, Joel Osteen, say that he used to do the same thing. He realized it didn't matter because if the end result was that his intent was good, what did it matter?

I used to be embarrassed to do or say some of the things I felt that I was being guided to do. Being a Christian inwardly is one thing. It's easier and there's no risk of ridicule. Acting out your Christian faith in the public eye is quite another thing. I'm not talking about being obvious or obnoxious or intrusive. I'm talking about the subtle things. After all, isn't that what a Christian is....a follower of Christ. If I get irritated while waiting in line or someone jumps into the parking space that I've been waiting patiently to pull into, will my behavior be indicative of a Christian—or not.

I will give a few examples of behavior and a few of the crazy errands I've been asked to do. Keep in mind it's taken me sixty-two years to get to the point where I hardly ever question. It's quicker to just do what I'm asked. I don't need to know the whys anymore. Although, in most cases I do find that out also.

Herb is a relatively new Christian, yet, he's not uncomfortable expressing it, like I used to be after being a Christian for decades. For instance, we were sitting at a sports bar and had ordered drinks, soup and sandwiches. The soup came and the waitress went back for the sandwiches. I had a spoonful of soup headed for my mouth when Herb reached over for my hand to say grace. We bowed our heads and prayed....in a sports bar. We always say grace at home. Yet, the first time saying it in public was a little disconcerting.

As if I needed encouragement, we went to Charlie Brown's for dinner one night. There was a group of about eight young adults celebrating someone's birthday. They were having a good time, laughing and enjoying a few drinks. When their dinners came, they all held hands, bowed their heads and said grace. What a shining example.

It's pride that inhibits us. What will people think, what will they say. Will they think I'm a nut. That image used to be so important to me. Now, I don't care what people think or say. I just care about pleasing God. There was a period of two weeks that I have to say God was really pushing me to what I felt was my limit.

MOTOR VEHICLE INSPECTION

It was the last week in March and I had to have my car inspected. I use the term 'car' loosely. It is the dullest, ugliest looking vehicle in the parking lot. The seats are ripped, the material above my head was hanging down so I just ripped it out. But it runs and I could care less what it looks like.

Before I left to go to the inspection station, I grabbed a book in case I had to wait. A thought popped into my head to take one of the rosaries that my mother makes. Why? I asked and the thought was repeated, only this time I felt that I was to take the pamphlet that explains how to say the rosary. I looked up to the heavens and said, "You *do* know I'm going to the Motor Vehicle and not church." Then I grabbed the pamphlet and rosary and put them on the front seat with my book.

I didn't need the book and actually had almost forgotten the rosary. I was waiting in a heated area with two men. One had a Lexus, the other, a Lincoln, beautiful cars. We could watch the inspectors as they tested the cars. The one guy was muttering about always failing the inspection. The other one had a newer car so he wasn't worried. Turns out the newer one failed. Then things weren't looking good for the other guy either. Out of nowhere, I blurted out that my car would pass. They looked at me, then my pathetic vehicle and laughed. Why do you think your car will pass they asked. I said because I prayed about it before I left the house. Both their cars failed, but I could see them hanging around to see what happened with mine.

In the few minutes I had remaining, a young woman came in to wait also. I usually make conversation with everyone and this time I asked the dumbest question. Are you from around here? Of course, she would be from around there if she was going to that station. However, she said that she wasn't from the area, but was taking her mother's vehicle through inspection. Her mother was sick, had had a heart attack, was losing her vision and had so many problems. I sympathized because her mother was the same age as me and that was scary.

I thought the inspector was signaling for me to come out so I excused myself and told Claudia I'd be right back. Turns out the inspector didn't want me and said that he wasn't done with this "thing" yet. On my way past the car I spotted the rosary peeking out from under my book and grabbed it and the pamphlet. I thought, am I supposed to give it it to this woman. She looked Jewish and I thought that I'd probably offend her if I gave it to her. Then I stopped worrying. In my mind I said that I was trying to do God's will. I told Him that He'd have to work out the details. He usually does and paves the way so smoothly.

I told Claudia that I would pray for her and her mother and before I could change my mind, I told her I felt that God wanted me to give her something and hoped that she wouldn't be offended. I handed her the rosary, she grabbed me and gave me the biggest hug. It turns out she had converted to Catholicism recently, wanted to say the rosary and had no idea how. Now she had the pamphlet as well. Oh, I almost forgot. My car passed.

DOLLAR STORE SLIPPERS

About a week later on April 2, 2007 I went to the dollar store and saw little gift sets of pink slippers and a white towel tied up in pink ribbon. They were half price at $2.50 each. They also had the cancer logo of a pink ribbon on them. They were so cute I got carried away and bought all sizes. I had about eight pairs. When I got in the car I thought "What am I going to do with all of these?." Some I'd give to my girls but I had way too many.

I then proceeded to my next errand, food shopping at Shop Rite. I finished my food shopping and was pulling out of my parking spot when the thought came to me to give the girl in front of me some slippers. She had just put her two toddlers in the car and was loading her groceries in the car. The thought came one more time. Give her slippers. I was going to listen but not before I let God know that I was willing to make a fool of myself for Him. I'll do it but she's going to think I'm crazy giving out slippers in a parking lot to strangers.

I went up to her and said "Excuse me, I feel that God wants me to give you something." She saw the bag I was holding and asked what it was. I opened the bag and said "Slippers". As if it was the most natural thing for me to do, she then asked what sizes. I said small, medium and large. She said "I'll have medium". I handed them to her and she started crying. I asked what was wrong. She asked if I knew that they had the American Cancer Society logo on them. I said, "Yes, but I bought them because I thought they were pretty." I told her I didn't mean to upset her, just to let her know that God was thinking of her. She said she knew *now* that He was. Everyone in her family had cancer, her mother, her father, her aunt. The list went on and on. She was so grateful. Her name is Destiny and she remains on my prayer list.

I was really beginning to see how God will just set things up when He asks us to do something. As bizarre as these incidents sound, I've never had anyone laugh or look at me like I'm crazy. Actually, some of my kids think I'm crazy. The girls don't and Rachele has her own stories. It's gotten to the point that it's exciting to see what God will do next. This is not something just for me. Anyone and everyone can do this if they're open to God working in their life. It does require letting go of pride. I'm getting better but still have a long way to go. I also stopped prefacing my little encounters with an apologetic "I'm not nuts, or I don't mean to be rude. I'll relate a few more incidents but can't tell them all. They happen so often, I'd be able to fill a book with them.

ACME

A few days after the above incident, I was at Acme in Sicklerville. I saw a young mother with a baby girl in the child's seat in the shopping cart. The baby had a helmet on and was obviously handicapped. I was told to give mom a rosary. I looked in my pocketbook for one of the rosaries my mother makes. They're plastic, but pretty and she has them blessed. I have dozens of them but didn't have one that day. I went down the next aisle and said, "Sorry, Jesus, I forgot to carry some extra rosaries." Then I was told "Give her yours." I had a rosary in my birthstones, sapphire blue with silver connecting the beads. It was in a leather pouch. I reasoned "This is *my* rosary, my favorite". Then the thought came that nothing I have is really mine. Everything is a gift from God.

I caught up with the young mother and said, "Excuse me, do you have a minute? She immediately thought I was going to ask what was wrong with her little girl. I told her that I thought her little girl was beautiful and I didn't need to know what was wrong. I explained that as a nurse, I've worked with children with disabilities for twenty years and they are very dear to my heart. She proceeded to tell me anyway. It was as if she needed to talk. Her daughter recently had brain surgery. I told her that I'd pray for her and her daughter and felt that God wanted me to give her something. I handed her the pouch and she pulled the rosary out and remarked how beautiful it was, too beautiful to accept. I closed my hand over hers and insisted. She had tears in her eyes and said "In case you're wondering, I *am* Catholic". Her name is Christina, her little girl is Fiona. My prayer list just keeps on growing.

ACME AGAIN

Several weeks later I was at Acme again and getting ready to leave the parking lot in Herb's little Volkswagen Beetle. A woman came up and asked how I liked the car. Her husband wanted a Beetle and she wanted a Jetta. I said that I'd prefer a Jetta but suggested she sit in the car to see how much room there was. She got talking about her husband who had had a heart attack. She had so many problems. She, obviously, needed to talk. She actually asked me what to do. I said, "Pray before you decide on a car." She said that she usually prays to St. Joseph, her favorite. I've been praying to St. Joe since eighth grade so that opened up another avenue for conversation. Meanwhile, my ice cream is melting in the ninety degree temperature. I was ready to leave when I was told to (guess what?) give another rosary away. I had since replaced my birthstone with a cobalt blue rosary with gold links. I pulled the leather case out and handed it to the woman. She opened the case and gasped. Her favorite color was cobalt blue. She wanted me to come to her house to see all the cobalt blue vases and accent pieces she had. She knew God was thinking of her that day. I, obviously, did not know her favorite color but He did. She hugged me and thanked me for taking the time to talk with her.

FURNITURE STORE

Most times I don't hear from these people. Sometimes, I'll call to see how they're doing.

Sometimes they call me. How uplifting and encouraging that is for me. One particular woman touched my heart. Herb and I were looking for furniture for our Pocono home. We came across a store almost by accident while looking for another one. We didn't find anything but I did see a club chair that was a possibility. I sat in it, sank in it and couldn't get out of it. Herb joked about my age. I told the salesgirl, Mary, it wasn't my age, it was my hip. I had a hip replacement. That started her talking. Her husband, in his early forties had both hips replaced. Several months later, he slipped off a curb and broke a hip. After the third replacement, he lost his job and was having difficulty finding another one. On top of that, they were going to lose their house if they didn't sell it soon. Mary said that her husband was home and they were having an open house but the house was on the market for six months and no offers. She was despondent and didn't want to go on.

Oh Lord, can we really be having this conversation in a furniture store?. I asked Him to give me the words to help her. I really didn't know what to say. I told her that Herb and I would pray for her, we'd get others to pray. I told her that the house would sell when the time was right. I checked on Mary after the open house. There were no offers. She was still depressed but not despondent. I promised to keep praying.

A month later Mary left a message. The house sold and her husband got a good job. She went back to church and her life is good… God is good.

OUR CARS

Herb always thought it was wrong to pray for material things. I told him otherwise. We would be needing another car and I knew if we prayed about it, God would help us. It was a couple of months later, we were doing yard sales and there was this Trooper with a sign on it. It was in mint condition, low mileage and $2900.00. Jillian happened to be home for a visit and she was with us. She is an avid yard saler also. We bought the car, then woke up the next morning in disbelief at what we'd done. Two days later the owner brought the papers over for us to sign. We told him how strange it was that we bought a car at a yard sale. He laughed and said that he and his wife felt the same way about selling it at a yard sale. Then he went on to say that he and his wife had been praying about selling it. Coincidence? I think not.

There was a time when Herb was skeptical about some of the occurrences in my life. Actually, there was a time when *even I* questioned whether it was God working in my life, or was I just imagining it. Again I was remembering Joel Osteen (minister) say that he used to pose the same questions about himself. God spoke to him, saying, what does it matter? If you think I'm guiding you or you're doing good on your own, don't worry about it. However, I was persistent, asked God for a sign and got an amazing answer, as did Herb also. There was a field nearby us on Route 73. The fellow we bought the house from told us we'd probably see deer there. Well we had been here about five years, having passed that field frequently. We'd also go when we knew the deer usually fed. We never saw one deer.

On the way home from the Tiki bar near us, Herb had his turn signal on to turn into our driveway when I blurted out, "Go straight, then to the field. There's three deer in the field." I clamped my hand over my mouth. I was just as surprised as Herb at what I said. He asked why I said it. I said I had no idea. I hadn't thought about it. It just came out. Of course, he said we were going to the field. I felt like an idiot, not even having a clue as to why I said it. We parked alongside the field as cars zipped by. There were two deer in the field. I was quiet for a few seconds. Then a third deer came walking out of the woods. We just looked at each other. Never do I hesitate to listen to that inner voice…the Holy Spirit.

'PRAY UNTIL PRAYER BECOMES LIKE BREATHING."

"PRAYER IS THE WORLD'S GREATEST WIRELESS CONNECTION"

Prayer is nothing other than communication with God. We need to keep in mind, that works both ways. We can't always be doing the talking, the asking. We have to listen too. "Be still and know that I am God." I'm not especially good at being still or quiet. Yet, I've made great strides in this area in recent years. I have learned to listen. I'm sure the sceptics will roll their eyes at this, but if you listen, placing yourself in God's presence, you will hear Him speak to your heart. I know. I used to be one of the sceptics.

How do you place yourself in His presence? I'm sure it varies for everyone. I can only speak for myself. Most times I find it easier to pray early in the morning. It gets me off to a good start. I'll sit in a comfortable chair, close my eyes and say, "I'm here, Jesus". I'll begin to thank and praise Him for everything. Once you start this, you'll be amazed at how many gifts you've been given. The list goes on and on. I do this regardless of how I feel. There will be days that everything goes wrong and you don't really feel grateful. Waiting until we feel better is not a good idea.

Rely on actions, not feelings. No matter how miserable or depressed we are, no matter how difficult our problems—even serious illness, I promise you that once you start thanking Him and praising Him, you will be amazed at the way your spirits will lift.

Some of my best prayer time has taken place in the car. When I'm by myself, I don't turn the radio on. I pray, which can be nothing other than talking to Jesus. When Herb and I would travel to New York or the Poconos, we'd talk or listen to soft piano music, like Danny Wright (thanks to my sister, Mary for turning us on to him). Not to get off track, but I find it interesting that Herb's appreciation for good music, including classical, has evolved from strictly country music, which we still love, especially my son Kevin's music.

Herb and I would also listen to Joyce Meyer's inspirational tapes. She explains so simply how to live your life with God as the center. One of the things she stresses is prayer. "Don't worry about the kids. Pray! Don't worry about the job, the bills, etc. Just pray! Pray, pray pray!" Worrying won't change things but prayer will. Someone once said that prayer was not a last resort but a pre-emptive strike. I love that.

Then, of course, there's prayer requests. I know that Jesus already knows my wants and needs even before I do. So why ask? I've heard it said that prayer is not for God but to open us up to Him.

There are times late at night when Herb is asleep and I'll soak in a bubble bath with a few lit candles and do my praying there. Now I am going to go off track because a memory came to me. I was in my early thirties with six children, creditors calling all the time, stressed out about everything. I was short-tempered with my children. I was losing it. I went to confession and reeled off my list of sins. I did not know this priest. He listened, was quiet for a few seconds, then asked a few questions. "What do you do for fun?" Play with the children, cook and do laundry. He got more specific. Did I go to movies, go out with my girlfriends, go to dinner, bowling....whatever. The answer was no. I never did those things. There was no time or money. He then gave me my penance. I was to take a half hour, preferably more, every day by myself. He suggested soaking in a bubble bath, locking the door and making it clear that I was not to be disturbed during that time. I did what I was told. I told the children not to knock or call me unless someone was bleeding. They actually listened and respected my privacy. To this day, I still take that time and look forward to it. I am so grateful for that priest who made me realize I had to take time for myself.

I just want to add, that despite the fact that I didn't get to go out, I rarely felt deprived. I loved being a wife and mother. It's just that once in a while it would have been nice to have a break from routine.

ANSWERED PRAYERS

I wouldn't even begin to entertain thoughts of telling about all my answered prayers—some yes, some no and some I'm still waiting for. However, one stands out because it's almost bizarre. It proves, undoubtedly, that if you trust God, no matter how bad or crazy the situation is, He can use the most mundane things to your benefit.

Herb had been seen by two cardiologists, considered to be the best in their field. Both concurred that Herb would need surgery in time, but there was no urgency. They both agreed that surgery posed a much greater risk than waiting a few months. They did tell him not to lift more than five pounds. The second opinion did nothing to ease my mind. I know that the doubt I was experiencing in spite of prayer, was probably God's urging me to disregard what we had been told. I told Herb that I would feel more comfortable if he made the appointment for a cardiac catheterization right away. He made it for that Monday, three days away.

We went to yard sales all day Saturday. We found a treadmill that Herb had wanted, but he couldn't lift more than five pounds without endangering himself and possibly having an aneurism burst. Keep in mind, that the week before, he was lifting and installing three commercial sized ceiling fans on our deck. He also had moved a one hundred and fifty pound slot machine by himself. He moved it twice! He must have had a bevy of angels surrounding and protecting him.

Anyway, I asked several people at the yard sale to help get the treadmill in our truck. Of course, to save embarrassment, I explained why my husband couldn't lift it. This opened up a conversation with one of the men who had experienced open heart surgery. He said, "You have to go to Graduate Hospital", and then for ten minutes he sang the praises of the staff and the care there. I thanked him and immediately disregarded most of what he said. I knew that we would be going to Our Lady of Lourdes Hospital.

We found furniture at another yard sale and again had to request help in loading it on our truck. There were four older couples at this house. They were all probably in their late seventies, early eighties. They were sitting around on beach chairs and all chimed in with information about the best hospital for open heart surgery. Two had actually undergone open heart surgery and two more had other surgeries at Graduate Hospital.

Two days later Herb had his catheterization done. He was getting restless, wanting to leave and go home. The doctor came in and said, "You're not going anywhere. We're transferring you for immediate surgery". He was amazed that Herb had been functioning so well. We were stunned. Then he asked what hospital we'd like to go to. I told him Our Lady of Lourdes. He asked about our insurance, then checked it himself. Lourdes did not accept our insurance. "Now where?" he asked. I can't even think clearly, I'm so upset. I said that I had no idea.

The doctor then took my insurance card and began making calls, which is unusual in itself. I've worked with doctors. They left things like that up to the nurses. After ten minutes he came back and told us we had two choices—Hahnemann Hospital or Graduate. My initial thought was that I knew that Hahnemann was excellent but I knew nothing about Graduate—except for what the yard sale people had told us. I rolled my eyes heavenward and said to Jesus, "You even work through yard sales?" I told the doctor, with every confidence, we'd go to Graduate. The doctor made the arrangements for Herb to be transferred by ambulance. As an after thought I asked the doctor which hospital he would have chosen, if it had been him having the surgery. Without hesitation, he said "Graduate". I asked him why and he said because they have the best doctors.

I drove home to pack a bag for Herb and make phone calls. I arrived to a flooded front walkway because the sprinkler had sprung a leak. I sloshed through the water to the front door, after turning the faucet off. My own tears by this time were nonstop. I was so scared. I didn't feel very strong spiritually now but I continued to pray as best I could. Inside I found that my daughter, Rachele, had set the table for two, put wild flowers (my favorite) in a vase and left lasagne in the frig as a surprise for Herb and me. I cried with gratitude but it was bittersweet. My husband wouldn't be sharing the meal with me.

Herb was transferred by ambulance to Graduate Hospital where I began scrubbing Herb's entire body, three times, with Betadine as was the routine for surgery. I needed to do something, so the nurses relinquished this task to me. I was shaky inside. Herb was calm and relaxed. "Be still and know that I am God" kept echoing in my mind.

Now we had no idea who the surgeon would be. Because of the urgency of the situation I had no time to research credentials. Yet, peace came over me. If God can pick out a hospital for us at a yard sale, surely, He can choose Herb's doctor. We prayed for Herb and for whoever the surgeon would be.

Dr. Gueratty walked in at 9:00 p.m. and sat with us for forty-five minutes explaining the procedure and answering questions. Once again, I know of no doctor who would spend this much time with a patient. Herb's aortic valve would have to be replaced and it was explained that this was a high risk surgery. He actually said that it made a quadruple bypass seem like nothing. It was that serious. Then before he left, he grasped our hands as a friend would and told us that he would be praying for Herb. Surely, God chose one of his angels to operate on Herb.

His surgery was by no means routine. In fact, complications arose that even Dr. Gueratty couldn't have foreseen. There was an anatomic anomaly on top of the anticipated problem, yet God guided his hands.

While I was in the waiting room at 6:00 a.m., I was alone except for the maintenance man who was emptying trash cans, cleaning tables and mopping the floor. I was desperate for more prayers for Herb. I put my rosary down and asked the man if he would do me a favor and pray for my husband. He asked for my husband's name, dropped his mop and bucket and left without another word. I looked down the hall to see where he went, just in time to see him enter the chapel. He returned ten minutes later, smiled and said, "Done".

I was on an elevator with my head down, tears trickling down my face. I had been in the ICU all day with Herb watching the monitors. At one point his blood pressure was dangerously high. By the time I got to the nurses' station, they had several doctors heading for his room. I was on my way to the chapel when a woman behind me placed her arm around me, squeezed my shoulder and said, "Your husband will be fine honey. He's in Jesus' hands." How could this stranger know why I was upset and assume it was my husband and not a brother or other family member. I believe with all my heart, that it was not a stranger, but an angel. I didn't know it then but I know it now.

Sometimes we don't always recognize God's hand in our lives. We may be too caught up in the physical aspect of our existence. If we place the spiritual facet of our life first, everything else falls effortlessly into place.

OUR MIRACULOUS POOL

THE PARABLE OF THE GOLD COINS LUKE 19:11-27

I thought of this parable and how it paralleled the way I hung on to my meager 401k, clenching my fists out of fear, afraid to let go of it. Wonderful things began to occur when I decided to share it.

Can you believe this! I'm sitting in the sun by our pool. It's a miracle. The economy is bad, we'll never have enough to retire and we're 67 years old. I had a very small 401K from Archway that I was obsessed with never touching. Probably because of all the money problems George and I had the entire time we were married, I clung to this money like a security blanket.

Herb and I prayed every night on our knees to thank God for his plentiful gifts of family, health, friends and country. We also ask Jesus to guide us in all that we do or say, or in people that we meet and in all our decisions. We're too old to do something foolish at this stage in our lives.

It was the day after our party for my CCD class and their families. We had about forty people here. It was sweltering. The temperature was 104 degrees. We were in the hot tub, which was actually filled with cool water when Herb said, "Tell me again why we got a hot tub instead of a pool". Obviously, it was cheaper. We had a little money left over from the sale of our Pocono home and our Franklin Ave. home. Plus we had so many aches and pains, we thought the hot tub would help, and it has. We've even been in it during a snowstorm.

Herb said "Let's get a pool now." I thought he was kidding. He wasn't. I said that I'd love it but we couldn't afford it. I didn't want to go into debt. He said that we should do it because we don't go anywhere or take vacations. We just have parties for family and friends. Big parties. He wanted me to think how nice it'd be to have the pool and how much use we would get out of it. No argument there, just concern about the cost. We both agreed that we couldn't make such a big decision without prayer.

We didn't pray to *get* the pool but for discernment in any decisions we made about it.

Several days later I woke up with a calm and peace and the decision to use my 401K. I couldn't believe it because all these years, I was paranoid about touching it. Now I realized that that small amount wouldn't do much to help us with Herb's retirement, so why not enjoy it. Herb had said that we didn't know how many years we had left together. It could be one or two or twenty. Let's enjoy it to the fullest. Life is so short. We know that only too well Jillian, because of the short time we've had with you and Markie.

Two days after I received my check, the market crashed. I would have lost most or all of my money. I had been losing some already. George lost a hundred thousand, Kevin lost a lot. It seems everyone but Herb lost because he plays it safe. Now here I sit looking at this crystal clear, cobalt gem in our yard and cannot believe this gift.

Shortly after this, I thanked God that I hadn't lost my money by greedily hanging on to it. I also opened my Bible to Matthew 19 vs 26, randomly. How appropriate. "With God all things are possible". This was no coincidence. This was truly Christ incidence. That Scripture is on the gate to our pool. Truly, this was confirmation that we did the right thing.

Since I was thirteen years old I used to say "I don't care what kind of house I live in when I grow up. I just want an in ground pool." I never thought I'd ever have one and certainly not when I was a senior citizen. Oh, the surprises God has in store for us. Because this pool was a gift, we wanted to share it not only with our family and friends, but others. We know so many wonderful people in church, our church family. They have young children, so we invited them to come whether we were there or not. I think at first they felt uncomfortable but they knew we really wanted them to enjoy it. It also allowed us to get to know them better.

I was in the pool at the end of October when the landscapers were wearing jackets against the chill of the air. They thought I was nuts. I was in my glory. I even found a wet suit at a thrift shop so I could continue to go in when it was colder. It is not a heated pool. The water was in the fifties. I soon opted to go without the wet suit. It was a pain to get into. Then I remembered Mark using my pantyhose under his wet suit when he went surfing in the winter. He said it helped the suit slide right on. We did have to cover it in November. I couldn't wait for spring.

We opened the pool April 1 and Ry, Kenzie, Jake and I went in on the third. We had just come home from the hospital, hours after George had passed. The frigid water was invigorating and healing at the same time. At least that's how I feel any time I go off the diving board and immerse myself in the crystal water. If I ever feel stressed, it evaporates the second I jump or dive in the pool.

I've done laps in the morning and watched the sun rise, filtering through the lacy network of trees. I've had some of the best conversations with Jillian and Mark while swimming. I know that they're with me. Herb and I have gone swimming in the moonlight and yes, we even have gone skinny dipping, or as Herb says, "chubby dipping". He loves it as much as I do. He just can't swim anymore because of his two torn rotator cuffs. But he goes in every day.

We especially love to see the water churn with Kenzie, Jake and their cousins and friends. Ryan loves it as much as I do. I love watching him do flips and somersaults and just enjoy himself. This truly is a heavenly gift and we treasure all the hours and months we're in it.

When we went to Niagara Pools to pick out our pool, they had two in ground sample pools. I fell in love with one and said just pick it up and place it in our yard. Herb pointed out that we didn't know if we had enough money and we should look at every option. I said I wanted this pool, the same liner, steps, shape etc. The salesman and Herb wanted me to look at other choices. I did. I didn't want them. When they figured out the cost of everything that I wanted, we had the exact amount. Coincidence?

DOCTORS

God has sent wonderful doctors into our lives. Our family doctor, Dr. Berger, came to our new home in Marlton Lakes on New Years Eve day because all four of our children had the flu. It was the first time we met him. He has been our doctor for thirty-six years. He has made house calls for us and even our grandchildren. He has stayed late (after 10:00 p.m.) in his office, when I needed someone to talk to. I was having difficulty dealing with the fact that my husband, George, was leaving. I was devastated and Dr. Berger's support was a godsend.

When I was in nursing school and panicked because I thought the children or I were experiencing symptoms of the current disease that I was studying, Dr. Berger came to his office. Unusual? He came on a Sunday morning right from the golf course, to walk me through the symptoms. He could have told me on the phone, but he didn't. I thought Ryan had meningitis. Dr. Berger agreed that he had all the symptoms then gave me a simple test to do that ruled it out.

He came to our home on Christmas day because George had an abscess. He even delivered Jillian at my request in 1976 even though he had given up that part of his practice. It required him taking late night calls and increased time at the hospital. We share a deep respect for each other and a love of books. He's recommended some of the best books I've ever read, like "Angela's Ashes" by Frank McCourt, which I think should be required reading for high school students.

We brag about children and grandchildren and admire each other's photos. Though Jillian lives in Georgia, she receives a birthday call from Dr. Berger every year. He's never forgotten the day he delivered her.

UPDATE

Dr. Berger is retired from family practice but is still teaching. He continues to keep in touch with me and with Rachele. He couldn't make it to her wedding in Missouri but offered her a week in his beach house as a wedding present, the next time they come to New Jersey.

URGENT CARE

These facilities are one of the greatest things to happen in the field of health care since it has been increasingly difficult to contact my primary care doctor for an appointment. I'm not the only one with this complaint. However, after trying a couple of facilities (whose names I can't recall) I was disappointed with the apathetic staff and vague diagnoses. Then I met Dr. Najafi and his professional, caring staff. Dr. Najafi has become someone I trust completely. My husband and I have been going to him for years now and have come to rely on his expertise. No matter how busy he is, he takes the time to inquire about family. I've shared my photos of family and have seen photos of Dr. Najafi's beautiful wife and his son and daughter. His smile and comforting manner make a visit something to look forward, instead of dread, and, always, he has been able to allay any fears as well as pain. We are blessed to have him in our lives.

DENTIST

We had a good dentist for almost thirty years and then found out inadvertently, that he would be retiring because of health issues. My concern about finding another good dentist was warranted. I had heard so many horror stories. How to choose a new one? There was only one way and that was prayer. Prayer and some 'footwork' and phone calls. It turned out to be so easy. I mentioned our dilemma to my daughter, Rachele, who told me about Dr. Leonetti. She had gone to him when one of her boys had a problem. She asked him about a payment plan because she didn't have the money, at the time. He didn't charge her anything. He said that her son's teeth were more important. I was so impressed with that story that I called the next day to make an appointment.

I was pleasantly surprised by the state of the art facility, the friendly and courteous staff and the prompt attention. I liked Dr. Leonetti and found him vaguely familiar, but couldn't place where I may have seen him. About two weeks later, Herb and I were at a yard sale and I saw Dr. Leonetti there. I was excited because I had been telling Herb about him and now I had the opportunity to introduce them. I pulled Herb over to Dr. Leonetti and was about to introduce them when Herb and Bob hugged like old friends. Then Bob's wife, Joyce came over and it struck me where I had seen him before. Bob and Joyce had been one of the presenting couples at our Marriage Encounter weekend. It was comforting to know that not only do we have a great dentist, but a faith filled caring friend.

ANOTHER ANSWERED PRAYER

We've had many prayer requests answered in unusual ways. Don't think we get all our prayers answered. We don't, obviously, or Mark and Jillian would still be here. Some of our answers are for small things and even material things, although in my eyes, there are no small miracles. There will be some who doubt the veracity of my stories. That's fine. I just ask that you, at some point, at every turn ask God to be in your life and give you discernment then be prepared to be amazed.

A couple of years ago Herb had several serious nosebleeds. He would have to get his arteries cauterized to stop the bleeding because normal methods were ineffective. One time, on a Saturday, (naturally, no doctors are available) it became so bad that I was concerned about the amount of blood he was losing. We went to the emergency room where he was told that the doctors there couldn't and wouldn't do anything for him. They wouldn't do cauterization. They suggested an ENT (Ear, Nose & Throat specialist). Of course, there was none in the hospital and none available on Saturday.

We left there totally frustrated. Herb was soaking through washcloths and hand towels, not tissues at this point. His blood pressure was within normal limits. I had an ice pack on the back of his neck and his nose was packed, and it continued to bleed. I called Rachele in Missouri to ask for prayers. Within an hour, she called back and said she had just seen a commercial on Fox News for "Bleed Arrest" for severe nosebleeds. I laughed because that's the channel we have on all day and I never saw the commercial. I never heard of the product. She said it was the first time she had ever seen it. She said Walgreens carried it. Since Rite Aid was closer to us, I went there. The pharmacist had never heard of it. I then went to Acme's pharmacy. They too, had never heard of it. Finally, I went to Walgreens and got it. It worked. I couldn't believe it. Neither Rachele or Herb and I have ever since seen the commercial. Coincidence? I think not. I do think God cares even about the little things in our lives. We're supposed to pray about everything!

CARS

We bought two Isuzu Troopers at yard sales for $2900.00 each, years apart. They were low mileage, great condition and have run beautifully with very few minor repairs. We've had one for eight years and the other five. We even got confirmation, as I call it on the second one. We passed it twice before stopping to look at it. By the time we were seriously considering it, Kevin called Herb on his cell phone and told him about a great looking Trooper for sale in Atco. We told him we were on it and thanks for thinking of us.

UPDATE August 2013

Several months ago we were talking about eventually needing another car. We still have one Isuzu and George's newer car, a Nissan Altima. Herb bought that from George's estate. However, even though it was newer and got better gas mileage, it was burning oil. Herb said it runs well. It just needs two quarts of oil a week. We couldn't afford an engine job so he opted to carry a case of oil with him. That turned out to be more trouble than it was worth so we sold it within a few weeks.

In anticipation of the twenty-two hour trip to Rachele's in September, I had concerns about the Trooper making its third trip to Missouri and back. It has almost two hundred thousand miles on it. Herb has no doubt it will serve us well. He did say that he'd like to get another car when he retires. Of course, we kept it in prayer adding to our list of things we're thankful for and asking Jesus to be in the center of any decisions in the future. When the time is right, we'll know.

It came sooner than expected. Herb happened to go on Craig's list and saw an ad by a mechanic for a Hundai, 2005 for $4,000.00. The mechanic works on nothing but Hyundai and Honda because they run for 300,000 miles or more. He's also gotten feedback on the cars he buys and repairs and he gets consistently good reports. We drove to Millville, N.J. which turned out to be a lot farther away than we had anticipated. The car was in good condition, looked great and drove well. One problem. It smelled of cigarette smoke, a deal breaker for us. We were disappointed but, obviously, it wasn't meant to be.

As we were driving back home we passed three churches in close proximity of each other. None of them was Catholic. Then a block away we passed a beautiful Catholic Church, St. Martin de Porres. I had heard of this saint but knew nothing about him. Save that information for future reference. Herb had printed out some other listings on Hyundai (because now we were armed with the information that they run well) before he had left work. He hadn't had a chance to look at them yet. He handed them to me and asked if there was anything else that looked good. I saw one in Hammonton, nearer to where we lived. It was the same year, a little less mileage and a little more money. We called and Barry said he'd meet us at the dealer's in a half hour.

We got there before Barry and had a chance to look the car over. It was classy looking, silver, loaded as the ad said, with heated seats sun roof and all the bells and whistles. I know nothing about cars but said we should ask for a car fax. Herb said that wasn't necessary. It would have made me feel better. I also like to have confirmation, from God, that we're doing the right thing. Yes, we can buy a car all on our own but we include God in everything.

The dealership was small. There were only about ten cars on the lot. When Barry came, we took the car for a drive. Herb was amazed that the engine was so clean. It really looks like a new car. He liked the way it handled and had no reservations. He wanted this car. We went in to the tiny office and the first thing I saw was a statue of St. Martin de Porres. Confirmation received. Then Barry asked if I wanted to see the car fax? Confirmation again, because that was important to me and I didn't even have to ask for it.

We went back the next day to get the temporary tags. Since I had mentioned our children and Mark and Jillian being in heaven, Barry was aware of our loss. He said, "RoseMarie, in light of what's happened with your children, did it cause you to question your faith?" Of course, I answered "No." I'm grateful to God for allowing me to be their mother for the years I had them. Our children aren't ours to begin with. They're God's". Though that was a very personal question, I loved that Barry asked it. It gave me a chance to witness to my faith and talk about our kids, and of course whip out all my pictures of them. It is amazing how God provides openings.

UPDATE

I called Rachele to ask her to look up St. Martin de Porres since I didn't know anything about him. It turns out that he was from Lima, Peru and was good friends with St. Rose of Lima, who is my patron saint. I guess she was looking out for me, more confirmation.

Our car is still running smoothly….however, the air conditioning died shortly after we purchased it. Again, prayer is essential in every situation but it doesn't mean there won't be problems. It cost us $1200.00 to repair. Even with that amount added to the cost of the car, Herb said we still got a good deal.

HERB'S DESK

My husband is 5'11 and weighs about 230 lbs. You would have to see it to believe it, how he even fits at his "desk", which is nothing more than a tiny closet, just big enough to house the computer and keyboard and not much else. He spends so much time cramped in this tiny alcove doing paperwork, that I thought it was time to get him a real desk. As usual, we kept even this request in prayer. My son, David was appalled that we would dare to ask God for such a thing. I said, "David, we have a very generous God and I believe that He wants to be included in every aspect of our life". Basically, I just say to Him, that He knows our needs and please be in the center of all our decisions. I do not give Him a checklist.

Anyway, we spent about two weeks checking out stores.....Staples, Boscovs, K Mart, Walmart, Ikea and many others. Nothing appealed to us and they all seemed to be cheaply made. We then went to a business furniture store but it was closed. We planned to go back, however, quickly changed our minds when we looked through the windows and could see some of the price tags--$1400.00, $1600.00.

A couple days later we stopped at Wendy's to get something to eat. As I got out of the car, I glanced down at a business card on the ground. I still don't know what made me pick it up since I'm obsessive about germs. We had had a storm the day before. The card was in a puddle but the printing was legible. It was for a business furniture outlet. Of course, we looked at each other and laughed. Is this our answer to prayer?

We went the next day. There were no signs on the building. We would never have found it on our own. There was just a number on the door. We walked into a massive warehouse with hundreds of desks. We didn't know where to start. After looking at several dozen, I spotted a huge cherry desk. It was beautiful. I loved it but Herb thought it was too big for our room. I said I would make it work. He agreed it was beautiful but was concerned about the size. Now, my only concern was for the price. This desk looked like the $1400.00 one we had looked at through the window. I turned the tag over and couldn't believe my eyes. It was $250.00 and there wasn't a scratch on it. We went into the office and the salesman wrote everything up.

On the way out, Herb passed another smaller desk and decided it was a better choice because of the size. I was so disappointed but I had to remember, it was his choice. Back to the office, ripped up the invoice and made a new one out. Herb was especially pleased because we could take this one home and wouldn't have to have it delivered. However, it not only didn't fit but when they turned it over, Herb realized it wasn't even wood, but fiberboard. We took it back, went back to the office again. The salesman tore up the second invoice and we went with our original choice.

It gave me a chance to witness to him. I thanked him for his patience with us and told him the story of how we had come across his shop. I said "God works in strange ways." He said he was going to start dropping business cards in parking lots. The desk did fit, by the way.

ONE CENT MULTIDIRECTIONAL HALOGEN LIGHT

Our hallway, though small, is an art gallery of family photos. I wanted to get a fixture that would enable us to direct the light in three different directions. I know that I'm repetitious, but think it's important to stress that Herb and I consistently ask Jesus to be in the middle of our day, to guide us whether we're talking to people, to help refrain me from inserting my foot in my mouth, which I've been known to do. We just invite him along, hoping He'll help orchestrate our day. On this particular day, I did NOT ask Him to find me a light fixture.

Actually, it was about a week after we had talked about getting one. Herb needed something at Lowes so while he was doing that, I went over to the light fixtures. I found the perfect one. It was on display. There was no price, no tag and no other ones in a box. I got a salesperson who was unable to help me. He told me to go up front by the registers and he'd get a manager. She came up and went through her inventory and couldn't even find the item. She then printed out a sticker with a upc label on it and handed the fixture to me. She said, "You're good to go."

The clerk at the register rang up all of Herb's items, then the lamp. It was one cent! The man just stared at the screen for several seconds before calling the manager, who happened to be near us. I said to the manager that this was crazy. She just smiled and said the price stands. She couldn't sell it without the box. I understood but asked her to let me pay something, offering $10.00. She said no. The clerk, even after being given the okay from the manager, had difficulty ringing it up. He said, "This is crazy. How does this happen?" I agreed, then added "Ask, and you shall receive." John 14 vs 12-14

Afterwards, we had to go to Home Depot for something that Herb needed. While in there, we looked at the light fixtures and found the exact one that we had just bought for a penny. It was marked $69.00. God does have a sense of humor. Of course, we thanked Him profusely for our new light.

JOYCE MEYER

Joyce Meyer is one of my favorite authors and speakers. She once said that we should stop holding onto things so tightly, unclench our hands and open them up to receive more of God's blessings, literally as well as spiritually. I've had some very significant things happen to me—big miracles. Yet, there are miracles everyday if we pay attention to them. A tiny seed growing into a beautiful flower, a rainbow, smiles from strangers, and icy drink on a hot day, should not be taken for granted.

Like everyone else, I do get attached to material things such as books, crystal pitchers obtained at yard sale prices, linens, vintage hankies and many other items. I had recently bought a red handbag from Marshalls. It wasn't a name brand and I didn't need it, however, I wanted it. It was $30.00. I think I must be a bulimic shopper. I buy things and then after a few weeks, I take them back. I took the red handbag back. I had never removed the tag and also, I already had three other handbags.

I'm switching gears here, for a reason. I will tie it together. I start teaching my CCD classes this week and I had thirty-five pencils to be sharpened with a manual sharpener that wasn't working very well. I said to Herb, maybe we should buy an electric one. He said that the classrooms would probably have a sharpener in them, so I scrapped that idea.

We've been trying to refrain from going to so many yard sales. We have enough "stuff" so I was taken aback when Herb said that there was a yard sale around the corner from us and we might as well go. It does become addictive. We went and I bought a beautiful, red, designer handbag in perfect condition for $8.00. Herb came walking over to me with his 'find', an electric pencil sharpener for $1.00.

This is not the first time this has happened, exactly when we needed or wanted something. Open up your hands in praise and thanksgiving to Jesus and be prepared to receive surprises.

I had found a wet suit at Red, White & Blue Thrift shop, shortly after we had our pool installed. It was the first time I had ever seen one and I've been going there for years. When Kenzie saw it she asked me if I'd get her one next time I went. I explained that I'd probably never see anything like that again. It was a fluke. However, next time I went, there it was in her size. I couldn't believe it. Then there was a request for children's crutches. Jake and Kenzie have an emergency room setup for when they play doctor. This has been educational for them because they want to learn what to do in all sorts of circumstances. They read my nursing manuals, have their own lab coats, stethoscopes and blood pressure cuff and, of course, a wheelchair. Kenzie knows how to apply an ace bandage correctly and a splint, if needed. Both she and Jake know more medical terms than most nursing assistants. So, of course, they needed crutches too. Ask and you shall receive. We got them. Aunt Rachele even made them an IV hookup from a water bottle. It amazes me how much they've learned by having fun. Oh, their favorite patient is Ringo, our cat who loves to be pushed in the wheelchair.

CHILDHOOD MEMORIES

Earliest memories I have are of waking up on the sofa after my nap. I was about four or five years old. My mother would give me a candy bar called a "Lunch Bar". It was chocolate and less than a nickel. Nobody from my age group seems to remember this item. I was beginning to think I had imagined this confection when Herb found the familiar wrapper on the internet, complete with "3 cents" on the wrapper. It has been discontinued.

My first day of first grade was frightening. There was a problem with the classroom not being ready so we had our orientation, so to speak, in the convent basement. I remember long tables and a dark, dreary atmosphere. The first instruction we were given was to write our name on the black and white tablet. I did not know how to spell my name. Then sister asked that we at least write our initials. I didn't even know what an initial was. I seemed to be the only one who didn't know how to do this. I was embarrassed to the point of tears. Not off to a good start. No wonder I always felt insecure.

When we finally got to our classroom, I felt more comfortable. Sister Josette Marie was a sweet, young nun. Over sixty years later I found out that one of the CCD teachers I worked with, went to St. Martin of Tours also and had the same nun. Small world. Second grade sister was Sister Mary Cyril. She was a little tougher. I remember she threatened to throw the trouble making boys out of the window if they didn't behave. I looked out the window of the second story room and refused to go back to school. I was terrified. I thought she meant it. There was a meeting with Sister, mom and dad and me whereby it was explained the threat was just a figure of speech.

Sixth grade nun was Sister Marie Grace. I remembered liking that class. It was when I first started to notice the good looking boys. We had sixty in our class, one nun, no aides. No wonder there were threats! In eighth grade we had a dance for our graduation. My best friend Dottie and I got the same exact pink dress. It was so pretty, however, I was so disappointed because it looked so much better on Dottie. She had a figure, I didn't unless you count "stick" figures.

I remember making mud pies and crunching in the leaves, all by the curb on my street—914 Brill Street in Philadelphia. I did well in school and usually got A's on my report card, yet, I was very insecure about my abilities and painfully shy. Even if I knew the answer to a question, I wouldn't volunteer it. I felt sure that I would somehow mess up the answer, stutter and appear stupid. Probably because I didn't volunteer answers, I was called on frequently. Even though I would answer correctly, my heart would be pounding and my face would flush—now I know that they were panic attacks. At home I wasn't allowed to voice my opinion if it didn't agree with my parents. I learned quickly to be quiet and submissive and it carried through to most of my life.

This next memory will give my age away. I remember in eighth grade we had inkwells! I wonder if the kids today even know what that was. Our desks had a hole in the upper right hand corner. A bottle of ink fit in there perfectly. We'd fill our fountain pens, then begin to write, carefully blotting the words with a blotter (another obsolete word). That was when we learned penmanship. So many things have gone by the wayside. It's sad. I recently gave a handout in my seventh grade CCD class. I was shocked to hear several students say that they couldn't read cursive writing.

Activities as an adolescent and young teenager were an occasional movie and roller skating. I used to love skating with my cousin, Loretta. We would also go to Boulevard Pools in Philadelphia to swim. These times were infrequent. Maybe that's why they are so special in my pool of memories. Loretta and I would try to synchronize our swimming like Esther Williams. I have another memory of Loretta and me when we were both married. She lived down the shore and she and I took out her small sailboat. If my memory serves me well, I think it was called a "Sunfish". I was amazed at her expertise in handling the sailboat amid the waves and the wind. That was really exciting.

Loretta's parents, my Aunt Rita and Uncle Earl have a beautiful love story. My Uncle Stan wrote a letter to his sister, Rita. Uncle Earl who was in the army happened to be the one censoring mail. In the letter, Stan was asking his sister why a beautiful girl like her was still single. Earl took it on his own, in a very respectful manner, contacting Rita. My cousin Loretta actually sent me a copy of that letter, which starts out "Dear Madam". Their relationship evolved from all the letters they had written over a long period of time. They fell in love before they even met. When they did meet in person, it just strengthened their feelings. They were married a short time thereafter.

Uncle Earl worked on the railroad, as did my father and other family members. He had a horrible accident when he was caught between two of the boxcars. He was literally crushed. Doctors told him that he would never walk again. He proved them wrong. He never walked without pain, but he did walk again. He took advantage of alternative medicine at a time it was considered ineffective by the medical profession. He had acupuncture and also went to a chiropractor.

EARLY TEENS

There was no middle ground when I was growing up. You obeyed your parents or there were consequences. Your parents had expectations and you were expected to rise to them. I believe that is good. My mother was the strict disciplinarian in the family. I will never forget the "talk" she gave me prior to my dating. I guess people of my age group refer to it as the "Birds and the Bees" talk. It consisted of one sentence that was seared into my brain. "Don't sit on a boy's lap and if you ever get pregnant, I will kick you the hell out!" At this time I didn't even know the facts of life but whatever they were I knew my mother meant what she said. Believe it or not, in hindsight, I'm glad she was so adamant about it. It was one cogent argument for me to behave. My palpable fear insured that I would remain a "good girl" until my wedding day. Of course, my Catholic upbringing also helped.

In a recent conversation with my daughter Rachele, she questioned how *did* I find out the facts of life? I remember distinctly that it was in the middle of Loretta Avenue in Philadelphia. I was with two girlfriends who were more informed than me. We were on our way to the drugstore to have vanilla cokes at the fountain. I stopped dead in my tracks amid traffic and people leaning on their horns for me to get out of the way. After digesting this information, I said "I'll never get married!!."

At fourteen, I could attend a church dance or have a date. I couldn't do both on the same weekend. I learned to make choices. I was not allowed to date anyone who had a car. Truth be told, I had less than ten dates before I met my first husband George. I loved family gatherings with cousins, aunts and uncles and grandparents on my father's side. The entire family would go to Washington's Crossing State Park on a Saturday. We did this often, rain or shine. There was a huge stone pavilion with a massive fireplace. On cool days we lit the fire. The adults would play Pinochle on the picnic tables. On warm days there would be softball games between the adults and the children. There was a wide stream to wade in and find fish and frogs and sometimes snakes.

There was a closeness to everyone in my father's family, young and old alike. Grandparents, aunts, uncles and cousins galore and an abundance of love transformed this simple gathering into a special occasion, each and every time. Even when it rained, our spirits were not dampened. We never got bored and always dreaded the goodbyes. With my mom, my grandmom Sophie and all my aunts providing the food—you can't begin to imagine the magnificent feast spread out, when it was time to eat. Sure we had the burgers, hot dogs and chicken. Then the menu went on and on, including Aunt Gene's gourmet dishes. There were so many phenomenal cooks in our family. There was always a hike to Bowman's Tower and the "butterflies" in my stomach as we ascended the circular, floating staircase up to the clouds. It's hard to believe that was so long ago, because the emotions and memories it evokes are still fresh in my mind.

I have a couple of memories of special times with my father. One took place on Christmas Eve. I was thirteen. Mom would go to the earliest Mass in the morning, which was usually 6:00 a.m. Dad and I walked the two city blocks to midnight Mass at St. Martin of Tours on the Oxford Circle in Philadelphia. It was snowing on the walk home. We held hands and I felt so special to have this time alone with daddy. When we got home, I was allowed to open one gift. It was a mint green sweater set that I loved. I can't help but add that I think having too many gifts today for children, makes it difficult to appreciate the thought that goes into one special gift. That sweater set is the only gift of significance that I can recall clearly after sixty years.

I just remembered another significant gift I received when I was a teenager. It was a manual typewriter. It really got a workout from me and my sister Mary. Mary still talks about how much it helped her to get ahead in school.

Another memory of my dad was of him in a Kelly green flannel shirt, visiting me in the hospital after my tonsilectomy. He brought ice cream for me but my throat was so sore that I couldn't eat it. Again, I felt so bad, thinking that I was somehow hurting him.

My dad was a powerful swimmer and swam across the Delaware River when he was young. I wanted to do the same. We had a boat that he and my uncle Stan had built. We learned to water ski and had picnics on the river. My dad said that I could swim across the river and he would be in the boat alongside of me keeping an eye on me. It was a much longer swim than I had anticipated because of the current, but I made it. It was a great accomplishment for me and I never fail to tell and retell the story every time we go over the Tacony Palmyra Bridge.

My dad would stop in a park, usually Burholme Park and find the highest hill and we would roll down. Years later when I was in my late fifties, Rachele took me to fly a kite which I had never done before. There was a hill behind our acreage on Blue Anchor and I couldn't resist the urge to roll down, with Rachele's encouragement, even though I was scheduled to have hip replacement surgery. I was glad that I did.

I also remember standing in line in the schoolyard at St. Martin of Tours School, waiting for the bell to ring. My mother had given me a small bouquet of roses to place before the statue of our Blessed Mother, in my classroom. The boys knocked all the petals off. I had nothing but stems and thorns left. How can I possibly recall this so vividly, fifty-seven years later and feel the pain—not for me but for my mother whom I felt would be so hurt by this.

I remember walking to the Deli on Halloween and our treat would be a huge Jewish pickle right from the barrel.

When I was in my early twenties, with four children we lived on Scattergood St. in Philadelphia.

In the summer, a huckster would drive his truck down our street, loudly calling out "Fresh vegetables, fresh fruit." I didn't have much money then but I always managed to buy a little something. We also had someone come down our very narrow street with a pony for the little ones to ride. I loved those days. One of my favorite memories of times long past is the milkman. I even enjoyed the clinking of the glass bottles as he picked up the empties and left fresh milk. It tasted so much better then. As a rare treat, he occasionally left ice cream.

One of the funniest memories was our "bread bag" boots. Boots back then were meant to be worn over the shoes. They were so difficult to get on. With four little ones to dress for the snowy weather, it took forever...until I discovered that a bread bag over the shoe would allow the shoe to slide right in place. Waxed paper also worked.

I remember Daddy rubbing whiskey on the gums of all my babies, when they were teething.

Rock & Rye whiskey with fruit and rock candy in the bottom of the bottle was an old fashioned remedy for coughs. For upper respiratory infections there was Vicks VapoRub on the chest and hot tea with honey, lemon and a shot of whiskey.

Ironically, my parents didn't drink much at all. The only time I remember them having a drink was when they would have family dinners (extended family) or company. In other words, special occasions. They'd also have a gin & tonic at a wedding. During Christmas daddy would invite the neighbors over for a drink.

I remember the Fuller Brush man coming to our house with his suitcase full of every type of brush imaginable. Mom always bought a little something.

One of the best memories was a once a month delivery from "Charles Chips & Pretzels." They were in large tin cans. Chips and pretzels never tasted so good. When the cans were empty, the delivery man would pick them up. We were recycling long before it was mandatory. I don't remember many treats. Mom did bake cakes but there wasn't much of a selection of goodies in the supermarket, like there is today. We had just a few choices of cereals also. If the kids today saw what it was like back then, they would be shocked and probably feel deprived. We never did.

I used to get a small allowance for doing chores. The worst job was cleaning the venetian blinds on Saturday morning. I was always getting small cuts on my hands from the metal slats. I would take my allowance, walk to the drugstore and get a "Veronica & Archie" comic book and a vanilla fudge ice cream cone. Sugar cones weren't invented yet. The taste was heavenly. Even the plain cone tasted great. They truly do not make them like they used to. I would also take any empty soda bottles to the drugstore to get a nickel refund—more recycling. Soda was just an occasional treat.

Daddy came home one day and said that the tavern on the next block had a sign advertising "Tomato Pie". He never frequented bars so it was a big deal when he went in there and brought home this new item, our first pizza.

PET PEEVES

I find the incessant use of a popular four letter word to be abhorrent. I cannot believe that educated people have such a limited vocabulary that they need to pepper their conversation with multiple slurs. I wonder if they even know that it's a legal term that was posted above the cells of prostitutes in medieval times, "Fugitive Under Carnal Knowledge." I actually saw a young girl in the supermarket with a shirt that had f_____ in huge letters on the front of her shirt. She was very proud of it, showing some friends. What is happening to our youth that this is acceptable?

Herb has a pet peeve also. Actually, I would have to say all the boys would agree. I talk too much. I repeat stories. Jake (age 8) and Kenzie (13) say I'm loquacious. I love that they use their advanced vocabulary. I was so quiet for most of my life that, in some way, I'm making up for it. My girls don't seem to mind. They have stories also. I have not mastered the art of brevity. I try and I fail miserably. I'm still working on it.

I'm sure there's someone else who would agree with the men in my life. Dr. Rothman told me that he would like me to be awake for my hip replacement. I wasn't real sure about that. Then he said, "Think of the story you'll have to tell your kids." That won me over. I was awake, alert and cognizant of everything that was going on. I had a clear plexiglass shield in front of me. I couldn't see anything, but the sounds alone piqued my interest. I remarked that it sounded like my husband's garage. Dr. Rothman would explain that he was indeed using tools similar to my husband's.

When a spray of blood hit the plexiglass shield, I asked what had happened. I was grilling him relentlessly, the nurse in me wanting to know every little thing that was going on. When he was measuring my leg for the fifth time, I questioned him yet again. He said, "Do you want to walk out of this hospital without a limp?" I said yes. He measured a sixth time. By the time he was stapling me back together, I said "I'll bet you're sorry I was awake for this Dr. Rothman." He replied "I'm getting there." He then handed me a phone and said to tell Herb I was fine. I thought he was supposed to do that. His ears must have been ringing from my incessant chatter. He is such an amazing doctor. I'm just glad that he has a sense of humor. Oh, I have no limp.

MEMORIES

When we lived in Atco, we'd frequent Annings Store. It was a five &dime store, a hardware store, grocery store and one of my favorite things to get was an orange ice cone—not orange sherbet. I have never been able to get it anywhere else. We'd take a large bowl and have them scoop ice cream to fill it. Ice cream never tasted so good.

Some memories may not have been funny at the time they occurred, but they are now. Case in point—did our kids get into trouble. Sure they did, but most of what they did I learned about years later. Mark would sneak out of the basement window, meet his friend Johnny from across the street and walk to the news store on Rte. 73, probably to browse through inappropriate magazines.

David and Kevin would sneak out after I went to bed. They would take my car through the woods. For the longest time I thought I had a leak in my gas tank. I'd fill it and it would always be close to empty. I was on a tight budget and I had to keep spending more and more of my money on gas. I never even thought that there was something untoward going on. I think I was trusting but the kids must have been laughing about how naïve I was.

LOVES IN MY LIFE

The loves in my life are God, husband, children, grandchildren, family, friends and country. One of the greatest gifts we have in life is our freedom. Don't ever forget that freedom wasn't free. Pray for our servicemen and women who keep us safe abroad and our policemen and women who risk their lives every day keeping us safe at home. One of the most powerful speeches ever given was by Ronald Reagan in 1961 and is even more appropriate for today considering the upheaval and numerous scandals eg. Fast & Furious, IRS, Benghazi, NSA, terrorist attacks that this administration refuses to label as such.

> "Freedom is never more than a generation away from extinction. We didn't pass it on to our children in the bloodstream. The only way we can inherit the freedom we know is if we fight to protect it, defend it and then hand it to men with the well fought lessons of how those in our lifetime must do the same. And if you and I don't do this, then who will. We may spend our sunset years telling our children what it once was like in America when men were free. WE ARE ON THAT PRECIPICE NOW."

> Ronald Reagan

The best things in life are not things at all. However, I do love many things, like sliding onto cool sheets, crisp linens that have caught the breeze on a clothesline. I love to inhale God's fabric softener as I burrow my face in a pile of freshly laundered clothes.

BOOKS are definitely high on my list. I echo Kathleen Norris' quote, "Just the knowledge that a good book is awaiting one at the end of a long day, makes that day happier." My tastes are varied. I've read a lot of Stephen King, biographies and self-help books. Just about anything that is in print. One of my favorite authors is Father Andrew Greeley. I've read most of his books. Though I'm not a fan of romances, his stories incorporate romance with factual history, even politics, though the books themselves are fictional. What I like the most that comes through in all his stories, is a love for God and a love and respect for the middle aged or older woman. He has also written many non-fiction books which were excellent reading.

Two other authors I thoroughly enjoy are Max Lucado and Joyce Meyer. They offer a wealth of spiritual insight which helps in my daily walk with Jesus. In the last eight years, Bill O'Reilly has risen to the top of my list. In his book "Killing Lincoln" I felt like I was present in the theatre and a silent spectator by Lincoln's deathbed. I actually cried while reading this book. Our children and grandchildren need to know about our history and real heroes. "Killing Kennedy", "Killing Jesus" and "Killing Patton" as well as "Killing Reagan" reveal history as if you were present. "A Bold Fresh Piece of Humanity" reveals Bill's experience during his school days and his Catholic upbringing, which he still adheres to. Herb and I are very proud of our library of books by all the Fox News contributors. The last two years alone I feel myself drawn to Military books especially those about Navy Seals. Chris Kyle "American Sniper" and Marcus Luttrell "Lone Survivor" give testament to the strength, endurance and risking life and limb for their love of our country. God bless our Military. Our granddaughter Kenzie has begun reading Bill's books. She has a ravenous appetite for books.

2015 POWDER KEG!!!

We have a presidential election coming up next year. I want to be informed. Right now, there are seventeen candidates campaigning to get the nomination. I am trying to prepare myself to make an informed decision. I have been voraciously reading their books, learning about their views and their background, how they voted on certain issues, especially pro life and military issues and if they had cogent reasons for doing so. I used to think politics was boring. Not anymore. This time around, it's explosive and volatile.

Though politics is not my favorite undertaking, I understand more and more that, as Dr. Charles Krauthammer attests to, politics affects just about everything in our lives, including our children's education, health care, taxes and on and on. We need to get the politics right or we will screw ourselves over. Vote people! Vote! But only if you know who and what you're voting for. Become informed. Just a note of interest, Dr. Charles Krauthammer is also a Fox News Contributor and author of an amazing book titled "Things That Matter."

MUSIC

I love music....to listen to or to play on my piano. It fills a special place in my heart. I missed the organ I had in the 70's. I received a treasured gift from my new hubby shortly after we were married. He bought me a beautiful Thoma piano. Finances were tight at the time, so the piano was bought second hand from a doctor in Haddonfield. There is nothing second hand about the quality of tone. Once again, I could play my forties music and the oldies as well as classical. I play my piano almost every day, sometimes for hours at a time. I have done this for over twenty years. Like the water in our pool, my music engulfs me with a calm I desperately need.

I especially enjoy the music from the forties, like "Stardust", "Ebb Tide", "Tenderly" and my mother's favorite, "Harbor Lights". Mom, in the last ten years likes to sing along with me when I play the piano. I don't recall where I read it, but I remember a quote that is so true, "Life without music is a mistake". Of course, Herb and I both love country music. Listening to my son Kevin's music is even more meaningful because we know the stories behind his songs and the people they're about.

I love to dance but especially favor swing or jitterbug and a good polka. Slow songs are great for getting romantic. Herb and I used to slow dance a lot in our first Lake Wynooska home, to Froggy 101, the only radio station we could get. Our song is "Always and Forever". Herb touched me deeply when, besides "our" song at our wedding, he requested "You Are So Beautiful".

There is a humorous story that took place at a Pocono bar near our home. Herb, George and I went for a drink and hamburger at this local "dive." The food was great and even the music was good. The jukebox had mostly country music. It was torture for me to hear these good dance songs and not be able to dance. Herb couldn't because of his torn rotator cuffs. George was having respiratory issues, although he used to love to dance. When Beer Barrel Polka came on, I couldn't take it any longer. I said I can't sit and listen to this and not get up and move, so I started getting my coat on to leave. Just then a tall good looking local man comes over, tips his cowboy hat and says "Maam, would you like to polka?" I threw my coat down and said "Yes, I would!" That country boy was really good.

It's 2016 now and we have more aches and pains but we still enjoy dancing to the slow songs, usually in our kitchen. If we're not dancing to Kevin's songs, it's George Strait and Rod Stewart. We recently went to a 4H Fair and concert tribute to George Strait and Alan Jackson in our neighborhood. We've lived here twelve years and didn't realize this place was ten minutes from us. We plan to attend the rodeo next month.

While we were checking out the animals and other booths before the concert started, I decided to have a butterfly painted (henna) on my arm in honor of Jillian and Mark's anniversary. The Indian woman was so gracious and, of course, I showed her photos. I also asked if she'd be able to do one for me in September before our daughter's wedding. She said she'd be honored and gave me her card. Her shop is close by in Voorhees. It's like a temporary tattoo, all natural and lasts about ten days. After she was done I turned around to see what everyone was looking at. It was the first time ever that I saw a double rainbow. I guess Jillian and Mark were pleased.

GEORGE

George was my first husband and the father of our six beautiful children. We met when I was fifteen and he was seventeen. I had gone to his brother Stan's prom and met him when I went over his house so his mother could take pictures. Their house was just a few blocks from my grandmother's house and my cousin's house. Shortly after that night, Stan backed out of a date to go to a party in my neighborhood, because it meant that he would have to take three buses to get to my house. Back then, teens rarely had their own cars. When George heard about this, he offered to take me to the party. I thanked him but declined since I already had another date. I went to the party with a friend who would be entering the seminary. George then asked me if he could take me to a movie the following week. I said yes.

Our first date was in February 1960. We walked over a mile to the Benner Movie in Philadelphia to see Doris Day and Rock Hudson in "Pillow Talk". It was bitter cold out. When we got back to my home, we went down to our finished basement to play records. Mom sent the twins, Mary and Joey, down to "chaperone". My little brother and sister were five years old. We had about ten dates before George enlisted in the Navy along with two of his friends from school. Most of our courtship was via letters. We'd both write several times a week. George would come home on leave most weekends, although my mother didn't want us spending too much time with each other. Her rule was either one date or one dance a week on either a Friday or Saturday, never both days.

My mother did allow me to have a very small party for George, when he came home on leave after a long separation. I still remember dancing to "Soldier Boy" and Sonny James "Young Love." However, Johnny Mathis, Elvis and Sinatra were my favorites. George gave me an engagement ring when I was sixteen. I think of that now with disbelief. At first, my mother was against it but then I argued that she was married at seventeen. Since my parents liked George, they finally gave their consent. George and I did care deeply about each other. Of course, keep in mind that we were sixteen and eighteen. Before the wedding I started to get cold feet. I remember telling mom I wasn't sure about this. I didn't think I could go through with the marriage. She said not to worry. Everybody gets cold feet. She also said that George was a good boy and that if I waited, I might end up with someone not so good. Again, I was seventeen.

George was going overseas in August of 1962. I graduated from Little Flower Catholic High School for Girls on June 9, 1962. Since we didn't want to wait until his deployment was over, we married on June 23, 1962, two weeks after my graduation. The ceremony took place at St. Martin of Tours Church on the Oxford Circle in Philadelphia. My brother Eddie was the altar boy. My cousin Loretta and my friend Dottie were my bridesmaids. My mother picked out my dress and I acquiesced. It was the first dress I tried on. I had no say in the matter. The reception was at a restaurant in Philadelphia. We had a jukebox for music and everyone had a good time.

After the reception, George's friends drove us to a motel in N.J. because George had a little too much to drink. One of his other friends came along so they could leave our car and go home in theirs. Next morning I couldn't wait to go swimming in the pool. I went alone. Then we headed for Bath, Maine where George had rented what he said was a beautiful farm house. He assured me it was in good condition and that he had been cleaning it up.

When we arrived it was dusk. It was a beautiful house on a tree lined street. I was so excited until he opened the door and hundreds of roaches scattered across the floor and kitchen counters. It was a two story house and I never even saw the second floor. It was so filthy I refused to go upstairs. Our first fight ensued. How could he expect me to live in this. Next day we found a tiny apartment. This was not what my romantic images of married life had conjured up. It was a rocky start.

George's parents were initially against us getting married. I don't know if it was just resignation or finally acceptance, but on the day of the wedding,

George's mom seemed very happy. His mom was a quiet person but I do remember her obvious pleasure anytime we visited. She spent most of her time sitting in a little chair in an alcove in their home. She had a little table with her cigarettes and her rosary. I felt a closeness with her over the years. She was a gentle, loving person. There didn't seem to be much happiness in her life, with the exception of our visits, especially with our children, her grandchildren.

I never became close to George's father. He had an overt disrespect and crudeness towards me. He was inappropriate when he kissed me one time so I tried to steer clear of him. His language and innuendos were off color. After that I avoided him. Actually, George wasn't even close to his dad. It was understandable because, in his dad's eyes, he could do nothing right. His dad criticized everything he did or didn't do. I remember George saying that he had to iron his dad's shirts and even make him breakfast. He used to iron while watching the Mickey Mouse Club.

George's dad was unreasonable too. I didn't have a car but his dad did. Yet, he would not come to visit us. He expected me to take three buses to visit them, while I carried diaper bags, was eight months pregnant and had a one year old, a two year old and a three year old in tow. He couldn't understand why I wouldn't do this, while George was at work. He was older and felt that, out of respect for him, I should have conceded. I thought, but never said that respect needs to be earned. Needless to say, that was one time when I said no. I never understood why George wasn't as upset over this as I was, nor would he come to my defense when his father insulted me. I realize now, as I'm writing this, that I was still being dependent on others instead of standing up for myself.

Even though there was no love lost between George's dad and me, we still visited because of his mother. One time I even attempted something that I thought would 'heal' our strained relationship. George's parents came to dinner, a rare occasion that I thought would be a very special dinner. I made a roast beef and Yorkshire pudding, an English specialty. I had gotten the recipe from our neighbor who was from England. I thought his dad would be surprised and appreciative of the special effort. He told me angrily that he wasn't English, but Welsh and that my roast was dry. Even George thought "Edwards" was English.

I remember when we moved into our beautiful split-level home in Marlton Lakes. We had a housewarming. George's aunt Betty (his mom's sister) and Uncle Art brought his parents to the party. The house must have seemed like a mansion to them—four bedrooms, two and a half baths, fireplace and lake view. I knew that this time George's dad would have to say something positive. I was so proud of George for having made this dream home possible. Everyone bubbled with praise and congratulations, including his mom and aunt and uncle. In front of all our friends and family, very loudly and sarcastically, his dad said, "You'll never make it!" Aunt Betty, also loudly, said, "Look around George. They already have!"

HUMOROUS MEMORY OF GEORGE'S

I'm sure our children will get a laugh out of this story. George loved telling it. When he and his friends were in high school they lamented that they did not have a car to get around in. They decided to remedy that by taking up a collection, door to door, for needy kids. They failed to tell people that *they* were those kids. After several weeks of collections, they were able to buy an old car that actually ran, at least for a few months. Knowing how staid and proper George was, it was hard to believe that he was that mischievous.

MADAME MARIE CURIE A surprising family link

This next fact is one of special interest to our family. George's maternal grandfather, Benjamin Sklodowska, was second cousin to Marie Sklodowska Curie, a Polish scientist who discovered how to measure radioactivity. During her lifetime Madame Marie Curie was the world's most famous woman scientist. Curie pioneered the study of radioactivity (a word she coined). She, her husband Pierre and French physicist Henri Becquerel shared the Nobel Prize in 1903, for physics for their work measuring the radiation of uranium and for discovering two new radioactive elements, polonium (named for her beloved Poland) and radium. In 1911 Curie became the first and only woman to win two Nobel Prizes. She earned, on her own, the award in chemistry for isolating pure radium.

Marie was a native of Russian-occupied Poland, but moved to Paris in 1891 to study. There she earned degrees in physics and mathematics. Both she and Pierre paid a high price for their work with radiation, which included a number of experiments in which they burned themselves with radioactive compounds to observe the effects.

Radiation sickness rendered Pierre an invalid. Their daughter Irene, their son-in-law and several lab assistants all died or were severely disabled by various radiation-linked diseases. Surprisingly, Marie lived well into her sixties but suffered poor health, blindness and deafness for years before she died of leukemia. One of her famous quotes is "Nothing in life is to be feared. It is only to be understood." 1867—1934

I gleaned most of this information from "100 Most Important Women of the 20th Century" which was compiled by Ladies' Home Journal with a foreword by Barbara Walters. There is an amazing movie, biography of Marie Curie titled "Madame Curie" 1942, with Greer Garson and Walter Pidgeon. It is well worth seeing.

OUR FAMILY BEGINS

Our first son, David, was born ten months after our wedding. George and I had very little time to get to know each other as a couple that first year because George left for Sicily five weeks after our wedding and didn't return until six months later. It was difficult going through the first few months of my pregnancy alone. I was still living in Maine. My dad came to drive me home to stay with him and mom. I couldn't help thinking about how difficult it had to be for my mom when she was pregnant with me. She went through the pregnancy and birth alone because my dad was in the Army, during World War II. At least, George would be home for the birth of our baby.

Although we were so young, probably too young (there's that hindsight again), we grew to love each other more. Friends and family believed that we were the perfect couple. So did we. We were happy. I was living my dream with a houseful of babies. George seemed to enjoy the children when they were babies and changed his share of diapers. He was also getting ahead in Xerox. When I look back I think that maybe the reason we reached a certain plateau and didn't go further was because we didn't actually nurture our relationship with 'dates' and time away from the children.

I sometimes think that George's social life was satisfied with business lunches and dinners, drinks after work etc. He even admitted to dancing when he went out. That really hurt. I, on the other hand, was a stay-at-home mom with no car. The only adult conversations I had were with my friends and neighbors, Lorraine and Miriam. We talked about kids. We did play cards once a week. I can't tell you how much I looked forward to that.

I realize now that I was a needy person, dependent on George for everything, just like I had been dependent on my parents. We only had one car so I couldn't just pick up and go. I would pack some snacks and take my four little ones to the park. Two sat in the coach, two held on to the side. It was about two miles to Wissinoming Park. I even would walk to my mother's house across the Roosevelt Blvd. That was a five mile walk.

We had one mini family vacation, a weekend down the shore with Lorraine and Paul and Frank and Miriam. Together, we had five toddlers. I was nine months pregnant with our third, our daughter Rachele. I was actually several days past my due date. I swam out past the breakers so the waves wouldn't pound me in the stomach. The lifeguard kept blowing the whistle for me to come in. I loved it.

George did win two trips from Xerox for his achievements. We went to Jamaica for five days and for a weekend in Florida. I was very proud of him but felt somewhat left out. It bothered George that all I could talk about were the children and our home. That's all I knew. At one point, I did a lot of reading about the history of Xerox. I figured that this knowledge would give me an edge up on conversing with George, his co-workers and superiors when we were at Xerox functions. It helped me to acquire more self-confidence and even George said he was impressed. Of course, my memory being what it is now, I'd need a refresher course about the Haloid Co., established in 1906, which became the precursor for Xerox. Actually, Chester Carlson made the first xerographic image in Queens, New York in 1938.

Our best years were the ones in Marlton Lakes. The children and I thrived there and spent the months from May to October swimming. George wasn't interested in swimming like we were, but he would come down when we had company, to show them the lake. He would go swimming occasionally but told me that it wasn't "his thing." He was also involved in the civic association. He would coach little league but wasn't interested in doing anything with our kids, like having a game of catch or going fishing. He'd have his name in the community paper and that meant a lot to him.

I made friends with some of the other mothers. We'd take turns having lunches and it helped me to hone my culinary instincts. I made everything from scratch, including bread. It's like everything else, practice makes perfect. Now those skills have gone by the wayside. I still do some things well, but now I cook as little as possible, maybe three times a week. Take out is a wonderful thing!

Our money problems were always present. George wanted me to get a job to help out. I reminded him that we only had one car. He said "You'll figure something out." I look back with embarrassment at my lack of self-esteem and find it difficult to believe that, once again, I did what I was told. It was humiliating borrowing my friends or neighbor's cars or bumming rides to look for a job. I was hired as a receptionist at a real estate office about five miles from home. Luckily, I was able to get a ride home from a neighbor who also worked there. I worked for a few months utilizing my typing and shorthand skills, then found another job at Archway School, five minutes from our home. Some time after that, my dad helped us get a second car.

We went for a Marriage Encounter weekend while we lived in Marlton Lakes. It was a great weekend and strengthened our relationship. Shortly after, when I was thirty-one and George was thirty-three, we became pregnant with Ryan, and a year later with Jillian. I was happiest when I was pregnant and having and caring for babies. I'm not saying that I didn't get stressed with the overwhelming responsibility, because I did, but I was doing what I loved most, being a wife and mother. I, however, never stopped wanting some time for us, a night out, dinner. It never happened.

One time I was so insistent on meeting George in down town Philly where he worked. I wanted us to go to lunch at one of the many places he was always talking about. He finally relented. It was difficult for me to even take the high speed line. I had never done that before. I was looking all around at the activity, the people and then George handed me a hot dog from a vendor. I said I thought we were going to lunch. He said, "This *is* lunch." I returned home, realizing that he probably knew everyone at the restaurants and didn't want them to meet me because of the other woman in his life.

George had a good, secure job at Xerox. Yet, with six children, there was never any extra money. We were always in a financial bind. Toys were bought once a year at Christmas. Clothes were bought once a year when we got our income tax return. There were no movies or fast food. All the children were great at entertaining themselves in the back yard or with friends. The boys had ramps and forts. Rachele had an old mattress that she did gymnastics on. We all made do with what we had. I don't remember complaints about what we didn't have.

I remember years later after George and I separated, he would take Jillian and Ryan for the weekend and he would take them out to eat. This was a treat that the older children never had, until they got jobs of their own and could treat themselves. They all had jobs by the time they were thirteen or fourteen. They had to grow up so fast. I remember at one point in time, they were all working at the Berlin Farmer's Mart. David was working at the tire place, Kevin was working next door at the stereo store, Mark was at a men's clothing store, and Rachele was unloading watermelons from a truck for the outside food stands. Working at the Berlin Mart was a rite of passage.

I'm not saying that we were poor, but things were tight...always. We never had steak or shrimp. We had lots of soups, chicken and hot dogs. No one complained. We lived in beautiful homes. George would work two jobs a lot of those years. That meant that most of the time I was alone in caring for the children.

In August of 1979 we would be married seventeen years. I sensed by now, there were problems in our relationship, but George wouldn't talk about them. He was coming home in the early morning hours. I was crushed but I hung on to a memory of a few months before when he came home from work. I was at the stove cooking, and he came up behind me, hugged me and said that he had had a bad day at work. Then he said "Thank God I have you to come home to." With that remark echoing in my mind, I found it confusing to say the least, that things began to go downhill after that.

Though the warning signs were many, I rationalized them away. I was in denial. Then there was a glimmer of hope. On 9/15/79, my thirty-fifth birthday, George told me he had made reservations for dinner at Pier111. I was ecstatic and in shock. Keep in mind that he had never taken me out to dinner or lunch in seventeen years. He rarely acknowledged birthdays, anniversaries and other holidays. Christmas was different. He would give me a card and gifts then. There also was one Valentine's day I remember that George *did* get me a gift. It was snowing and he walked to Montgomery Ward to pick up a black bikini he had bought for me. My appearance was so important to him that he would be concerned about my weight gain when I was pregnant. One time the doctor, knowing that George kept after me, was so pleased that I hadn't gained anything, that he said to George, not me, "Good job George!" That same Valentine's Day he also gave me a heart shaped box of chocolates which he placed on top of my washer. I was thrilled.

We differed greatly on our views on special days. Money was scarce but I did enjoy trying to make birthdays and holidays special. Sometimes there were small gifts, but mostly cards, a cake and a special meal. Looking back, I suppose I was trying to impose my ideas on him. The first Mother's day card I ever received from George came after we were divorced. I appreciated it but couldn't understand why he waited until then. He had always reminded me on mother's' day that I wasn't his mother. I responded that as the mother of our children, some acknowledgement would be greatly appreciated.

With all this in mind, you can imagine why this dinner invitation on my birthday seemed so significant, such a positive thing. I was mistaken. We hardly talked at dinner and I ended up getting food poisoning. Two weeks later when Jillian and Ryan were three and four years old, and David, Kevin, Rachele and Mark were young teenagers, my world and theirs crashed. I just thought George was overworked. He had become a workaholic. On October 6, 1979 I felt something inside of me that was frightening, to put it mildly. A wave of nausea hit me with such force, then palpitations (panic attack) when George admitted that there was another woman in his life. My head pounded. I remember punching him repeatedly, I was so angry and hurt."

I thought that we would grow old together. I was in disbelief as George told me "It's not you Rose. You've been a great wife and mother." He went on to list many of my attributes going so far as to say that he was still attracted to me, then ended by saying that he just didn't love me anymore. I was devastated, in shock. We remained together, to some degree, for another four years. At the end of those years, our marriage of twenty-one years was over.

Years later when I was in nursing school, I had to do a term paper on male mid-life crisis. We were given a list of books from which to draw our material. I attempted several times to utilize these books, but unsuccessfully. My train of thought was in a state of stasis. I then proceeded to write of my own experience with George, because by now I was aware that this had to be what he was going through. I got an A+ on my paper.

During these tumultuous years, there was a glimmer of hope when I actually thought we might get back together. George had asked me out for dinner on Valentine's day. About a week before, we met at the roller skating rink. While skating, George fell and I fell with him, breaking my wrist. He took me to the hospital that night. Next day he took me to the doctor to get the cast on. A week later, Valentine's day had come and gone with not even a call.

At this time, George was doing renovation work on the Hoppe's house, right behind our house. I couldn't believe that he never called to see how I was doing or to explain about why he stood me up on Valentine's day. I was so frustrated because I had difficulty in even making lunch for myself. I couldn't open tuna or a can of soup because of the pain and swelling. I couldn't drive because I was on pain medication. I was limited even more because I was right handed. I finally lost it and called George at the Hoppe's house. I blasted him for standing me up, for being so insensitive that he never even called to see if I was okay or needed something. I ranted about how I couldn't even manage to open a can of soup or drive to get milk and bread. Then I hung up. That afternoon he came over with a grocery bag. In it was a loaf of bread, milk and an electric can opener. He left without another word. I went back to work the next week. It was over a month before I heard from George. Dating was never mentioned again.

CRUISE

When George would take Jillian and Ryan for a weekend, I would ask if they had a good time. Other than that I did not want to know anything so I did not pump them for information. Truth be told, I didn't want to know what was going on. It hurt too much. However, one time Ryan and Jillian were talking about their father going on a cruise with his girlfriend.

I was not very Christian like then. I was furious and called to tell him so. I prefaced the conversation with "It's your life, your money and I know that I have no right to say anything but I'm going to." I continued, "I was a good wife to you, always putting you first. You admitted that. We never did anything or even go out to dinner, unless it was a Xerox function. Yet, we talked of doing things, like a cruise or traveling or even a vacation once in a while. It was always going to be later. Now you're taking someone you've known a couple of months and I've given you twenty-one years. I then said "You are one lousy son of a b-------" and hung up.

He called back and said "Please don't hang up. Just listen." He wanted to take me on a cruise when he got back from the first one. I laughed and told him that he was crazy and hung up again. Mark and his friend were in the kitchen when he called back. I was so upset and Mark wanted to know what happened, so I told him. Mark thought I should go. He said that I deserved it. I looked at him with disbelief. I said absolutely not.

He couldn't understand why I wouldn't just go. His friend (I think it was Sal) said, "Mark, don't you get it?" Mark said, "Get what?". He said, "Your mom doesn't want to sleep with the guy.!" We all cracked up laughing and I confirmed it. I finally got over it. I had to. There were so many other vacations. He took his friend to England (My dream was to have high tea in England and go to a pub). He took her to Hawaii, the islands and skiing in Colorado. You name it. He was there. Now I can laugh about it but not back then when the "green eyed monster" bared its fangs.

I wasn't upset with the other person in his life. She is actually a good friend of mine. I felt that she was too good for George. Keep in mind this transpired many years after our divorce. I just felt cheated that I never got to visit those special places. There would never be the money to do those things on my own. Decades have passed and I am at peace with my husband on our three bucolic acres, inhabited by scores of wildlife. It really couldn't get any better than that.

THE RENAISSANCE; GEORGE'S DREAM COME TRUE

George had always wanted a boat. He had remote controlled boats but he wanted a real one. He said if we had a boat, it would be a family centered activity—fishing with the boys and he thought it would give us quality time. I wanted him to spend more time with the kids and for us to do something as a family once in a while. While it sounded good there was one problem. We didn't have any money.

He asked me to ask my mother if we could borrow the money. I didn't want to do that, but I did. He named the boat "Renaissance". I love the water as much as the kids but the boat was not a pleasurable experience for me. The only exception was when Lorraine and Paul would come down and spend time with us on the boat. I could relax then. George was more laid back when they were there. Normally, he would get upset if the kids were diving off the boat in the slip after we cleaned it. He didn't want them dripping water on it??? It's a boat!! One of the men who had a boat in another slip heard George yelling and invited the kids to dive off of his boat.

Though the older children did come down on the boat in the beginning, it wasn't long before they opted to stay home. One good thing did happen while we were the marina. The owner's cat had kittens and we got to pick the best of the lot. "Misty" was a Siamese and the most amazing cat. The owners' daughter would throw the kittens off the dock and they'd swim to a ramp and climb up. They would go over to the girl again, crying until she repeated this little feat. The mother cat would jump in the water, on her own. As much as we love the water, we knew "Misty" was a good match for our family.

We did have a frightening experience when Lorraine and Paul were with us. George was moving rapidly in the water and his wake swamped another boat. We watched as people on the other boat fell down from the force of our wake. They were furious and came after us. Jillian and Ryan were around four and five years old and, of course, they had life jackets on. When Lorraine and I saw the other boat heading for us, we grabbed the kids and went below just as a glass bottle crashed through a window in the galley, spraying glass all over. We were all shaken up.

George took friends out on the boat for fishing trips several times but never took our boys. That was a huge disappointment to me and to them. However, I found out many years later that David had taken the keys to the boat and he and Kevin went down and took it out. I was actually glad to hear that. They apparently were more adept at maneuvering the boat in and out of the slip than George was. More often than not, he had trouble and would always blame it on the current.

My mother did lend us the money for the boat but when it came time to pay her back, George didn't have the money so I got a job as a bank teller and paid her back. As far as I'm concerned, a boat is nothing but a big hole you sink money into. There was always something going wrong with it.

THE DIVORCE

The decision to get a divorce was a difficult one especially because of my faith. I actually believed that, at age 37, my life was over. I knew that I would never be able to share it with anyone else. I honestly believed that. After years of counseling and tirades of emotional abuse, I found the strength to make a decision and say "Enough!"

Of course, I had all my children but as they graduated, they began to strike out on their own. Things were increasingly difficult for them as I relied on them so much more. They were like young parents to Ryan and Jillian, babysitting while I worked or went on job interviews, or even shopping. I remember the first supermarket to stay open until midnight. I'd do my shopping after work and would get home at 10:00pm then clean the house. That's really the first time I realized I had a serious problem with insomnia.

One night I got home early to witness a scene I'll never forget. Mark had the dining room table set with the linen table cover and napkins and my good wine glasses. He had a white hand towel over his arm, like a waiter and was pouring "wine" (grape juice) for Jillian and Mark and serving them spaghetti. I cried tears of joy. He was enjoying his little brother and sister. Markie, I miss you sooo much!

Rachele took them to Los Amigos, a restaurant within walking distance of our home. She treated them to nachos and sodas with her own money. The Mexican setting was so exciting to them. Kevin and Trudi would take

Jillian and Ryan over their house when they got married. Did I mention that my children are exceptional?

David took Rachele and Ryan under his "wing" teaching them to hunt. Rachele remembers sitting on the roof of our house and David drilling her to never take a shot unless it was a good one. He said that you don't want to injure or maim an animal. She talks often of all he taught her, how to track, how to make sure the sun wasn't at your back because it would silhouette you and the deer would see you.

From the onset of our problems to the end result, it was actually four years before I was sure that divorce was inevitable. There were many ups and downs along the way. Actually, it had been a little more than two years of this emotional trauma when an event occurred that helped me to focus clearly on the fact that our relationship was over. It happened in an emergency room. I was there with Kevin and was frantic because the injury was to his eye. His contact lens, in the process, became imbedded to the point that the doctors were having trouble getting it out due to swelling. I feared for his sight. Keep in mind, he already has serious problems with his eyes.

I called a friend and asked if they would get a message to George. He was in a local bar. He did show up at the hospital but was not supportive. He was actually sarcastic, asking how the other guy looked. I told him that if he couldn't be there for his son, then leave. I remember seething about his attitude and behavior. Prior to this incident, I was ambivalent about what to do, even though a priest had suggested a separation. The guilt I knew I would feel if I ended our marriage would be debilitating. Yet, I wasn't ending it, was I? George had already chosen to do that.

I made up my mind that when he came in that night I would ask for a divorce. Now I wasn't vacillating nor was I feeling any guilt. I knew it was the right decision. I'd never been so sure of anything. When George came in I calmly stated that I wanted a divorce. Imagine my shock when he said "I'll do anything you want. Just don't get a divorce." This is crazy. He's playing games with me. For two years he's been telling me he doesn't love me and dating someone else. So in answer to his request, I said the only thing I knew he wouldn't do and that was to go for counseling with a priest. Shock hit me again as he said okay. Now the guilt resurfaces because if he wants to try, I felt I had to. It was like a roller coaster ride of emotions. We did go for some counseling but it was short lived.

One of the priests I went to wrote for the Catholic Star Herald. He was in another town. I was still feeling the stigma attached to having marital problems. I told the priest my story. I was so riddled with guilt about even thinking about a divorce. When I was done talking, he said to me "You're either Polish or Italian". Remember, my last name is Edwards at the time. He did not know that my maiden name was Wawrzyniak. I told him I was Polish and asked how he came to that conclusion. He said that the Polish and Italians have a unique way of inflicting guilt on their children through religion.

He suggested a separation. I was shocked. I said that marriage is forever. He agreed and then said that marriage was between two people. He pointed out that I was alone in this. He suggested I stop doing George's laundry and saving meals for him and giving him haircuts. He said that as long as nothing changed at home, there was no reason for George to change. He had his cake, so to speak, and was eating it too.

NEARING AN END

This whole book has been written with prayers for guidance. My intent is not to hurt anyone, though some of the chapters in this book may be difficult to recall, not only for me but for my children. It's been cathartic, writing about my life and painful at times. It's helped me to face issues that I may have been in denial about. Hopefully, it may even help someone else who reads my story. I believe it is a testament to my faith, that no matter how bad a situation is, keep trusting God and He will bring good out of it. I have seen that happen over and over again. It doesn't make the difficult times any less difficult though when you're experiencing them.

The next two years were strange for lack of a better word. Through counseling, I knew I had to start doing things for myself instead of depending on anyone else. I took a CPR class, I joined the YWCA to swim. No matter what I did, it caused problems. Since I had asked for a divorce George was now super vigilant. He never used to call me from work. Now he'd call several times a day. Most of the time I was home, however, if I wasn't, a barrage of accusations would surface. I reminded George that I wasn't the one who was cheating.

He assumed I was swimming with a young, good looking guy. He wanted to know if my CPR partner was young and good looking. I said he should walk over to the school and look in on the class. It was two blocks from our home. As for the people at the Y, they looked to be in the age range from middle age to their seventies. This was the Y, not some exclusive spa. I was the youngest one there. He wanted to know how long I swam. I told him. After that, he timed me and would yell at me if I was late getting home. The Y was across the street from the Echelon Mall, so I would go over there and get a piece of pizza before coming home. Then I'd be accused of meeting someone there.

I'm getting close to my last straw. I couldn't live like this. We went to a Xerox function and as I was coming back from the rest room, I passed a man who smiled at me. I smiled back. George saw it and made a scene. Where do you know that guy from!! I said I didn't. Why did you smile at him? He had a Xerox name tag on. He was one of George's co workers.

The following is the last incident that I would tolerate. George had a good friend, Bob. We had gotten together socially in earlier years, with Bob, his wife and his children. Later, Bob left his wife for another woman. George spent so much time with the two of them. I'd remember he'd get calls late at night from one or the other. He'd get dressed and leave and be gone for hours. He didn't have time for the children and me but he had time for his friends.

I can remember talking with friends when I was young, as women will do, about what we'd do if we found out that our husband was cheating on you.

409

My answer, as well as everyone else's was that I'd kick him the hell out. I didn't. I prayed continually....daily rosaries, visits to the church, brown scapular tucked under his side of the bed. Yes, I still shared a bed with him.

I had benchmarks that were forever changing. When he came home in the early hours, two days a week, I was grateful for the other five. Then it became four days, then three. Finally, the only day he seemed to stay home was Sunday and it was agonizing for me because he would spend hours with the Real Estate section, circling apartments in red then making phone calls. He never found one. Maybe he wasn't even looking. I never knew.

In years previous, we had always gone to Mass together. Before I found out about the other woman, we were at Mass (summer of "79). By now, he was very cold and distant to me but I was grateful that he was beside me at Mass. God was still working in his life. Mass was in the school gym at that time. I remember it as if it was yesterday. Just before Communion, he got up and said "I can't do this anymore" and left. The sinking feeling, the nausea, shaking and tears that ensued are still clear. Did God stop working in George? No, I think George did.

For two years we lived like that...ups, downs and in the gutter emotions. I am aware that he must have been going through his own hell. But my concern was that he chose to put me and the kids through hell. I'm ashamed to say that there were times that I was so focused on my own pain that I just assumed the kids would be fine, resilient. That was selfish of me. They were also experiencing some of the most difficult times that they would ever have to go through.

After two years I stopped sharing a bed with George. For the next two years I slept on the sofa in the living room. When he did move out after four years, he took the bed. My friend Pat was watching from her kitchen sliding door. She was taking inventory. I said let him take it all. I didn't care. Then she said he was taking my library table. That was important to me. David had picked it up out of someone's trash, when I spotted it. It was beautiful. It was a memory of David and me when we lived on Dock Rd....and so began our fruitful adventures of trash picking.

I ran over to George and fought for that table and kept it. I've changed the positioning of our furniture so much that Herb threatens to nail everything down. Anyway, that table remained. When Herb and I moved two big houses of furniture (Pocono house and Franklin Ave. house) to a smaller home, we had to purge and the library table would not fit anywhere. So I did the next best thing. My friend Pat has it in her dining room and since I was cleaning her house at that time to make extra money, I'm still the one who polishes it, lovingly.

I'm off track again. Back to George's friends Bob and Candy. I had known this girl casually from Xerox functions. This time we were at a party at a friend's house. I was smiling and socializing but my heart wasn't in it. I went to use the rest room which was in proximity to the bar and tables in this small, finished row house basement. As I was about to close the door, Candy pushed past me, came in and locked the door and said she wanted to talk to me. I said that this was so inappropriate and rude. She said that she didn't care. She proceeded to tell me that she knew more about my husband than I did. I said, "He's still my husband." She said "Not for long. George wants nothing to do with you."

I stormed out and there was dead silence in the room. Since everyone had heard her shouting and it was a small room, I was publicly humiliated. Our host was a friend to both of us and he tried to console me as I ran up the stairs. George stayed down as if nothing had happened. I asked Bernie to go get George and tell him I wanted to leave. George was furious with me that I would make such a fuss. He came to Candy's defense and said that she just had too much to drink. I said that didn't take away the information he had given her, drink or no drink. I said, "I am your wife and the mother of your children and you are defending this woman's cruelty to me. There was no response. I reached my breaking point. I was done.

I still didn't understand why this had to happen. I thought George had it all. He had a wife who loved him and was there for him always, in every capacity. He had six extraordinary children who loved him, a beautiful home, and exciting job and his health. Isn't that everything? Maybe because we were so young when we married, he may have felt that he missed something in life. Was it all his fault? Of course not. Maybe I was too passive and too content—even though there were times that I pushed to have more communication. Whatever the reasons, it's twenty-five plus years later and it doesn't matter.

There are times, as with the writing of this book, that the residue of bitterness will surface. All I can do is keep turning everything over to God, again and again. He did apologize years later and said that he regretted what he had done. I did accept his apology. I made a conscious decision to do so but that's not the same as feeling it. I had to keep turning it over to God. I know that I'm being redundant, but in reality, that is exactly how it was, over and over.

I just had a disturbing thought. I said that I may have been too passive at times....content to be in George's presence. I seem to recall jumping all over Herb for that. Sorry hon.

Life goes on, wounds heal and with God's help, relationships are forged anew. Despite the difficulties and emotional trauma, the ensuing resentment and bitterness began to dissolve over the years, probably close to ten years. I emphasize that it didn't just 'happen'. My prayers for healing were constant. I didn't want our children to ever have to walk on eggshells because their divorced parents were both in the same room. I prayed even though, at times, I didn't see any thing positive occurring.

A cordial relationship developed in time. I still was insecure and listened to others, assuming they knew so much more than me. Despite our financial problems when George and I were together, I assumed that he was doing something right. He was traveling, taking cruises, visiting Europe so when he came to me with an offer to help me, I acquiesced, though not right away. I was still a single parent at this time and was frugal out of necessity. George wanted to know if I had any money saved. I was so proud that I had saved a thousand dollars. It was the first time I had any money in the bank. It was my safety net.

George had been making investments and making quite a bit of money on them. He said that if I gave him the thousand, he was almost sure he could make an extra five hundred in a few months. I am the first to tell you that I am unknowledgeable about investing. It was very scary to take that step and trust him, but the thought of the extra money won out. I started losing money. When I got down to five hundred, I told George I wanted out. He said to hang in there. It will be well worth it. He felt sure it would start to pick up again. I lost the whole thousand. He didn't even bat an eye.

Looking back over the years, it seems there's a pattern with me and even Herb and me, losing money in increments of $1000.00. My investment, Herb's and my investment in land at Marlton Lakes and the loss of a $1000.00 down payment for a vacation (our first in fifteen years), that was cut short because I came up with a case of "Shingles" the first day. There are a couple others, but this is beyond boring. Enough.

God's ways are not our ways. God's timing is different from ours, but His timing is perfect. I knew, without a doubt that His timing would be best. During that time we've had numerous family gatherings, even a family vacation on an island in Connecticut. Our children always have both parents there. Early in my marriage to Herb, one of the kids posed the question "Why is daddy hanging around so much?" It was a development that wasn't expected. Not only do Herb and George get along, they are the best of friends. Yet, knowing Herb, it is understandable. He always felt that with my six children in the picture, children he loves and accepts as his own, he expected George, as their father to be involved and included in everything. What is a simple concept for Herb, would be impossible for most men. When I said that George didn't have time for the kids when we were together, Herb just said that everyone makes mistakes and deserves another chance. There is no jealousy in Herb. He's very secure in our relationship.

I honestly believe that George's relationship with our children and grandchildren became so much better because of Herb. There were many times that George expressed openly to me, jealousy because of the close relationship Herb had with the kids. I told him that he should work on and nurture any relationship that he wanted to improve. He didn't like me telling him that but I did begin to see him make a concerted effort to do just that.

He really did expect people to rally around him. He was used to that in the work environment. He did have an air of superiority that was evident with the women he dated. I knew this firsthand because I was friends with one of them. He would tell me that someone needed to wear more makeup or more stylish clothes or get a better hair style. He even paid to have them do this and became upset if they went back to the way they were. I told him that he was shallow and superficial. He said, "I know I am."

I honestly believed that he wanted to change. He would make remarks to me about Herb and how patient he was. He admired Herb for so many reasons and told me so. It wasn't always this way. George looked down on Herb in the beginning. Yet, in the ensuing years, Herb was the first one George would come to for help. He told me that he was so appreciative of the relationship he had with me and the kids. He said that it would not have been possible without Herb. In the last few years that George was here, he actually went to Herb for advice about investments on his 401K. Herb was the only one not losing anything. I guess that makes up for the previous losses due to our naivete.

There was one incident I recall that was upsetting for our family. It was the day of Jillian's funeral. We came back home after the luncheon and quite a few members of our extended family came also. It helped so much to see Jake and Kenzie and their little cousins playing together. They even went in the hot tub and had a ball. Of course, all our children were here and my niece, Melanie.

Then something happened to change the tone of things. Some inappropriate language was used by someone and George flipped out, for lack of a better term. I didn't hear it, nor did Herb. No little ones were within earshot. Yet, George was trying to get everyone involved, at least our kids who hadn't even been present. To condense this story, he got in altercations with David, Rachele and Ryan and they weren't involved. There was so much yelling going on, I remember sitting in the living room with Melanie while she was changing baby Ryan and just shaking my head. I couldn't believe that this was happening today of all days. He stormed out of the house.

George called me the next day and asked if he could come over. He wanted to talk. I said yes. He started out by saying, "You *do* understand why I had to do what I did yesterday?" I said, "No." He couldn't believe I wasn't agreeing with him. He asked what he was doing wrong. I said that first of all, if he had a gripe with someone, he should go to them discreetly and address the issue, not embarrass them like a child in front of everyone. I also pointed out that Herb would not have tolerated offensive language either, had he heard it, which he hadn't.

To try to get several of the kids involved was wrong. He just wanted someone to side with him. This wasn't the first time he lost his temper and caused a scene. It's happened in restaurants when the wine wasn't brought out with the meal. He is very exact in his expectations. I told him that from my observation, we were being knocked over one by one like bowling pins. He asked if I had any advice, which was a first. I said "George, we're you're family, not your employees. Stop trying to manage everyone and just love them. Accept that none of us is perfect."

How is my relationship with George now? We communicate more than we did before. We are friends. He's grown more patient over the years and is now enjoying retirement, although he keeps active with rental properties and spending time with our children and grandchildren. The three of us frequently go to Mass together then out to breakfast afterward. I also recently found out that George prays the rosary, every day, on his knees for everyone in our family. To date, George has not remarried.

Do I have regrets? Many, don't we all, but never a regret about the result of my marriage with George...David, Kevin, Rachele, Mark, Ryan and Jillian, the closest we ever came to doing something perfect.

Slowly, the joy began to seep back into my life. I always enjoyed having the kids friends around, at least most times. Obviously, I needed my quiet time also. George's job was so stressful and our household always active. Surprisingly, it wasn't all that noisy. Our children were well behaved.

George preferred quiet time when he came home—as much quiet as you can have with six children. So the children tended not to bring their friends home often.

That started to change after we were separated. Mark was always bringing someone home. I remember one night in particular. Kevin had a "jam" session. I think that's the word. It was on the back deck. He and David had friends over. I can't recall everyone who was there, but there was a crowd. Kevin had his guitar and others had instruments too. It was loud! You could feel the vibrations in the house. I thought we'd have some complaints from the neighbors. We had one. I knew most of the police in our township because they all did their banking where I worked as a teller. I forget which officer it was, but he just laughed and said to "Turn it down after 11:00 pm Roe." He was glad to see the kids having a good time.

That same night I was tired and achy, still dealing with residual effects of Lyme disease. Since it was getting late I decided to take a hot bath, my remedy for everything. I was watching the "waves" from the vibrations actually moving the bath water. Since we had another bathroom for guests, I was surprised by a knock on the door. The other bathroom was occupied and a few of the girls just wanted to comb their hair and put lipstick on. I pulled the shower curtain over to give me privacy (of sorts) and they came in, babbling excitedly as teenage girls will do, even talking with me. I smile at the memory. Shades of normalcy were reappearing.

HEAVY TRIAL FOR GEORGE

George has been diagnosed with small cell lung cancer and emphysema. This cancer was aggressive. He asked me to go with him to Fox Chase Cancer Hospital, probably because of my nursing background and also because we remain friends. The doctor explained everything and didn't mince words when George asked for a bottom line. He was told that he had one year to live. The doctor left us alone for a few minutes. I placed my hand on George's shoulder and asked if he was okay. Surprisingly, he said an emphatic "Yes!" He had been afraid that the doctor was only going to give him a few months. A year was good in his eyes.

George's last year was a good one in his eyes. He felt well and was not having many side effects from the chemo. There was no nausea at all for which he was grateful. Initially, he had sores in his mouth for a week, then that resolved itself. He was blessed with good neighbors, Andrea and Kevin. Andrea would come over to me when she saw me leaving George's house. I would check up on him and bring soup or something that I had made. She also, would bring him food. She'd always want an update on his condition. That was not forthcoming from George, because of his pride. Although, as his condition deteriorated, he did take Kevin, Andrea's son up on his offer to take his trash out.

Our family pitched in. Trudi did a lot of driving to Philly to take George to appointments when he couldn't drive himself. While she did that, Kevin would clean up his house. I would change his linens and do laundry. I cleaned for the first two months but it got to be too much for me so George hired someone else to come twice a month. Herb would stop on the way to work at 5:00am (when George was in the hospital) to clean the litter box and feed his cat, Sabrina. When George was home, Herb would stop after work to do it. The litter box was downstairs in the basement, George couldn't navigate the stairs but didn't want the box upstairs.

George remained ambulatory for most of that year. He attended T-ball and soccer games for Kenzie and Jake. Ryan would take him fishing and called him daily. David and Rachele live in other states but called regularly. David, in New York is five hours away. Rachele in Missouri was 20 hours away. Kevin sent lots of e-mails.

George asked our Jenny to shave his head when he started losing his hair. Kenzie and Jake were with her when she did it. He wanted pictures taken to record this event and we have some very touching shots. It was actually becoming to George when he got a tan. He loved that it was no maintenance.

We were anticipating Kenzie's First Communion party at our home. Ryan and Jen and the kids were here helping us to get ready. Also, Ry needed his brake pads done. Herb supervised. George also came. I was surprised that he stayed as long as he did, since he tired easily. He made lemon martinis and we had potluck. Jake and Kenzie and I rolled down the hill until we were dizzy. Then Jake helped with the car. His little hands were black with grease, just like a mechanic's. George remarked that it was one of his most enjoyable days.

George was still getting around slowly, until the last few days. He called Ryan when he couldn't get to his bedroom. Ry went over and called 911. He was admitted to Virtua Hospital in Voorhees, N.J. Ryan would visit him every morning. I'd go in the afternoon. On the fifth day, Ryan called and said that the doctor said he didn't have much time. I immediately called Father Jose and asked if he'd be able to administer the last rites or as we call it now, the Sacrament of the Sick. He told me he'd leave right away.

Father arrived minutes after me. I stayed with George while Father Jose anointed him with oil. He held his other hand while we prayed the Our Father. George actually prayed with us in halting, hushed tones and even made the sign of the cross. Father talked with him, offering words of comfort. He had gotten to know George when he came to parties at our home, so he wasn't a stranger. George thanked Father for coming and thanked me profusely for having him come. He said it was so comforting to have him there.

Kevin and Trudi arrived next, then the rest of the family. At one point, George told the nurses he wanted to be alone, no visitors, not even us. We went down to the waiting room for our vigil. The doctor came in and explained what to expect. Someone asked how long he had. The doctor answered "Only God knows."

Herb left the airport as soon as I told him what was happening. When he arrived, the nurses said George was adamant about not wanting to see anyone. I asked if they would just tell him that it was Herb who wanted to see him. The nurse came out with a smile and told Herb to go in. Herb was in for quite a while. It's not for me to ask what was said. They were friends. I do know that Herb held his hand while he was in there and was emotionally moved. I believe that Herb was the last one to speak with him.

I know that there were phone calls from Rachele and Melanie. I held the phone to his ear while they talked. Our nieces Melanie and Regina came from Philly to the hospital, but George was already in his new home (heaven). I went in with Herb to see George after he had passed and the vision that surfaced in my mind was of George walking hand in hand with Jillian and Mark and for a moment I......

George fought a valiant battle. This may seem like a paradox, but the weaker he got, the more obvious his strength was. He stayed strong in his faith to the end.

The next day Rachele, Jake and I saw a white dove outside the dining room window. I couldn't believe it. Eleven years we had been in this house and never saw a pure white dove, just the clay colored ones. This dove hung around for two days. Ironically, he perched on our bar which was on our deck. The bar was George's favorite place to be when we had family gatherings. He was always the bartender. It was obvious to us that this was a sign that George was happy in his new home.

George's funeral Mass was beautiful in so many ways. Kenzie and Jake as young as they were, participated. Kenzie was the altar server. After Communion, the hymn "Fly Like a Bird to the Lord My Soul" was played and Kenzie fluidly and expertly signed the hymn. She has been learning sign language since the age of six months. I was so proud of her. Herb went up on the altar to do a reading and Jake went with him, holding his hand and standing on a stool beside Herb. Then after Mass, a military salute outside and the handing over of the American flag to David. Kenzie and Jake watched intently as the flag was folded into a triangle. I had taught them how to do it and it actually meant something to them because of the significance. It was a great sendoff for George.

FRIENDS Proverbs 17:17 A friend loves at all times.

EVELYN

I visited my friend Evelyn today. She's eighty six years old and suffering from Alzheimer's. Thankfully, each time I see her or call her, she recognizes me and recalls memories of years past. She worked as a switchboard operator for Archway School until her late seventies. She was, in part, responsible for me securing my job as a nurse at Archway. She was asked to place an ad in the newspaper for a Pediatric nurse for the Pre School Program. I would be graduating from nursing school in two weeks. Prior to placing the ad, Evelyn wanted to know if I would be interested in that position. Absolutely!

The job entailed riding on the bus as we picked up the children. Some of the children were in wheelchairs, some on oxygen, some had tracheostomies and required frequent suctioning. Many needed tube feedings. School hours and a ten minute ride to work made this the perfect job. My interview took place by the outdoor pool as my medical director did laps. She, too, was handicapped. She had multiple sclerosis. I got the job and worked there for twenty fulfilling, rewarding years.

Anyway, Evelyn became a second mother to me. Ironically, she's the same age as my mother and their birthdays are a day apart. She gave me the support I wanted and sometimes needed. Evelyn attended my nursing graduation as did Mark and Jillian and Ryan. No one came from my extended family. I felt like the pariah in the family, because I was the first one to ever to separate and get a divorce. It didn't matter what the reason. The fact that my husband had another woman in his life didn't seem to enter into the equation. Evelyn "adopted" me into her family.

She was beginning to have difficulty walking and she didn't like to go out and socialize, even though she was warm, caring and social to everyone she worked with. She had a sense of humor that wouldn't quit. She always looked at the positive side of things. I was especially appreciative when she came to Herb's and my wedding. Again, my mother and brothers and sisters did not come.

The reason my family didn't attend was because our wedding, though it took place in a church, wasn't in a Catholic church. Herb wasn't Catholic and the Methodist Church he was baptized in didn't recognize annulments. The Catholic Church said he had to go through the annulment process with the Tribunal. I still don't understand that. However, he did go through the proper channels to obtain it. I had already gotten my annulment and was free to marry in the Catholic Church. Due to the fact that someone didn't do their job properly, his paperwork sat neglected for three months, even though he did make follow-up calls to see how it was progressing. Our wedding in the Catholic Church took place three months later. My mother did come to that service.

Though not everyone qualifies for an annulment, Herb's situation established sound reasons for one. He and his wife married because, as they said back then, "they had to."

However, Herb found out, early on, that the baby was not his. Yet, he cared for this little boy as his own son, even after the divorce. He paid support all through high school, took him every weekend and on vacations. That's the kind of person Herb is.

Now to get back on track, Herb's paperwork was submitted in plenty of time for our scheduled wedding date. The tribunal failed to process it, thereby delaying approval of the annulment. It was too late to cancel the reception hall, so we went ahead and had the wedding at the Chapel in the Woods, Church of All Faiths, in Medford, N.J., a quaint log cabin church in the woods...a perfect setting. My pastor from my Catholic Parish said that if he hadn't already scheduled a trip to Ireland to visit his family, he would have attended the wedding. That did afford me some comfort.

Most importantly, my children and our friends were all there. It was so beautiful. Herb had tears in his eyes, by the time I reached him on the altar. My first born son, David, gave me away.

I remember my mom saying, "You understand why I can't come?" I responded that I would never understand. I didn't want approval, just acceptance, especially since we were going about things the right way and someone else messed up. I believe that things happen for a reason. What the reason was, I may never know. The pain and rejection surfaced years later when my entire family *did* attend weddings that weren't in the Catholic Church.

Also, even more painful than my own rejection, was that of my daughter, Rachele. Nobody from my family came to her wedding either. She had a beautiful church wedding, but it was in the Methodist Church. I was grateful it was a church service. After all, it's the same God.

These incidents hurt deeply. Yet, being passive, as I still was back then before therapy, I don't think anyone ever knew the extent of my pain. I knew I had to forgive or I'd have no peace. I wasn't able to do it on my own. As always, I turned to Jesus and my pastor. Of course, it wasn't immediate. Nothing is ever that easy, but time and prayer are very effective healing aids.

I hesitated to write anything so negative in my book. It was my sister, Diane, who reminded me that it's an autobiography. My life is the end result of positive and negative events and how I handled them. I ruminated on that for a long time, as well as praying about it. It made writing more difficult, although cathartic. My "feel good" book now may cause tears instead of laughter. Isn't life a combination of both?

I guess you're wondering how my relationship with my family is today. I will elaborate, but if I were to sum it up in one sentence, suffice it to say "God does work miracles."

As for Evelyn, I felt so blessed that God brought Evelyn and me together at a time I needed her most. She has since passed away. I miss her…

LORRAINE AND PAUL were our closest friends. Paul has since died and Lorraine and I remain close after fifty years. We don't see each other often but we're always there for each other emotionally. Sadly, we share an experience that is devastating—losing our sons to tragic accidents, my Mark and Lorraine's Patrick.

Years ago our families spent an extended weekend at our home in Marlton Lakes. After two days we commended our children, our four and their three, Paul, Patrick and Colleen. We were so proud of the fact that with seven kids together constantly, there were no problems. We no sooner voiced that appraisal and there was a knock at the door. It was the lifeguard reporting that the kids were smoking on the beach. We were shocked and issued the appropriate lecture. Nowadays, that doesn't even seem like a problem.

Keep in mind, that the kids were constantly interacting and going off on little adventures. They fished, they swam, caught turtles and made up their own games. The television was not their entertainment. Lorraine, Paul, George and I spent a large part of the weekend singing while I played songs on the organ. We laughed so hard we cried. We took walks at night to the lake. Of course, Lorraine and I had our wine and the guys had their beer. We bonded like never before.

Fast forward....Lorraine and Paul also came from Philly to be with me when they heard that George was leaving me. Paul cried and sympathized with me. Lorraine was all business. She asked, "What will you do now? What are your plans?" I was in shock. I didn't have any plans. She helped me to deal with the issues in a way, I didn't want to, even lending me money for a lawyer. I saw her as being harsh. I was on the "pity pot" and wanted sympathy. Yet, even then I knew that she was helping me. Her common sense attitude was what helped me to deal with everything.

A female lawyer told me that even with six children I wasn't entitled to any help from the government. She suggested that I stop on the way home and submit applications to different businesses. I passed Woolco on the way home, and did what she told me. I was hired for seasonal help as a salesgirl. I was at the jewelry and cosmetic counter, the worst possible place to be. Men were asking me to help them decide what to buy for their wives.

They were enthusiastic in wanting to please their wives. It just rubbed salt in my wounds.

After Christmas I started looking for a better paying job, hoping to utilize my secretarial skills. Lorraine continued to "mentor" me. She'd ask me what I wanted to do. I'd tell her that George thought I should go here or there for a certain job. She would say, "That's what George wants. What do *you* want?" Again I'd say "Well George thinks if I....." She'd interrupt several times, extremely frustrated, asking the same question. Finally, she made me realize that I needed to do what *I* wanted. I had always done what George had wanted. Old habits die hard. She made me realize that I had to grow up and make my own decisions.

I ended up getting a secretarial job at an electrical company in close proximity to my home. I took it on my own to learn all the electrical symbols. My boss was also a pilot and had his own twin engine Beech. Once we flew to Delaware on business. That was the one and only time that he took me. He was a nice guy, a perfect gentleman. After that one short flight, the mood of the office changed. The girls I worked with were not happy with me, thinking I was getting preferential treatment.

I had gotten a raise after three weeks. I enjoyed the responsibility and the contact with the builders and inspectors, who were always calling in for me to arrange for inspections on housing developments. Despite the positives, I was unable to handle the emotional stress so I left after six weeks.

I then got a job as a bank teller and really enjoyed that. However, no job is ideal. We had auditors come in and close the bank down and start counting all the money at our stations. I really was naive at that time in my life. It seems everyone but me knew that the assistant manager was in trouble for kiting. She was fired. There always seemed to be something unethical going on. It was like a soap opera.

I remember one humorous incident at the bank. David had come to the back door of the bank, after hours. The doors were locked and we were all counting our money to settle for the day. There were piles of money everywhere. Since my manager knew my kids, she let David in. He didn't stay long. He told me later that he had broken out in a cold sweat on seeing all that money laying around. I worked at the bank for several years.

Back to Lorraine and Paul. They came to our home on Dock Road when they heard that I was sick with a 104 degree temperature and "milk fever", and old diagnosis for nursing mothers. Ryan was about six weeks old. I was still able to nurse him without complications. Lorraine and Paul helped with the house, with the kids, with the meals. I remember hearing her ask what the kids had wanted from MacDonalds. When everyone wanted something different, she said, "Never mind!' Everyone will get the same thing. She calmed the chaos with her authoritative voice.

The following year when Jillian was born, they came down several times. Jillian had an umbilical hernia and the doctor didn't want her to cry and exacerbate it. Uncle Paul held her close and walked her for hours.

Paul came once in a while to see how I was doing, after the separation from George. At this time, he and Lorraine were also having problems. One time my fridge went on the blink and there was Paul with groceries to replace the ones I lost. I miss him and his smile, his great hugs and his gentle, endearing way....to this day.

UPDATE Lorraine and Russ have been together for over twenty years. They are among our dearest friends even though visits are infrequent. Thank you God for telephones.

MAUREEN

"A sweet friendship refreshes the soul." Proverbs 27:9

Suffice it to say that Maureen was a lifesaver to me. We met at Our Lady of Mount Carmel church and school, where our children were attending. She is a quiet unassuming person. Little did I know that she would become my "rock", my fortress in the storm, during the trials that George and I were undergoing. She listened, she advised, she prayed. She made sure that I listened, took her advice and prayed too. Her faith is unshakeable, her love unconditional. She had me do things that made no sense—like listening to John Denver records. She must have been inspired by the Holy Spirit because John Denver's music struck a chord with me. It released a flood of tears, anger, then blessed healing.

She insisted I get help. When I did go to frequent counseling sessions with Father Bourke, it helped, but not enough to suit Maureen. She then had me go to Camden County Catholic Social Services. I was terrified to go to Camden so she went with me the first time. After that I went for an hour a week for one year. It was difficult, yet liberating. God blessed me with an excellent counselor. It was the best gift I gave myself.

When I first called to make an appointment, they asked me if I wanted a lay person or clergy, male or female, psychiatrist or counselor. I was caught off guard. I was going because my mind and my life were so unstable. Now I'm being asked to make decisions I hadn't even thought about. I did the only thing I knew how to do—pray. In my mind, I asked Jesus to choose for me, then told the person to give me the first person available. The earliest appointment wasn't for three weeks. I need help now. I took the appointment and was sorely disappointed at the time frame but accepted that Jesus was in control. The next day I got a call and was told that there had been a cancellation and there was an opening that Friday. My counselor, Kevin was amazing at helping me to help myself, so to speak. It was not an easy undertaking, but it was productive.

At the start of our relationship, I didn't want Maureen there. I was in clinical depression, functioning by rote. She showed up at my home with her daughter, told me that we were going to Batsto Park. I was to get Gene Ryan and Jillian. I was angry and didn't want to go. I told her so. She didn't care what I wanted. We were going to do it anyway. I cried most of the day because I would see couples holding hands, a reminder of what I didn't have. She said things would get better but it would take time.

Years later when Mark died, she was there again. She must have had a direct line to God. Although, I realized now that we all have a direct line, if we choose to use it. She took me to Atsion Lake, knowing how I loved the water. She did not like the water. Yet, I did not want to be anywhere near the water. My Mark's accident had happened at a pool. I sat on the blanket crying quietly. Then I got angry (not at God, not at anyone). I literally stomped towards the water, threw myself in and swam hard and fast, back and forth, back and forth, almost in a frenzy, with a rage. Then I found myself sobbing as hard as I was swimming. I swam until I was physically exhausted and my tears spent. I came out of the water, and miraculously, the self pity was gone. With no further words, just a hug, we packed up and went home.

Maureen continues to be there for me. When Herb had his open heart surgery she brought several delicious meals over. I thank God every day for bringing this loving, devoted friend with unbelievable strength into my life. Since she was there for me, I have made it a point to be there for others in similar situations, passing it on so to speak. She truly is a blessing.

PAT AND DAVE

Pat and Dave were our neighbors in West Berlin for twenty-five years. To date, we have been friends for almost forty years. I would always talk with both of them and thought they were really good people. Although, during the years that George and I lived there, we didn't get together socially. George kind of kept to himself, other than to say hello when we were out in the yard. I honestly can't remember a time they weren't there for me. I became even closer to them when George and I were going through our breakup.

There was one incident they witnessed while they were eating dinner. Their sliding door by their kitchen table gave them a birds-eye view of our picnic table in the back yard (our yards joined together). George and I had been arguing and to avoid any more yelling, I went outside to our picnic table. I had a tall glass of iced tea. George followed me out and continued arguing. I said please just stop. He then picked up my glass of tea, ice and all, and threw it in my face and walked away. Pat almost choked on her dinner.

Pat was easy to be with, so giving of her time. She was never too busy to talk with me. She also included my children and me in family dinners. We were part of her extended family. Jillian, Ryan and I even went to Florida with Pat to visit her mom and her sister, Barbara. We had had a fire in our home, in our family room. George said if I would give him all the insurance money from homeowners he would repair the damages. Since we were separated at the time, Pat came up with that idea for all of us to go to Florida and visit her mother and sister, so I didn't have to be in the house while George was working there.

Her children Laura and Mark and my Jillian and Ryan grew up together. (Mark is now married with two children and Laura has two daughters. Laura touched me deeply on her wedding day when she came off the altar to give her mother a rose, and also gave me a rose in honor of Jillian and mentioned her name to the congregation. She calls me her second mom.

Dave could always make me laugh with his dry sense of humor. He also made wonderful drinks and would bring you up to date on happenings in the neighborhood. I could have a difficult day at work and just looking across my back yard at the light in Pat's house, gave me a sense of comfort. It amazes me now, that looking back Pat was never too busy for me, because it was an almost daily occurrence that I'd show up at her door. She has the patience of a saint. I am so grateful for the ongoing support she gave.

We moved away years ago, ten miles away. We do keep in touch and talk regularly and get together for dinner or often Pat and I will meet for lunch. It took Herb and me two years of living here and saying how much we missed them both, to finally accept that we still have them.

When Herb came into my life he was also accepted by Pat and her family. We've had so many friends come visit at our first Lake Wynooska home. One of the most memorable times was when Pat, Dave, Laura, Pat's sister and mom came. I can only describe Pat's mom as a "spitfire". She made us laugh and wasn't afraid to take chances.

The timing was bittersweet because Jean (Pat's mom) had terminal cancer. She knew it, accepted it and continued to live with cancer, instead of dying with cancer. I'll always remember her standing by the glass sliding door in the kitchen, watching our beautiful, fluffy white skunks. She was amazed at these little creatures.

Barbara spent her time in the living room, reading and listening to the gentle sounds of classical piano music. Next day I was playing the piano and glanced out at Barb trying to get her mom in the canoe. She almost fell in twice. I yelled for Herb and Dave to get out there and steady the boat. Our nerves were shot, worrying about her. Jean loved gliding around in the canoe. They even picked some berries in a little cove, while touring our lake.

As I recall memories, some long ago, some more recent, I realize that the scripture that says to Trust God and He will bring good out of bad, has manifested itself in my life, over and over again. I didn't understand why I had to go through all that I did, yet I can honestly say I never stopped trusting God. He has brought so much good into my life through family and friends.

As I write this, I'm looking forward to spending time with Pat and Dave for the weekend in our new Wynooska home. We'll probably read a lot, out by the lake. We're all avid readers. I'm sure we'll even play Pinochle. Time marches on, we grow older and friendships grow deeper.

UPDATE 2013

Pat literally saved my life. We were leaving Ott's Restaurant after one of our lunch dates. Pat was walking slightly behind me and noticed a mole on my upper back. She was very concerned. I thought it was a tiny birthmark. I had never been to a dermatologist and did not plan to see one. Herb had seen it but said it was nothing. It did not fit the description that we're told to look for. There were no irregular borders and it was not raised. Pat was insistent and made me promise to see a dermatologist. I did and was diagnosed with melanoma. As Dr. Berger reminded me, twenty years ago melanoma was a death sentence. It still is, if not discovered early. Thank you Pat for saving my life.

UPDATE 2013

Recently had dinner with Pat and Dave and their family. Laura and Kahoya were home from Texas with their beautiful daughter Priscilla, for a visit. They are expecting their second child. Mark and Heidi were there with Gavin. It was so good to see them. I had seen their daughter Kaitlyn just a few weeks ago when Pat brought her over to swim with Kenzie. Friends really are an extension of our family and such a blessing. Mark was reminiscing about me swimming across the Delaware. I love that he remembered that.

UPDATE CHRISTMAS EVE 2015

Laura and her husband Kajoya were home visiting for Christmas. They live in Texas and they came to our Christmas brunch with their two beautiful little girls, Priscilla and Gracie. It was so good to see them and, of course, Pat and Dave.

DINNER FROM HELL (as dubbed by Dave)

The Twin Towers had fallen days before. Our country was numb with grief and disbelief at this terror attack. I had been crying off and on for days. We went to our Pocono home with George and Dave. They had offered to help Herb paint the house outside. I talked with our neighbor Snookie and we both cried again. I felt drained. We did plan to go out to dinner that night because it was my birthday.

We arrived at the restaurant and ordered drinks. Everyone's drink came except for mine. I called a busboy and ordered again. He said he was underage and would get the waitress to bring it. The waitress comes back and refills George's, Dave's and Herb's drinks. I'm still waiting for my first.

Then we order our meals. We all ordered the same thing, prime rib, because they were noted for it. Their dinners came. Mine did not. Dave offered me his drink. I said no, that I wanted my own. The thought entered my mind that I was being petty. How could I even get upset just days after 9/11 but I did.

I finally got my drink and my meal and proceeded to choke on a piece of meat. At first, I was coughing and hacking, which we know means that I'm still getting air. Then the coughing stopped. I picked up my cloth napkin to cover my mouth to catch anything I might expel, and Herb calmly says "Who is that masked woman?" and they all laugh. A lady at a booth yelled at her husband to help me. She said "That woman's choking." Dave waved at her and said, "She's fine. She's not turning blue yet." George kept on eating. By then I had expelled the food in my napkin/mask. I was furious. I was also scared that no one seemed to care.

I excused myself to go to the ladies' room and splash water on my face. I thought the door was locked. Much to my surprise, while I'm on the toilet, the door opens to face the dining room filled with people. I raised my hand and said "Occupied." I didn't have the energy to even be embarrassed. This was the final humiliation. I washed my hands and exited to a room full of stifled laughter. We got our desserts and next round of drinks for free.

UPDATE 2016 Pat's retired!! We get together twice a month for lunch. The four of us will be going away for a long weekend in the fall to Annapolis. Also, on the agenda is the Ford Theatre.

CLARE AND BILL

Our friendship with Clare and Bill came about in our senior years. We met at Our Lady of Mount Carmel's RCIA classes. Herb and Bill were attending classes to convert to Catholicism. There was an immediate rapport with them. We began getting together socially and thoroughly enjoy their company. The closeness we feel with them defies the short time we've known them. God has all kinds of surprises for us when we keep Him in the picture.

431

Clare and Bill love to entertain and are excellent hosts. They have a Christmas brunch each year and always invite not only us, but also Trudi, Kevin, their children as well as Ryan, Jen and their children. In other words, they make us feel like part of their family and I believe that feeling is mutual.

When Clare and Bill come here to our parties, they make it a point to speak with everyone no matter how many people we have. My niece Melanie and her husband Brian hit it off with Clare and Bill. I have no idea what they talked about for a very long time, but Mel and Brian expressed how much they enjoyed them. Everyone does, they are so caring and loving.

Clare has had a difficult year, having undergone surgery for melanoma, partial breast mastectomy. She also has a detached retina. Her demeanor never changes. She and Bill are strong in their faith and it shows. Clare and I were both going through some difficult medical issues around the same time. Bill, upbeat as always, hugged me and said that we would both be fine because he and Herb were here to take care of "their girls". We are truly blessed to call them our friends.

MARYANN

MaryAnn and I met when I was engaged to Ed. She was our realtor when I planned to sell my house and move in with Ed after the wedding. There are some relationships that defy explanation. You just have to experience them.

We became very close and have remained so for almost thirty years. We get together a few times a year for lunch. Just recently she came in between appointments, as usual, laden down with gifts, sweet treats for Herb, flowers for me. We ate lunch, swam and talked about our families and my upcoming job with our church, as a pastoral associate of the sick.

MaryAnn is a Eucharistic Minister in her church and visits the nursing home each week so we have our church ministry in common. She is sensitive, caring and truly Christ-like and has a calming influence on me. She was there for me when Jillian went home (heaven). I was an emotional wreck but MaryAnn took me to lunch, listened while I talked incessantly about my baby girl and just provided comfort.

We talk about anything and everything and share stories of how the Holy Spirit is working in our lives. We both believe that there are no coincidences in life. Herb loves MaryAnn as much as I do. He trusts her completely. I've wanted to go to an accountant for guidance whether it was at the time we were contemplating selling our home or just legal advice. Herb adamantly refuses. MaryAnn has stressed to us that she is a realtor not an accountant, yet, Herb will trust no one but her with all our financial information. This puts tremendous pressure on her, but she has given us excellent advice in the past, for which we are both grateful.

Herb and I both love MaryAnn as if she was family....she is.

DENNIS

Dennis is a friend from church. I met him when I volunteered to help out at the St. Vincent de Paul Thrift Shop. I worked there briefly, but long enough to know that Dennis is a very caring person. When he learned that I had worked with a child at Archway, who had a diagnosis of Epidermolysis Bullosa, he gave me two books with spiritual inscriptions by the author addressed to me personally. The books were "Tough Cookie" and "Don't Cry For Me" written by Lillian Sparks, about her son Byron who suffered with this horrible disease. The book is a beautiful testimony to faith, and how she and her faith-filled family lived with this ongoing battle. Their son Byron went to heaven at age twenty, as my Mark did. Dennis thought this book would help me. It did.

Years later when my Jillian went to heaven, Dennis was there again. We would see each other at church. Dennis attends daily Mass. I'd also stop by St. Vincent De Paul Thrift Shop which he manages for our church. Sometimes I'd just stop in to say hello. He dropped everything one day and said we were going to lunch. When he said that he was taking me to an Indian restaurant, I cried. He had no way of knowing that Jillian had said that she wanted to take me to an Indian restaurant next time she came

433

home. Jillian and I shared such a love of all things edible and savored new eating experiences. At the risk of being repetitious, she'd send me photos of her plate at any new restaurant. She wanted me to see the presentation and would describe the tastes. We never got to go but, obviously, she whispered in Dennis' ear.

I would also see him when we went to Jake's soccer games. He was coaching another team. Again, he gave of himself.

STEVE

Herb hired Steve to put a roof on our new deck. He had said that there were a few options on how to do this. Fast forward a month later and I'm in Berlin shopping. I was ready to turn out of the K Mart shopping center and head towards West Berlin to pick up prescriptions at Shop Rite. That inner voice of mine, that I've come to know as the Holy Spirit, said "Go home." I rationalized that I was halfway to West Berlin and if I went home, I'd be wasting gas and time since I'd have to turn around and come back anyway for the prescription.

The thought came again and again so strongly, that I heeded it. I've had so many of these 'discussions' with the Holy Spirit that I knew it was best to listen. It does get easier each time. Apparently, I had been talking out loud while I was idling the car. Someone stopped to ask if I needed help. Suffice it to say that walking with our Lord can be a humbling experience.

I turned to head home, mumbling as I went, "Why am I doing this, Jesus?" I pulled into my driveway. There was a white truck with no lettering on it and no sign of anyone in the truck or at my front door. I went out back to see a man standing in my yard looking out at the woods. I assumed that it was Steve. I walked up to him and said, "You must be trying to figure out the best way to do the roof. He said, "No, I already know what I'm going to do." Then why was he here?

It was windy, cloudy and cold and as I glanced towards my car with the groceries, I uttered something, more to myself, about disliking food shopping, then apologizing to God at the same time, about being grateful that I had the money to go shopping and the car to get me there.

Steve asked if I prayed about everything. I replied yes, but was surprised that he took my complaints and regret about them, as a prayer. Not everyone would recognize it as such. I asked this stranger, this good looking pensive man if he'd like to come in out of the cold. He did.

We had been talking about anything and everything for about twenty minutes, when my Rachele came in with my groceries. I had forgotten all about them. I introduced Steve and Rachele to each other. She sat down and for another forty-five minutes the three of us discussed kids, faith, likes and dislikes as if we had known each other forever.

Later, I questioned why Rachele wasn't the least bit curious about how this man came to be in my kitchen. With Jesus at the wheel, the unusual becomes ordinary, even to be expected. Again, living with Jesus in your life is an ongoing adventure--the ride of your life, if you let go and let God. She also refreshed my memory about the UPS guy showing up at our Christmas party. Nothing would surprise her.

Rachele left, Steve stayed a little while longer then said he had to get back to work. He thanked me for my hospitality then paused. He told me that he had no idea why he had come to my house. He had no intention, no reason and ended up in my driveway, not knowing why. He also said that if I had been five minutes later, he'd have missed seeing me.

I began laughing and he thought that I was laughing at him. Then I told him my story. We knew we were meant to be there together. Steve said that I helped him with some of the things I had said. It really wasn't clear why we were brought together at that time.Sometimes, God may use us or our words to help others and we're not even aware of it.

A week later Steve began work on the roof. I tried to stay out of his way and just offer him something to drink or eat once in a while. He asked if I was avoiding him. I said that I was because I knew that our son, David, preferred no distractions or conversation when he was working on something. I assumed Steve would want it that way too. He laughed and I discovered that he was the complete opposite. We'd talk an hour before he started and enjoyed it when I came out to talk even while he worked. We had many in-depth conversations about marriage, children, faith and prayer.

To condense this somewhat, suffice it to say that Steve, Herb and I have become close friends. It's years later and Steve will still stop by to visit or join me sometimes for lunch or in the evening for a glass of wine. He's invited to our parties because we consider him, family. He even had an opportunity to meet and talk with Jillian on one of her visits.

Steve was in farming before he worked in construction with his dad. He has two sons and a daughter who are his pride and joy--understandably so. We've been to his mom and dad's home and shared some of his dad's homemade wine. They're such a warm, loving family. Steve's faith is strong although he would deny that. We don't try to figure out why we were drawn together. We're grateful for the mutual support we give each other.

UPDATE 2015 Steve marries Karen and is deliriously happy! I'm happy for them. They are a very special couple.

JOANN AND JERRY

Joann and Jerry came into our lives when George and I moved to Marlton Lakes in the early seventies. They and their five children were our neighbors and became close friends, as well as another couple, Maryanne and Pete. Jerry was a builder and Joann knew everything else about the business. She also had her realtor's license.

We all went to the same church, Assumption in Atco, N. J. We began to attend charismatic prayer meetings at St. Edwards in Pine Hill because Assumption did not have prayer meetings. Eventually, due to low attendance, the prayer meetings were discontinued. We spoke to our pastor about having them in our homes. He said that it was preferable to have a priest at the meetings but not necessary. There were three absolutes that should take place: 1. Praise and thanksgiving, 2. Reading of Scripture, and, of course, applying that Scripture to our daily lives and 3. utilizing the gifts of the Holy Spirit which are: healing, tongues, wisdom, knowledge, faith, prophecy, discernment, and working of miracles.

Meetings lasted anywhere from an hour or more. We always asked the Holy Spirit to guide us. We sang hymns and sometimes I played the organ. At times, it was just our families, other times neighbors and other friends came. It was the most joyful and peaceful time in our lives.--ever! I can honestly say that even though we were in dire straits financially. We prayed about anything and everything. Sometimes it was a quiet meeting. Other times, our kids ran wild. There were times that the older children would participate. We even ate a lot of our meals together, modeling ourselves after the apostles.

This part of practicing our faith was anything but boring. It was exciting to an extreme. I can remember one time our mortgage payment was overdue, as usual. I was concerned about this. Since we shared everything with Joann and Jerry, I mentioned it to them. Their solution was to pray, not for money, just that we were given a sense of peace and whatever else God thought we needed. Amazing to this day. How prayer will calm and comfort, in spite of the problems.

Our payment might be late but it really wasn't the end of the world. Ironically, the amount that was so huge at the time seems insignificant now. It was the early seventies. The amount was $242.63 for our beautiful four bedroom, three bath split level on half an acre. I had spoken to Joann on Sunday afternoon. Early Monday, the mailmen delivered a check for the exact amount. I was near joyful hysteria when I called George at work. At first he thought it might have been from Joann and Jerry, but since the postmark was days before I had even mentioned it to them, that was impossible. In all my excitement I never checked where it was from. I was so focused on the amount and this obvious answer to prayer. Turns out it was a refund from Allstate. We never did figure out why. We did, however, thank and praise God.

George and Jerry eventually built us a beautiful rancher on two acres in close proximity to Marlton Lakes. The house was gorgeous, though smaller, even though I was pregnant with Gene Ryan. It was a three bedroom, one and a half bath home with a huge living room and kitchen, with a massive brick fireplace between the two rooms. There were also built in shelves in the brick wall which held my cookbooks in the kitchen. It was so cozy to have the fire crackling while we ate dinner, while looking out at the view through the sliding doors, especially when it was snowing. The living room was just as cozy. To date, that house was my favorite, with the see-through fireplace.

George even took David rabbit hunting on our property. It was great having so much room for the children. Rachele made friends with some of the neighbors and she would ride horses with them. She still dreams about having her own horse in Missouri. We did miss the lake though. Of course, with Joann and Jerry still in Marlton Lakes we were able to go swimming there.

The children all went to Assumption school in Atco, N.J. I'd drive them to school everyday and everyday, no matter how slowly I went over the railroad tracks, my muffler would fall off one end. It was always David, in his white dress shirt and navy dress pants, who had to fix it. He was one of those kids who could do just about anything.

Through almost constant prayer, George and I and Joann and Jerry felt we were being led to take a trip to Missouri to look at and purchase farmland. The details of this decision and trip were voluminous and would require another book, so I'll try to condense it. Believe me, the confirmation we received through prayer and Scripture was extremely convincing.

In the Conley's old Volkswagon bus, Joann and Jerry and George and I and our nine, yes, nine children drove straight through to Mountain View, Mo., almost twenty three hours. Can you even begin to conceive how uncomfortable this was and what a test of our patience. I remember turning around once and seeing Rachele and Michele's faces smashed up against the window. There were no empty spaces available and no seatbelts.

We prayed the whole way, said rosaries, read Scripture and sang hymns. George and Jerry took turns driving. One time George got carried away and was going 80mph in a 45mph zone. A police officer pulled him over. The officer was ready to write the ticket, then noticed the rosaries and Bible. He said, "The angels must be with you buddy. Slow down." He let him go with that warning.

As we neared Mountain View, we were so close and yet so far. We just couldn't find the farm we were looking for. We were all hungry, achy and starting to get irritable. We pulled over and parked outside of a charcoal factory, then pulled out the map. The chimneys in the charcoal factory were billowing smoke and scenting the air like a giant barbecue. It made us even hungrier.

On that note, we decided to go back to a diner we had passed and see if any of the locals knew where the farm was. First, though, Joann said, "Let's see what the Lord has to say to us." She randomly opened the "Good News" (New Testament) and read out loud, "You are to stay where you smell the charcoal fires burning...." Dead silence! The four of us were stunned. Of all the Bible verses to read....coincidence? I think not. More like Christ incidence. Again, if you ask God to guide you with His Holy Spirit, expect answers.

Joann then handed the "Good News" to someone else. We asked Jesus if there was anything else we should know. Another random opening, "You are to stay here and become fishers of men." Hmmm. Shortly after buying the farm, Joann and Jerry found out that the people in their community intensely disliked Catholics. They went to the priest, prayed with him and did indeed build a church, becoming fishers of men.

Anyway, we went to the diner, ordered, held hands and said grace. We asked the waitress to look at our map and the address of the farm we were looking for. She knew of the farm and said we were minutes from it. It was just past the charcoal factory. We told her we had found the charcoal factory and the scent of it had whetted our appetite. She laughed and said that the factory had been closed down for ten years. We said that there must be another one because the one we saw and smelled was indeed functioning. She said that there was only one factory in Mountain View. It had to be the same one. Yes, God can do anything. His special effects are phenomenal. Thirteen of us did not have visual and olfactory hallucinations.

We went back to the farm and fell in love with the three hundred rolling acres, the horses in the field, the sun setting over the pastures. It was surreal and dreamlike. Then we saw the house we would have to live in, all thirteen of us. It was a tiny two bedroom house. Joann and Jerry were already planning to build on, saying, positively we can do this! George and I cosigned the agreement of sale along with them. Back in N.J., however, fears set in, George was given a financial incentive to stay at Xerox, and we gradually stopped listening to our Lord. George said that we couldn't possibly do this. I always felt that it was my job to support my husband, so we backed out of the agreement.

Joann and Jerry's families thought they were crazy taking such a risk, leaving a very successful business. Joann and Jerry were confident that God would take care of them. Now, years later, most of their family is out there with them. Jerry did build a beautiful five bedroom, two story house.

Partly because of embarrassment at putting Joann and Jerry in such a bad position, having to handle the huge mortgage by themselves, we began to spend less time with them. I kept in touch on a frequent basis but George began putting in late hours at work and going out with friends after work. He now had no time for prayer meetings. Our problems in our marriage began insidiously at this time.

More financial stress caused us to sell our beautiful home on Dock Road and move to a bi-level on Franklin Ave. in West Berlin, N.J. I was so tired of moving--three times in less than ten years.

Contact, once our friends were in Missouri, was rare. Eventually, we lost all contact. Twenty-five years later, Rachele and our friend, Steve were discussing the "Left Behind" books, a series of twelve books written by Tim LaHaye and Jerry Jenkins. Although they were labeled fiction, they are based on Scripture and written from the authors' viewpoint. Since both are biblical scholars, I and everyone else who has read them, found them to be more truth than fiction.

They are exciting, frightening, yet full of hope and trust in God. The characters lived extremely difficult lives in a society mostly devoid of God. They witnessed to their faith at the risk of persecution and death. Yet, there was a closeness and support among the believers that was to be envied. They shared meals and everything else and prayed together. In discussing the books, we all remarked how comforting it would be to have that kind of life in this secular world.

A light bulb went off in my head. We had had that kind of life. Memories flooded in and emotions poured out. How had we let that go. I started wondering how Joann and Jerry were after all these years and felt a strong desire to get in touch. I didn't even remember the name of the town they were in, but George did. I called information and got the number and left a message. That night Joann called and we spent an hour and a half on the phone. She was so glad to hear from us. They still prayed for us after all these years.

They had had three more children, bringing their total to eight, They, too, had lost a son. They are dairy farmers and have about sixty cows. We watched them when we later visited, as they milked and did their chores. It is grueling work with no days off. Joann said it was so difficult, initially, because they had expected us to be there and eventually others. She took her new baby Melissa to the top of a hill, was holding her and nursing her and crying out to God. "Why did You want us here?" There's nobody here, no family or friends and most of the people hate Catholics. She was actually sobbing and then when she was willing to listen, she heard God's answer, "I want you to depend on Me, not others."

We shared stories, some painful, some uplifting and the twenty-five year separation evaporated. We made plans to visit Joann and Jerry. I wondered how awkward it would be since I was now with Herb. They had only known George. It would have to be uncomfortable for them. Herb didn't seem the least bit concerned. He just wanted to meet them after all he had heard about them. I also found out that we had owed Jerry $3000.00 for materials he purchased for our Dock Road house. Remember, Jerry was the builder. I was not aware of this outstanding debt. Jerry thought this was why George wouldn't return his calls. He was too embarrassed that his check bounced. Jerry said all he cared about was the friendship but George's pride got in the way. Even though it wasn't his responsibility, Herb agreed to take our savings and pay a third of that.

We flew into Springfield then rented a car for the two hour drive to their farm. We stepped out of the car and I was almost crushed by Jerry's bear hug. We were crying and hugging and just absorbing the unconditional love that has always been forthcoming from these wonderful people. I need not have worried about Herb. He was welcomed with embraces from both Joann and Jerry and accepted as family.

Herb had his first prayer meeting around the kitchen table as we all held hands. Keep in mind, this was foreign to him. He had not converted to Catholicism yet. We'd pray together at home but this was a whole new experience. Surprisingly, he said that he felt very comfortable.

All of the Conleys' children were warm and loving. Some, I was meeting for the first time, Melissa, Nathan and Kathleen. Still etched in my memory were Brian, Michele and Maureen, Ricky and Robbie. They and our kids were inseparable growing up. It was like going home. The span of decades was connected in seconds. Amazing what happens when God is in the middle of it.

Rachele and I went out to visit the Conleys the following year. She wanted to see, as Maureen put it, "her long ago childhood friend." Today Rachele and her sons live in Mountain View just down the road apiece from the Conleys. She and Brandon, her youngest lived with the Conleys for a year and a half while she was going through her divorce.

Michele and Rachele picked up where they left off, as little girls. Now they're grown women. Michele and Rick have four children. Their families are integrated as if it's one big one. Michele and Rachele walk an average of five miles a day. They never run out of stories and memories, all the while making new ones. Rachele loves her new life. Can hardly wait to visit her again.

HARRY FROM COMCAST

Harry came into our lives when we were having ongoing problems with our phone and cable service. I needed dependable service whether I was babysitting my grandchildren or in case of an emergency. Keep in mind, we did have to call an ambulance twice for Herb. We have over three acres so our neighbors aren't as close as in a development.

Anthony came twice and couldn't resolve the problem. When he was here he remarked on Jillian's picture on Herb's screensaver. He said that she was so beautiful. I told him her story. Then, of course, Mark's story ensued. He was beside himself, not knowing what to say except for "I'm sorry." He promised to get the best technician out here to fix our problem. Third time out, he came with Harry. He left before Harry was done. Harry said that Anthony had told him about Jillian and Mark.

Harry asked questions and he also said he knew that I was Catholic because of the rosaries he had seem laying around, but he remarked that I didn't talk like I was Catholic. When I asked him what he meant, he said that it was obvious that I had a personal relationship with Jesus Christ. I responded, "Of course I do." That's how I deal with all this.

It was an interesting conversation and we both shared a lot. He was studying to become a minister, had a wife and two sons. Our phone problem is still not resolved. Harry had the outside wires and telephone pole checked, not only at our house, but in the neighborhood, since the problem may have been elsewhere. No one else was having a problem, just us. Coincidence?

I was getting frustrated at this point. Herb was not. He even said that maybe there was another reason Harry was here. Now he's sounding like me. There was so much more monitoring of our house before the issue was resolved. The last day that Harry was here, I was on the front porch with him. He asked if we could pray together. I said I'd like that. We held hands, bowed our heads and talked to Jesus on our front porch. Our problems were finally resolved with two new modems. It seems God provided the time to establish yet another spiritual friendship.

A few weeks later, Harry was in the area and stopped by to see how things were. He stayed for lunch and we talked some more. While we were eating, our friend Steve came walking in with some wood for a job he was doing for us. He shook hands with Harry and hugged me and said, "Roe, your neighbors will be talking. You've got the Comcast truck and my construction truck. We all laughed. He forgot the septic truck from two days before. Joey Randanella has been coming here for twelve years to pump out our septic system. We have a mutual friend whom I worked with at Archway. Also, we'd both talk about our families and Joey would update me with photos of his little daughter. There was always a hug and a promise to pray for each other before he left.

Herb got a chance to meet Harry one day when he came home from work. He took an instant liking to him. Even Ryan got to meet him. I even got a photo of Jake on the Comcast truck. They had heard so much about each other that I didn't even have to introduce them.

ROSEANN AND AL

Our friendship began twenty-five years ago. RoseAnn was one of my bridesmaids in my wedding. She and Al were married a year before Herb and me. We keep in touch regularly and get together a few times a year. The last several years have been a heavy trial for RoseAnn with neck and back surgeries. Al's had his share of health issues also. You'd never know it to look at them. RoseAnn is as beautiful as ever. It must have been all those years of teaching dance that keep her in shape. They are both retired now. Al was a Philadelphia Police Officer and a very talented composite artist before the computer images were used.

They are friends on a spiritual level also. We can always count on prayers from them. They have a special devotion to Our Blessed Mother. It's so comforting to be able to share the good, the negative and uplifting occurrences in our lives, that parallel each other. Obviously, they're a constant on our prayer list.

MICHELE AND AL

Michele and Al are Ryan and Jen's next door neighbors and good friends. We got to know them under dire circumstances. Sadly, parents who have children who have gone to heaven before them, share a sacred bond with other parents in the same situation. Al and Michele's son Joey was in a tragic car accident, that his father witnessed on the way home from work. They had worked together that day but were in separate vehicles.

I don't even recall how we started our friendship. If memory serves me right, Ryan told Michele about losing Mark and Jillian and thought it might be good if we both met. We went to lunch and talked about our kids. I see Michele as strong and determined and in constant emotional pain. I recognize that because I live with it. Yet she brings joy to anyone who is blessed to be in her company. She and Al also have a daughter Jess, who is dealing with serious medical issues. On Joey's birthday, Al and Michele have a butterfly release. Their home is packed with Joey's and Jess's friends as well as family and friends of Al and Michele's. We're felt honored to be among them.

Though we've only known Al and Michele a few years, it feels like we've been friends for a long time. There is a closeness, warmth and love that comes through, not only in their hugs, but their words. Ironically, those who have lost the most, seem to be able to love others more intensely. This is another relationship where time is not of the essence to the depth of the feelings. That, I believe with all my heart, is because we all have a strong faith. Yes, our faith has been tested, excruciatingly. We're human. We hurt, we cry, we mourn, we love and we go on and continue to live, knowing we'll be with our kids again.

UPDATE Christmas Eve 2015

It was so good to see Al and Michele on Christmas Eve. It's one of the busiest days for everyone but they made time to come to our brunch. Ironically, even though they live next door to Ryan and Jen, they see more of them at our house. Their friendship is truly a gift from God.

Al and Michele's daughter will be getting married in May!

SAMANTHA

Sam is also a close friend and neighbor of Ryan and Jen, as well as Al and Michele. They all live in a wonderfully close knit community. I remember the day Ryan called to tell me about Sam's husband Brad having a heart attack. He asked me and Herb to pray for Brad and his family. I didn't know Sam then but I could discern that Ryan was extremely upset so I assumed that he and Jen were close to them also. Brad was in his early forties, much too young. Sam and Brad have two beautiful children, Nick and McKenna. They're good friends with Jake and Kenzie.

Four days later, we were in upstate New York at David's home. He was having his annual summer weekend celebration for family and friends. Since Trudi's sister Allison is also a neighbor of Ryan and Jen's, she called Trudi to tell her of Michele and Al's son Joey. Two precious souls in four days, taken to heaven so unexpectedly left their families and community reeling. We were in David's kitchen when Trudi got the call. I got sick to my stomach and I didn't even know them. But seeing Ryan and Jen, I knew they were in shock and hurting. I remember sitting at the kitchen table and saying we should say a prayer. I didn't know what else to do.

I eventually came to know Sam, McKenna and Nick and become friends with them also. It seemed that everybody was connected emotionally. Sam is a beautiful woman, inside and out and bears a heavy loss at so young an age. Looking at her children, she's doing a great job. Sometimes I look at Sam and I see an adventurous side to her. She reminds me of my Jillian. That's probably one of the reasons I feel so connected to her.

We were all at Al and Michele's butterfly release on Joey's birthday which, by the way, is an amazing thing to witness. Everyone is given an envelope and opens them up at the same time. These sleepy, dormant butterflies wake up and fill the air with their beauty. They hang around flitting from one person to the next, a miracle in progress, and Joey, once again reassuring mom and dad and Jess that he's with them always.

Somehow Sam and I got talking about getting together for a dip in the pool when the weather and the water got colder. Sam recently got a pool and she loves the water like I do. Thus, the Polar Bear Plunge evolved. As I told Al and Michele, I believe because this started at Joey's birthday party, he was there in that icy pool as were Jillian and Mark, laughing at their crazy parents.

POLAR PLUNGE October 19, 2013

We waited until it got dark because the pool looks so dramatic with the lights on in it. You could feel an almost tangible excitement as we headed for the pool with towel and robes, wondering who would back out and who would surprise us. Jen was the biggest surprise. She doesn't like to be cold and I just thought she might not do it. But then, look whom she's married to. Those who didn't go in had jackets on. The air was chilly. Hot chocolate and marshmallows for the kids, and wine for the big girls, were awaiting us on the deck and Herb turned up the propane heaters. We're good to go.

Ry and Jen, Jake and Kenzie went in, as did Sam, McKenna and Nick. Nick was the first one in, then Steve Raiker who came with a jacket that actually had a Polar Bear Plunge patch. He has been in the ocean when the water was 37degrees and the air 38 degrees. He said the water in the pool felt like it was in the forties even though Herb said it was higher. I think we have a broken thermometer. Bea Raiker declined, as did Herb, who thought his heart couldn't stand the shock. Clare and Bill seemed to have as much fun watching the crazy people in the pool. Nick and Jake were floating around in a tube like it was the middle of summer. Michele went in, Al watched. We have some daring women in this gathering.

Nobody got chilled because you were so numb you couldn't feel anything. We did have plenty of warm towels and robes. One of the pictures Herb took was of Michele, Jen, Sam and me in our robes. He said we looked like we were at the spa. He made copies of the picture for each of us. I love this picture and find myself looking at it often. I feel gratitude when I look at it, for the wealth of friendship and love we share. Thank you God.

MEMORIES SHARED BY MY CHILDREN

During the writing of this book, my girls were always suggesting that I put this incident in or another. They'd say, "Remember this mom?" Although I did usually recall these times when they jarred my memory, I realized that they had their own special memories. I suggested that they write them down in their words and I'd have a special section in my book just for them. The following are in their own words.

MY DAUGHTER RACHELE WRITES

December 2007 GRANDPOP WAWRZYNIAK

My grandfather passed away when I was twelve. I still remember him well... every detail, his dark hair, his bright smile, rough hands from working on the railroad. The way his eyes crinkled at the corners when he'd smile and call me by my pet name, "Shelly Bird". I don't remember any other grandchild having a pet name from him. I remember the acrid smell of his cigars and the yellow/ orange glass ashtray he used. Somedays I swear I still smell his wonderful cigars when I'm feeling down.

My mom's father was a special man. He never said a bad thing about anyone and was unfailingly happy. His larger than life joy was contagious—from days diving into the waves at the beach, to pinochle games, to picnics at Wissahickon Creek. Grandpop's favorite place was wherever his grandkids were. I used to sit up against him as he lay on his side, head propped up on his hand, watching football with my dad. He'd rub my back and just smile at me once in a while. I was safe and life in this world was perfect because he was in it.

See, my grandfather didn't just live life. Life had a hard time keeping up with him. During the summer we'd all pile in the car and go to the beach. We kids had our sailor hats, sunglasses and "Good & Plenty" tote bags. Grandpop had his Nomad sunglasses and big green car. He'd join us kids in a dozen rounds of bouncing in the seat, chanting, "I smell the seashore, I smell the seashore", as we got to the salt marshes.

I even remember the small white Blessed Mother statue that sat on the dashboard. At the beach we'd get extra treat—Neapolitan coconut candy and a white nougat candy with fruit flavored jelly pieces in it. My brothers and I would bury Grandpop and feed him pretzels, while just his head stuck out above the sand. Then off to the water we'd all go. He'd carry me out to where the water was up to his chin and put me on his shoulders. I'd stand on him and flip and dive off his shoulders. I was only four years old. The water was way over my head but I was never afraid because my grandpop was with me.

At the end of the day he'd walk me down to the water and rinse the sand off me, then carry me to the blanket. Once we dried off, grandmom held a towel around me while my mom put us in dry clothes, after dusting us with baby powder. The two scents, the ocean and the baby powder evoke such strong emotions and memories of grandpop. David, Kevin, Mark and I all had plastic drawstring bags with the Good & Plenty logo on them. We carried our clothes in them,.

There were other memories too, simple things. The Eisenhower silver dollars he would give us kids every time we went over grandmom and grandpop's house. This was weekly. The way his freezer was on the bottom of the fridge. Sitting at the table drawing sticker people and laughing. These were not stick people, but sticker people. We'd draw stick figures and then add stickers all over them. We'd laugh so hard.

There is no one word that would describe my grandpop. He was the warmest, kindest, most gentle and loving man I ever knew. He had no enemies, only friends. He was a joy to be around and was so generous and giving. He was always the first one to see the good in everyone and the positive in every situation. He once told me "Shelly Bird, don't ever marry someone who can give you only what you can give yourself. Find someone who can give you more than what you can give yourself."

On top of everything else, grandpop was a wise man. I miss him to this day and still love him fiercely. Somehow my safe, secure, happy world was never the same after he died. It felt like the whole seam was ripped out of the fabric of my life. Somehow the repair job just never came close to the original.

OTHER MEMORIES OF RACHELE

There are so many memories it's hard to choose just a couple. So I've decided on one lesson handed down and one memory. The lesson is one in simplicity. Mom loves and gets a thrill from the simple things in life—a card, a gesture, wildflowers etc. Oh, don't get me wrong. Mom loves her fine china and elegant table settings. I mean, God forbid you should have lunch on a paper plate, her world would crumble (ha, ha). She gets that from my grandmom who would take silverware and the good salt shakers to the beach.

I remember no matter how poor we were or how many meals mom gave up so we could eat, she always gave us the ability to be grateful for simple and kind acts. When mom was in the hospital after hip replacement surgery, I went to visit her on the second day. I knew what made me feel better after my surgeries. Again, it was a simple thing. I filled a basin with warm soapy water, filled a cup with water and fixed her toothbrush, and took them to her bed table with a washcloth and towel. She washed her hands and face and arms and brushed her teeth. She then proceeded to cry. At first, I thought I had offended her. She simply told me that little gesture was done without her asking, and it felt so wonderful to her after being unable to get a full shower yet. It was a lesson in love and faith. Jesus washed the feet of the disciples. I love my mom and wanted her to feel better. Sometimes actions speak louder than words. That's a true gift my mom passed on to me. Be humble and do simple acts of kindness.

As for my memories, there are hundreds. I guess I'd have to pick a couple that encompass the family attitude as a whole—simple, fun, caring and a bit mentally challenged, in a good way. With all the different personalities, it's surprising we don't all clash. Instead, we complement each other in some way. As scary as it sounds, we all think alike.

We had all decided to go to Strathmere beach one day in separate cars. My kids and I were going early and Mom, Herb, Jillian and a host of others were leaving later. I thought up a way to let them know exactly where we were, along the miles of beach. I made a huge sign and taped it to the back window of my car. "CHELE IS HERE". They saw it immediately. Mom was still laughing as they trudged onto the beach loaded down with coolers, chairs and umbrellas. She was laughing because she had told Herbie, "I should have called Chele and told her to make a sign, or we'll never find her."

Our family always finds humor in any situation. They got so used to my shoulder popping out of joint, they'd simply point and say "Go find your wall". Thrusting my shoulder against the wall would get it back in place. We'd laugh at Herb's laugh, which sounds like Mr. Magoo, or mom's weak bladder. Kevin was always coming up with funny songs or we'd pick on dad's fishing ability. It's fun to laugh at ourselves and each other.

Poor Herb got a real taste of this a few years back. We were all up the Poconos for the annual family reunion. This year my sister Jillian came from Georgia and my cousin Josh came and brought his kayak. Well Herb decided to try to get into it while it was still on dry land. Problem is, Herb's body type was not meant for a kayak. Regardless, he got stuck—for real. He was lodged in so tight, he could not get out. Knowing how caring and helpful we are, he asked for help. That set off a chain reaction like a string of fireworks on Chinese New Year!

Kevin and Trudi laughed and I ran to get mom, laughing and shouting like Paul Revere on steroids, to the thirty or so people there, "Herb is stuck in a kayak". Well they paused long enough to grab cameras, anything to mark this in history. We all ran back to Herb who was red from laughing. There was my family circled around Herb, who was stuck like Winnie the Pooh in Rabbit's hole, all taking pictures. The flashes looked like the paparazzi on Grammy night's red carpet. Taking photos of anything and everything was a learned behavior from my mother. Her obsession with the camera and the

451

flashes in our faces was probably the cause of all of us kids needing glasses or contact lenses.

Mom laughed until Herb said he couldn't feel his legs anymore. I think it was Josh and Kevin who helped first. When they tried to pull him up by the arms, the whole kayak lifted. The moral of this story is, don't do anything around my family if you don't want it on permanent record in photographs. Our with him. That brought more laughter and pictures. They eventually did free Herb, though I was laughing family gatherings are never dull. If you want to fit in, grow tough skin, get a sense of humor and a strong bladder.

RACHELE'S POEM TO ME

Rachele has written volumes of poetry and has had some of it published. In this one, she talks about what it will be like when I'm gone from this life. We both are very comfortable in discussing this topic. After all, death is a part of life. In reality, there is no death anyway, just crossing from one life to another.

WHEN YOU ARE GONE

When you are gone I will miss your smile, but I will have your picture.
When you are gone I will miss the flash of your camera, but I will still have the photographs.
When you are gone, I will miss your wisdom. I will be grateful for all you have taught me.
When you are gone, I will miss your grace and beauty, but as the autumn sun retreats beyond the splashes of red and gold, and the geese pierce the sky, I will be reminded of you.
When you are gone, I will miss our long talks, but I will carry with me the security of them.
When you are gone, I will miss your laughter, but it will echo in my heart for eternity.
When you are gone, I will miss your strength. However, this memory will carry me when I cannot carry myself.

When you are gone, I will miss your faith. It taught me to believe in all things.

When you are gone, I will miss your compassion for others, but I will be surrounded by those whose lives you touched.
When you are gone, I will miss your knowledge but thank you for my love of books and poetry.

When you are gone, I will miss you....the mother, the woman, the friend. I need not be concerned about your memory fading, life will keep you alive, The scent of lilacs in May and roses in June, Nat King Cole and chestnuts, I love you in sign language, yard sales, the changing of the seasons, snow angels and baking. And if these should fail, I will close my eyes and pass gently over my lips, the words, my mother. For you are forever etched in my mind and have left a legacy of love...and your grandchildren thank you...for my mother will never really be gone!

IN TRUDI'S WORDS

I have been with the Edwards-Dalbow clan for almost twenty-five years. Of course, I married the best one of them all, Kevin Brice. I met Kevin through David, the oldest son, with whom I have been friends and a sister-in-law for all these years. David had been dating a friend of mine and wanted to introduce me to his younger brother...Guess who? You're all thinking of Kevin. Wrong, it was Mark. Mark is only three months younger than me. So, as it goes, David sets up a date for me and Mark.

It was the summer of 1982. I was down in the family room of the Edwards house on Franklin Avenue in West Berlin, anxiously waiting to meet Mark. I still remember the minute and the setting of what, would turn out to be life changing for the rest of my life. As I sat on the couch waiting to meet Mark, in walked a young, muscular, gentle, sweet-talking man. As I listened to him engage in conversation with David, he stood in the doorway and was lifting himself up by the frame of the door. Wow! The muscles, the long hair, the eyes that melted me and sent an alarm through me—I quietly stared, hoping that David would say, "This is Mark." Finally, what seemed like forever, (I think I was actually holding my breath waiting) David introduced me to....Kevin.

About ten minutes later I did meet Mark and immediately felt like we were friends forever. I adored his sense of humor. We went to the movies and Mark bought me everything I wanted. Now, those who know me, understand that probably cost Mark a lot. Mark and I became friends for the rest of his short, wonderful life. We both knew that we had a friend in each other. There just wasn't a spark for either one of us. Mark, being the sensitive young fifteen year old, let me down gently by saying, "We will be friends." This was great because we both felt the same way. I immediately began asking Mark about Kevin. The funny part of the story is that Mark thought that he was meeting Eva, another friend of mine. I guess you had to be there to see the unfolding of it all. I still laugh inside when I think of it.

A couple of weeks go by and another encounter arises for me to see Kevin. It was not a date. David had a group of all our friends get together and invited Kevin to be the driver. At the time, David had his green pickup truck, with no bed on it because he raced it at Atco Raceway, and yes, being an Edwards, he had won many times. Before Kevin arrived to pick us up, I told David and our friends that I would sit next to Kevin in the car. I don't remember a lot from that night. However, I do recall the infatuated, in love, hanging on every word and movement that Kevin made.

Did I mention that Kevin fills out a pair of jeans like a man should. I was in love with this guy that I didn't know much about. I just knew that he and I belonged together. Kevin wrote a song about our first kiss. The rest of the story becomes history.

Along with Kevin, David and Mark, there was Chele, their sister who is one year older than I. Kevin used to get jealous of Chele because when I was over the Edwards house, Chele and I would always hang out and take walks to the store. Through the years. We have had the normal sister-in-law issues, but we both admire and love each other...for life. Chele is extremely talented with crafts, writing poetry, drawing etc. Chele and I have an unspoken bond and know that we can count on each other no matter what, where or when.

Then there are the "babies", Ryan and Jillian. They were labeled the babies because of the fact that RoseMarie and George had Ryan, eleven years after

Mark was born. Jillian was born sixteen months after Ryan. Kevin and I had always taken the babies with us to the candy store, sleep overs etc. They were like our Steven and Nikki. What great kids they were, with imaginations you can only read about. Ryan and Jillian are very special to me. The love that I feel for them is so deep that it goes to the core of my soul. I am so proud of the "babies" that have now grown into amazing adults. I will always be there for them.

George Edwards, AKA G-Pop, is a wonderful father-in-law and grandpop to our kids. He appears as the Rock of Gibraltor, always steady, knowing where he's going. Under the perfectly kept appearance lies a man with a heart as big as Mount Everest. His children have picked up many of his talents. David and Ryan, following in G-Pop's love of fishing, Kevin, for his love of music and picking up G-Pop's guitar at a young age. Ryan for staying strong through his career as a police officer. Jillian picked up her love of travel and the unknown. Mark had his charm and perfection. Chele had his unchallenged strength to endure all that may try to rock her world. Nikki, my daughter has G-Pops love of the arts and adventure. To sum it up, G-Pop has given his children and grandchildren variety, spice of life, strength and love.

RoseMarie Edwards-Dalbow—Wow! What a woman. The challenges and losses that she has had to face are incredible. The loss of a son, Mark and recently, the loss of her daughter Jillian. We all share the pain, but for her who carried them, gave birth, nurtured and watched them grow…to have to let go and give them back to God….words cannot express it. Through the last twenty years since Mark has left us, I can only see that mom's faith is what helped her with that loss. Of course, having all of us and Herbie helped, but mom's faith is one I would never challenge. She gives everything, good, bad, sad, happy to God's will. I wish I could have her faith.

Along with her faith, is her unconditional love, love for her kids, grandkids, family, friends, nature and even strangers. Her unconditional love sometimes warrants remarks like "We've heard this before." Yes, mom, you've told us that story ten times now. We all know that mom has given to us her love of life, the love for each other, the love to endure, the love of laughter, the love of tears, the love of compassion and the love of others.

To go on about mom would take a separate book and I have been accused by my Nikki, more than once, that I am "turning into grandmom". I only hope that someday when my children start their families, that they will enjoy coming to visit Kevin and me as much as we enjoy going over mom's. I know that my house will never be as "magazine perfect" as mom's, and may not smell of homemade stuffed potatoes (my favorite), but if it is filled with the same love that mom has shown us all, then I will be grateful for that.

Herbie the "Love Bug" is a kind, loving, happy go lucky man. Quietly, patiently, adoring mom and accepting all of us as a "package deal", knowing his life would never be the same—or should I say sane. He has embraced all of us and we have become a huge family. Add in the sisters-in-law, Beverage and Jenny, the grandkids Steven, Nikki, David, Duane, Jamie, Jason, Tyler, Brandon, Makenzie and Jake and all our little critters. With all this said, I am glad to be a part of the Edwards-Dalbow clan.

MISSOURI TRIP JUNE 5, 2010

We're on the road to Rachele's in Mountain View. Last time we saw Rachele was two years ago when she flew in for Jillian's funeral Mass. It's been even longer since we've seen our grandsons, Jamie, Tyler and Brandon, since they did not come for the services. The cost of airline tickets is prohibitive. We're so anxious to see them. We had such a great visit last time and are looking forward to the time together.

We'll also be looking at homes and properties. As much as we love our home in New Jersey, we may not be able to afford to retire here. Therefore, we need a backup plan. We're stepping out in faith and have been praying every day for guidance and discernment as to where God wants us and the time frame in which everything will take place.

We'd like enough acreage and bedrooms to accommodate our whole family for a visit, at one time. So there will be no downsizing. Crazy, isn't it? We'll both be 66 in four months and here we are contemplating a major life change--a new adventure. Whoever said that asking God to guide you in every undertaking was boring, has obviously never tried it.

My head is spinning. I have so many "what ifs" roiling around in my head that it feels as if I have a blender in there, set on high speed, frappe to be exact. What if we don't find a house or property. What if we do? How will we know it's the right one. What if our home in New Jersey doesn't sell? I don't even want to think about carrying two mortgages. This scenario plays over and over until I remind myself to focus on Jesus and His Words (Phillipians 4, verse 6) "Don't worry about anything, but in all your prayers ask God for what you need, always asking Him with a thankful heart. And God's peace which is far beyond human understanding, will keep your hearts and minds safe in union with Christ Jesus." We need to place all our trust in Him and then heed His promptings.

I am missing Jake and Kenzie already. That will be the most difficult part of any move. The trip itself is interesting with Herb cheering loudly and waving his arms in celebration of hitting each 100 mile mark. His outbursts are so loud, I jumped in my seat. Only 1200 miles to go. He's also started his mid-western drawl. He's a nut, but a very happy one.

We finally exited Pennsylvania and will now go through West Virginia, Ohio, Indiana and Illinois. We made it to Mountain View by 2:00am. We hadn't even used the GPS because it was such a straight run. However, at the last minute, Herb wanted to try it and see if it would take us a different way to Rachele's home. It did and half the community is still laughing about it. We were directed to a gravel road which became narrower as we went along. Not only that, but there were no houses, no lights, no place to even turn around. The woods became denser and then we came to a creek. Now what! No cell phone reception either. I thought about blowing the horn in the hopes that someone would hear us. Herb got out of the car, determined that the stream was shallow, so we crossed it. We came out on the Conley's property, two miles from Rachele. Next day the Conleys remarked about hearing someone go through their property in the middle of the night.

We arrived at Chele's at 2:30a.m. Our grandsons came running out to greet us with hugs and kisses. Chele said they had insisted on staying up to welcome us. Bear hugs all around. We had a relaxing four days, playing

Scrabble, talking, reminiscing and house hunting. Jillian would have met her match in Scrabble with Jamie. His command of language is impressive. We went to an amazing, inexpensive restaurant, "Ryan's" with Rachele, our grandsons and some of their friends. We had a great meal and a lot of laughs, as usual.

As for the house hunting, Rachele and sometimes Michele and Maureen came along. There was one house that we came so close to putting a deposit on. It was a 5 bedroom, 3 bath house, all hardwood floors, two master suites, 2 car garage, plus a shop for Herb that would have housed a small airplane. It had a pool, a huge screened in living area, pond and 10 acres. It was in mint condition. They also had fruit orchards and a large screened in chicken house which is a must, should we move. We want fresh eggs. Price was $199,000.00, taxes on all this, an unbelievable $824.00 a year.

We prayed about it, talked about it, but in the end we decided to wait until we have no other choice but to move. Considering the economy, that very well may happen. Right now there are four states on the verge of financial collapse, New York, California, Illinois and New Jersey. Back to Philippians 4.

MISSOURI TRIP 2008

We stayed with Rachele and our grandsons and had a great time. Rachele and I walked most of her twenty acres and just talked. What else is new. We all did something to Herb that I still can hardly believe we got away with. It was my idea but it took only seconds for the boys and Chele to jump on board. He was so exhausted that he went to bed early. I happened to spot a wine bottle on the kitchen counter. I asked if there were any more bottles. We quietly went in the bedroom, placed one bottle near Herb's hand, and the boys sat on the floor in front of him with a bottle in their hands. Party time!

Next Jamie the artist and graphic designer got his paintbrush, his easel and a French beret which we placed on Herb's head, along with his sketch pad. Paintbrush we slid in Herb's hand. Artist!

Rachele got a black and red plaid hunting hat, her shotgun and stuffed rabbit. Herb the Hunter! All the time we're doing this we were taking pictures. There were flashes of light everywhere. Once in awhile Herb would start to move and we'd all drop down to the floor. He never woke up. We had to leave the room several times because we were laughing so hard. Rachele and I peed ourselves, but we didn't stop. We were on a roll.

Rachele got her Bible, a large crucifix, white collar and Herb became a priest. Tyler or Jamie said we could keep going and have enough photos for a calendar. The funniest was the antlers we placed on the pillow above Herb's head. It looked like they were growing out of his head. Then the finishing touch—a red bottle cap on his nose made him "Rudolph". He never woke up and we were laughing still, an hour after it was all over.

The best part was the fact that Herb would never see these pictures until we got home and he made a slide show of all the photos he had taken of the kids. I was dying to tell him, but waiting to see his expression was worth the wait. I was so disappointed when Herb wanted to wait until the next day to view them. We were looking at the photos together. When suddenly, the first one of him with the bottles came up. He said, "What the heck? What is that? What did you do?" By the time he got to Rudolph, he was laughing just as hard as I was. He found it hard to believe that we did all that to him, without him waking up....Great memory.

TIME WARP (of sorts)

I've always tried not to take anything for granted. Yet, we were sorely tested this summer. There was a rainstorm on June 25, 2015 and we lost power for three days. Ryan and Jen lost it for five days. We were blessed not to have any serious damage done. Some people had trees fall on their houses and cars. We had a lot of downed branches, enough to fill ten trash cans the first day. We would be cleaning up for days to come.

Our beautiful pool is littered with leaves and pine needles, an easy fix. As hot as it has been without fans and air conditioning, we can cool off in the pool. The pump didn't run for three days but the water remains crystal clear. Love that salt water pool!

We still have running water so we're able to take ice cold showers and shampoos. No blow dryer, though so I looked like I rolled out of bed when I went to church. No power in church. Mass is by candlelight. It's a weekday so there were only about two dozen people there. A beautiful way to start the day. Afterwards, I had to take Communion to Gladys. Trying to navigate the streets in Berlin was like being in a war zone. Each street I turned on was blocked by fallen trees and police cars. I eventually got there.

Some areas looked like a tornado had created a swath of debris. Don't know for sure because we have no radio, TV or phones. Land lines are dead. I have no cell phone. Herb left the house at 4:00 am, driving to three different stores, looking for ice for our ice chests. He couldn't find any and as a result, we lost about $300.00 worth of food. Ironically, he found out there was plenty of ice at a farm market at the end of our road. By then, it was too late to save our food but the farm market kept us supplied for the next few days when we replaced some of that food.

Ten pounds of chicken nuggets, salmon and eggs and a delicious ragout I had made were put out in our feeding area for our "Busters" (turkey buzzards) and the raccoons and skunks. Thank God for the amazing cleanup job the animals do, otherwise we'd be smelling garbage for days.

Initial estimate of when we will have power is five days! At first, I was extremely upset. Food has spoiled, laundry can't be done and is piling up (that alone could put me into withdrawal). One of the first lessons learned as a Christian is that we should thank and praise God for everything and He will bring good out of it. Trust Him. Thanking Him for this chaos almost seems inane. Traffic lights aren't working. How is that good? My daily devotional "Jesus Calling" confirms that we should thank God for everything.

So I do it. How's that working? It's working, believe it or not. Drivers are actually very patient at the lights, even smiling as they wave me on. I am so grateful to Herb for keeping both our cars filled with gas, because most gas stations have lost power and can't pump gas.

I was picking up branches when Jim (part of our church family) stopped by to see if we needed anything. He still had power. He gave me his cell phone to use to call Herb and wanted to leave it with me, but I declined. Later that afternoon he called Herb's cell phone and extended a dinner invitation from AnnMarie. Herb had come home early and we were already at Olive Garden, imbibing and eating our stress away. He had no way of charging his cell phone. Meghan, our waitress from another town, had also lost power. We talked about our mutual dependency. She ended up offering to charge Herb's cell phone while we ate. It went from 14% to 73%, another good deed.

I'm doing lots of reading as usual, only now I read by candles or our oil lamps. We've always kept flashlights in every room, so that is not a problem. Herb even has little lanterns on the floor by the cats' bowls. I so admire the Amish for their independence of modern conveniences.

I woke up early this morning relaxed and peaceful. No clock watching. Screens of digital clocks remain blank—no pressure. I drive to the end of our road to get ice and fresh fruit from our farm market. Justin helped carry everything to the car. We talked. He's not so dependent on the gadgets that most guys and girls in their twenties are obsessed with. He said that he enjoys the quiet. It was refreshing to hear.

Went home to wash down the frig, now that it was empty. Breakfast was a bowl of freshly picked blueberries from the farm market.

Another visitor comes, Joe Cook. We met him at our yard sale. Herb and Joe keep in touch by e-mail. He, too, lost power but has a generator and offered help. It was a good visit. Of course, as always we talked about Fox News. It was a year ago that Judge Janine had guests from the FBI on her show, as well as a head of Homeland Security, from a previous administration. They talked about how easy it'd be to incapacitate us and our economy by collapsing the power grid.

461

I don't want to even think about that seeing how difficult these few days are. They also said that it is relatively easy to take precautions to prevent this. Our president is aware of this, but, as usual isn't concerned about anything except global warming. The experts believe it WILL happen eventually but can't do anything without his okay. As for global warming, we call it change of seasons.

Jugs of water warming in the sun were perfect for doing dishes by hand. A trip to Berlin and I found a laundromat open. There were so many people there for the same reason. They were from Berlin, Atco, Clementon, Winslow and Sicklerville. Everyone is inconvenienced, it's hot and humid, in the high eighties, yet all were pleasant. I even had an opportunity to use my sign language skills with a young girl there.

I guess the lesson learned is that we don't need all these material things, like phones, dishwashers, TV and internet. They do make our lives easier but they usurp a lot of the human experience. I've been enjoying the smiles and conversation that comes with a less hurried pace.

Photo was texted by Jen of Jake and Kenzie reading by the light from their headbands with lights (like a miner's cap), They were reading in an otherwise dark room curled up on their couch. What a beautiful sight! I love that they love their books as much as I do. In the words of Henry David Thoreau, "Books are the treasured wealth of the world and the fit inheritance of generations and nations."

Dinner with Ry and Jen, Jake and Kenzie at "Racks" bar and grille. No power at home means no cooking. Yeah! Afterwards we went to Home Depot and got a generator. Herb hooked it up and thought I'd be thrilled we had lights. I wasn't prepared for the noise. I couldn't concentrate to read because the noise was so distracting. Herb found me in the office reading by candlelight. He couldn't believe I preferred that. He said, "Basically, I was sitting by a $700.00 candle." He turned it off. We had already lost the food in the frig. That would be the only thing the generator would be good for, as far as I'm concerned. Except for my washing machine, of course. Shortly after, the power came on. Herb had joked that if he bought a generator, once we had spent the money, he knew the power would come back on. Though our lights are now on, we still do not have phone service or cable.

Next day phones and cable are on. Jen, Ry, Jake and Kenzie come over to do laundry and take hot showers after a refreshing swim. They weren't so lucky. They have a well and without electric, they had no running water because of the pump. That night our phones and cable go out again. Ryan and Jen would still be without power for another two days. This scenario is becoming a lesson in patience. It also makes me very appreciative of what I have.

Thank you God for all our modern conveniences, for surrounding us with nature, for our pool and for all the smiles, conversations and quiet moments I experienced through this power failure, which revealed a power surge of sorts from others I had contact with. I love You…

DATING

I was working as a bank teller in our neighborhood. I got to know a lot of the people because they would come in every week. Some, I knew from our parish. There was one man I met that I was very grateful to. I think if it wasn't for him, I would have been fired that first week. It was a Friday and the first of the month. The line at the teller's windows extended out the door. I was a nervous wreck.

This man hands me his check and deposit slip. I was supposed to deposit a large amount and give him a small amount in cash. I reversed it and gave him several hundred dollars too much. He actually went outside, got back in line and when he finally came back to my window, he said very discreetly, I think you made a mistake. After that incident, he'd always smile and ask how I was. Then he asked me out. I said "No, I'm married." This happened while George had been seeing another woman for well over a year.

My manager knew this man and said he was divorced, had four children and was just a nice guy. She made him aware of my situation and he asked me out for lunch at a diner across the street from the bank. I told her and him I wasn't interested. She said, "You have to eat. Go." I was so stupid but once again I was listening to someone else in charge and went. It was terrible. I couldn't eat and asked Bill to take me back to the bank. He apologized for not listening to me the first time. I also remember him saying "We're not doing anything wrong." Of course, I felt like I was.

A few days later he sent flowers to the bank thanking me for being so honest with him. I took the flowers home, hoping it was an opportunity to make George jealous. He laughed and told me to go out with him. Probably because he knew I wouldn't. Anyway, months later I did end up talking with Bill, on the phone, usually when I was done working late on Friday night. The older kids were all out with their friends and Jillian and Ryan went to bed early. I was lonely and that one phone call was something to look forward to. Even though I had several friends, they were all married and I didn't want to intrude on their time together at the end of the day. It ended up that Bill was just a friend even though he would have liked to date me. He did take Jillian, Ryan and me out for dinner once at the Ground Round. I was amazed that this place actually catered to children. I wasn't aware that there were restaurants that were "family friendly." I really lived a sheltered life. Bill helped David get a job in construction and he taught Kevin how to wire houses since he was an electrician. I'm grateful that he was there at that time in my life. He died about twenty years ago.

I dated more in my forties than I ever had as a teenager. Actually, I only had a handful of dates before I met George. After George left me I started going to Parents Without Partners, which was at the Silver Lake Inn in Clementon. The counselor I was seeing once a week for an entire year, suggested it. I loved to dance and they had great music. I felt very uncomfortable at first so I struck up a conversation with some of the other women there. I met some very nice men and I met some jerks. The good ones would warn me about the others. It seemed that even in this area, God was looking out for me. If I had it to do over again, I wouldn't have dated until years later. In hindsight, because of George's rejection, I was probably looking for someone to validate me and my serious lack of self worth. That was very immature thinking on my part.

Shortly after breaking up with Herb, whom I had met at Parents Without Partners, I met Ed at Mama Venturas. It was the only high class place around, where the men wore suits and the women dressed "to the nines" and were treated respectfully. I had gone there with my friends RoseAnn, who was single and a dance instructor, and Florence who was a widow. We all loved to dance. RoseAnn eventually met her husband there. Years later, she and Al would stand for Herb and me when Fr. Bourke officiated at our second wedding in the church. RoseAnn also was in our wedding party at our first wedding in the Church of All Faiths.

Ed was Italian and with me being Polish, we shared many of the same family and traditional values. He was a great dancer and played the sax. The huge common denominator for us was that both our sons went to heaven at age twenty. Unlike my Mark's sudden death, Ed's Steven was bedridden for seven years. Ed was Steven's primary caretaker. We also shared a strong faith. We talked incessantly of our sons and shared photos and stories. He was a perfect gentleman and I appreciated the respect that was not always forthcoming in others had met. I met his parents and his sister, his children and his friends. I was warmly accepted and embraced.

Most of my children liked Ed. Ryan towered over him and would pat Ed on the head like he was the little kid. Ed had a great sense of humor and was good to my kids. Jillian was going through a rough patch as a teenager and would challenge Ed on many issues. One time she was sarcastic and he called her on it. He said "I've always shown you respect, Jillian, and I expect the same in return, even if we disagree on something.

It wasn't until months later that she told me how much she respected Ed. She said he didn't let her manipulate him or get away with anything. He also challenged her intellectually, more than any other adult. She loved the banter between them. Years after I had broken up with Ed, I found out that Jillian had kept in touch with him by e-mail, when she was in Georgia.

Rachele liked Ed but did have some reservations about him, even having him checked out by a friend of hers who was on the police force. Of course, there was nothing of interest. I found this out long after I married Herb. She also had a surprise engagement party for us at her home. She said she had no reservations at all, after meeting Ed's family. His mom and sister were helping with the cooking and Rachele said they just reminded her of our family. She said they were wonderful.

Ed had a boat. I think by the size of it, it was probably classified as a yacht, but to him, it was the boat. Jillian and Ryan would come with us and Rachele would even meet us at the marina. David and Bev came down once. David got along well with Ed. Even when we went to Mama Venturas, Rachele would come. One time, Kevin and Trudi came and another time George showed up. Our dates were strange, to say the least. It seemed like no one wanted to let me out of their sight. It didn't bother me. I thought it was neat.

Kevin and Trudi did not like Ed. I'm not fully sure of the reasons but I know that they were very upset when I broke up with Herb. Also, Ed was very generous with money and gifts and I think (I could be wrong here because it wasn't discussed) they may have questioned his motives. Whatever the reasons, they chose to stay away for the time that I was dating Ed. Contact with them was severed and it was an extremely difficult time for me, not seeing them or my grandchildren. I ended up seeing Fr. Bourke once again for counseling. He told me that there was nothing I could do about the situation. I would have to learn to live with it and continue to pray. Those prayers were eventually answered and Kevin, Trudi, Steven and Nikki and Herb and I reconciled before my wedding to Herb. One of the most touching moments during our wedding was when little Nikki handed me a pink rose. Beautiful gesture Trudi.

Ed was a devout Catholic, which meant a lot to me. Besides his son Steven, who was in heaven, he had another married son and a teenage daughter. They were great kids and we got along well. However, putting things into perspective, I foresaw a potential problem—a big one. Ed was very liberal with his daughter, who was older than Jillian. Jillian was already testing me and pushing boundaries I had set—normal teen behavior. Having two extreme opposing philosophies on disciplining our children would not work. I knew I'd have to end our relationship but emotionally, I wasn't strong enough.

One day I prayed so fervently for Jesus to help me. I didn't want to do this but if it was the best thing, I asked Him to give me a sign. Although Ed did know of my concerns, he felt sure we could work things out. The next day after work I turned on the last fifteen minutes of Oprah and I couldn't believe the topic. It was about women who cancelled their weddings at the last minute. None of them had any regrets. I thanked Jesus for this obvious sign but told Him that it still wasn't enough. I was so afraid of doing the wrong thing. If I wasn't supposed to marry Ed, I would need a BIG sign. I got it a week later.

It was six weeks before our wedding. The cruise was booked. I had our invitations ready to mail. Then New Year's Eve came. Ed and I went out for a quiet dinner. Afterwards, he asked if I'd mind if he stopped at his house to wish his daughter a happy New Year before taking me home. We seldom went to his house so of course, I agreed. I asked what plans his daughter had and he said that she had planned to have a couple of girlfriends over to watch a movie. When we got to his house, we couldn't even pull in the driveway. There were cars everywhere. The front door was open despite the cold air. There were dozens of people drinking, smoking and I thought I smelled marijuana.

I was shaking as Ed took my hand and walked in the house. I knew immediately that, in a strange way, this was my answer, my big sign. His daughter hugged us both and when he asked what was going on, the answer was vague. So and so told someone else and it snowballed. I knew Ed was upset and I waited to see how he handled this. He said that he was too angry to handle it now. I said that maybe that's the best time to address this. He wanted to take me home. I pointed out that these were mostly underage kids and he'd be responsible for them. He took me home and went right back.

Next day, there was no need for an explanation when I handed my engagement ring to him. He understood but wasn't happy about it. I do believe that God brought us together for a reason when we both needed someone to lean on, after our sons went to heaven. I even realized early in our relationship that I had taken care of Ed's son for a short time at Voorhees Pediatric. Steven, at twenty, was the oldest patient there. As a rule, they only accepted children up to eighteen years of age. However, since Steven didn't have much time left, they made an exception. It afforded Ed some measure of comfort to know that I had met and cared for his son even though it was such a brief time. Ed and I had not yet met, when I was caring for Steven.

The breakup was devastating for both of us, even though I saw no other way. It didn't negate the good that came out of our relationship. Ed said that he just wanted me to be happy and that was all he cared about. Hopefully, in time I would be but I was so raw that I honestly believed it would never happen.

YEARS LATER

One of Ed's good friends was a musician. He, also, was a man of strong faith and he put his career on hold to raise his daughter. Years after Herb and I were married, we received an invitation from him, to a dinner dance to benefit an animal shelter. Herb wanted to go. I said it may be uncomfortable and maybe we should pass on this because Ed would probably be there. Herb, always the optimist, said it would be fine. It was.

We were sitting at a table talking when Ed walked over, complimented me, kissed me on the cheek and shook Herb's hand and engaged him warmly in conversation as if it was the most natural situation. As always, he was a class act, no bitterness just respect. When I pray for my Mark and Jillian, I can't help but remember Ed's Steven too.

NIECES AND NEPHEWS

I have five nieces and twelve nephews. I've lost count of great nieces and nephews, which is still growing and at last count, well over thirty. I cannot write about all of them. Some I hardly ever see. I love and pray for them all but I do have my favorites. Am I allowed to say that?

My favorite niece, **MELANIE**, (my sister Mary's daughter) is nearest my heart for so many reasons. We share the heartache of losing a child and the comfort of knowing they are with God. Mel and Brian have four children. Their firstborn, Matthew, was welcomed into heaven the same day that he was born. Collin, Gabrielle (Gabby) and Ryan came after. Mel is beautiful, compassionate, sensitive to other's needs and has a strong faith.

Some in our families, including my sister Mary, think Mel and I are more alike in looks and personality. What a great compliment for me! She never fails to call and write on Mark's and Jillian's birthdays and anniversaries. I do the same on Matthew's birthday and anniversary. Mel and Brian's children know that their older brother Matthew is in heaven, looking after them. They also celebrate his birthday as they would any birthday.

There are probably many who don't understand this. We can't talk to everyone about our children. That's why Mel is such a blessing to me. We are on the same wave length or, more accurately phrased, the same prayer length. Herb and I feel very close to all their children. Colin seems to be the most sensitive to others, like his mom. I had a short but very telling conversation with him recently. I felt like I was conversing with an adult, not a child. He had to write an essay in school. If he could have anything for Christmas, what would it be? He wanted his brother Matthew...heart wrenching. Gabby is warm, loving and so huggable. Ryan, like our Jake, is bubbly, adventurous and affectionate. Actually, all of Mel and Brian's children are warm and affectionate.

I love when our Kenzie gets together with her cousins Gabby and Makayla. They're all the same age and get along beautifully. Herb just loves watching them together. From the time they were five, they enjoyed doing things together, whether it was in the hot tub, on the golf cart or just talking animatedly as little girls will do. One of my fondest memories is helping them to gather mint and lavender from my garden and then making sachets in little organza bags. They are so appreciative of every little thing which is unusual for girls so young. Whenever I see Makayla and Gabby, they run to me, giving me the best hugs ever! I hope that they know how much I love them…Uncle Herb too.

One of the cutest things they ever did, took place in the summer by our pool. They had asked me if I had any tights they could wear. I thought this a strange request when it was ninety degrees and they were in bathing suits. They each took a pair of tights and put both their legs in one leg of the pants, hiding the free hanging leg in their waistband. I love their creativity. They became "mermaids" and posed on the diving board.

I have another memory that is forever etched on my heart. It took place on the day of Jillian's funeral, at the luncheon at Mama Ventura's. I was having a meltdown and was hurrying to the restroom to cry alone. I opened the door to a scene I will never forget. I stopped dead in my tracks. There was a long vanity with a long mirror over it. In front of the vanity were chairs. Kenzie, Gabby and Makayla were standing on the chairs because they were so little. They were all five years old. They were giggling and primping in front of the mirror, like little teenagers. I should have gone back for my camera but I was mesmerized and just watched, thanking Jesus for this beautiful moment. I knew, without a doubt, that Jillian was watching from above.

UPDATE July 2016 Impromptu visit with Mel and the kids. Jake and Kenzie were here with me and Melanie, Colin, Gabby, Ryan and their friends stopped by on their way down to the shore. It afforded time for Mel and me to catch up on family things while watching the kids in the pool.

They were in for hours laughing, diving, playing Marco Polo and thoroughly enjoying each other's company. Mel got a bit melancholy watching Kenzie and Colin pair off for quite awhile. It reminded her of previous family gatherings where she and my Ryan would connect when they were their age.

It was a beautiful, unplanned day. We ordered pizzas, had snacks and the kids took a walk through the woods. Simple things... I am so grateful for the simple things and for this beautiful setting in the woods that we are blessed to live in.....and to share.

It got even better when Ryan and Jen came after work and they were able to see Mel and the kids. Although, their families do stay in touch. Herb made it home in time to see everyone. He also was able to take my camera and put the dozens of photos I had taken on the TV slide show we have on our deck. The kids enjoyed watching themselves. It was a great end to a beautiful day.

JOSH

I would be remiss if I didn't mention my favorite nephew, Josh. Josh and his wife Julie have two children, Haley Ryan and "Bear" (Little Josh). Julie is an R.N. and works long shifts in the NICU (Neonatal Intensive Care Unit). Despite rigid schedules they find time to remain in touch regularly. Considering all the responsibilities of his own, Josh was here with us and was especially concerned about me, calling several times a week in the weeks and months after Jillian went home (heaven). He even made me laugh through my tears. I was explaining how disoriented I was becoming and forgetful. I'd find myself out back staring into space. He said, "Aunt Rose, keep your phone with you. If you find yourself out on the road in your pajamas, call me. I promise I'll come and get you."

He'd bring Haley over and she and Makenzie would play together, getting to know each other for the first time. This was the first time these little cousins had met. Despite the age difference, they were drawn like magnets to each other. Josh drove three hours with Haley to be with us in our home in the mountains, even though he had had other plans. Makenzie and Haley were certainly getting to know each other well. Another example of good coming out of bad, if we trust God.

I have a precious memory of Kenzie (Ryan called her "Bug") and Haley, called "Scwag" by Josh. These two gorgeous little girls with the craziest nicknames. Anyway, they were in the back of Josh's SUV which they called the "Clubhouse". Josh was playing Kevin's CD's. Haley knew all the words to all of Kevin's songs. He taught her well. They were having a ball singing and dancing.

Josh was there, not only for me, but for his cousins. He picked Rachele up from the airport when she flew in from Missouri. He kept in touch with her and Jillian over the years. He has always nurtured family relationships. Family is a priority to him and his beautiful wife Julie. Josh, Rachele and Josh's dog Sullivan hiked the Appalachian Trail in Pennsylvania. Rachele and Jillian were both over Josh and Julie's house for a party when Jillian came home from Atlanta one time. He even offered to drive to Atlanta and bring Jillian home when she was going through a difficult time.

Ryan and Josh are cousins and share so many similarities. They are both amazing fathers. They also have extremely high expectations of their children. Their children do excel at most everything they undertake probably because of that. There are no whiny kids in our family. I've often joked that if my arm was hanging by a thread, Ryan would say "Get over it mom. You need to exercise more." Exercise and pushing yourself beyond what you think you are capable of seems to be a mantra with Josh and Ryan.

It's filtered down to their children. An example of this occurred recently when Josh and Julie's four year old son, unbeknownst to them, decided to cut an apple up for a snack, self-sufficiency. The knife slipped and Bear cut his fingertip badly. There was a lot of blood, but unlike most four year olds, there was no screaming. He wrapped up his finger then cleaned up the blood before telling his mom what had happened.

There was also an incident with Kenzie that parallels this attitude. She was playing softball and was on the pitcher's mound when her teammates were concerned because blood was running out of her mouth. She spit a tooth into the dirt and brushed off any attempt to help her. She continued playing with no interruption. One of her teammates retrieved the tooth and gave it to Kenzie when the game was over.

JOSH (Insight into Josh's work ethic)

Josh joined the Navy to pay for college. After four years active duty, he got out and worked full time as a police dispatcher at night and went to school full time during the day. He interned part time with the Export Assistance Center. He graduated with a degree in Economics, with honors. He then started working full time for the District Attorney's Office, while going to Law School at night. He was elected class president three years in a row. The fourth year he did not run for office. No time.....you think??

Josh founded the running group "The Animal Camp" which, at present, has thirty-three members. You have to run a hundred miles to get in. His biggest running accomplishment was running the "McNaughten in Vermont", two hundred mile trail race in 2011. He finished in third place. Only three people finished the race. Ten had started. He finished in 67 hours of non-stop running, with the exception of a three hour break after the first hundred miles. Josh's brother John finished second. Josh is now an Assistant Prosecutor.

UPDATE 2015

Haley and Bear are kept busy with competitive activities. Haley swims year round and recently completed a two mile swim, non- stop. Keep in mind that she's only eight years old. She also plays soccer, is in gymnastics and ballet. Both she and Bear have won their division in at least one of the kids triathlons. One year Haley finished first in her age group beating all the boys and girls. (There's that strong girl/women link in our family, once again.)

Both children paddle their own kayaks, are proficient on skis and have completed "mud obstacle courses." Bear is also in the Scouts and in wrestling. Bear's best was finishing second place overall in triathlon when he was five. He was in the four to six bracket. He also skis expert level slopes. Recently Julie was scheduled for a benefit run but was called into work at the last minute. Haley took over for her mom, running with all adults and came in second. Josh calls regularly and Julie calls occasionally.

Julie was there for Herb when he had his open heart surgery. Since she worked at the hospital, she would make middle of the night visits to check on Herb. They are a beautiful, caring family and very close to my heart, as well as Herb's.....literally.

UPDATE, NOVEMBER 2015

I received a quick phone call from Josh. He and the kids had been camping in the Delaware River Water Gap area. Temperatures at night were in the low thirties. He wanted to let me know that he and Haley and Bear had just come back from a swim in the river! He said that he knew I'd appreciate that (considering I love my Polar Plunge before we close the pool). If I was there Josh, I'd be in the river too.

When I attempt to praise Josh for all he does, especially keeping the families close, he'll bring up his brother Pete as a phenomenal father. Pete thinks nothing of taking his four young children camping even without his wife Jen. Jen is a flight attendant and not always home on weekends. Jonathon and Jacob are in grade school. The youngest are Luke and Charlotte, ages one and three! That is amazing.

SUMMER 2013

This summer I got to know my nephew Peter's wife Jen and their three sons a little better. Pete is Diane's son. Jen brought my sister Diane down and of course Diane's grandsons Jonathon, Jacob and Luke. Our Jen and Ryan came over with Jake and Kenzie and they got to know their cousins. The only time they had met was at one of our Halloween parties. Jake and Jonathon were cowboys. Those parties were crazy and big (one year I counted 85 people), so you really didn't have much time one on one, with that many people.

Later Julie, Josh's wife came with Haley and Bear (little Josh), Diane's grandchildren also. I feel like I have to keep clarifying who's who because there are so many little ones in our family. We had such a good time in the pool and playing volleyball. This ever-increasing family is such a blessing. Of course, because Josh is my favorite nephew, I've always felt close to his family. Haley and Bear even left me messages on the phone, after my recent surgery.

I also feel close to Eddie (Diane's son) and his wife Renee though I don't see them as often. They are both so thoughtful. When I had my hip replacement they came down on two different occasions, with delicious meals that Renee had made. They lived quite a distance away at that time. Their children are Jackson, Olivia and Mason. They also are very devout in their faith. Herb was so enamored with Olivia when they visited. Olivia seemed to gravitate towards Herb also. She's a little chatterbox....like her mommy and her Aunt Rose.

UPDATE; Pete and Jen have added a beautiful daughter, Charlotte, to their family.

UPDATE A few days after Christmas (2015) we had a mini reunion of sorts. Diane's son Peter came with his four children. Jen, who is a flight attendant, was working. Eddie (also Diane's son) and Renee came with their three children. It was a special treat having them all together. Of course, Herb was entranced with Olivia, just like old times.

JANUARY 2016

There was an assassination attempt on Philadelphia Police Officer, Jesse Hartnett. My niece, Debbie (Diane's daughter) is a Critical Care Nurse and was one of the first ones to administer care to him. I thank God that this officer had the best. I am so proud of Debbie. Pray for Officer Hartnett, his family and all doctors and nurses and, always, our police.

RoseMarie Dalbow

FAMILY FAVORITES/RECIPES

FETTUCCINE ALFREDO Mark's favorite

¼ lb. butter
¾ cup parmesan cheese
½ cup light cream
1 egg salt & pepper
Melt butter. Add cheese cream, beaten egg and blend until slightly thickened. Do this over low heat. Toss with noodles and serve immediately.

I made this meal for Mark's birthday when I was in the beginning stages of labor with Jillian. He also wanted an angel food cake, which I frosted with chocolate whipped cream. Just beat heavy cream, a little sugar and cocoa powder. He loved it.

CHEESECAKE (makes its own crust) 350 degrees Rachele's favorite

2 8 oz. pkgs. Philadelphia Cream Cheese (room temp.)
1 cup sugar
4 eggs
2 tsp. cornstarch
1 tsp. vanilla
1 cup whole milk
Mix cheese & sugar until creamy. Add eggs vanilla and cornstarch. Beat until creamy then add milk. Mixture will be watery. Butter 10" glass pie plate. Bake until crust starts to brown slightly and knife inserted halfway between center and edge of plate comes out clean. Center will set later. Remove from oven and spread topping on. Return to oven for five minutes.
TOPPING
1 cup sour cream
2 Tablespoons sugar
½ tsp. vanilla
Pinch of salt

476

ITALIAN VEGETABLE SOUP Jillian's favorite

3 cups chopped cabbage
3 cups sliced celery
3 cups sliced carrots
3 bunches sliced scallions (can substitute a chopped onion)
3 large garlic cloves, crushed (I now use the chopped garlic in a jar)
3 8 oz. cans stewed tomatoes.(cut tomatoes into small pieces with kitchen shears)
2 46 oz. cans chicken broth
1 ½ tsp. thyme
1 ½ tsp. basil
Salt and pepper to taste
I saute the onion & celery in butter for 10 minutes before adding to the rest of the ingredients.
When soup starts to boil, turn down to a simmer and add wide egg noodles and green beans (NOT French cut). Can be canned or frozen. Cook until noodles are tender. If I have left over chicken, I'll cut that up and add it. Lots of chopping, well worth it.

DAMN GOOD CHILI Ryan's favorite I think he just felt empowered saying the title.

4 lbs. ground beef
2 8 0z. cans tomato sauce
2 8 oz cans water (use the tom. Sc. Cans to measure)
2 large onions
2 large green peppers, chopped
2 tsp. cumin
1 tsp. oregan
6 cloves garlic
2 tsp. salt
2 Tablespoons chili powder
½ tsp. cayenne or tabasco sauce to taste
4 cans kidney beans, drained

Update on chili: Recently had Pat's chili and it's better than mine. I've since altered the above, substituting the water and tomato sauce with Prego or Ragu sauce. It makes for a thicker consistency.

Saute onions and peppers in olive oil. Set aside. Brown meat and drain fat. Add all other ingredients including peppers and onions. Cook for one hour. Serve topped with shredded cheddar cheese.

SPINACH SALAD & DRESSING Kevin & Trudi's favorite

¾ cup sugar

1 cup canola oil or olive oil (canola is milder)

½ cup red wine vinegar

2 Tablespoons Worcestershire sauce

1/3 cup ketchup

½ tsp salt

¼ tsp pepper

Mix ingredients in blender. Assemble salad with:

Spinach leaves (If you use bagged salad, check for the latest date)

Hard boiled eggs, sliced

Mushrooms, sliced

Red onion, sliced

Water chestnuts, sliced (can) drain them

1 lb. crisp bacon, crumbled (add at last minute)

TEXAS SALSA This is David's wife, Jayne's recipe. Everyone loves it and it keeps well in the frig (if it lasts more than a day). I'm so glad she shared it with me. It's a hit at barbecues. It's healthy to boot. I'll eat it for breakfast, lunch and dinner.

2 cans shoepeg corn (white), drained

1 can black eyed peas, drained

1 can black beans, drained

¾ cup green pepper, chopped

1 ½ cups sliced celery

1 cup red onion, chopped

BOIL;

1 cup sugar

¾ tsp. pepper

½ cup corn oil

½ cup red wine vinegar

¼ cup white vinegar

Pour over veggies when sugar is dissolved. Keep in frig until ready to serve.

LASAGNE Herb's favorite This is actually Pat Hoppe's recipe and it is great!

1 lb. ground beef

1 lb. ground sausage

1 lb. shredded mozzarella cheese

1 15 oz. container ricotta cheese

Salt, pepper and Italian seasoning to taste

I use fresh parsley, about a Tablespoon (half if dried)

Use any sauce and doctor it up. I might add a lot of garlic, a little wine and tsp. sugar

I use the noodles that don't need to be boiled ahead of time.

BAKED BEANS Florence Hoppe's recipe (Dave's mom) People that don't usually like beans, get hooked on this. This is another of Herb's favorites. This recipe is over a hundred years old.

1 can butter beans, drained

1 can cut green beans, drained

1 can kidney beans, NOT drained

1 lg. can Bush's baked beans, NOT drained

¾ cup brown sugar

½ cup cider vinegar

1 tsp. dried mustard

½ tsp. garlic powder

4 huge onions (softball sized)

½ lb bacon fried crisp (I use 1 lb.)

Cook the chopped onions in the bacon fat
This can be frozen. They actually taste good hot or cold, anyway you can get them.

A favorite of Rachele's and mine are homemade Pierogies. We don't really have a recipe. Rachele makes them like her great grandmother did. She dumps a 5 lb. bag of flour on the table, makes a well in the center and breaks her eggs and other ingredients in that. I tried that once and got more flour on the floor. I stick to using a bowl. Our favorites are the ones we fill with cottage cheese. We used to make them for the Christmas Eve dinner. It is an all day job. I make them about once a year. It's frustrating when Herb says he'd rather have spaghetti sauce on them. I think his taste buds are dead.

BANANA BREAD This is an old standby of mine. Rather than waste over ripe bananas, this can be made in about ten minutes. Paul used to say I had them stacked like bricks in the freezer.

1 stick butter, softened
1 cup sugar, cream with butter then add
2 eggs
2 large bananas (just break in chunks)
2 cups flour
1 teaspoon baking soda
½ teaspoon salt
I like to add walnuts but have also added diced apple
Sprinkle cinnamon sugar on top and bake in 350 degree oven until knife in center comes out clean

STUFFED POTATOES Trudi's favorite

Bake six large Idaho potatoes, slice in half lengthwise
Scoop insides out into large mixing bowl. Leave thin layer of potato on bottom
Place small slice American cheese on bottom of potato skin

Mix potatoes with butter and sour cream (I don't have a recipe so amounts are approximate)
1 and a half sticks butter, six ounces sour cream
Chopped parsley
Spoon mixture into skins, top with cheese and return to oven until slightly crusty on top.
Crumble bacon on top
If mixture is too stiff, add more sour cream

CAT WHISPERER

Herb was adamant about not having any other cats, now that we were down to a lone male cat "Bandit." Prior to this, we always had at least two. Bandit is a sweet affectionate black and white cat. He loves to cuddle. We're beginning to think that Mark and Jillian, from heaven's vantage point are orchestrating an animal shelter in our back yard. Both of them loved animals but Jillian worked at the shelters, volunteering her time even though she had two jobs. Caring for abused and neglected animals was a passion with Jillian. She would send us videos to encourage us to help out the shelters in our area. We have followed through on that either by monetary donations or items that are needed at our local shelters.

We have three acres of woods so we have a variety of animals, deer, fox, raccoons, turkeys, skunk. There have been feral cats in the area but I had never seen them. My neighbor had told me about them. Herb and I "met" Jillian's gray tabby "Little Girl" when we visited her in Atlanta. Jillian wasn't surprised when Little Girl just cuddled with Herb. He's such an animal lover. Strange occurrences started happening within days after Jillian's funeral.

David (Jillian's brother) was going to have Little Girl flown home for Herb to take care of. However, I received a phone call from Jillian's boyfriend (also David) asking if we would consider leaving Little Girl with him. We talked it over and agreed to let him have her. He was hurting also and this helped him in some way. I found out later that he had some allergy issues with cats but he didn't care. He gave me updates and if he had to go on a business trip, his mother took care of her.

The day after we made that decision I saw what I believed to be a feral cat in our yard. She was Little Girl's twin. She even had the same odd markings. I compared this cat with the photo of Jillian's Little Girl. Herb saw the cat and was going to take food out for it. I cautioned him to keep his distance because the cat could be dangerous. Shortly after, I went outside to see Herb with Little Girl in his lap. She was purring contentedly. It seems that Jillian wanted Herb to have Little Girl, one way or other. We kept her and she had kittens in our bedroom closet, four of them.

Most of our cats have been black and white. "Pokey" and "Penny" were unique. They acted more like dogs. Poke would play "fetch" with a toy mouse, retrieve it and drop it at our feet. Unlike most cats they would come when Herb called, not when I called. Penny was protective of the kids. If I raised my voice to them, she would come over and bite me (no broken skin) until I lowered my voice. She would do the same if I raised my voice to Herb. He thought it was funny. I didn't. It was a warning that I heeded. We even had a friendly skunk that would come at dusk and eat side by side with Poke and Penn in the back yard. He never sprayed.

We've lost so many cats over the years, it looks like Stephen King's "Pet Cemetery" out back. Up until two years ago we were down to Bandit and Silas. Herb had been keeping an eye on a couple cats out back that he knew to be feral. We checked with neighbors to see if they belonged to them. They did not. There was "Ginger" an orange cat that looked like a Maine Coon. Ginger was Herb's sidekick and followed him everywhere.

Then there was a soft gray cat that was so skittish, she'd run if she saw us. She was pregnant when Herb went into the hospital for cardiac surgery. The weather was brutally cold so Herb made me promise to try to get her on our screened in deck so she wouldn't have her kittens in the dirt under the deck, which is where she would run to. I did not want to do this because I knew what was coming. Herb is a soft touch and has a heart of gold. His surgery was a matter of life and death. He knew I couldn't refuse his request. "Gracie" and I didn't get along but I fed her and took care of her for Herb.

Herb was home for six weeks, recuperating. He installed pet doors in just about every door that we have (five in all). He doesn't believe in keeping them in when they have all of nature around them. The vet bills were exorbitant because they all got their shots, even the three kittens, two of which he couldn't give up. All this after we were down to one cat and he said, no more. A friend took the third kitten, which Herb said we should have just kept him too. They were all boys.

Now, in 2015, we have five cats. The kittens "Oreo" and "Ringo" (because he has a perfect white ring on his black tail) are bookends to Herb when he's working at his computer. They have to lie on the desk. Oreo actually heels like a dog. They all get along which is amazing. They love climbing trees. Ringo is the most unusual. He loves to be pushed around in a wheelchair by Kenzie. When we have company and most of the cats scatter and hide, Ringo goes from person to person, sometimes begging for food. Bandit is an old soul at fifteen years and likes to raise his paw and gently tap anyone who will take the time to pet him.

Gracie, the feral cat has been domesticated by Herb. He's the only one who can carry her around. Initially, she wanted nothing to do with coming in the house. Little by little, Herb gained her trust. Now, she's the one who rarely goes out. In the evening if we're watching television or playing Scrabble or reading in our office, Herb has a ring of cats at his feet and usually Ringo in his lap.

At one time, Kevin had a couple of cats and his dog Zoey. Zoey rules. Anyway, Trudi said he came up with a plan to find a new home for the cats. He was going to put them through one of our pet doors when we were out, thinking we'd never notice one or two additional cats. After all, any animal from outside has access to our garage through a pet door. We've actually had a skunk come through. Thank goodness they're friendly.

We're not the only ones that Jillian and Mark seem to be sending animals to. Rachele has twenty acres in Missouri. She already had one dog and raises chickens. On Halloween (Mark's favorite holiday) a black kitten showed up on her porch. She named him, very appropriately, "Boo". He started growing by leaps and bounds. She took him to the vet who said he was a rare breed, a Siberian Forest Cat. He told her to expect him to grow much bigger than an ordinary house cat. To date, he is 25 pounds. He looks like a small panther.

He's a gentle soul but mischievous, can open drawers and doors. He's a pack rat and Chele will find her rosaries, jewelry and other items that he takes, in places you wouldn't expect. I did some reading up on the breed and they're very intelligent. This summer Rachele sent several small photo albums with pictures of Boo and captions or stories under them. She wanted Kenzie and Jake to get to know Boo. When I heard Jake laughing out loud, I knew that the "Boo Books" have the makings of a great children's series. Hopefully, Rachele will publish them.

It did not end there for Rachele. Several other cats showed up, playmates for Boo. But only Boo is allowed inside. The others have nests made of straw and blankets. Then "Penny" a pure bred beagle showed up. We used to have a beagle when the kids were little. No one in the area was missing a beagle. What is so strange is that this pup showed up on Rachele's doorstep, because to get to her house in the woods, you have to drive a mile down a dirt road. Really strange. Jillian??Mark?? What *are* you doing up there?

FOOD FOR THOUGHT

"You are never so high as when you are on your knees." James 4

"A day hemmed in by prayer is less likely to unravel."

"Courage is resistance to fear, mastery of fear, not the absence of fear." Ephesians 6:13-14

"The only necessary thing for the triumph of evil is for good men to do nothing." By Historian Edmund Burke. I like to quote this when people say they don't vote because one vote isn't going to make a difference. Think of your children and grandchildren's future before you use that excuse again. God gave us this wonderful country. Let's not lose it for future generations.

"You gain strength, courage and confidence by every experience in which you really stop to look fear in the face...you must do the thing you think you cannot do." Eleanor Roosevelt

For me, the completion of this book is something I thought I couldn't do.

"Keep God in your heart, a prayer on your lips and God will enlighten your mind"

Do you ever ask yourself how we have reached such a low point in our society? I do. We legislate against saturated fats but not against pornography. We forbid smoking in public places (I'm all for that) but don't forbid foul language or taking God's Name in vain. As a school nurse, I could not administer Tylenol without a parent's permission. Yet a young girl can get birth control and even an abortion without permission. Hundreds of times I have told people to "have a blessed day" as I'm checking out of a store. Most people look surprised, then issue a sincere thank you. Only once did I receive a negative remark when I said "God bless you." We're not allowed to mention God was the response. My comeback was "then give me back my money which has "In God we trust" all over it". You can imagine how well that went. We need to place God first, then everything else will fall into its rightful place. Think about this.....then pray.

"The tragedies of life, small and large, carve contours in our character that draw us to a different way of living, one that God intends to both use and transform" Dan Allinder

I remember saying this on the day of Jillian's funeral. "If my life is this bad with God in it, I sure don't want to ever imagine what it would be like without Him."

"With respect, love can come. Without respect, love will go."

Governor Chris Christie's mother

"Trouble is inevitable, misery is optional."
"You may be disappointed if you fail, but you are doomed if you don't try." Beverly Sills

"I cannot live without books." Thomas Jefferson

"There are only two ways to live your life. One is as though nothing is a miracle. The other is as though everything is a miracle." Albert Einstein

"Living in the past paralyzes the present and bankrupts your future."

"A mother who radiates self-acceptance and self-love, vaccinates her daughter against low self-esteem."

I wish I had known this years ago. I never heard this until my girls were adults.

"If your way is not working, try God's way."

"We have room for only one sole loyalty and that is loyalty to the American people." Teddy Roosevelt

"Some people see a problem, others, an opportunity.

Where some people see an obstacle, others see a challenge. Choose wisely".

This is oft repeated by Rachele. Her karate instructor used her as a living example of this, when she finally got her black belt despite her handicap (her shoulder). She is the epitome of tenacity.

"A good question for an atheist is to serve him a fine dinner and then ask if he believes there is a cook." "For the Benefit of Clergy" as seen in The Anglican Digest.

"Second hand faith is not second rate. All knowledge is second hand, history, geography, science and math."

"The greater the power, the more dangerous the abuse." Edmund Burke

I find this a very cogent argument against big government, which is what we have now.

"What if you woke up tomorrow with only the things you thanked God for today?" This is so thought provoking and profound, yet simple. When I posed this question to my CCD students, the silence was palpable.

"One day your life will flash before your eyes. Make sure it's worth watching."

"The happiest people don't *have* the best of everything. They just *make* the best of everything."

"Great spirits have always encountered violent opposition from mediocre minds." Einstein

EPILOGUE 2016

Herb and I will be 72 this September. He continues to work at the airport. This is his fortieth year. To date, he has no plans to retire. However, he has cut down his hours to a four day week. The three day weekend makes a huge difference. We enjoy a simple life which includes going out to lunch with friends and our children, watching Jake and Kenzie compete in sports and (as Herb puts it) raising our five cats (or as Rachele would phrase it, children with fur). Reading, swimming and Scrabble remain high on our list.

As I review the pages of my book, that is my life, and all the memories it evokes, perhaps that "brass ring" we all hope to attain, has been in my keeping all along. I claim, close to my heart, my successes and my failures, because without the failures I would not be able to appreciate the successes.

Or, in the words of Francis Bacon, "In order for the light to shine so brightly, the darkness must be present.".

REMNANT: small fragment of something; what is left over, last remaining indication of what has been

The remnants of my life are made up of all my experiences, good, bad, happy, sad, exciting, quiet and sometimes devastating. Sometimes laughter and joy overtake me, more often than not. Then tears and ever present grieving for Mark and Jillian and more recently, my grandson David. I'm living a paradox. As I grow older, I remind myself that I'm moving closer to being with them again and that thought is comforting.

All these experiences have combined to create a beautiful tapestry that is my life….the precious life that God has gifted me with. The remnants have become whole because God is by my side, has been and will always be…. Trust Him….completely.

Author is donating a portion of her proceeds to St. Jude Children's Research Hospital

Printed in the United States
By Bookmasters